Shadow over the Promised Land

Sheldon Brivic

Shadow Over the Promised Land

Slavery, Race, and Violence in Melville's America

CAROLYN L. KARCHER

Louisiana State University Press

BATON ROUGE AND LONDON

Grateful acknowledgment is given to the *American Quarterly* for permission to
republish "Melville's 'The 'Gees': A Forgotten Satire on Scientific Racism"
(Copyright 1975, Trustees of the University of Pennsylvania); to *Essays in
Literature* for permission to republish "Melville's 'The Bell-Tower' and 'Benito
Cereno': Companion-pieces on Slavery" (1979); and to the *Southern Review* for
permission to republish "Melville and Racial Prejudice: A Reevaluation"
(Spring, 1976). This book is from a dissertation to be submitted to the
Graduate School, University of Maryland, in partial fulfillment of the
requirements for the Ph.D. degree in American Studies.

Design: Dwight Agner
Type face: VIP Monticello
Composition: Graphic Composition, Inc.
Printing: Thomson-Shore, Inc.
Binding: John H. Dekker & Sons, Inc.

LIBRARY OF CONGRESS CATALOGING IN PUBLICATION DATA

Karcher, Carolyn L   1945–
   Shadow over the promised land.

   Bibliography: p.
   Includes index.
      1. Melville, Herman, 1819–1891—Political and social views.   2. Slavery and
slaves in literature.   3. United States in literature.   I. Title.
PS2388.P6K37   813'.3   79-14861
ISBN 0-8071-0565-1
ISBN 0-8071-0595-3 pbk.

TO MARTIN

Contents

℘reface

THE RECENT proliferation of monographs on Melville's racial views and attitudes toward slavery, war, American ideology, and class conflict reflects a growth of political consciousness among scholars. Until the mid-1960s, there was almost no interest in Melville's racial views, and very little recognition of the prominent place that social criticism occupies in his writings. Even critics actively committed to racial egalitarianism insisted that a work like "Benito Cereno," for example, was not about slave revolt, but about good and evil, and that Melville's alleged use of blacks to symbolize evil and whites to symbolize good had no racial implications.[1] The few critics politically conscious enough to object to the racism inherent in such symbolism did not challenge the prevailing interpretation of Melville's fictional themes and strategies, but instead accused Melville himself of racism.[2] Only since the Civil Rights and anti-Vietnam War movements have forced us to read our national history and literature afresh has it become possible to approach

1. See, for example, Yvor Winters, *In Defense of Reason* (Denver, 1947), 222. See also Rosalie Feltenstein, "Melville's 'Benito Cereno,'" in John P. Runden (ed.), *Melville's "Benito Cereno": A Text for Guided Research* (Lexington, Mass., 1965), 124–33.
2. For example, F. O. Matthiessen, *American Renaissance: Art and Expression in the Age of Emerson and Whitman* (New York, 1968), 508 (Matthiessen does emphasize Melville's social criticism, however); Sidney Kaplan, "Herman Melville and the American National Sin: The Meaning of 'Benito Cereno,'" *Journal of Negro History*, XLI (1956), 311–38, XLII (1957), 11–37; and even so recent a critic as Kingsley Widmer, *The Ways of Nihilism: A Study of Herman Melville's Short Novels* (Los Angeles, 1970), 59–90.

Melville with a different set of questions and assumptions about him as an artist, thinker, and moralist.

This book is the product of such a rereading. Indeed, it originated as a study of Melville's apocalyptic vision and did not acquire its present form until I discovered a side of Melville I had always overlooked while concentrating on his religious thought—the Melville who had written impassioned indictments of American and European imperialism in *Typee* and *Omoo*, slavery in *Mardi*, pauperism and mistreatment of emigrants in *Redburn*, flogging and militarism in *White-Jacket*, the betrayal of American Revolutionary ideals in *Israel Potter*, the complacency of the rich and the exploitation of the working class in "Poor Man's Pudding and Rich Man's Crumbs" and "The Paradise of Bachelors and The Tartarus of Maids"; the Melville who had extolled the "democratic dignity" of the "arm that wields a pick or drives a spike," and had proclaimed: "Men may seem detestable as joint stock-companies and nations; knaves, fools, and murderers there may be; men may have mean and meagre faces; but man, in the ideal, is so noble and so sparkling, such a grand and glowing creature, that over any ignominious blemish in him all his fellows should run to throw their costliest robes"; the Melville who had paid eloquent homage to the courageous endurance of a woman victimized by the greed and lust of men: "Humanity, thou strong thing, I worship thee, not in the laureled victor, but in this vanquished one."[3]

In exploring this Melville, I found that criticism of slavery and racism was more pervasive in his works than I had ever imagined. It became obvious that the handful of black characters and explicit statements about slavery over which critics had deadlocked were part of a much larger picture, integrally related to Melville's democratic and religious ideals, his attitudes toward authority and violence, his personal experience of oppression as a sailor, and his unique opportunity to observe a nonwhite society at first hand. Further investigation revealed that Melville was reacting against current theories about race and that some acquaintance with those

3. Herman Melville, *Moby-Dick; or, The Whale*, ed. Harrison Hayford and Hershel Parker (New York, 1967), 104; "The Encantadas," in *Great Short Works of Herman Melville*, ed. Warner Berthoff (New York, 1970), 132.

theories was a prerequisite to understanding Melville's exposé of them.

I do not, of course, mean to claim that criticism of slavery and racism is central to all or most of Melville's writings—simply that they were pressing concerns of his that he kept bringing up in his antebellum novels and tales. In some works—*Pierre*, for example—slavery and race are unquestionably peripheral, and focusing on them illuminates but a small aspect of the whole—an aspect chiefly important for clarifying Melville's position on these issues. In others, such as "The Paradise of Bachelors and The Tartarus of Maids," black slavery is closely associated with the major themes of wage slavery, working-class alienation, and disparities between rich and poor. Here the focus on slavery and race serves to explain a more significant portion of the text. In a few works—notably *Moby-Dick* and *The Confidence-Man*—I will be bold enough to assert, notwithstanding the weight of scholarly opinion to the contrary, that slavery and race are crucial themes and that concentrating on them not only takes us to the heart of the text, but radically transforms our perceptions of its total meaning.

My approach in this book has been to examine Melville's treatment of slavery, race, and violence as it evolved from *Typee* through the major fiction of the 1850s to the late poetry and *Billy Budd*. Except in two cases—"The Town-Ho's Story," which I have analyzed in connection with *White-Jacket*, rather than with *Moby-Dick*, where it belongs, and *Israel Potter*, which I have bracketed with *Pierre* because of their complementary perspectives on the American Revolution—I have adhered to chronology.[4] I have begun by trying to place Melville in the spectrum of contemporary attitudes toward slavery and the Negro, and by discussing biographical factors that may have influenced both the stand Melville took on the slavery question and the mode he adopted of promulgating his egalitarian views.

That mode was an indirect one, relying on many ingenious techniques of subverting his readers' racial prejudices and inducing them to identify with victims of oppression, regardless of race. Ini-

4. In the case of "The 'Gees," I have followed chronology of publication, rather than of composition.

tially, Melville seems to have believed that if his compatriots could be aroused to a sense of fellowship with the Negro, a solution to the slavery problem would naturally follow. *Moby-Dick*, in which he dramatizes a love marriage between the races as the means of averting apocalyptic doom for the nation, marks the climax of this hope. As the decade inaugurated by the Fugitive Slave Law of 1850 wore on, Melville's vision of America grew increasingly pessimistic. His later novels and tales no longer seek to convert readers to an ideal of human brotherhood. Instead, they exhibit a perverse relish for entrapping readers in the toils of their own racism and for compelling them to experience the consequences of blinding themselves to the humanity of their nonwhite victims. Thus in "Benito Cereno" and "The 'Gees," Melville limits readers to the myopic viewpoint of racists. This technique reaches its culmination in *The Confidence-Man*, where a character who masquerades interchangeably as a white and as a black, and whose "true" racial identity remains unfathomable, disseminates the theories about Negro character enunciated by proslavery apologists and lures his interlocutors into staking their very souls on these pernicious tenets. After the Civil War, Melville, like so many northerners of his generation, seems to have been overcome by a sense of guilt toward the defeated South that drove him to transfer his allegiance from the Negro to the southerner as America's chief victim. Not until the end of his life did Melville recover his youthful dream of human brotherhood. In the opening pages of his last novel, *Billy Budd*, written after a thirty-year retreat from prose fiction, Melville once again portrays a dark-skinned sailor—this time not a Polynesian, but an African—as a heroic savior and fuses his image with that of the white "Handsome Sailor," Billy Budd.

A word, finally, about my omissions. Among the tales I have not discussed are several whose relevance to slavery and race has already been demonstrated by other critics: "I and My Chimney," "The Piazza," "The Happy Failure," "Bartleby" (one of Melville's finest achievements), and the Indian-hater episode in *The Confidence-Man*.[5]

---

5. See Marvin Fisher, *Going Under: Melville's Short Fiction and the American 1850s* (Baton Rouge, 1977), for provocative interpretations of the first four of these tales. See

The truth is that, having very little to add to the brilliant interpretations that these writings have lately inspired, I preferred to
limit myself to works more important to my line of argument and
to elucidate facets of them that other critics have neglected.

I would like to reverse the usual order of acknowledgments by
placing the tribute to the greatest personal debt first. This book
owes most to my husband, Martin, who believed in me long before
I had begun to believe in myself, has always taken my work and
professional aspirations seriously, and has provided constructive
criticism at every stage of composition. My greatest intellectual debt
is to H. Bruce Franklin. Having introduced me to Melville in the
most exciting college course I ever took, and having later, through
his own political odyssey and revolutionary writings, stimulated me
to read Melville with new eyes, Professor Franklin is in a sense the
spiritual father of this book. Both its style and its substance have
also benefited incalculably from his having taken the time to comment in detail on the entire manuscript. Other mentors I take pleasure in thanking for vital encouragement are: Edgar A. Dryden,
who read several early versions of the manuscript; John M. Wallace,
whose work on the literature of the English Civil War first taught
me what historical criticism is all about; and Donald Stanford, Beth
Brownlow, and Louise Y. Postman, who in different ways showed
confidence in my work when I needed it most. Several friends,
colleagues, and academic advisers suggested reworking various passages: Marvin Fisher, Michael T. Gilmore, Joyce Sparer Adler,
James B. Gilbert, Leonard I. Lutwack, Dorothy Ross, Simone
Vauthier, and above all Linda Hess, whose preliminary editing
smoothed out many rough spots. I also wish to thank the Library
of Congress staff, particularly Herbert Davis and Anne Hallstein,
for their help, and the University of Maryland for financial assistance

also Laurie Jean Lorant, "Herman Melville and Race: Themes and Imagery" (Ph.D.
dissertation, New York University, 1972), 145–65, on "The Happy Failure" and "I and
My Chimney"; Scott Donaldson, "The Dark Truth of *The Piazza Tales*," *PMLA*, LXXXV
(1970), 1082, 1085–86; and William J. Sowder, "Melville's 'I And My Chimney': A
Southern Exposure," *Mississippi Quarterly*, XVI (1963), 128–45. The best explication
I have read of the Indian-hater episode is Joyce Sparer Adler's "Melville on the White
Man's War Against the American Indian," *Science & Society*, XXXVI (1972), 417–42.

and the privilege of publishing this manuscript before presenting it as a dissertation. Finally, I would like to express my gratitude to Nirmal Singh for his valiant typing and to Margaret F. Dalrymple for her extremely sensitive editing.

List of Abbreviations

BB	*Billy Budd*
BC	"Benito Cereno"
BD	"Bridegroom Dick"
BP	*Battle-Pieces*
BT	"The Bell-Tower"
C	*Clarel*
CM	*The Confidence-Man*
E	"The Encantadas"
G	"The 'Gees"
IP	*Israel Potter*
M	*Mardi*
MD	*Moby-Dick*
O	*Omoo*
P	*Pierre*
PBTM	"The Paradise of Bachelors and The Tartarus of Maids"
PMP	"Poor Man's Pudding and Rich Man's Crumbs"
R	*Redburn*
T	*Typee*
TI	"Timoleon"
WJ	*White-Jacket*

ONE   ℳelville and the Slavery Controversy: The Biographical Context

TWO FORMATIVE experiences gave Herman Melville a distinctive perspective on the issues of slavery and race that dominated his age. The first was a long stint as a common sailor, beginning with a voyage to Liverpool at age nineteen, that exposed him to some of the nineteenth century's most oppressive working conditions—conditions that put Melville on a footing with men of all races, most of them from the bottom of society, and that taught him what it was like to be a slave.[1] The second was the famous sojourn among "cannibals" in the Marquesas that inspired Melville's first book, *Typee*. This experience, as *Typee* attests, reversed the cultural assumptions Melville had inherited about the relative merits of civilization and savagery, Christianity and heathenism, white and nonwhite. On the one hand he discovered a primitive, heathen, nonwhite people who "deal[t] more kindly with each other, and [were] more humane," than many who professed to live by the Sermon on the Mount—a people whose society seemed to run by itself "with a harmony and smoothness unparalleled . . . in the most select, refined, and pious associations of mortals in Christendom."[2] On the other hand, he saw that wherever "civilization" and Christianity had penetrated the South Sea islands, the natives had

1. H. Bruce Franklin, *The Victim as Criminal and Artist: Literature from the American Prison* (New York, 1978), 31–34, describes these conditions and their impact on Melville.
2. Herman Melville, *Typee: A Peep at Polynesian Life*, ed. Harrison Hayford, Hershel Parker, and G. Thomas Tanselle (Evanston, 1968), 200, 203. All further page references to this edition will be given parenthetically in the text.

been decimated by imperialist wars and white-introduced venereal diseases, their "depopulated land" invaded by "rapacious hordes of enlightened individuals," and their "small remnant" literally "civilized into draught horses, and evangelized into beasts of burden" (T, 195–96). As a result, never again did Melville take for granted either the superiority of white Christian civilization or the benefit of imposing it on others. Never again did he judge nonwhite peoples by ethnocentric standards. On the contrary, he began to reexamine his own society through the eyes of "savages."

These complementary experiences of quasi enslavement and cultural reeducation shaped the approach Melville adopted toward handling the slavery question in his fiction. Instead of making slavery his single, overriding concern—as did abolitionist novelists like Richard Hildreth and Harriet Beecher Stowe—Melville focused on the oppression and exploitation he had known as a sailor and generalized about slavery by analogy. Instead of making American Negro characters his primary vehicles for challenging his compatriots' anti-Negro prejudices, he created fictional counterparts for them among the South Sea cannibals, American Indians, native Africans, Cape Verdeans, Europeans, and white Americans he had encountered on his voyages.

Melville's oblique and eclectic treatment of slavery has seldom been recognized by critics. Too often, critics have tried to determine where Melville stood, in the controversy over the Negro's rightful status in America, by isolating all references to slavery, blacks, abolitionists, and southerners, totaling them up, and averaging out the inconsistencies. Confusion about Melville's stance has also arisen from another source, however. One of the thorny issues slavery raised, especially in the 1850s, was whether abolition could be achieved by any means short of violence, and if not, whether opponents of slavery ought to countenance violence. On this issue, Melville was extremely ambivalent. The view he presents of slave revolt in "Benito Cereno," for example, is hardly that of an enthusiastic partisan. Some critics have construed this as ipso facto evidence of racism and irresolute antislavery feelings.[3] Yet Melville betrays the same qualms about endorsing violent rebellion in all his

3. Kaplan, "Melville and the American National Sin," 27; Margaret M. Vanderhaar, "A Re-Examination of 'Benito Cereno,'" *American Literature*, XL (1968), 184; Eleanor

works, be the rebels black or white. At the same time, he consistently exhibits tyranny as unbearable and resistance to it as essential if the victim of oppression is to preserve his manhood.

The conflict between these two positions, in my opinion, is central not only to Melville's art, but to his life as well. By temperament Melville seems to have been at once a refractory conformist and a reluctant rebel. His erratic career as a sailor, besides taking him aboard four different ships in less than four years (not counting the voyage to Liverpool), included a desertion, an escape from "civilization" to a tribe of noble savages, a flight in turn from this tribe's attempt to possess him, a mutiny, an imprisonment and jailbreak, an interval as a beachcomber, another brief stint aboard a whaler, and finally a cruise on a man-of-war, which he later described as the ultimate in shipboard despotism.

The two autobiographical narratives in which Melville recounted most of these adventures—*Typee* and *Omoo*—reveal highly ambivalent reactions to the avenues of escape he had taken from the onerous discipline sailors had to bear. *Typee* begins by trying to explain what drove him to jump ship on a cannibal island fifteen months after setting out on his first whaling voyage, choosing "rather to risk my fortunes among the savages . . . than to endure" another four years under a captain whose word was law and against whose ill treatment there was no redress (T, 20). "The usage on board," Melville asserts, "was tyrannical; the sick had been inhumanly neglected; the provisions had been doled out in scanty allowance; and [the ship's] cruizes were unreasonably protracted." He attributes these abuses directly to the captain, whose "conduct . . . was arbitrary and violent in the extreme," and whose "prompt reply to all complaints and remonstrances was—the butt end of a hand-spike, so convincingly administered as effectually to silence the aggrieved party" (T, 21).

Melville considers in turn three possible responses to this situation—rebellion, adjustment, and desertion. Rebellion is the first course to be rejected, though for politic rather than moral reasons: "unfortunately, with a very few exceptions, our crew was composed of a parcel of dastardly and mean-spirited wretches, divided among

E. Simpson, "Melville and the Negro: From *Typee* to 'Benito Cereno,'" *American Literature*, XLI (1969), 33.

themselves, and only united in enduring without resistance the un-mitigated tyranny of the captain. It would have been mere madness for any two or three of the number, unassisted by the rest, to attempt making a stand against his ill usage" (T, 21). Adjustment is given equally short shrift. It might have been conceivable, Melville argues, "had we entertained the hope of being speedily delivered . . . by the due completion of the term of our servitude." But the ship had barely started on her expedition, and the "longevity of Cape Horn whaling voyages is proverbial, frequently extending over a period of four or five years." Indeed, even as Melville was writing *Typee*, three years after having jumped ship, the *Acushnet* was still at sea (T, 21, 23).

Hence the only alternative open to him, Melville concludes, was desertion, which he justifies on the grounds that the abuses to which the crew had been subjected constituted violations of the contract under which he had sailed, thus absolving him of the obligation to "perform his share of the compact" by serving out his full term (T, 20). Yet the defensiveness with which Melville belabors this point and seeks to vindicate himself from the "no way flattering" imputation of having "run away" suggests that he may have been trying to assuage a sense of guilt and shame that still haunted him.

A much stronger sense of guilt imbues Melville's account of his escape from the Typees. Idyllic as he perceived Typee society to be, his "indulgent captivity" was evidently not a happy one. Melville may not have actually feared cannibalism, but he seems to have been plagued by psychosomatic symptoms of tension.[4] Above all he shrank from the natives' constant importunities to let them tattoo and "make a convert of me" (T, 220). Rather than lose his cultural identity, Melville finally chose to return to the very tyranny from which he had earlier fled. This, however, meant betraying a people whose culture he rated superior in many respects to his own. In fiction the betrayal takes the form of abandoning a father figure (Marheyo), a devoted friend and brother (Kory-Kory), and a mistress (Fayaway), and culminates in the murder of a Typee chieftain,

---

4. Edgar A. Dryden, *Melville's Thematics of Form: The Great Art of Telling the Truth* (Baltimore, 1968), 40–45, analyzes Melville/Tommo's inflamed leg as a psychosomatic ailment "tied to his desire . . . to have the advantages of both the primitive and civilized worlds." Since Melville mentions this ailment in the first chapter of *Omoo*, it seems to be biographical fact, not mere invention.

reflecting Melville's awareness of reenacting the white man's depredations against these South Sea island paradises. Melville spent the rest of his life "upbraiding" himself for having repeated "Adam's flight" from Eden, though "without compulsion or the sin."[5]

His regrets began as soon as he joined the crew of the *Lucy Ann*: "Safe aboard of a ship—so long my earnest prayer—with home and friends once more in prospect, I nevertheless felt weighed down by a melancholy that could not be shaken off. It was the thought of never more seeing those, who, notwithstanding their desire to retain me a captive, had, upon the whole, treated me so kindly. I was leaving them forever."[6]

Meanwhile, to add to his conflict of loyalties, Melville found himself aboard a ship that was ripe for the mutiny he had dismissed as "madness" in *Typee*. The setting: a rotting, unseaworthy vessel, infested with rats and furnished with worm-eaten provisions. The cast: a "sickly" captain, "no more meant for the sea than a hairdresser"; a drunken, headstrong first mate, "who, as the story went, had been given his captain in charge"; and an unruly crew, reduced by desertions from thirty-two to twenty sailors, of whom half were suffering from venereal disease, some to the point of being "wholly unfit for duty" (o, 6, 10).

The mutiny, or rather strike, that Melville fictionalizes in *Omoo* breaks out when the captain falls seriously ill, and the sailors discover that instead of bringing the ship to port in accordance with normal usage, the mate intends to put the captain ashore and temporarily continue the voyage without him. Several of the sailors, disappointed in their hopes of respite from duty and outraged by the mate's highhanded tactics, advocate seizing the ship on the spot and sailing her into port at Papeete, even "if they all swung for it" (o, 70). Forced to choose between standing with his shipmates and risking disciplinary action, or forfeiting his self-respect and going against his sense of justice by siding with his officers, Melville reluctantly casts his lot with the mutinous sailors. Here is how he summarizes his dilemma:

5. Herman Melville, *Clarel: A Poem and Pilgrimage in the Holy Land*, ed. Walter E. Bezanson (New York, 1960), III. xxix. 74–78.

6. Herman Melville, *Omoo: A Narrative of Adventures in the South Seas*, ed. Harrison Hayford, Hershel Parker, and G. Thomas Tanselle (Evanston, 1968), 7. All further page references to this edition will be given parenthetically in the text.

For my own part, I felt that I was under a foreign flag; that an English consul was close at hand, and that sailors seldom obtain justice. It was best to be prudent. Still, so much did I sympathize with the men, so far, at least, as their real grievances were concerned; and so convinced was I of the cruelty and injustice of what Captain Guy seemed bent upon, that if need were, I stood ready to raise a hand. (o, 73)

I must explain myself here. All we wanted was to have the ship snugly anchored in Papeetee Bay; entertaining no doubt that, could this be done, it would in some way or other peaceably lead to our emancipation. Without a downright mutiny, there was but one way to accomplish this: to induce the men to refuse all further duty, unless it were to work the vessel in. The only difficulty lay in restraining them within proper bounds. Nor was it without certain misgivings, that I found myself so situated, that I must necessarily link myself, however guardedly, with such a desperate company; and in an enterprise too, of which it was hard to conjecture what might be the result. But any thing like neutrality was out of the question; and unconditional submission was equally so. (o, 83–84.)

Although in life prudence had won the upper hand, in fiction Melville struck the balance in the opposite direction, indicating that this time he felt guilt, not at having defied authority, but at having played a less active role than he would have liked in championing his fellow sailors. In life, Melville joined the strikers' ranks only after failing to obtain exemption from duty on medical grounds. In *Omoo*, on the contrary, Melville glorifies himself as a ringleader of the strikers who articulates their grievances in a round robin that they all sign. But mirroring the discrepancy between his real-life and fictional roles in the mutiny, even Melville's romanticized version of it reveals a dichotomy between flamboyant rhetoric and guarded behavior, imaginative identification with rebels and inability to envisage acting on it. Thus he represents himself as a leader who shuns violence and attempts to pacify the hotheads of the group by pleading that "a little patience and management would, in the end, accomplish all that their violence could; and that, too, without making a serious matter of it" (o, 73–74).[7] As we shall see, the tensions in Melville's

7. Gordon Roper's "Historical Note" in the Northwestern–Newberry edition of *Omoo*, 320–22, distinguishes between fact and fiction on the basis of British consular documents on the *Lucy Ann* affair. See also Charles R. Anderson, *Melville in the South Seas* (New York, 1966), 204–15.

self-image that pervade his fictional account of the one mutiny in which he participated reappear in all the confrontations between abused seamen and overbearing commanders that he dramatizes in later works, including his controversial narrative of a revolt aboard a slave ship.

Almost equally relevant to the issues raised in these later confrontations is the ambivalent attitude toward authority figures that Melville evinces in *Typee* and *Omoo*, on the one hand through his nostalgic characterizations of the Typee chieftains who befriended him, and on the other hand through his overwhelmingly negative portrayals of the captains whose tyranny and meanness drove him to desertion and mutiny. Whether or not he exaggerated the brutality of his first captain and the effete incompetence and unreasonable obduracy of the second, as some of his biographers have opined,[8] the gallery of sea captains Melville displays in his subsequent fiction contains a preponderance of petty despots and weaklings, ranging from Captain Riga and Captain Claret to Amasa Delano and Benito Cereno. The two memorable exceptions—the "grand, ungodly, godlike" Ahab who leads his crew to death and destruction in his mad hunt for the white whale, and the fatherly Vere who, in the name of martial law, decrees the execution of the young sailor he knows to be morally innocent—are authority figures whose embrace proves as fatal as Melville feared the Typees' might be.

The authority figures with whom Melville had to contend for the rest of his life, however, were not sea captains, but publishers, editors, readers, and the family members he had to support by producing salable fiction. Nowhere did he more dramatically act out his deep inner conflict between complying with and resisting their demands on him than in alternately yielding to and defying the outraged evangelicals and worldly-wise publishers who pressured him into issuing a revised (or as he ruefully put it, "Expurgated?—Odious word!") edition of *Typee* in 1846. Although he dutifully accepted the view that "the interest of the book" consisted in "the *intrinsick merit of the narrative alone*" and proceeded to suppress his impassioned attacks on the missionaries, his tributes to the moral superiority of primitive peoples, and "all passages

8. Leon Howard, *Herman Melville: A Biography* (Berkeley, 1967), 48; Anderson, *Melville in the South Seas*, 111–12; Roper, "Historical Note," *Omoo*, 321.

... calculated to offend the tastes, or offer violance [sic] to the feelings of any large class of readers,"[9] his "earnest desire for truth and good" had the last word.[10] The very next year Melville threw expediency to the winds, unburdening himself more fully in *Omoo* than he had dared to even in the first edition of *Typee*, and lashing out more unsparingly than ever against the missionary and imperialist despoilers of Polynesia.

Melville's warring tendencies toward rebellion and conformity are also apparent in the staid marriage on which he embarked after returning home from four adventurous years at sea which had thrown him among rough sailors and voluptuous Polynesian natives. The epitome of dull, conventional, well-bred Victorian womanhood, Elizabeth Shaw could hardly have presented a more striking contrast to the naked Polynesian nymphs whose charms Melville had celebrated with such gusto. As one genteel acquaintance of the Shaws confided to another, "After his flirtations with South Sea beauties it is a peculiar choice." A more romantically inclined feminine admirer of *Typee* and *Omoo* fantasized that "Mistress Melville might wince sometimes if she attaches much credit to his accounts of his romancing," though "she *may* like him the better, for the adventures he has passed and he loves her that she doth *laugh* at them—as I suppose she does."[11] Whether Elizabeth Shaw overlooked or laughed off Melville's youthful dalliances, she certainly does not seem to have provided a very satisfactory outlet for either his amorous or his intellectual needs. Indeed one can almost date Melville's marriage as the starting point for his covert mode of expressing himself and assailing the taboos of his stifling milieu, be it in airing his private sexual frustrations and religious doubts, or in articulating the forebodings he shared with his contemporaries over his nation's entrapment in the slavery dilemma.

If Melville seemed to be betraying the adventurous, heterodox

9. Merrell R. Davis and William H. Gilman (eds.), *The Letters of Herman Melville* (New Haven, 1960), 39, 43. For an illuminating discussion of the passages Melville was forced to delete from *Typee*, see Franklin, *The Victim as Criminal and Artist*, 34–35, 39–41.
10. From Melville's preface to *Omoo*, xiv; see also Roper, "Historical Note," *Omoo*, 327–28.
11. Jay Leyda, *The Melville Log: A Documentary Life of Herman Melville, 1819–1891* (2 vols.; New York, 1969), I, 305, II, 917; Roper, "Historical Note," *Omoo*, 337.

side of himself when he married Elizabeth Shaw, he was clearly fulfilling his aspirations toward social and family sanction, respectability, status, and even, as it turned out, financial security. The daughter of Chief Justice Lemuel Shaw of the Massachusetts Supreme Court, Elizabeth Shaw represented the birthright of which the Melville family had felt itself cruelly dispossessed by the tragic death and bankruptcy of Allan Melvill, Herman's father. The two families, moreover, had been united by close ties since before Herman's birth. As Allan Melvill's most intimate friend, Judge Shaw had helped the family through a financial crisis in Allan's lifetime and loyally supported his widow and her children after Allan's death. Meanwhile, Elizabeth had remained a close friend of the Melville daughters. In marrying Elizabeth, who was all but a sister to him, Herman Melville was thus reclaiming his patrimony and, perhaps more important, recovering a father.[12]

Noting how prominent a part the quest for a father plays in Melville's fiction and how many of Melville's characters are orphans or Ishmaels, several biographers and critics have linked these fictional themes with the trauma Melville must have undergone when his father died, leaving him destitute at the age of twelve.[13] As Newton Arvin has pointed out, Melville, like most bereaved survivors, especially children, must have felt abandoned and experienced not only grief but resentment toward his father for dying. This ambivalence, which unmistakably shapes Melville's fictional characterizations of fathers and father figures, also seems to have driven him to choose a surrogate father who incarnated the dual aspects of the loving protector Melville craved and the heartless deserter against whom Melville retaliated by transmuting him psychologically into an oppressive tyrant whose yoke he had to cast off. Accordingly, Judge Shaw, who generously continued to tide over

12. This analysis has grown out of a stimulating paper on Melville and Dana given by Robert F. Lucid at the Melville Society Meeting in Nantucket, 1969. According to Leyda, *Melville Log*, I, 53, the Melville family changed the spelling of the name in 1832, after Allan Melvill's death. Elizabeth Shaw's friendship with the Melville sisters is documented in the *Melville Log*, I, 120, 125–26, 140, and 175–76.

13. Newton Arvin, *Herman Melville* (New York, 1957), 23; Charles Olson, *Call Me Ishmael: A Study of Melville* (San Francisco, 1947), 82; Robert L. Carothers, "Herman Melville and the Search for the Father: An Interpretation of the Novels" (Ph.D. dissertation, Kent State University, 1969), 3–6 and *passim*; Edwin Haviland Miller, *Melville: A Biography* (New York, 1975), 69–72.

the expenses Melville incurred in writing unpopular books and even to finance the voyages prescribed to restore his son-in-law's flagging health and spirits, was at the same time a "man of intense & doating biasses, in religious, political & social matters," as Melville's friend Richard Henry Dana, Jr., confided to his diary.[14]

Shaw's most glaring biases were those he manifested on racial prejudice and slavery in his official capacity as chief justice. During the very years Melville was writing *Redburn*, *White-Jacket*, and *Moby-Dick*, Shaw was trying two controversial cases on which he delivered verdicts that abolitionists would anathemize. In the first, *Sarah C. Roberts* v. *the City of Boston* (1849), Shaw upheld the Boston Primary School Committee's right to enforce segregated schooling on the grounds that "the law had not created and could not alter the deep-rooted prejudice which sanctioned segregation"— a ruling that helped establish a basis for the notorious "separate but equal" doctrine in American law. In the second, the celebrated case of the fugitive slave Thomas Sims (1851), Shaw became the first northern judge to order a fugitive returned to his master in conformance with the recently passed Fugitive Slave Law.[15] Hence, had Melville openly attacked racism and the federal government's policy of buttressing slavery, he would have had to brave not merely public opprobrium, but the reproaches of a betrayed mentor. No wonder, then, that Melville found himself repeatedly dramatizing situations in which seamen faced the choice of either abjectly submitting to tyrannical officers at the price of their manhood, or else exercising the "privilege, inborn and inalienable, that every man has, of dying himself, and inflicting death upon another"[16]—alternatives that equated rebellion with murder and represented submission and rebellion as equally suicidal. Only through his art did

14. Leyda, *Melville Log*, II, 514.
15. For a full treatment of Shaw's role in the slavery controversy, see Leonard W. Levy, *The Law of the Commonwealth and Chief Justice Shaw* (Cambridge, Mass., 1957), Chaps. 5–7; on the Roberts case, see Leon L. Litwack, *North of Slavery: The Negro in the Free States, 1790–1860* (Chicago, 1961), 147–49. Among critics who have related the Roberts and Sims cases to *Redburn*, *White-Jacket*, and *Moby-Dick* are Charles H. Foster, "Something in Emblems: A Reinterpretation of *Moby-Dick*," *New England Quarterly*, XXXIV (1961), 6–7, 11–14, 17–20; and Simpson, "Melville and the Negro," 25–27. The quotation is from Litwack, p. 148. I consulted the Shaw Papers at the Massachusetts Historical Society in the hope of finding correspondence about the Sims case, but the search proved fruitless.
16. From Herman Melville, *White-Jacket; or The World in a Man-of-War*, ed. Harrison Hayford, Hershel Parker, and G. Thomas Tanselle (Evanston, 1970), 280.

Melville achieve an uneasy truce between his conformist and rebellious selves by creating a series of fictional personae who chafe
at tyranny but manage to resist it without consummating suicidally
murderous impulses against their oppressors.

So far we have been concentrating on how Melville's family life may
have influenced his covert way of tackling the issues of race and
slavery in his fiction. It remains to situate Melville with respect to
his northern literary contemporaries, most of whom shared Judge
Shaw's racial views and tolerated slavery as an apparently intractable
evil, but some of whom publicly championed the antislavery cause.
Poignantly attesting to Melville's extreme sense of isolation is the
almost total silence he maintained on the subject of slavery in his
letters to family members, friends, publishers, and fellow writers,
even while he was formulating his impassioned fictional indictments
of it. One is struck by the way Melville seems to straddle intellectually diverse worlds and to feel at home in none. His religious
skepticism and irreverence alienated him from most of his contemporaries. including the intellectuals of the Young America circle
revolving around the New York editors Evert and George Duyckinck, who had taken Melville into their fold in the flush of *Typee*'s
success and whose politics resembled Judge Shaw's. At the same
time, Melville's allegiance to the principle of "unconditional democracy in all things"—meaning in practice, as he wrote to Nathaniel Hawthorne, that he would consider a "thief in jail . . . as
honorable a personage as Gen. George Washington"—set him at
variance with the few intellectual peers who shared his religious
doubts.[17]

His Pittsfield neighbor, Oliver Wendell Holmes, a like-minded
rebel against the "one-hoss shay" of Calvinism with whom Melville
enjoyed spirited discussions on "East India religions and mytholo-
gies," cherished memories of "slavery in its best and mildest form"
passed on to him by his slaveholding grandfather, and flirted as well
with the theories of an ethnological school claiming that human
races were distinct species. The unflattering portrait Melville drew

17. Davis and Gilman (eds.), *Letters of Melville*, 127. On Melville's relationship with
the Duyckinck circle, see Perry Miller, *The Raven and the Whale: The War of Words and
Wits in the Era of Poe and Melville* (New York, 1956). On the political differences between
Melville and Hawthorne, see Foster, "Something in Emblems," 8–15.

of Holmes as a heartless scientist in "I and My Chimney"—a cour-
tesy Holmes is said to have reciprocated with a savage caricature
of Melville in *Elsie Venner*—indicates that hostility toward Holmes's
unconcern for human values outweighed the intellectual affinities
that might have alleviated Melville's loneliness in Pittsfield society.[18]

Nathaniel Hawthorne, with whom Melville talked deep into the
night of "time and eternity, things of this world and the next, and
books, and publishers, and all possible and impossible matters,"
remained an aristocrat of the mind who, as Melville ruefully noted,
seemed to "feel a touch of a shrink" on encountering "my ruthless
democracy on all sides."[19] For an artist whose insight into "the
protean guises of the devil in his New England haunts" Melville
rightly admired, Hawthorne proved strangely blind to the devil's
"presence in the slave-pens of Carolina" (as Daniel Aaron so aptly
phrases it).[20] As late as 1851, Hawthorne felt justified in maintaining in a campaign biography of Franklin Pierce—the college
friend whose presidency would be remembered for serving the interests of slaveholders—that southern masters and their black slaves
"dwelt together in greater peace and affection . . . than had ever
elsewhere existed between the taskmaster and the serf."[21] Even
during the Civil War, Hawthorne never ceased to feel that it was
"'sentimental nonsense' to risk American lives in order to liberate
slaves." Hawthorne, of course, was exceptional in remaining unable
to commit himself to the Union cause that most of his northern
literary contemporaries ultimately championed, whatever their attitude toward the Negro.[22] Nevertheless, Melville's closest associ-

18. Leyda, *Melville Log*, I, xxviii, II, 506, 636. Melville may be caricatured as Dick
Venner, a wild, adventurous New Englander turned "gaucho" after a stay in South
America. On Holmes's views about slavery, see Howard R. Floan, *The South in Northern
Eyes, 1831 to 1861* (New York, 1973), 74–75. On Melville's caricature of Holmes, see
Merton M. Sealts, Jr., "Herman Melville's 'I and My Chimney,'" *American Literature*,
XIII (1941), 153–54.

19. Quoted from Hawthorne's *American Notebooks*, in Eleanor Melville Metcalf, *Herman Melville: Cycle and Epicycle* (Westport, Conn., 1970), 113; Davis and Gilman (eds.),
Letters of Melville, 126–27.

20. Daniel Aaron, *The Unwritten War: American Writers and the Civil War* (New York,
1973), 44.

21. Cited in Randall Stewart, *Nathaniel Hawthorne: A Biography* (New Haven, 1948),
133; see also Allen Flint's excellent article, "Hawthorne and the Slavery Crisis," *New
England Quarterly*, XLI (1968), 393–408.

22. Aaron, *The Unwritten War*, 44, 53–55.

ates—and those with whose social background and literary tastes he had most in common—were men who did not share his ardent fellow feeling with the slave and would hardly have provided a sympathetic audience for the egalitarian racial ideas Melville sought to promulgate in his fiction.

A notable exception is Melville's inspiring forerunner in both seafaring and sea literature, Richard Henry Dana, Jr., who risked the flourishing law practice he had taken up after writing *Two Years Before the Mast* to plead the case of Thomas Sims. Yet for some reason Melville's relationship with Dana apparently never developed very far, despite his affinity with one "who like myself, [had] experienced in person the usages to which a sailor is subjected," as Melville wrote Dana, and despite Melville's gratification that the "Siamese link of affectionate sympathy" he had felt for Dana on reading *Two Years Before the Mast* "should be reciprocated . . . and be called out by any White Jackets or Redburns of mine."[23]

Besides Dana, two literary men whom Melville ought to have greeted as kindred spirits on the slavery question, though there is no evidence that he did so, were George William Curtis and Frederick Law Olmsted, both connected with *Putnam's Monthly*, the magazine in which Melville published his principal short stories. Curtis, as ex officio literary adviser to the editors of *Putnam's*, appreciatively reviewed "Benito Cereno," "The Bell-Tower," and "I and My Chimney" for them. He also recommended publication of *The Piazza Tales*, singling out "The Encantadas" and "Bartleby" for special praise. Strangely enough, considering that *Putnam's* had become an organ for moderate antislavery views and that Curtis was at this time an active antislavery partisan, he did not comment on the relevance "Benito Cereno" and "The Bell-Tower" had to the slavery controversy, but simply characterized the one as "ghastly & interesting" and the other as "picturesque & of a profound mo-

23. Davis and Gilman (eds.), *Letters of Melville*, 92–93, 106–108. On Melville's relationship with Dana, see William H. Bond, "Melville and *Two Years before the Mast*," *Harvard Library Bulletin*, VII (1953), 362–65; James D. Hart, "Melville and Dana," *American Literature*, IX (1937), 49–55; and Robert F. Lucid, "The Influence of *Two Years before the Mast* on Herman Melville," *American Literature*, XXXI (1959), 243–56. On Dana's role in the Sims case, see Foster, "Something in Emblems," 11; and Robert F. Lucid (ed.), *The Journal of Richard Henry Dana, Jr.* (3 vols.; Cambridge, Mass., 1968), I, xxiii–xxx, II, 420–25.

rality." Nor does it seem that Melville, on his part, was even aware of Curtis' role in his literary career.[24]

Curtis' friend and colleague, Frederick Law Olmsted, who had just completed a well-publicized journalistic tour of the slave states for the New York *Times*, joined the firm of Dix and Edwards, the new publishers of *Putnam's*, in April, 1855, the very month that Melville submitted "Benito Cereno." The following year Dix and Edwards issued both Melville's *Piazza Tales* and the book version of Olmsted's *Journey in the Seaboard Slave States*, which Harriet Beecher Stowe hailed as "the most thorough *exposé* of the economical view of this subject which has ever appeared," "calculated to do more good with less friction" than any book to date. "An antislavery man of strong conviction, but temperate . . . [political] outlook," Olmsted expressed views on slavery and racism very close to Melville's, if not quite as radically egalitarian. Like Melville, Olmsted did not call for immediate abolition, but concentrated on convincing northerners that their duty was to "demolish the bulwarks of this stronghold of evil by demonstrating that the negro is endowed with the natural capacities to make a good use of the blessing of freedom; by letting the negro have a fair chance to prove his own case, to prove himself a man entitled to the inalienable rights of man." Olmsted also made liberal use of irony in refuting the proslavery apologists' assertions of the Negro's intellectual inferiority and biological adaptedness to slavery, as Melville would in "The Bell-Tower," "The 'Gees," and *The Confidence-Man*. Although the two men arrived independently at the same conclusions (already implicit in Melville's earlier writings), Melville must have read at least some of Olmsted's much-discussed letters to the *Times* in 1853 and 1854. That his path apparently never crossed Olmsted's bespeaks Melville's curious isolation.[25]

24. Leyda, *Melville Log*, I, xxiv, II, 499–502, 504, 507–508, 510. On *Putnam's* as an organ of moderate antislavery views, see Floan, *The South in Northern Eyes*, 123–30. On Curtis' antislavery politics, see Gordon Milne, *George William Curtis and the Genteel Tradition* (Bloomington, 1956), 85–86, 90–91.

25. For an account of Olmsted's literary career and southern travels, see Laura Wood Roper, "Frederick Law Olmsted in the 'Literary Republic,'" *Mississippi Valley Historical Review*, XXXIX (1952), 459–82. Citations are from pp. 471, 460, and 465. For examples in Olmsted's works that parallel Melville's satire on racism, see Frederick Law Olmsted, *A Journey in the Seaboard Slave States, with Remarks on Their Economy* (1856; rpt. New York, 1968), 191–200, 226, 388, 478–79, 552–53; and *A Journey in the Back Country*

Of the other major writers who embraced the antislavery cause in the decade when Melville was writing the bulk of his fiction, none was personally known to Melville; and he seems on the whole to have found them all as incompatible philosophically as he found Holmes and Hawthorne politically. Melville objected to Ralph Waldo Emerson's facile rationalization of evil and suffering, which, as he noted in his copy of Emerson's *Essays*, indicated a "defect in the region of the heart" and a "self-conceit so intensely intellectual and calm that at first one hesitates to call it by its right name."[26] Melville also felt strongly enough about the icy selfishness Emerson's philosophy fostered to caricature the "Grand Master" as a "non-benevolent" mystic in *Pierre* and as a "cross between a Yankee peddler and a Tartar priest" in *The Confidence-Man*, where a "practical disciple" (Henry David Thoreau) puts Emersonianism "into action" by refusing a loan to a friend in need.[27]

As for pietists like John Greenleaf Whittier and evangelicals like Harriet Beecher Stowe, Melville's notorious aversion to the missionary programs and temperance crusades they supported presented an insuperable barrier for both parties to any alliance between them, while Melville's skepticism precluded his espousing the abolitionism they preached as a means of inaugurating the millennium in America.[28]

(1860; rpt. New York, 1970), Preface and 64, 83, 287, 382–85, 432–46. Other critics who have linked Melville with Olmsted are Jean Fagan Yellin, *The Intricate Knot: Black Figures in American Literature, 1776–1863* (New York, 1972), 216, 225; and Sowder, "Melville's 'I And My Chimney,'" 128–45.

26. Cited in William Braswell, "Melville as a Critic of Emerson," *American Literature*, IX (1937), 331; see also Davis and Gilman (eds.), *Letters of Melville*, 77–80.

27. Herman Melville, *Pierre; or, The Ambiguities*, ed. Harrison Hayford, Hershel Parker, and G. Thomas Tanselle (Evanston, 1971), Bk. XXI, 289–93; Herman Melville, *The Confidence-Man: His Masquerade*, ed. H. Bruce Franklin (Indianapolis, 1967), Chaps. 37–41. Melville's satire of Emerson and Thoreau has been discussed by Egbert S. Oliver, "Melville's Picture of Emerson and Thoreau in *The Confidence-Man*," *College English*, VIII (1946), 61–72; Elizabeth S. Foster (ed.), *The Confidence-Man: His Masquerade* (New York, 1954), lxxiii–lxxxii, 351–61; Brian Higgins, "Mark Winsome and Egbert: 'In the Friendly Spirit,'" in Hershel Parker (ed.), *The Confidence-Man: His Masquerade* (New York, 1971), 339–43; Hershel Parker, "Melville's Satire of Emerson and Thoreau: An Evaluation of the Evidence," *American Transcendental Quarterly*, No. 7, Pt. 2 (Summer, 1970), 61–67.

28. On the evangelical and Garrisonian abolitionists' involvement in revivalism, missionary programs, temperance, and other Christian reform movements, see Gilbert H. Barnes, *The Antislavery Impulse, 1830–1844* (New York, 1964); Louis Filler, *The Crusade Against Slavery, 1830–1860* (New York, 1963), Chaps. 3 and 6; and Aileen S. Kraditor, *Means and Ends in American Abolitionism: Garrison and His Critics on Strategy and Tactics*,

Nevertheless, Melville had more in common with the abolitionists than has generally been recognized. He explicitly upheld the charges of cruelty and sexual exploitation that the abolitionists leveled at slaveholders,[29] and he condemned slavery as a monstrous betrayal of the American Revolution's egalitarian ideals. Again and again Melville warned that failure to abolish slavery would bring an apocalyptic judgment on America. He may even, at some point, have shared the abolitionists' belief in America's millennial destiny, if we are to credit his eloquent invocation of it in *Redburn*:

> Settled by the people of all nations, all nations may claim [America] for their own. You can not spill a drop of American blood without spilling the blood of the whole world. . . .
>
> On this Western Hemisphere all tribes and people are forming into one federated whole; and there is a future which shall see the estranged children of Adam restored as to the old hearth-stone in Eden.
>
> The other world beyond this, which was longed for by the devout before Columbus' time, was found in the New; and the deep-sea-lead, that first struck these soundings, brought up the soil of Earth's Paradise. Not a Paradise then, or now; but to be made so, at God's good pleasure, and in the fullness and mellowness of time. The seed is sown, and the harvest must come; and our children's children, on the world's jubilee morning, shall all go with their sickles to the reaping. Then shall the curse of Babel be revoked, a new Pentecost come, and the language they shall speak shall be the language of Britain. Frenchmen, and Danes, and Scots; and the dwellers on the shores of the Mediterranean, and in the regions round about; Italians, and Indians, and Moors; there shall appear unto them cloven tongues as of fire.[30]

Although Melville scouted *Redburn* as a comedown after his allegorical epic *Mardi*—a financial flop—there is no evidence that he wrote such passages merely to enhance the book's popular appeal.

1834–1850 (New York, 1969), Chap. 4. Melville's feelings about missionary programs and temperance can be gleaned from *Typee*, Chaps. 17 and 26; *Omoo*, Chaps. 44–46; *Pierre*, Bk. XXII, Chap. 1; and Davis and Gilman (eds.), *Letters of Melville*, 128.

29. See, for examples, Herman Melville, *Mardi: and A Voyage Thither*, ed. Harrison Hayford, Hershel Parker, and G. Thomas Tanselle (Evanston, 1970), 515, 531–35; *White-Jacket*, 275, 378; and *Pierre*, 261. Further page references to *Mardi* will be given parenthetically in the text.

30. Herman Melville, *Redburn: His First Voyage, Being the Sailor-boy Confessions and Reminiscences of the Son-of-a-Gentleman, in the Merchant Service*, ed. Harrison Hayford, Hershel Parker, and G. Thomas Tanselle (Evanston, 1969), 169.

Indeed, in the same letter to his father-in-law that disparages *Redburn*, Melville asserts: "yet, in writing these two books [*Redburn* and *White-Jacket*], I have not repressed myself much—so far as *they* are concerned; but have spoken pretty much as I feel."[31]

Granted Melville's sincerity in envisioning "the estranged children of Adam restored" to Edenic harmony in America, there is nonetheless a major difference between the millennial note he strikes in this passage from *Redburn* and the millennialist credo to which most abolitionists subscribed. Melville is looking forward to a new dispensation of human brotherhood, whereas the abolitionists looked forward to the Kingdom of Christ. Moreover, Melville did not long cherish the hope that America would become a Paradise. By the time he wrote *Moby-Dick* two years later, he expected apocalyptic doom, rather than millennial jubilee, for America. In the last analysis, Melville's disagreement with the abolitionists boils down to this: to Melville, slavery came to epitomize the vanity of America's millennial aspirations; but to most abolitionists, slavery was the primary obstacle in the way of fulfilling these aspirations.

If Melville could neither embrace abolitionism as a program nor abolitionists as fellow travelers, he could and did join them in dramatizing the evils of slavery, in refuting the rationalizations by which southerners defended it and conservative northerners tolerated it, and in tracing its insidious corrosion of American democracy. Melville actually verges on the genre of the abolitionist tract in *Mardi*, which contains his first literary protest against slavery. Not only does he depict slaves being whipped by their overseers and masters, forced to wear collars around their necks, and advertised as runaways in the very "Temple of Freedom" (the U.S. Capitol); he also adopts the abolitionists' evangelical language, condemning slavery as a "sin . . . foul as the crater-pool of hell" and prophesying the damnation of slaveholders: "conscience or no conscience—ere he die—let every master who wrenches bond-babe from mother, that the nipple tear; unwreathes the arms of sisters; or cuts the holy unity in twain; till apart fall man and wife, like one bleeding body cleft:— let that master thrice shrive his soul; take every sacrament; on his bended knees give up the ghost;—yet shall he die despairing; and live again, to die forever damned" (M, 534–35).

31. Davis and Gilman (eds.), *Letters of Melville*, 92.

True to the ambivalence we have already encountered in *Omoo*, Melville's poet-spokesman retreats rather quickly from urging slaves to revolt, "though they cut their chains with blades thrice edged, and gory to the haft!" (M, 533). But when he and the other fictional personae bow to Melville's philosopher's qualms and shy away from the violent solution that their "sympathies" call for, lamenting that "not one man knows a prudent remedy" for this "vast enormity," they are acknowledging an impasse at which abolitionists like Garrison had also arrived.[32] "The head is dull, where the heart is cold" (M, 534), concludes Melville's poet, while his philosopher faces the terrible insight that in their helplessness to suppress the evil they denounce, his various personae "weeping, all but echo hard-hearted Nulli" (the proslavery politician John C. Calhoun). The lame appeal to a deus ex machina in which Melville's personae ultimately concur—"Time—all-healing Time—Time, great Philanthropist!—Time must befriend these thralls!" (M, 535)—departs further from abolitionism rhetorically than it does in substance.

Melville's antislavery jeremiad in *Mardi*, unique among his writings for its outspoken sermonizing on the subject, provoked an immediate retort from a southern member of his friend Duyckinck's Young America circle, the eminent South Carolina novelist William Gilmore Simms. To compound the blow, Simms was among the minority of critics who had appreciated the allegory of *Mardi*, with its "many glowing rhapsodies, much epigrammatic thought, and many sweet and attractive fancies." Thus when Simms ended his otherwise complimentary review of Melville's first original creation by expostulating that "he spoils every thing to the Southern reader" with his "loathsome picture of Mr. Calhoun, in the character of a slave driver, drawing mixed blood and tears from the victim at every stroke of the whip,"[33] Melville must have felt himself confronted anew with the conflict that persisted in dogging his literary career.

---

32. See John Demos, "The Antislavery Movement and the Problem of Violent 'Means,'" *New England Quarterly*, XXXVII (1964), 501–26; also Kraditor, *Means and Ends in American Abolitionism*, 185–217; and Truman Nelson (ed.), *Documents of Upheaval: Selections from William Lloyd Garrison's "The Liberator," 1831–1865* (New York, 1966), xvi–xx, 4–31. Floan, *The South in Northern Eyes*, 134–36, interprets Melville's critique of slavery in *Mardi* as a burlesque of abolitionist rhetoric but presents no evidence for this reading.

33. "*Mardi: and a Voyage Thither*," *Southern Quarterly Review*, XVI (October, 1849), 260–61.

"Try to get a living by the Truth," he complained in a letter to Hawthorne while in the midst of writing *Moby-Dick*,"—and go to the Soup Societies." By his own standards, Melville never satisfactorily reconciled the financial compulsion he was under to write books that would have popular appeal with his creative need to tap his deepest inner resources and to fulfill the truth-telling mission he conceived to be his as an artist: "What I feel most moved to write, that is banned,—it will not pay. Yet, altogether, write the *other* way I cannot. So the product is a final hash, and all my books are botches."[34] Although few of us would consider Melville's books artistic botches, the continuing critical debate about his attitudes toward slavery and race does raise questions about how effectively he succeeded in making his art serve as a vehicle for truth.

Whatever propagandistic merit we may ascribe to Melville's oblique indictment of the prejudices that paralyzed his countrymen in the face of slavery, we will surely be impressed with its thoroughness. Beginning with *Mardi*, in almost every piece of fiction Melville wrote, he addressed himself directly or indirectly, concertedly or in passing, to refuting the racist assumptions that justified slavery in the South and racial discrimination throughout the United States. Before we can understand Melville's manner of discrediting racism, however, we must familiarize ourselves with the various contemporary beliefs about the Negro against which he took his stand.

These beliefs fall into three main categories: proslavery ideology, scientific racism, and romantic notions of innate racial character. The most blatantly racist beliefs about the Negro, of course, were those promulgated by the southern apologists of slavery in their dry and endlessly repetitive treatises on slavery and, more influentially, in their romanticized fictional accounts of plantation life.[35]

According to the proslavery argument, certain intellectual, temperamental, and physical peculiarities shared by no other race pre-

34. Davis and Gilman (eds.), *Letters of Melville*, 127–28.
35. My résumé of the proslavery argument is based on the following works: William Sumner Jenkins, *Pro-Slavery Thought in the Old South* (Gloucester, Mass., 1960); William R. Taylor, *Cavalier and Yankee: The Old South and American National Character* (New York, 1969), Chap. 9; and *The Pro-Slavery Argument; as Maintained by the Most Distinguished Writers of the Southern States, Containing the Several Essays, on the Subject, of Chancellor Harper, Governor Hammond, Dr. Simms, and Professor Dew* (1852; rpt. New York, 1968), 26–27, 32–34, 48, 56, 74–77, 81, 128–33, 160–61.

disposed the Negro toward slavery and disqualified him for freedom. Intellectually, maintained the proslavery apologists, the Negro had always shown himself inferior to other races. In Africa, they asserted, he had immemorially been enslaved by neighboring peoples and had never evolved a high civilization of his own. In America, they affirmed, no Negro, even when exposed to white influence and education, had ever attained intellectual stature superior to an average white man's. The Negro, moreover, was conscious of his inferiority, they insisted, and did not aspire beyond humble status unless incited by meddlesome ideologues.

Temperamentally, apologists held, the Negro tended to be child-like, happy-go-lucky, and generally docile, with the result that he depended for his well-being on a master's care, suffered but fleetingly, if at all, from such emotional vicissitudes of slavery as the sundering of family ties, and submitted to discipline with equanimity. The Negro's pauperized condition in the free states, they pursued, testified to his inability to fend for himself, while the rarity of slave revolts in the American South betokened the Negro's contentment with his servile rank. The few violent outbreaks that had indubitably occurred apologists dismissed as fomented by outsiders, restricted to a very small number of slaves, and easily nipped in the bud, not infrequently with the help of loyal slaves. Most slaves, indeed, went the refrain, reciprocated their masters' paternal guardianship with unequalled devotion and love, making the relationship between master and slave more heartwarming to behold than any save that between parent and child. Nevertheless, apologists warned, once released from the domesticating and civilizing bonds of slavery, these same childlike creatures degenerated into bloodthirsty savages, as the "horrors of St. Domingo" all too painfully attested. Hence emancipation would unleash the very evil that abolitionists mistakenly sought to avert under slavery: a vengeful uprising of black against white, ending in the extermination of the one race or the other.

Physically, claimed the apologists, the Negro was hardier than other races, being inured to hot climates and immune to such tropical diseases as malaria and yellow fever, which precluded the use of white laborers in the Deep South. Some apologists went so far as to allege that the Negro was even resistant to abuse. They hastened to add, however, that abuse was the exception rather than the rule, if only because it was contrary to the master's self-interest to damage his own property, and they pronounced slaves better housed, fed, and clothed, and better provided for in sickness and old age, than free laborers.

Although the vast majority of Melville's fellow northerners decried slavery in principle and repudiated the more extreme assertions of the Negro's insensibility to suffering, many found it tempting both to imagine, as Holmes and Hawthorne did, that southern slavery was on the whole benign in practice and to bask in the sunshine of the Negro's proverbial cheerfulness whenever slavery clouded their mental horizons. As James Fenimore Cooper wrote in substantiating the claim that black slaves in America were not unduly dissatisfied with their lot, and were "better off, so far as mere animal wants are concerned, than the lower order of the European peasants": "They are a race proverbial for their light heartedness. The laugh of the negro is merriment itself."[36]

Abolitionists, of course, had long been waging a vigorous campaign against the proslavery argument on both factual and moral grounds. In championing the Negro's right to freedom and equal treatment under the laws, they contended that blacks shared all the feelings whites would experience if subjected to the same fate, and that the intellectual capacities of blacks and whites were at least comparable, if not yet demonstrably equal in every respect. In the late 1840s and early 1850s, however, the emergence of a discipline known as ethnology provided proslavery apologists with scientific grounds for disputing these egalitarian assumptions.[37]

Ethnology, as one prominent authority, Dr. Josiah C. Nott of Mobile, Alabama, defined its aims, sought to "know what was the primitive organic structure of each race?—what such race's moral and psychical character?—how far a race may have been, or may become, modified by the combined action of time and moral and

36. Robert E. Spiller, "Fenimore Cooper's Defense of Slave-Owning America," *American Historical Review*, XXXV (April, 1930), 580.
37. For a history of antebellum ethnology, see William Stanton, *The Leopard's Spots: Scientific Attitudes toward Race in America, 1815–59* (Chicago, 1960). George M. Fredrickson, *The Black Image in the White Mind: The Debate on Afro-American Character and Destiny, 1817–1914* (New York, 1971), Chaps. 1–3, discusses the influence ethnology had on the slavery controversy and provides a useful corrective to Stanton's tendency to minimize the ethnologists' proslavery affiliations.

physical causes?—and what position in the social scale Providence
has assigned to each type of man?"[38] In practical terms this meant
that ethnologists attempted to trace the racial differentiation of
mankind back to the very genesis of the human species, even pos-
tulating a separate creation for each race; that they extrapolated
intrinsic moral and intellectual propensities from the physical differences they observed; that they assumed the quasi permanence of
both physical and psychological characteristics; that they ranked
the races of men according to ethnocentric standards of beauty and
innate intelligence that allegedly entitled each race to a particular
station in life—the Anglo-Saxon at the top and the Negro at the
bottom.[39]

As Nott's definition suggests, the founders of American ethnology
were closely associated with the southern apologists of slavery and
were directing their study of race (or allowing it to be directed)
primarily toward proving the Negro's historical subservience and
biological inferiority to other races. The most overt racist among
the pioneers of American ethnology was undoubtedly Nott himself.
A South Carolinian by birth and a slaveholder, Nott privately referred to his field as "niggerology." He also confided to a notorious
proslavery apologist that he had been using the trappings of "eth-
nography, etc." to mask his true concern, "the negro question . . .
that I wished to bring out."[40]

More debatable is the racist bias of the Philadelphia Quaker
Samuel G. Morton, whose monumental *Crania Americana* (1839)
had inaugurated the large-scale comparative study of cranial capacity and conformation in the various races. Though a genuine
scientist with no personal animus in favor of slavery, Morton did
not shrink from an alliance with Nott; nor did any conscientious
scruples prevent Morton from supplying the leading proslavery
politician, John C. Calhoun, then secretary of state, with ethnological data that proved instrumental in furthering proslavery ex-

38. Josiah Clark Nott and George R. Gliddon, *Types of Mankind: or, Ethnological Researches, Based upon the Ancient Monuments, Paintings, Sculptures, and Crania of Races, and upon Their Natural, Geographical, Philological, and Biblical History* . . . (1854; rpt. Miami, Fla., 1969), 49.
39. Nott and Gliddon, *Types of Mankind*, 79, 456–61, 465.
40. Jenkins, *Pro-Slavery Thought*, 257, 259–60, cites Nott's letters to Ephraim Squier and James H. Hammond.

pansionism. Moreover, when Morton turned from measuring and classifying American Indian skulls to examining the skulls of Egyptian mummies, the problem he devoted himself to solving was whether or not the ancient Egyptians were a negroid race—an issue hotly contested between antislavery and proslavery partisans and considered crucial to assessing the Negro's capacity for achieving a high level of civilization. Morton's conclusion that the Egyptians were a predominantly Caucasian people who had themselves practiced Negro slavery represented a major victory for proslavery apologists and a crushing setback for racial egalitarians.[41]

No less implicated in the defense of slavery were two international figures who joined forces with American ethnologists in the 1840s: the English-born Egyptologist George R. Gliddon and the Swiss biologist Louis Agassiz. Gliddon collaborated in Morton's study of the ancient Egyptians by furnishing mummified crania and translating hieroglyphic inscriptions, and he explicitly promoted their findings among southerners as ammunition against the abolitionists. Agassiz, upon settling in the United States, where he quickly imbibed American Negrophobia, began extending his theories about the independent origins of plants and animals in separate geographical spheres to include the human race. He eventually helped Nott to formulate a concept of hybridity applicable to racial intermixture as well as to animal crossbreeding. Both Gliddon and Agassiz later cooperated with Nott in compiling that summum of antebellum ethnology, *Types of Mankind*, which appeared in 1854.[42]

On the fringes of ethnology as a science was the Louisiana doctor Samuel A. Cartwright. Like Nott, Cartwright specialized in diseases supposedly peculiar to the Negro, among which he listed "drapetomania" (a mental aberration inducing black slaves to run away) and "dyaesthesia aethiopica, or hebetude of mind and obtuse sensibility of body" (causing what overseers called "rascality"). More strident than Nott in his polemics on the white race's destiny to rule and the black's to be ruled, Cartwright dropped all pretense

41. Nott himself gives details of Morton's and Gliddon's correspondence with Calhoun in *Types of Mankind*, 50–51. On the significance of Morton's classification of the Egyptians, see Fredrickson, *Black Image in the White Mind*, 74–78; also Stanton, *The Leopard's Spots*, 50–51, 99.

42. Stanton, *The Leopard's Spots*, 45–46, 50–53, 102–103; Fredrickson, *Black Image in the White Mind*, 76–77.

of scientific neutrality and subordinated ethnology to the mission of perpetuating black slavery. His long-winded ruminations on the "ethnical elements" fitting the Negro for slavery were almost an inadvertent caricature of Nott's ethnology. Nonetheless, Cartwright was extensively quoted (Frederick Law Olmsted devoted several pages to refuting Cartwright's theories) and taken seriously enough as an ethnologist in the South to be chosen to write the section on ethnology in the Old South's crowning testimonial, *Cotton Is King, and Pro-Slavery Arguments*.[43]

The speed with which the magic wand of science could transmute racial prejudice into accredited fact in the right intellectual atmosphere was ominously presaged by a lengthy review of *Types of Mankind* featured in *Putnam's Monthly*. Heading the July, 1854, issue of *Putnam's* that carried the first installment of Melville's *Israel Potter*, the review, provocatively entitled "Is Man One Or Many?" was bound to catch Melville's eye.[44] Indeed, its repercussions, as we shall see in "Benito Cereno," "The Bell-Tower," and "The 'Gees"—all written within the next two years—indicate that it gave Melville much food for thought.

The reviewer's hesitant endorsement of the thesis propounded by *Types of Mankind* typified how ineffectual the moderate antislavery sentiments that *Putnam's* stood for would prove against racism, once white supremacists abandoned the bludgeon of the proslavery argument for the scalpel of science. Except for a tribute to the spiritual unity of mankind symbolized by the biblical account of creation, the reviewer agreed that the "scientific" evidence presented by ethnologists pointed irresistibly toward "fixed and primordial distinctions among the races." He remained troubled, however, by a vague presentiment that "to deny the identity of the

43. Samuel A. Cartwright, "Diseases and Peculiarities of the Negro Race," *De Bow's Review*, XI (July, 1851-January, 1852), 64–69, 209–13, 331–36, 504–508; *Essays, Being Inductions Drawn from the Baconian Philosophy Proving the Truth of the Bible and the Justice and Benevolence of the Decree Dooming Canaan To Be Servant of Servants . . .* (Vidalia, La., 1843); "Slavery in the Light of Ethnology," in E. N. Elliott (ed.), *Cotton Is King, and Pro-Slavery Arguments: Comprising the Writings of Hammond, Harper, Christy, Stringfellow, Hodge, Bledsoe, and Cartwright, on This Important Subject . . .* (Augusta, Ga., 1860), 691–728. Fredrickson, *Black Image in the White Mind*, 87–89, discusses Cartwright's influence as a popularizer of Nott's theories. Olmsted quotes and refutes Cartwright in *Seaboard Slave States*, 191–93, 199–200, 226–27, 552–53, and *Back Country*, 92–96, 437.
44. "Is Man One or Many?" *Putnam's Monthly Magazine*, IV (July, 1854), 1–14.

human species seems like denying the manhood of men"—a presentiment which, though he promptly dismissed it, made him go out of his way to emphasize that no member of the human species, not even the "lowest Alforian or Guinea Negro," had more in common with the chimpanzee than with "Shakespeare and Washington."[45] Having fended off the bugbear of animal kin that peered through the breach the new ethnology made in human unity, the reviewer assented readily to the principle of a biological hierarchy in which the Negro occupied the lowest human rung. Clearly *Types of Mankind*—with its authoritative array of statistics, charts, craniological and anatomical illustrations, etymological disquisitions, and archaeological findings, all contributed by specialists of uncontested eminence—threatened to legitimize the view of the Negro as an inferior human being, radically different from the white man, that had hitherto occupied the more vulnerable ground of prejudice and proslavery apologetics. By supplying a scientific rationale for racism, the book gave a new impetus to segregated schooling, housing, and transportation facilities, and to restrictive job policies and suffrage laws—forms of racial discrimination to which northerners clung as tenaciously as southerners did to slavery.[46]

Paralleling the onset of scientific racism during this period was the growing popularity among abolitionists of a more benign form of racism, which George M. Fredrickson calls "romantic racialism."[47] A product of the historical theories about "inbred national character and genius" that the romantic movement had diffused, romantic racialism—like ethnology—dwelled on the contrast between the Anglo-Saxon and the Negro, but credited the Negro with moral virtues compensating for his alleged intellectual inferiority to the Anglo-Saxon. Romantic racialists accepted the southern plantation romancers' stereotype of the Negro as an affectionate, docile child, adapting it instead to the antislavery argument. In the words of the moderate Unitarian abolitionist William Ellery Channing: "Of all races of men, the African is the mildest and most susceptible of attachment. He loves, where the European would hate. He watches

45. *Ibid.*, 5–6, 14.
46. Fredrickson, *Black Image in the White Mind*, 90–91; Litwack, *North of Slavery*, Chaps. 2–4.
47. The following paragraphs are based on Fredrickson, *Black Image in the White Mind*, Chap. 4.

the life of a master, whom the North American Indian, in like circumstances, would stab to the heart. . . . Is this a reason for holding him in chains? . . . let not this manifestation of a generous nature in the slave be turned against him. . . . Let it not be used as a weapon for his perpetual degradation."[48]

This sentimentalized image of the Negro—most memorably personified in Harriet Beecher Stowe's Uncle Tom—appealed to the sympathies of humanitarian whites, but also fostered condescension, if not contempt, toward a creature so lacking in the indomitable spirit, energy, independence, and pride that supposedly characterized the Anglo-Saxon. Channing himself recognized that "even love . . . becomes in the slave a weakness, almost a degradation," and admitted to finding in the slave's attachment and devotion "to a man who keeps him in the dust and denies him the rights of a man . . . a taint of servility, which makes us grieve whilst we admire."[49] Stowe similarly expressed ambivalence toward the long-suffering Christian meekness and pacifism she extolled in Uncle Tom by glorifying rebelliousness in her mulatto characters and predicting that "if ever the San Domingo hour comes," mulattoes would initiate it: "Sons of white fathers, with all our haughty feelings burning in their veins, will not always be bought and sold and traded. They will rise, and raise with them their mother's race."[50]

As Fredrickson points out, the romantic notions of racial character articulated by Channing and Stowe represented a dangerous departure from the original premise of abolitionism expounded by leaders like William Lloyd Garrison, Wendell Phillips, and Theodore Weld—that blacks and whites possessed the same basic capabilities and weaknesses, and that the Negro's alleged peculiarities resulted merely from the environmental influences of slavery and pariah status, under which all human beings were likely to develop similar emotional and intellectual limitations. Instead, romantic racialism implicitly denied the Negro "the inherent ability to compete on equal terms with the ruggedly aggressive Anglo-Saxons" and thereby "indirectly encouraged a fatalistic attitude toward any fail-

48. "Slavery," in *The Works of William Ellery Channing* (6 vols.; Boston, 1841), II, 93.
49. *Ibid.*
50. Harriet Beecher Stowe, *Uncle Tom's Cabin; or, Life Among the Lowly*, ed. Kenneth S. Lynn (1852; rpt. Cambridge, Mass., 1962), Chap. 23, p. 274.

ure of freed Negroes to rise to white levels of practical competence and worldly success." Hence like scientific racism, it contributed to the tragic perpetuation of anti-Negro discrimination after the Civil War.[51]

The primary assumption held by proslavery apologists, ethnologists, and romantic racialists alike was that innate physical, temperamental, and intellectual characteristics unmistakably distinguished human beings of different races from each other and determined their respective destinies. It was this assumption, which Melville recognized as underlying his fellow Americans' failure to resolve the dilemma of slavery, that he devoted himself to combating throughout his antebellum literary career. From *Redburn* onward, Melville created fictional parallels between all the situations the Negro faced in America as a slave and second-class citizen and the situations faced by exploited groups of other races. He showed whites developing the same traits under these conditions as the Negro was thought to exhibit by nature; and he dramatized the various ways in which people of all races react to exploitation, from adjustment to passive resistance to outright rebellion. More subversively, Melville continually undermined the very concept of race that lay at the basis of racial prejudice: at first by subjecting white characters like Redburn and White-Jacket to the same forms of discrimination they naïvely suppose reserved for the black objects of their pity; later by confronting white characters like Ishmael with the difficulties of determining the racial identity of some of their fellow men; still later by trapping readers in the dangerous racial misconceptions they share with characters like Amasa Delano and Benito Cereno; and finally by blurring the racial lines between black and white characters altogether, as in *The Confidence-Man*, where whites masquerade as blacks and blacks as whites, leaving the reader with no means of defining race or recognizing racial identity.

51. Fredrickson, *Black Image in the White Mind*, 125–26.

TWO   *T*erspectives on Slavery and
Rebellion in *Redburn*, *White-Jacket*,
and "The Town-Ho's Story"

MELVILLE first began experimenting with less direct
techniques of speaking out against slavery and racial prejudice in
Redburn, which he wrote within a few months of publishing *Mardi*.
Although two well-known passages in *Redburn* still appear to raise
these issues quite openly, they nevertheless exhibit a marked change
in tone and emphasis from the abolitionist rhetoric of *Mardi*, with
its stereotyped references to shackled bondsmen groaning under the
lash. No longer are southern slavery and southern slaveholders the
direct objects of Melville's censure. Instead, he has shifted his attention to the areas of northern guilt.

In the first passage, Melville draws an implicit analogy between
the crusade against the slave trade in Britain and the parallel
"struggle between sordid interest and humanity" currently engaging
northern merchants and southern planters in America. He thus
discreetly holds up the "triumph of sound policy and humanity" in
which the British crusade had culminated as an incentive to American antislavery action.[1] The topic is broached circuitously, via Redburn's account of a monument in Liverpool "representing Lord
Nelson expiring in the arms of Victory." After describing the principal figures of Lord Nelson, Victory, and Death, Redburn focuses
on the evocative statues at the base of the pedestal: "four naked

1. Herman Melville, *Redburn: His First Voyage, Being the Sailor-boy Confessions and
Reminiscences of the Son-of-a-Gentleman, in the Merchant Service*, ed. Harrison Hayford,
Hershel Parker, and G. Thomas Tanselle (Evanston, 1969), 156. All further page ref-
erences to this edition will be given parenthetically in the text.

figures in chains, somewhat larger than life . . . seated in various attitudes of humiliation and despair." Although "these woe-begone figures of captives" merely emblemize Nelson's chief victories, Redburn finds himself unable to "look at their swarthy limbs and manacles, without being involuntarily reminded of four African slaves in the market-place." One association leading to another, he continues:

> And my thoughts would revert to Virginia and Carolina; and also to the historical fact, that the African slave-trade once constituted the principal commerce of Liverpool; and that the prosperity of the town was once supposed to have been indissolubly linked to its prosecution. And I remembered that my father had often spoken to gentlemen visiting our house in New York, of the unhappiness that the discussion of the abolition of this trade had occasioned in Liverpool; that the struggle between sordid interest and humanity had made sad havoc at the fire-sides of the merchants; estranged sons from sires; and even separated husband from wife. And my thoughts reverted to my father's friend, the good and great Roscoe, the intrepid enemy of the trade; who in every way exerted his fine talents toward its suppression; writing a poem ("*the Wrongs of Africa*"), several pamphlets; and in his place in Parliament, he delivered a speech against it, which, as coming from a member for Liverpool, was supposed to have turned many votes, and had no small share in the triumph of sound policy and humanity that ensued. (R, 155–56)

This series of associations concludes on a note that sends the reader's thoughts back to "Virginia and Carolina," where black slaves, like the immovable statues of Nelson's monument, remain in chains notwithstanding the abolition of the slave trade: "How this group of statuary affected me, may be inferred from the fact, that I never went through Chapel-street without going through the little arch to look at it again. And there, night or day, I was sure to find Lord Nelson still falling back; Victory's wreath still hovering over his swordpoint; and Death grim and grasping as ever; while the four bronze captives still lamented their captivity" (R, 156).

Immediately afterwards, Redburn undergoes an experience that vividly illustrates how the existence of slavery threatens the liberties of all citizens, as the abolitionists were continually preaching:[2] "Now,

2. For a representative formulation of this argument, see William Ellery Channing, *Works*, II, 119–20; also Harriet Martineau, *Society in America* (3 vols.; 1837; rpt. New York, 1966), II, 343–52.

as I lingered about the railing of the statuary . . . I noticed several persons going in and out of an apartment, opening from the basement under the colonnade; and, advancing, I perceived that this was a news-room, full of files of papers. My love of literature prompted me to open the door and step in; but a glance at my soiled shooting-jacket prompted a dignified looking personage to step up and shut the door in my face" (R, 156). In short, Redburn learns that as long as society tolerates the violation of human rights, his own human rights will never be secure. Since freedom of the press and freedom of speech had been among the chief casualties of the American public's effort to avoid controversy over slavery during the 1830s and 1840s, it may not be coincidental that the privilege from which Redburn is excluded is that of entering a newsroom.[3]

Complementing this passage is a later episode in *Redburn* that draws the same moral about racial discrimination. Here, too, Melville's manner of bringing up this explosive subject is disarmingly tactful. While exploring Liverpool, Redburn is dogged by the spectacle of "poverty, poverty, poverty, in almost endless vistas." What particularly strikes him about this spectacle is "the absence of negroes; who in the large towns in the 'free states' of America, almost always form a considerable portion of the destitute." The victims of poverty in Liverpool, on the contrary, are all whites, "and with the exception of the Irish . . . natives of the soil . . . as much Englishmen, as the dukes in the House of Lords" (R, 201–202). Apparently Redburn has taken it for granted that pauperism is a fate mostly restricted to blacks, and he finds it a shock to discover that in England pauperism is no respecter of color. His first reaction is to pride himself on the favorable contrast his native land offers to England: "[in America] such a being as a native beggar is almost unknown; and to be a born American citizen seems a guarantee against pauperism; and this, perhaps, springs from the virtue of a vote" (R, 202).

His next reaction, however, is to realize that the relegation of blacks to pauperism and pariah status can no more be taken for

3. For a general account of the muzzling of antislavery criticism in an era that saw mob attacks against abolitionists, vandalism against schools established for blacks, destruction of abolitionist presses, and censorship of the mails, see Russel B. Nye, *Fettered Freedom: Civil Liberties and the Slavery Controversy, 1830–1860* (rev. ed.; Urbana, 1972).

granted than the exemption of whites from such misfortunes. The obverse of the contrast between America and England, as Redburn notices, is that "in Liverpool . . . the negro steps with a prouder pace, and lifts his head like a man; for here, no such exaggerated feeling exists in respect to him, as in America." So conspicuously lacking, indeed, has Redburn found racial prejudice in England that he has several times encountered the ship's mulatto steward (here characterized as "black," as if Melville wanted to make sure that quibbles over degrees of color would not becloud the basic principle) "walking arm in arm with a good-looking English woman." Whereas the British have greeted this sight with equanimity, "in New York," Redburn points out, "such a couple would have been mobbed in three minutes; and the steward would have been lucky to escape with whole limbs."[4] Meeting this challenge to his American prejudices, Redburn starts to question his former assumptions about the proper relationship between the races: "Being so young and inexperienced then, and unconsciously swayed in some degree by those local and social prejudices, that are the marring of most men, and from which, for the mass, there seems no possible escape; at first I was surprised that a colored man should be treated as he is in this town; but a little reflection showed that, after all, it was but recognizing his claims to humanity and normal equality; so that, in some things, we Americans leave to other countries the carrying out of the principle that stands at the head of our Declaration of Independence" (R, 202).

Redburn's ruminations present a carefully worded but nonetheless radical answer to those who sanctioned racial prejudice and discrimination as human instincts that neither Christianity nor legislation could overcome—the premise on which Judge Shaw would base his ruling in favor of racially segregated schooling later that

---

4. Melville may have been thinking of the antiblack and antiabolitionist riots of July, 1834, in New York, blamed on abolitionists for publicly consorting with blacks. See Nye, *Fettered Freedom*, 204–205. For a first-hand account and postmortem by abolitionists, see Gilbert H. Barnes and Dwight L. Dumond (eds.), *Letters of Theodore Dwight Weld, Angelina Grimké Weld, and Sarah Grimké, 1822–1844* (2 vols.; Gloucester, Mass., 1965), I, 153–56, 270–77 (hereinafter cited as *Weld-Grimké Letters*). For an analysis of a fictionalized version of these riots, in which they are touched off by an attempted interracial marriage, see Simone Vauthier, "'Marie ou l'esclavage aux Etats-Unis,' par Gustave de Beaumont: Ambiguités américaines, ambiguité française," *Recherches anglaises et américaines*, III (1970), 99–126, especially 113.

year.[5] Avoiding the use of the loaded word *race*, Melville implicitly ranks racial antipathies with other "local and social prejudices" that few would consider so tenacious. Although he acknowledges that "for the mass, there *seems* no possible escape" from such prejudices, he refuses to concede that there *is* none. Moreover, he pointedly condemns prejudice as "the marring of most men," just as abolitionists denounced it as sinful. Nor does Melville quail at the bugbear of "amalgamation" that dismayed all but the most stalwart friends of the Negro in antebellum America. Countenancing intermarriage, Redburn decides, is only the logical consequence of recognizing the Negro's "claims to humanity and normal equality."[6]

More radical than Redburn's words, however, are the implications of their context. First, anti-Negro prejudice emerges as an American failing, rather than as an attitude that comes naturally to all whites; hence it immediately assumes less awesome proportions. Second, Redburn himself demonstrates by his change of heart that everyone is potentially capable of overcoming his prejudices with "a little reflection." The ultimate tour de force Melville achieves in this episode is to show that the "local and social prejudices" that victimize the Negro in America can also relegate Redburn to inferior status in England. On the very page following his repudiation of discriminatory practices toward the Negro, Redburn tells of his own experiences with social ostracism in Liverpool churches, where his poverty-stricken appearance assigns him to an obscure seat:

> I used humbly to present myself before the sexton, as a candidate for admission. He would stare a little, perhaps (one of them once hesitated), but in the end, what could he do but show me into a pew; not the most commodious of pews, to be sure; nor commandingly located; nor within very plain sight or hearing of the pulpit. No; it was remarkable, that there was always some confounded pillar or obstinate angle of the wall in the way; and I used to think, that the sextons of Liverpool must have held a secret meeting on my account, and resolved to apportion me the most inconvenient pew in the churches under their charge. (R, 203–204)

5. Litwack, *North of Slavery*, 147–48; Levy, *The Law and Chief Justice Shaw*, 113–17.
6. On contemporary attitudes toward amalgamation and racial prejudice, see Fredrickson, *Black Image in the White Mind*, Chap. 1, and pp. 121–27, 172–74. On abolitionist attitudes toward social equality with blacks, see Litwack, *North of Slavery*, Chap. 7.

Reminiscent of Frederick Douglass' mortifications in the churches of New Bedford,[7] Redburn's trials as a second-class Christian in Liverpool warn the reader that the stigmas attached to race can as easily be applied to class, and that wherever the principle of discrimination is allowed to operate, anyone is liable to suffer from it.

In both these episodes, Melville avails himself of fairly conventional methods of influencing his readers. At the same time, however, he was developing a far more subversive technique of showing his readers the evils of slavery by using the demeaning conditions to which white seamen were subject as analogues for the degradation slavery inflicted on the Negro, and then inviting his readers to extend the sympathetic insight he had given them into the mind of the white "slave" to that of the black. This technique, which soon became Melville's primary mode of indicting slavery and racial prejudice, first appears in an early chapter of *Redburn* where Melville confronts the central paradox of slavery—that one man can exert enough power over others to keep them in bondage, though they may be individually, as well as collectively, stronger than he. In characterizing Jackson, the diabolical sailor who terrorizes the crew of the *Highlander*, Redburn remarks that "he was the weakest man, bodily, of the whole crew" (R, 57) and wonders "what it was that made a whole ship's company submit so to the whims of one poor miserable man like Jackson" (R, 59). Melville associates Jackson's tyranny with slavery at the very outset when Redburn notes that Jackson had earlier "served in Portuguese slavers on the coast of Africa." In keeping with this, one of Jackson's means of bullying the sailors is to dilate with "diabolical relish" on the "*middle-passage*, where the slaves were stowed, heel and point, like logs, and the suffocated and dead were unmanacled, and weeded out from the living every morning" (R, 57). Redburn's account of how the sailors "stood in mortal fear of [Jackson]; and cringed and fawned about him like so many spaniels" recalls Frederick Douglass' description of "the living and lingering death to which cowardly and slavish souls" on a plantation condemned themselves by succumbing to their master's bullying. Among the sailors who put themselves at

7. Cf. Frederick Douglass, *My Bondage and My Freedom* (1855; rpt. New York, 1969), 350–53. The resemblance must be coincidental, however, since *Redburn* was written six years earlier.

Jackson's beck and call, Redburn reminisces, "those who did the most for him, and cringed the most before him, were the very ones he most abused; while two or three who held more aloof, he treated with a little consideration" (R, 59). Similarly, one of the lessons Douglass reported having learned as a slave was that "he is whipped oftenest, who is whipped easiest; and that slave who has the courage to stand up for himself against the overseer, although he may have many hard stripes at the first, becomes, in the end, a freeman, even though he sustain the formal relation of a slave."[8]

Resembling slaves in another respect are those of Redburn's shipmates who, like him, are ranked as "boys." As Redburn tells us: "In merchant-ships, a *boy* means a green-hand, a landsman on his first voyage. And never mind if he is old enough to be a grandfather, he is still called a *boy*; and boys' work is put upon him" (R, 60). In short, these sailors experience the same systematic denial of their manhood as the male slaves who were called "boys" until well into old age.[9]

Melville's allegorical exposé of slavery acquires yet another dimension when Redburn begins to speculate about the relevance of physiognomy to a sailor's status. In attempting to explain Jackson's mysterious predominance, Redburn ascribes it to his physical appearance: "I have no doubt, that if he had had a blue eye in his head, or had had a different face from what he did have, they would not have stood in such awe of him" (R, 59). Belying the apparent naïveté of this explanation is its ironic reversal of the racist clichés that rationalized slavery and white supremacy. On the one hand, the ugly, yellow-skinned, decrepit Jackson obviously does not owe his sway over the crew to the physical superiority that allegedly marked the white race as destined to rule over other races.[10] On the other hand, as Redburn notices with astonishment, a Belfast sailor whose "great

8. *Ibid.*, 95.
9. Kenneth M. Stampp, *The Peculiar Institution: Slavery in the Ante-Bellum South* (New York, 1956), 328.
10. The idea that physical superiority marked the white race for mastery is usually the implied corollary of the argument that physical and intellectual inferiority marked the Negro for slavery, although racist writers concentrated on proving the latter. See, for examples, Thomas Jefferson, *Notes on the State of Virginia* (1785; rpt. New York, 1964), 133, 138; Nott and Gliddon, *Types of Mankind*, 49, 79, 106–107; Cartwright, "Slavery in the Light of Ethnology," 705; Matthew Estes, *A Defence of Negro Slavery As It Exists in the United States* (Montgomery, Ala., 1846), 63–64.

strength and fine person, and . . . red cheeks"—the very picture of
Caucasian beauty— ought by conventional white supremacist standards to entitle him to superior status is instead a laughingstock
among the crew for his poor seamanship and the particular butt of
Jackson's abuse *because of* his good looks. Compounding the reversal, Redburn shortly afterwards compares Jackson to a baboon—
a species of animal racists commonly linked to the Negro[11] —while
depicting him in the classic pose of a slavetrader examining a piece
of human merchandise:

> After [two sailors] had been disputing some time about who had
> been to sea the longest, Jackson . . . bade one of them open his
> mouth; for, said he, I can tell a sailor's age just like a horse's—by
> his teeth. So the man laughed, and opened his mouth; and Jackson
> . . . made him throw his head back, while he looked into it, and
> probed a little with his jack-knife, like a baboon peering into a junk-
> bottle. I trembled for the poor fellow, just as if I had seen him under
> the hands of a crazy barber, making signs to cut his throat, and he
> all the while sitting stock still, with the lather on, to be shaved. . . .
> Somehow, I felt as if [Jackson] were longing to kill the man;. . . after
> concluding his examination, [Jackson] said, that the first man was
> the oldest sailor, for the ends of his teeth were the evenest and most
> worn down; which, he said, arose from eating so much hard sea-
> biscuit; and this was the reason he could tell a sailor's age like a
> horse's. (R, 60)

This episode in *Redburn*, where Melville first uses the analogy
of sailor life to dramatize the way slavery violates the manhood of
the slave and the humanity of the master and to dispute the inherent
superiority that supposedly entitled the white man to enslave the
black, foreshadows many of the themes and images we shall find
in his subsequent works. Jackson's hatred of sailors like the Belfast
man and Redburn himself—who are younger, handsomer, and more

11. Nott, for example, juxtaposed sketches of Negro faces and crania with those of
the chimpanzee and orangutan and claimed that these apes were no "more widely separated
from certain African and Oceanic Negroes than are the latter from the Teutonic or Pelasgic
types" (*Types of Mankind*, 457–59). Cartwright, "Slavery in the Light of Ethnology," 707,
denominated the Negro "the Prognathous species of mankind" and described him as "a
genuine human being, anatomically constructed, about the head and face, more like the
monkey tribes . . . than any other species of the genus man." Apparently responding to
such writings, a satiric article in *Putnam's Monthly Magazine*, VI (December, 1855), 608–
12, entitled "About Niggers" and addressed to racists, ends with the words: "The nigger
is no joke, and no baboon."

manly than he—sets Melville's pattern for exploring the conflicts that arise when a system elevates some men over others regardless of their intrinsic merits as human beings, and consequently gives meanspirited, base men unlimited power to tyrannize over subalterns to whom they feel inferior, as Radney does to Steelkilt in "The Town-Ho's Story," and as Claggart does to Billy Budd. Jackson's manner of treating the sailors as if they were horses evokes the brutalization of the Negro furthered by proslavery ethnologists like Samuel A. Cartwright—a subject Melville took up again in "The Bell-Tower" and "The 'Gees." Embodying slavery at its ugliest and reversing the stereotype of white superiority, Jackson himself is a precursor of the hermit Oberlus, that hideous European tyrant of the Enchanted Isles who exhibits "qualities more diabolical than are to be found among any of the surrounding cannibals." Finally, Redburn's vision of Jackson as a hate-crazed barber, about to cut his client's lathered throat, prefigures the macabre shaving scene in "Benito Cereno," where a slave called Babo (a name many critics have associated with "baboon") flourishes a razor over his master, whose "usual ghastliness was heightened by the lather."[12]

In *Redburn* the subtlety and tact with which Melville appeals to his readers' consciences on slavery and urges the principle of racial egalitarianism never obscure his views on these issues. Even critics who accuse Melville of shilly-shallying on the issue of slavery and evincing ambivalence toward the Negro in other works have given him credit for taking a bold stand on Negro rights in *Redburn*. Their only reservations have centered on Melville's failure to rise above comic stereotype in portraying black characters like the ship's cook and steward, although no one denies that these characters are sympathetically treated.[13]

In trying to gauge Melville's racial views by his characterizations of blacks, we do indeed encounter certain problems. We may object, for example, to Melville's stereotyping the mulatto steward as a

12. Recently Charles E. Nnolim, *Melville's "Benito Cereno": A Study in Meaning of Name Symbolism* (New York, 1974), 40–47, has challenged the common association of Babo with "baboon," plausibly arguing that Melville may have been aware that "the word 'babo' in the Hausa language . . . means 'NO.'"

13. Kaplan, "Melville and the American National Sin," 319–20; Widmer, *The Ways of Nihilism*, 69–70; Simpson, "Melville and the Negro," 23–25. A recent exception is Edward L. Margolies, "Melville and Blacks," *CLA Journal*, XVIII (1975), 368, note 7, who sees Melville as frankly conceding his prejudices in *Redburn*.

dandified, "sentimental sort of a darky," who weeps over a "lock of frizzled hair" he carries in his vest pocket and is addicted to romantic novels and fancy clothes of "every kind of color and cut" (R, 83). However, we must remember that Melville also uses the steward to illustrate the increased pride and self-esteem blacks display in England, where they are not discriminated against, and to defend the Negro's right to full equality with whites, not barring intermarriage.

Melville's treatment of the ship's black cook presents similar difficulties. This Bible-reading black man reminds us of Harriet Beecher Stowe's Uncle Tom, and we find him making "a scrape of the foot, and such a bow as only a negro can make" (R, 305). More disturbing is Redburn's remark: "It was well for him that he was a black cook, for I have no doubt his color kept us from seeing his dirty face; I never saw him wash but once, and that was at one of his own soup pots one dark night when he thought no one saw him" (R, 43). Here the issue is whether Melville is expressing his own racism or satirizing Redburn's. Only after examining the immediate context of this passage, the narrative treatment of both the cook and Redburn elsewhere in the book, and the substance and style of Melville's commentary on race can we answer this question intelligently. Most of the evidence, in fact, indicates that Melville is satirizing Redburn's racism as well as the snobbery and superciliousness with which the boy at first reacts to his shipmates.[14] Redburn's attitude toward the cook, whom he pronounces "a very suspicious looking sort of a cook, that I don't believe would ever succeed in getting the cooking at Delmonico's in New York" (R, 43), recalls the spirit in which he recoils from the sailors' profanity and drunkenness and complains of the "severe affliction" of having to associate with "such a parcel of wicked hard-hearted rascals" (R, 47). Moreover, the cook serves to expose the shallowness of the Sunday School piety that Redburn personifies. "A serious old fellow, much given to metaphysics," and prone to "talk about original sin" (R, 81), the cook, like Melville himself, shows himself to be a good deal more

14. Edward S. Grejda, *The Common Continent of Men: Racial Equality in the Writings of Herman Melville* (Port Washington, N.Y., 1974), 55–66, reaches the same conclusion in his fine analysis of *Redburn*, which traces the progression in Redburn's racial attitudes from prejudice to egalitarianism.

skeptical of easy answers to religious questions than Redburn. Among the minority of the crew who can read at all—though Redburn observes that "reading must have been very hard work for him; for he muttered to himself quite loud as he read; and big drops of sweat would stand upon his brow, and roll off, till they hissed on the hot stove before him"—the cook pores over his Bible. Unlike the stereotyped pious slave, he is not merely seeking spiritual comfort, but struggling with the meaning of obscure passages. One day, perplexed by a "mysterious passage in the Book of Chronicles," the cook approaches Redburn, his most literate shipmate, and reads the passage aloud, "demanding an explanation" (R, 82). Redburn glibly replies that "it was a mystery that no one could explain; not even a parson," but the old cook refuses to be satisfied with such an evasion and continues to ponder the enigma. True to his Sunday School training, Redburn proceeds to lament that "notwithstanding his religious studies and meditations, this old fellow used to use some bad language occasionally" (R, 82). Nevertheless, at the end of the voyage when Redburn and the rest of the crew find themselves nearly penniless, the cook pockets "the goodly round sum of seventy dollars as his due," his piety having "proved profitable in restraining him from the expensive excesses of most seafaring men" (R, 305). This "fortune," which Redburn imagines him at once investing in a "grand, underground oyster-cellar," gives the cook the opportunity to escape the fate that meets the majority of sailors.

These examples show how careful we must be to assess Melville's black characters in context if we wish to use them as indices of his racial attitudes. In *Redburn*, the process remains relatively simple, since Melville speaks out quite straightforwardly against slavery and racism. In subsequent works, however, Melville begins to discredit racist misconceptions about the Negro obliquely, by creating parallels between black and white characters to demonstrate that whites subjected to the same demeaning conditions as blacks develop the same allegedly racial traits. If we miss these parallels and focus exclusively on Melville's black characters, we end up distorting his message.

Of course, we should not minimize the significance of Melville's opting to preach racial egalitarianism via symbolic analogues rather than via black characters portrayed without race consciousness. It suggests that he never actually achieved the degree of color blindness he advocated in theory—an impression reinforced by the race consciousness we sense in his treatment of the cook and the steward. (To say this, however, is still a far cry from maintaining, as Sidney Kaplan and Kingsley Widmer do, that Melville in any way endorses the racist images of the Negro that he presents through characters like Amasa Delano and Benito Cereno.)[15] Melville's increasing reliance on such subversive techniques as the use of Negro analogues and myopic racist protagonists to teach the reader the pitfalls of racism also increases the risk of misinterpreting his intent. It is possible that his satires on racism may have backfired with his nineteenth-century audiences, just as they have with some modern critics.

Exemplifying this problem of interpretation is the black slave who appears in a chapter of *White-Jacket* entitled, perhaps ironically, "The Manning of Navies."[16] Read in isolation, Melville's description of this slave seems to express anti-Negro sentiments similar to those of people who feared the economic competition with which the Negro, whether slave or free, threatened white working men, and who joined proslavery apologists in contending that slaves fared better than free laborers.[17] The passage begins with an exposé of conditions in the navy that deterred white Americans from volunteering for it and that consequently favored the practice, contrary to an edict of Congress, of shipping black slaves as man-of-war's-men. Melville then cites the slave belonging to the *Neversink*'s purser as an instance he has personally witnessed of this abuse:

> On board of the United States ship Neversink . . . there was a Virginian slave regularly shipped as a seaman, his owner receiving his wages. Guinea—such was his name among the crew— belonged to the Purser, who was a southern gentleman; he was employed as

15. Kaplan, "Melville and the American National Sin," 17–28; Widmer, *The Ways of Nihilism*, 70–73.
16. Herman Melville, *White-Jacket: or The World in a Man-of-War*, ed. Harrison Hayford, Hershel Parker, and G. Thomas Tanselle, Chap. 90. All further page references to this edition will be given parenthetically in the text.
17. This was the position Hawthorne took in a letter cited in Flint, "Hawthorne and the Slavery Crisis," 399–400. On anti-Negro sentiments among labor leaders, see Lorman Ratner, *Powder Keg: Northern Opposition to the Antislavery Movement, 1831–1840* (New York, 1968), 62–64; also Filler, *The Crusade Against Slavery*, 114, 255–57.

his body servant. Never did I feel my condition as a man-of-war's-man so keenly as when seeing this Guinea freely circulating about the decks in citizen's clothes, and, through the influence of his master, almost entirely exempted from the disciplinary degradation of the Caucasian crew. Faring sumptuously in the ward-room; sleek and round, his ebon face fairly polished with content; ever gay and hilarious; ever ready to laugh and joke, that African slave was actually envied by many of the seamen. There were times when I almost envied him myself. (WJ, 378–79)

Capping this stereotype, Melville goes out of his way to praise the purser's "pleasant, kind, indulgent manner toward his slave" and to give him credit for treating Guinea well, even "under circumstances peculiarly calculated to stir up the resentment of a slave-owner" (a cryptic allusion to an actual incident of Melville's cruise on the United States, the freeing of the purser's slave ordered by Judge Shaw in accordance with Massachusetts law when the ship landed in Boston).[18]

Not surprisingly, at least one critic has singled out this passage in accusing Melville of manifesting insensitivity to slavery and "ambivalence toward the Negro," if not outright racism. Melville's caricature of this pampered black body servant is incontrovertibly distasteful. Offsetting and redefining it, however, is a portrait four pages later of a white seaman named Landless, whom Melville describes as Guinea's exact counterpart.[19] Like Guinea, Landless illustrates the way men provided with the basic necessities of life somehow adjust, or appear to adjust, to a servile existence shorn of dignity: "notwithstanding the iniquities of a man-of-war, men are

18. The historical incident is discussed by Anderson, Melville in the South Seas, 432–33; Kaplan, "Melville and the American National Sin," 323–24; and Priscilla Allen Zirker, "Evidence of the Slavery Dilemma in White-Jacket," American Quarterly, XVIII (1966), 482–83. Zirker interprets Melville's praise of the purser as an antiabolitionist gesture placing him "even farther to the right than Judge Shaw." Melville may have merely been echoing Shaw's tribute to the purser (cited in Anderson) for agreeing to let his slave choose between slavery and freedom irrespective of the court's decision. In any case, a tribute to a kind master need not indicate antiabolitionism; even the fervent abolitionist John Greenleaf Whittier addressed such a tribute to "Randolph of Roanoke." See Hyatt H. Waggoner (ed.), The Poetical Works of Whittier (Boston, 1975), 303–304.

19. Zirker, "Slavery Dilemma in White-Jacket," 482–83, 485. Zirker notices both Melville's disparagement of the "Jack Landless type of sailor" and the "contrasting kinds of allusions to the Negro" that he makes in the same chapter, but interprets such "contradictions" as evidence of Melville's "ambivalence."

to be found in them, *at times*, so used to a hard life; so drilled and disciplined to servitude, that, with an *incomprehensible* philosophy, they *seem* cheerfully to resign themselves to their fate. They have plenty to eat; spirits to drink; clothing to keep them warm; a hammock to sleep in; tobacco to chew; a doctor to medicine them; a parson to pray for them" (WJ, 383; italics added). In short, such seamen are "happy slaves" in another guise.

Granting that men of this type exist, Melville still holds that their cheerful resignation to their lot is incomprehensible rather than natural, and that it may, after all, be deceptive. He then shows how relative "happiness" can be by pointing out that the navy life White-Jacket finds so irksome is for Landless full of amenities which would strike "a penniless castaway . . . as a luxurious Bill of Fare" (WJ, 383)—in the same way that Guinea's material comforts and freedom from naval discipline seem enviable to White-Jacket.

Many verbal echoes develop the analogy between the slave whose sobriquet, given to him by the crew, brands him as a product of the Guinea Coast slave trade and the tar whose name symbolizes the sailor's rootless life as one of society's outcasts. Just as Guinea, "though a bondman, liable to be saddled with a mortgage, like a horse," appears "ever gay and hilarious; ever ready to laugh and joke," so Landless, "though his back was cross-barred, and plaided with the ineffaceable scars of all the floggings accumulated by a reckless tar during a ten years' service in the Navy . . . perpetually wore a hilarious face, and at joke and repartee was a very Joe Miller" (WJ, 379, 383–84). Guinea is "accustomed to light and easy duties"; Landless is privileged with "many idle hours." Guinea, "in India-rubber manacles, enjoyed the liberties of the world"; Landless "enjoyed life . . . and, though cribbed in an oaken prison, with the turnkey sentries all round him, yet he paced the gun-deck as if it were broad as a prairie."

Not only does Melville relate Landless to Guinea in particular, but to the Negro in general; for he describes him as a white man manifesting all the traits thought to be racially peculiar to the Negro. Echoing the Southern cliché that "slaves are perpetual children," Melville ascribes to Landless "the zest of everlasting adolescence" (WJ, 383). Investing Landless with the unshakable mirthfulness believed to indicate that the Negro by nature bore hardships lightly,

Melville asserts that "nothing could transmute [Landless'] laugh into any thing like a sigh." Matching the callousness under the lash that proslavery apologists attributed to the Negro, Landless submits to scourgings, reports Melville, "with the same invincible indifference" he displays when "ordered to the main-truck in a gale; or rolled by the drum to the grog-tub" (WJ, 384). Melville even mimics the dehumanizing jargon of the pseudoscientific treatises written on the Negro when he refers to Landless' habit of chewing tobacco as if it were the quirk of a strange animal: "Those glandular secretions, which in other captives sometimes go to the formation of tears, in *him* were expectorated from the mouth, tinged with the golden juice of a weed, wherewith he solaced and comforted his ignominious days" (WJ, 383).[20]

While depicting Landless as a real-life white analogue of the Negro, Melville also invites the reader to compare Guinea and Landless as literary stereotypes that glorify an oppressive regime by romanticizing its victims. Guinea, of course, is a character straight out of plantation romances and the slave melodies of Stephen Foster. As for Landless, Melville explicitly identifies him with the British man-of-war's-man immortalized in the sea chanteys of the eighteenth-century songwriter Charles Dibdin. "Full of sea-chivalry and romance," the "patriotic verses" Dibdin put in the mouths of sailors like Landless, Melville observes, "would lead one to think that man-of-war's-men are the most care-free, contented, virtuous, and patriotic of mankind." The fact is, Dibdin's ditties were "composed at a time when the English Navy was principally manned by felons and paupers." Comments Melville cynically: "Dibdin was a man of genius; but no wonder Dibdin was a government pensioner at £200 per annum" (WJ, 383). The perniciousness of this kind of literature, in Melville's view, lies especially in the slavish mentality it inculcates in the class on whose degradation the regime reposes. Dibdin's ditties, for example, written expressly for sailors, "are pervaded by . . . a reckless acquiescence in fate, and an implicit, unquestioning, dog-like devotion to whoever may be lord and master."

20. *The Pro-Slavery Argument*, 32, 34, 128–29, 217–19, 459–60; Taylor, *Cavalier and Yankee*, 302–303. See also Floan, *The South in Northern Eyes*, 117, 121, for northern versions of this cliché. Cartwright, "Diseases of the Negro," 67, provides the closest analogue to Landless' tobacco chewing in his description of the Negro's peculiar sleep habits.

Melville stresses that the conditions Dibdin idealizes in these songs, "which might be sung with equal propriety by both English and American man-of-war's-men," still prevail in the American navy of his own day, where "skulkers and scoundrels of all sorts" predominate (wj, 382). Accordingly, Landless' favorite song turns out to be Dibdin's "True English Sailor," the first line of which strikingly telescopes the images that societies like Dibdin's England and the antebellum South cherish of their working classes: "Jack dances and sings, and is always content" (wj, 384).[21]

Melville does not further spell out the analogy between the English and American stereotypes represented by Landless and Guinea. Instead, he develops his criticism of the ideals Dibdin celebrated, forcing the reader to reevaluate the concept of a worker who is "always content," to confront his unconscious motives for finding any merit in it, and to assess the psychic cost a man like Landless has paid for his adjustment: "This Landless was a favorite with the officers, among whom he went by the name of 'Happy Jack.' And it is just such Happy Jacks as Landless that most sea-officers profess to admire; a fellow without shame, without a soul, so dead to the least dignity of manhood that he could hardly be called a man" (wj, 384). Melville then explains why officers cannot tolerate a subaltern who shows self-esteem, but "instinctively" feel that such a man threatens the very essence of an institution like a man-of-war: "a seaman who exhibits traits of moral sensitiveness, whose demeanor shows some dignity within; this is the man they [officers], in many cases, instinctively dislike. The reason is, they feel such a man to be a continual reproach to them, as being mentally superior to their power. He has no business in a man-of-war; they do not want such men. To them there is an insolence in his manly freedom, contempt in his very carriage" (wj, 384–85).

At last specifically applying this analysis to the slave system, Melville pronounces the self-respecting seaman as "unendurable" to officers "as an erect, lofty-minded African would be to some slave-driving planter" (wj, 385). He must have meant the reader to complete the analogy by contrasting such an "erect, lofty-minded Af-

---

21. See Taylor, *Cavalier and Yankee*, 300–307, on the stereotyped Negro slaves of plantation romances; also Yellin, *The Intricate Knot*, Chaps. 2–5, especially pp. 17, 29, 54, 59.

rican" with the servile, grinning Guinea—the latter the product of a system that crushes men's spirits and turns them into mere lackeys, the former the symbol of the innate human dignity that sustains some men against the worst forms of tyranny and thus portends the ultimate triumph of the human will to freedom over the power that holds men in bondage.

Melville hastens to add that these strictures do not "apply to *all* men-of-war": "There are some vessels blessed with patriarchal, intellectual Captains, gentlemanly and brotherly officers, and docile and Christianized crews. The peculiar usages of such vessels insensibly soften the tyrannical rigor of the Articles of War" (wj, 385). Yet this concession is surely intended for the readers whose prejudices Melville was attempting to overcome. Like the earlier tribute to the purser for his kind treatment of Guinea, it seems to be Melville's way of saying that he was indicting a tyrannical institution, not personally attacking the individuals comprising it.[22] Nowhere does Melville suggest that the relatively comfortable lot of individual subordinates can redeem a fundamentally degrading system. Indeed, in another episode of *White-Jacket*, as we shall see, Melville openly challenges the "well-known poetical" comparison "between a sea-captain and a father" (wj, 276).

The same combination of rhetorical tact and ideological militancy marks the concluding paragraph of this chapter. Even while Melville apologizes for not counterbalancing his unflattering picture of the navy with praise for its successes, he hints that he does not share the prevailing regard for military glory, and he doggedly reaffirms his commitment to exposing naval abuses:

> Wherever, throughout this narrative, the American Navy, in any of its bearings, has formed the theme of a general discussion, hardly one syllable of admiration for *what is accounted* illustrious in its achievements has been permitted to escape me. The reason is this: I consider, that so far as *what is called* military renown is concerned,

22. Zirker, "Slavery Dilemma in *White-Jacket*," 485, interprets this passage as an "explicit withdrawal of [Melville's] former militancy." For evidence of Melville's solicitude to distinguish between indictment of an institution and personal criticism of individuals, see Davis and Gilman (eds.), *Letters of Melville*, 107, where Melville refuses to name his officers in writing, even privately: "I have never indulged in any ill-will or disrespect for them, personally; & shrink from any thing that approaches to a personal identification of them with characters that were only intended to furnish samples of a tribe."

the American Navy needs no eulogist but History. It were superfluous for White-Jacket to tell the world what it knows already. The office imposed upon me is of another cast; and, though I foresee and feel that it may subject me to the pillory in the hard thoughts of some men, yet, supported by what God has given me, I tranquilly abide the event, whatever it may prove. (WJ, 385; italics added)

Ironically, although many modern critics have missed the antislavery message underlying Melville's rhetorical ploy of depicting the best aspects of slavery while equating it with a nonsouthern authoritarian institution, at least one of the contemporary readers Melville may have been trying to reach sensed enough of that message to take offense. William Gilmore Simms, who had previously castigated Melville for portraying John C. Calhoun as a slave driver in *Mardi*, now accused him, in a review of *White-Jacket*, of taking a "most unjust and wanton fling at the South, in compliance with the stereotyped prejudices of his own region." Far from appreciating the conciliatory tone Melville had attempted to strike when he praised the purser as a kind master and elsewhere credited southern officers with being "much less severe, and much more gentle and gentlemanly in command, than the Northern officers" (WJ, 141), Simms juxtaposed such statements with the obnoxious reference to slave-driving planters and charged Melville with inconsistency: "It is somewhat strange that a writer who can think so shrewdly and observe so well should still be so infatuated with his own local prejudices, as to forget subsequently what he has just said, and reflect upon the Southern slaveholder, as one necessarily more tyrannical than any other class of persons." In short, Simms distorted the parallel Melville had drawn between tyrannical sea officer and tyrannical slave driver into a malicious slur on southern character. He also managed to endorse Melville's indictment of what Simms himself called "the unceasing severities and cruelties of a system which has no solitary reason or necessity for its continuance" (meaning flogging) without perceiving the relevance of that indictment to the slave system.[23] If Melville had hoped that indirection and tact would win over readers hostile to abolitionist propaganda by in-

23. *"White-Jacket; or the World in a Man-of-War,"* *Southern Quarterly Review,* XVII (July, 1850), 515, 520.

ducing them to see the black slave's plight in other than racial terms, Simms's reaction must have profoundly dismayed him.

For the modern critic, however, the significance of Simms's review of *White-Jacket* lies not in its conjectural impact on Melville, but rather in the question it raises about Melville's technique of condemning slavery by analogy. Are we to evaluate these analogies as propaganda aimed at converting the reader or as private double-talk aimed at "hoodwinking" the "superficial skimmer of pages" while satisfying Melville's compulsion to tell the truth? [24] Whichever way we view the subversive mode Melville perfected in such extended parallels between black and white character types, it does not seem to fulfill its purpose. On the one hand, Melville's prevailing tone of moral outrage—which his contemporaries, including Simms, recognized as the keynote of *White-Jacket* [25] and which stamps his overt message in a chapter like "The Manning of Navies"—demands that we take seriously the propagandistic intent of the covert message. Yet as propaganda the analogy between Guinea and Landless has apparently proved oversubtle, perhaps to the point of counteracting its purpose. When even a critic as familiar with *White-Jacket* and the conditions to which it refers as Priscilla Allen Zirker has overlooked the parallel that redefines Melville's use of the "happy slave" stereotype, it seems unlikely that many contemporary readers would have realized, even subconsciously, that Melville was not reinforcing, but subverting their assumptions about racial traits as opposed to environmental conditioning. On the other hand, if Melville sought merely to veil his criticism of slavery from unfriendly eyes, in the manner that he dissembled his attacks on Christianity beneath a facade of conventional piety, it is hard to explain why he indulged in such outspoken antislavery rhetoric as the reference to slave-driving planters that alienated Simms.

We seem to face a paradox: having begun by adopting a technique of subverting proslavery arguments that is so elaborate as to be ineffectual, Melville ends by giving himself away in a burst of

24. From Melville's essay, "Hawthorne and His Mosses," reprinted in the Norton Critical Edition of *Moby-Dick*, ed. Harrison Hayford and Hershel Parker (New York, 1967), 548–49. See Dryden, *Melville's Thematics of Form*, 21–29, for a fine analysis of Melville's view of fiction as the "great Art of Telling the Truth."

25. Simms, *"White-Jacket,"* 514–15. Other contemporary reviews are excerpted in Leyda, *Melville Log*, I, 370–75, 381–82.

bravado and welcoming the "pillory." This paradox suggests at least a basic confusion in his intent, if not a still deeper conflict. Perhaps while his rebellious self identified with the unbowed slave and the unpopular antislavery orator, his conformist self balked at throwing off the yokes that chafed him, and recoiled from social ostracism.

In any case, Melville's rebellious self continued to seek more direct methods of both dramatizing the effects of servile status on black character and portraying self-respecting blacks who command the esteem of their white fellow seamen. Many critics have commented on the unusual number of black characters in *White-Jacket*. True, as some critics have objected, most of these characters are mere stereotypes.[26] Nevertheless, they differ considerably from each other, as well as from the black characters in *Redburn* and *Moby-Dick*. The ship's cook in *White-Jacket*, for example—"a dignified colored gentleman, whom the men dubbed '*Old Coffee*'" (wj, 58)— is very unlike his unkempt, Bible-reading counterpart in *Redburn*, even though he appears too briefly to be individualized as a character. His hallmark is the "dignity" with which he stars in the daily ritual of presenting the deck officer with a sample of salt beef or pork to be tasted for healthfulness before the men begin their meal. In describing the scene, Melville de-emphasizes Old Coffee's racial traits and eschews the low comedy that black cooks and stewards invariably provoked in contemporary man-of-war narratives.[27] "He preserved the utmost rectitude of carriage; and when it was 'Duff Day,' he would advance with his tin truncheon borne high aloft, exhibiting a pale, round duff surmounting the blood-red mass of beef;—he looked something like the figure in the old painting of the executioner presenting the head of St. John the Baptist in a charger" (wj, 285–86).

26. Kaplan, "Melville and the American National Sin," 321–23; Simpson, "Melville and the Negro," 25; Zirker, "Slavery Dilemma in *White-Jacket*," 484.

27. Cf. the offensive description of a "coloured gemman" serving as ship's cook in Henry James Mercier, *Life in a Man-of-War, or Scenes in 'Old Ironsides' during Her Cruise in the Pacific, By a Fore-Top-Man* (Philadelphia, 1841), 224; also cited in Zirker, "Slavery Dilemma in *White-Jacket*," 484–85. As Zirker points out, Melville draws on Mercier's account of the "nigger pugilists" Chuffy and Grubbings (*Life in a Man-of-War*, 193–200) for his own account of the rivalry between Rose-Water and May-Day, yet he suppresses all the crude racist elements and instead makes the story serve to indict Captain Claret for fomenting quarrels between seamen. It is hard to see why Zirker concludes, "To say that Melville did not descend to the lowest form of racial humor . . . is not to say much for his attitude toward the Negro" and toward slavery.

Old Coffee's three assistants, in contrast, are patently minstrel-show stereotypes: "negroes also, [they] went by the poetical appellations of 'Sunshine,' 'Rose-water,' and 'May-day'" (wj, 58). Yet Melville dissociates himself somewhat from their demeaning names, implying that the crew are responsible for them. Furthermore, he takes pains to differentiate among the three. He singles out Sunshine as "the bard of the trio," who enlivens their work with "some remarkable St. Domingo melodies" while all throw "themselves into a violent perspiration" polishing the copper caldrons in which the ship's coffee and salt meat are boiled. Though verging on romantic racialism, Melville's description of "these jolly Africans, thus making gleeful their toil by their cheering songs" develops in another direction; for White-Jacket, while listening to Sunshine, is reminded not of slaves singing in the fields, but of the way sailors on merchant vessels "sing out . . . when pulling ropes, or occupied at any other ship's duty." To White-Jacket, it is the unnatural "rule of men-of-war, which forbids the sailors to sing out" at their work that calls for comment, rather than the propensity for singing at work that blacks share with other men. Of the two other cook's assistants, Rose-Water is "a slender and rather handsome mulatto" (wj, 275) who seeks to escape the stigma of blackness by identifying himself with his white father and cultivating white tastes. He lends White-Jacket Moore's "Loves of the Angels," recommending it as "de charmingest of wolumes," and denounces the "sad taste" of another shipmate "in admiring such vulgar stuff" as a Negro songbook (wj, 168–69). May-Day, on the contrary, is "a full-blooded 'bull-negro,' so the sailors called him" (here, too, Melville makes a point of dissociating himself from the term), proud of his brute strength, which he flaunts against Rose-Water as his means of improving his status among whites, and hence in his own eyes (wj, 275). Both Rose-Water and May-Day are rather pitiable in their servility toward whites, but they are clearly a step ahead of Guinea, the pampered slave. As a free black, Rose-Water allows himself a discreet protest against the captain's injustice in arraigning him for a misdemeanor directly attributable to the animosity the captain has fostered between him and May-Day: "'Please, sir,' said poor Rose-Water, 'it all come of dat 'ar bumping; May-Day, here, aggrawated me 'bout it'" (wj, 276). Guinea, on the other hand, avails himself of his exemption

from witnessing floggings with a slave's immemorial obsequiousness: "'Scuse me, massa!' said the slave, with a low salutation; 'I
can't 'tand it; I can't, indeed, massa!'" (WJ, 379).

The most distinctive of the black characters in White-Jacket,
however, is an "old negro, who went by the name of Tawney, a
sheet-anchor-man." Tawney, as most critics concede, has "a solid
individual existence as character rather than as stereotype." One of
the few blacks Melville describes without a trace of race consciousness, and the only black in White-Jacket not to speak in dialect,
Tawney is "a staid and sober seaman, very intelligent, with a fine,
frank bearing, one of the b'est men in the ship, and held in high
estimation by every one" (WJ, 311). Moreover, Melville shows Tawney associating with White-Jacket and his friends on an equal footing or, perhaps we should say, a superior footing, since Tawney is
among the "oldest Tritons" on the ship, whose "narratives of the
war-service they had seen" are highly valued by the younger sailors.
Invited into the main-top on calm nights to tell of his experiences
in the War of 1812, Tawney recounts some incidents of naval battle
that Melville in fact lifted out of a white fellow seaman's published
reminiscences, Samuel Leech's Thirty Years from Home, and that
serve not only to dignify Tawney but to dramatize Melville's conviction that "the whole matter of war is . . . utterly foolish, un-
christian, barbarous, brutal, and savoring of the Feejee Islands,
cannibalism, saltpetre, and the devil" (WJ, 315). Throughout Tawney's narrative, nothing but his name and Melville's occasional references to him as "the negro" remind the reader that this venerable,
battle-scarred seaman, who has shared in the making of American
history side by side with whites, is black.[28]

Tawney is so successful an attempt at breaking down racial bar-

28. Zirker, "Slavery Dilemma in White-Jacket," 484; Simpson, "Melville and the Negro," 25; Kaplan, "Melville and the American National Sin," 322–23; Anderson, Melville
in the South Seas, 389–94. Zirker objects to Melville's having given Tawney a "racially
descriptive" name, and one which he had used elsewhere "for the purpose of a racial joke."
Yet both the word tawny, which Melville applies to many sun-tanned white sailors in his
fiction, and the joke—a letter Melville wrote in Negro dialect and signed "Tawney,"
probably referring to the "deep tan he must have acquired in his four months as a sailor"
in 1839 (see Davis and Gilman's note, Letters of Melville, 17)—emphasize that the difference
in color between "whites" and "blacks" is one of degree, rather than kind, and that it can
vary to the point where racial differentiation on the basis of color becomes meaningless.
This is precisely the point Melville develops in Moby-Dick, "The 'Gees," and The Confidence-Man.

riers and inculcating color blindness in human relations that one could wish Melville had availed himself of this technique more often, instead of relying so heavily on Negro analogues to show that blacks were identical with whites in their capacities to develop admirable character traits in a favorable environment and to retain them in an unfavorable environment, as well as to succumb to degradation. Perhaps he did not do so because he had not in fact known many Tawneys. Or perhaps it was simply that he became more interested in exploring the minds of black rebels and feared his readers would feel too threatened if he were to have black characters express their rebellious sentiments directly. Whatever the reason, when Melville turned, as he did in one of the most memorable episodes of *White-Jacket*, to dramatizing the dilemma of the "slave" faced with the alternatives of submitting to the violation of his manhood or of resisting it to the death, he chose to do so via a white character with whom his readers could more easily identify.

Entitled "Fun in a Man-of-War," the episode begins with a sardonic account of the gladiatorial games which the captain allegedly licenses to divert the crew, but which, according to Melville, a crew seldom elects "when a navy captain does not happen to be an admirer of the *Fistiana*" (WJ, 274). In describing these games, Melville once again parodies the pseudoscientific jargon of ethnological studies, which served to reduce blacks from sensitive human beings to brutes or mere objects on the pretext of giving a scientific view of the Negro.[29] The sailors, writes Melville, play at "*single-stick*," equipped only with the "helmets . . . nature had furnished them," in lieu of the "heavy, wired helmets" usually worn to protect participants against injury in this game. They practice "*sparring* [which] consists in playing single-stick with bone poles instead of wooden ones," by pommeling each other "with their fists (a hard bunch of knuckles permanently attached to the arms, and made globular, or extended into a palm, at the pleasure of the proprietor)." They perform "*hammer-and-anvil*" by having "patient No. 1" get down on "all-fours . . . while patient No. 2 is taken up by his arms and legs, and his base is swung against the base of patient No. 1"; and they conduct "*head-bumping*" matches, "an especial favorite with the Captain,"

29. See the examples of scientific racist writings cited in Chap. 6.

by setting "two negroes (whites will not answer) butting at each other like rams" (WJ, 274–75). Thus at the outset Melville puts white sailors on a par with blacks: both are subject to dehumanization by a captain who takes advantage of his authority.

The only superiority the white sailors can claim is their exemption from head-bumping, which, of course, is intrinsically no more mortifying than the other sports. This point, however, is apparently lost on the white seamen; not until later does White-Jacket realize how effectively he has blinded himself to his own "degraded condition" in imagining that others are still "lower in the scale" than he (WJ, 277). Meanwhile, secure in the immunity his white skin affords him against this particular indignity, White-Jacket enjoys the luxury of pitying Rose-Water, one of Captain Claret's Negro victims, who abhors head-bumping but is unfailingly pitted against the pugnacious May-Day, who "much fancied the sport," thanks to "a skull like an iron tea-kettle" (WJ, 275). At the same time, Rose-Water and May-Day console themselves with their illusory sense of superiority to each other. Rose-Water prides himself on not being a "'nigger,' which, among some blacks, is held a great term of reproach . . .; for his mother, a black slave, had been one of the mistresses of a Virginia planter belonging to one of the oldest families in that state." May-Day, on his part, "lifted up by the unaffected, though verbally unexpressed applause of the Captain," takes to despising Rose-Water "as a poltroon—a fellow all brains and no skull; whereas he himself was a great warrior, all skull and no brains" (WJ, 275).

Anticipating black writers like Richard Wright and Ralph Ellison, Melville dramatizes the function of the brawls that whites encourage among blacks to divert the aggressions of the blacks away from whites and toward each other. He also shows how whites use the blacks who best conform to the approved brutish stereotype to humiliate those who rashly aspire to rise above that stereotype through "white" pursuits, at the same time ensuring that even the winners under this system never get out of hand.[30] Thus as long as the rivalry Captain Claret has incited between Rose-Water and May-Day takes the sanctioned form of "play," he allows May-Day

30. Cf. the episode of fist-fighting between Richard Wright and a fellow office worker, instigated by their white boss, as described in *Black Boy*, Chap. 12, pp. 255–66 (Signet edition), and the "battle royal" scene in Ralph Ellison's *Invisible Man*, Chap. 1.

almost unlimited license to bully Rose-Water. But as soon as it develops into a genuine enmity that is no longer subordinate to his pleasure, the captain reasserts his primacy over both blacks by invoking a rule against fighting on shipboard and having the two antagonists "flogged . . . in the most impartial manner" (WJ, 276).

Sensitively though Melville renders the racist aspects of this situation, he consistently refuses to let the reader dismiss the fate that befalls Rose-Water and May-Day as one that cannot overtake whites. Instead, he reminds the reader of a previous incident that had taught the entire crew "with what facility a sea-officer assumes his wonted severity of demeanor after a casual relaxation of it" (WJ, 95, 276). He then moralizes on the deceptiveness of a captain's paternalism:

> For any landsman to have beheld him in the lee waist, of a pleasant Dog-Watch, with a genial, good-humored countenance, observing the gladiators in the ring, and now and then indulging in a playful remark—that landsman would have deemed Captain Claret the indulgent father of his crew, perhaps permitting the excess of his kind-heartedness to encroach upon the appropriate dignity of his station. He would have deemed Captain Claret a fine illustration of those two well-known poetical comparisons between a sea-captain and a father, and between a sea-captain and the master of apprentices. . . .
>
> But surely, if there is any thing hateful, it is this *shipping of the quarter-deck face* after wearing a merry and good-natured one. (WJ, 276)

Having called into question the very solace he seems to offer the reader at the end of the chapter "The Manning of Navies"—that "patriarchal, intellectual Captains" and "gentlemanly and brotherly officers" can take the sting out of life aboard a man-of-war—Melville invites the reader to extend this insight to slavery; for he concludes the chapter by drawing an analogy between the officer who unships his "quarter-deck face" for a paternal mask, "to be merely sported for a moment," and "the temporary condescension of a master to a slave"—"the most outrageous and galling" of insults (WJ, 276).

Melville does not content himself, however, with reiterating in general terms his conviction that a man-of-war regime oppresses white sailors as much as blacks. In the next chapter, he brings this truth home to the reader by casting his persona White-Jacket in a plight similar to Rose-Water's. Furthermore, Melville makes the reader share White-Jacket's thoughts and feelings as he learns that he is liable to the same indignities and injustices for which he has complacently pitied Rose-Water, and as an "instinct diffused through all animated nature" prompts him to strike out at his oppressor, though he pay for it with his life.

The chapter opens with White-Jacket's reflections on Rose-Water's unmerited flogging: "When with five hundred others I made one of the compelled spectators at the scourging of poor Rose-Water, I little thought what Fate had ordained for myself the next day. Poor mulatto! thought I, one of an oppressed race, they degrade you like a hound. Thank God! I am a white" (wj, 277). Some critics have taken this "sympathy . . . of a rather condescending sort" at face value as another manifestation of Melville's ambivalence toward blacks.[31] White-Jacket's rhetoric, however, seems too blatant to be anything but self-parodying. Indeed, in the next sentence White-Jacket implicitly deprecates his own complacency: "Yet I had seen whites also scourged; for, black or white, all my shipmates were liable to that. Still, there is something in us, somehow, that, in the most degraded condition, we snatch at a chance to deceive ourselves into a fancied superiority to others, whom we suppose lower in the scale than ourselves" (wj, 277). The self-parody becomes unmistakable when, after recognizing that he is no less subject to degradation than Rose-Water, White-Jacket repeats: "Poor Rose-Water! thought I; poor mulatto!"

As it transpires, White-Jacket soon finds himself arraigned at the mast to be flogged for failing, both literally and symbolically, to know his place; for White-Jacket has, on paper, been assigned a particular "station" aboard the *Neversink*, although in practice he has been given the impression that he can occupy any station he finds convenient. Nor is White-Jacket the only sailor in this predicament. "Such was the state of discipline" on the *Neversink*, as he subsequently discovers, "that very few of the seamen could tell where their proper stations were" (wj, 278). Like Rose-Water and May-Day, after being allowed to persist in ignorance of his "proper"

---

31. Zirker, "Slavery Dilemma in *White-Jacket*," 482, asserts that "the idea that White-Jacket and Rose-Water, a Negro, are equally oppressed in the world of the man-of-war trembles on the threshold. . . . But the incident does not take this direction." See also Kaplan, "Melville and the American National Sin," 322.

station for almost the entire voyage, and after scrupulously obeying orders in an attempt to "avoid the possibility of the scourge," White-Jacket is arbitrarily singled out for punishment on an occasion when Captain Claret happens to be in "ill humor" (WJ, 279–80).

Yet unlike Captain Claret's gladiators, who submit to his whims at the cost of their manhood, White-Jacket is no Happy Jack. He is evidently a seaman of the type whose "manly freedom" is as intolerable to sea officers as "an erect, lofty-minded African['s] would be to some slave-driving planter" (WJ, 385). Deliberately eschewing the usage that man-of-war's-men have adopted of "obsequiously touching their hat at every sentence they address to the Captain," White-Jacket risks further provoking Captain Claret's displeasure in the teeth of his impending flogging. He also dares to contradict the officer who claims to have assigned him to his station. On being sentenced to a flogging, White-Jacket feels "wild thoughts" enter his heart—of the kind that make a man seem "almost irresponsible for his act and his deed." As he tells the reader, the impulses that surge through him when he feels driven to choosing between abject surrender and foredoomed mutiny are the instinctive impulses that any man retaining some "dignity within" would have under the circumstances. Hence, in articulating them he speaks not only for himself, but for all such men, be they sailors or slaves, white or black:

> The thing that swayed me to my purpose was not altogether the thought that Captain Claret was about to degrade me, and that I had taken an oath with my soul that he should not. No, I felt my man's manhood so bottomless within me, that no word, no blow, no scourge of Captain Claret could cut me deep enough for that. I but swung to an instinct in me—the instinct . . . that prompts even a worm to turn under the heel. Locking souls with him, I meant to drag Captain Claret from this earthly tribunal of his to that of Jehovah, and let Him decide between us. No other way could I escape the scourge.
> Nature has not implanted any power in man that was not meant to be exercised at times. . . . The privilege, inborn and inalienable, that every man has, of dying himself, and inflicting death upon another, was not given to us without a purpose. These are the last resources of an insulted and unendurable existence. (WJ, 280)

Nothing, however, more poignantly reveals Melville's own deep conflict over defying authority than the alternatives with which he confronts White-Jacket—the psychological suicide of submitting to the scourge or the literal suicide of plunging into the ocean, symbolically locked body and soul with Captain Claret in an embrace fatal to them both. So powerful does the conflict appear that in Melville's imagination acceptance and rejection of the authority figure have become intertwined, and the necessity of dying has become a prerequisite for the privilege of killing the authority figure.

Ultimately, Melville can conceive of no solution to such an impasse short of invoking destiny itself. As in *Mardi* he had opted out of deciding between the poet's ardent revolutionary sympathies and the philosopher's heavy-hearted resignation to "present woes for some" rather than "future woes for all," appealing instead to "all-healing Time" to befriend the slave, here Melville falls back on the self-confessedly improbable expedient of having an officer intervene to vindicate White-Jacket, obliging Captain Claret, "as if a slave to Fate," to call off the flogging before White-Jacket need consummate his suicidal rebellion.[32]

Apparently the question of whether slave revolt could be justified, at least as a last recourse, continued to preoccupy Melville, for he returned to it two years later in his next book. "The Town-Ho's Story," a chapter of *Moby-Dick* which Melville first published separately in *Harper's Monthly*, raises this issue through the same analogy between the white seaman and the black slave that Melville had used in *White-Jacket*, roughly recreating White-Jacket's confrontation with Captain Claret. It also manifests the same conflict on Melville's part between identifying with the rebellious slave or acknowledging the authority of his oppressor. "The Town-Ho's Story" dramatizes a mutiny more extendedly and endorses it more decisively than any of Melville's previous works. At the same time its very format—as a story secretly confided by the crew of the *Town-Ho*

---

32. Zirker, "Slavery Dilemma in *White-Jacket*," 486–91, discusses the ambivalence toward revolt that Melville shows in the "anticlimax of this dénouement," as well as in the "mutiny of the beards."

to the Gayhead Indian harpooneer Tashtego, then inadvertently communicated by Tashtego to his shipmates on the *Pequod* when he talks in his sleep, and finally narrated by Ishmael, not directly to the reader of *Moby-Dick*, but in "the style in which I once narrated it at Lima, to a lounging circle of my Spanish friends"[33] —eloquently bespeaks Melville's need to dissociate himself from rebellion.

The tale of a proud seaman's feud with his overbearing officers, its initial stage illustrates White-Jacket's contention that a seaman who carries himself with "manly freedom" is a "continual reproach" to his officers "as being mentally superior to their power" (WJ, 385). Melville goes much further in "The Town-Ho's Story" than in *White-Jacket*, however; for he expressly challenges the theory that society's power structures correspond to a prior gradation in nature itself, subordinating the lower forms of life to the higher—an argument used to rationalize the domination of one class by another ever since Aristotle.[34]

Melville maintains in this story that worldly hierarchies often violate natural orders of merit, elevating mediocre men over their betters, and consequently causing friction between insecure authority figures and resentful subalterns. "Now, as you well know," he explains, "it is not seldom the case in this conventional world of ours—watery or otherwise; that when a person placed in command over his fellow-men finds one of them to be very significantly his superior in general pride of manhood, straightway against that man he conceives an unconquerable dislike and bitterness; and if he have a chance he will pull down and pulverize that subaltern's tower, and make a little heap of dust of it" (MD, 211). When Melville proceeds to define Steelkilt's superiority to his commanding officer in physical terms, he unmistakably extends this challenge to the racial sphere. Reversing the racist stereotypes that identified the white master with the thoroughbred horse and the Negro slave with the lowly mule, Melville confers the master's Roman bearing, royal spirit,

33. Herman Melville, *Moby-Dick; or, The Whale*, ed. Harrison Hayford and Hershel Parker (New York, 1967), 208. All further page references to this edition will be given parenthetically in the text. "The Town-Ho's Story" appeared in *Harper's New Monthly Magazine*, III (October, 1851), 658–65, a few weeks before the publication of *Moby-Dick*.

34. Jenkins, *Pro-Slavery Thought*, 120–21, 137, 289, discusses the proslavery apologists' derivation of this theory from Aristotle.

beauty, and intelligence on the common sailor Steelkilt, and endows the mate Radney with the ugliness, endurance, obstinacy, and spiteful cunning traditionally ascribed to the slave:[35] "Steelkilt was a tall and noble animal with a head like a Roman, and a flowing golden beard like the tasseled housings of your last viceroy's snorting charger; and a brain, and a heart, and a soul in him, gentlemen, which had made Steelkilt Charlemagne, had he been born son to Charlemagne's father. But Radney, the mate, was ugly as a mule; yet as hardy, as stubborn, as malicious" (MD, 211). Melville thus implies that if physiognomy, rather than inherited privilege, were indeed the basis for relegating some men to mastery and others to subservience, as racist theorists like Cartwright claimed, many a slave might find himself a master, and many a master a slave. Although Steelkilt is a white "slave," Melville develops him into an analogue for the "erect, lofty-minded African," using the same technique by which he had earlier made Landless a counterpart to the stereotyped Negro menial.

As a "Lakeman and desperado from Buffalo," Steelkilt hails from a physical and spiritual wilderness in many ways akin to Africa. His native Great Lakes region covers "leagues and leagues" of "ancient and unentered forests . . . harboring wild Afric beasts of prey," and is cut by a "green-turfed, flowery Nile," the Erie Canal, where "your true Ashantee" flourish and "your pagans" howl, in the guise of wild, swart-visaged Canallers (MD, 209–10, 214–15). The "grand fresh-water seas" that dominate this wilderness also encompass many of the "rimmed varieties of races and of climes" found in the two great oceans that the African continent straddles (MD, 209). Steelkilt himself, as Melville describes him, is as much a barbarian at heart as the fabled African savage—and at the same time as successfully domesticated. "Though a sort of devil indeed," he can be "retained harmless and docile" if treated with "inflexible firmness, only tempered by that common decency of human recognition which is the meanest slave's right" (MD, 210).

Correspondingly, "the tyrannical Radney," as Alan Heimert has pointed out, has the notorious "southern characteristics" of a fiery,

35. See Cartwright, "Slavery in the Light of Ethnology," 723; Estes, *Defence of Negro Slavery*, 64, 80.

vindictive temperament and a penchant for violence.[36] Contrary to the notion that the white man exerted a civilizing influence over the African, Radney and Steelkilt appear to be equally subject to primitive passions.[37] Radney, despite his Vineyarder's upbringing, is "quite as vengeful and full of social quarrel as the backwoods seaman, fresh from the latitudes of buck-horn handled Bowie knives" (MD, 210). The inevitable collision between the two men thus becomes a paradigm of master-slave conflict, and the mutiny in which it culminates a paradigm of slave insurrection.

Trouble first erupts when the mate overhears his handsome subaltern Steelkilt making fun of his homeliness. Determined to avenge the gibe, Radney in turn seeks to demean Steelkilt by issuing him an "order . . . almost as plainly meant to sting and insult Steelkilt, as though Radney had spat in his face" (MD, 212). While showing that both men are initially at fault, Melville generates more sympathy for Steelkilt by dwelling on the "strange forbearance" the goaded seaman exhibits in spite of his officer's "most domineering and outrageous manner" (MD, 213). Repeatedly "smothering the conflagration within him," Steelkilt at first quietly refuses to obey the mate's unwarranted command, retreats when the "infatuated" Radney threatens him with a hammer, warns his persecutor to desist, and at last retaliates only after the mate grazes him with the hammer. Radney, on his part, behaves throughout as a "fool . . . branded for the slaughter by the gods" (MD, 214). Hence Melville clearly intends the reader to endorse the blow with which Steelkilt finally crushes Radney's jaw.

Even when Steelkilt's personal feud with his abusive mate develops into a general mutiny threatening the safety of the already unseaworthy *Town-Ho*, Melville seems to identify with Steelkilt in his defiance of the captain and his refusal to be flogged for the insubordination to which he has been provoked. Steelkilt pleads his case with dignity (echoing the argument Melville had used to claim his discharge in *Omoo* [38]), and his demands sound eminently rea-

---

36. Alan Heimert, "*Moby-Dick* and American Political Symbolism," *American Quarterly*, XV (1963), 529–30.

37. *The Pro-Slavery Argument*, 273–74; also Jefferson, *Notes on Virginia*, 134–35.

38. *Omoo*, 6, 103. According to Roper, "Historical Note," 321, "The crew list of the *Lucy Ann* does not confirm Melville's claim that he signed on for the cruise only."

sonable: "'Look ye, now,' cried the Lakeman, flinging out his arm towards him [the captain], 'there are a few of us here (and I am one of them) who have shipped for the cruise, d'ye see; now as you well know, sir, we can claim our discharge as soon as the anchor is down; so we don't want a row; it's not our interest; we want to be peaceable; we are ready to work, but we won't be flogged'" (MD, 216). In contrast to Steelkilt, the "valiant captain" cuts a sorry figure as, "standing out of harm's way," he dances "up and down with a whale-pike, calling upon his officers to manhandle that atrocious scoundrel, and smoke him along to the quarter-deck" (MD, 215). His intransigence about making no promises to let the rebels off without a flogging if they lay down their arms and return to work seems petty and rancorous.

Despite having presented the mutineers so sympathetically and laid such a solid groundwork for justifying their recourse to violence, Melville apparently could not bring himself to let them enact a successful mutiny. Once again, he has his hero choose a self-defeating form of rebellion. Rather than lift a hand against the captain, Steelkilt persuades his reluctant compeers to allow the captain to lock them all in the forecastle, where they intend to remain until guaranteed amnesty. As might be expected, the unity of the group breaks down after several days of confinement on a "famishing diet," and all but two of Steelkilt's fellow mutineers desert him (MD, 217). Only when the chances of success have thus been reduced to almost nil does Melville have Steelkilt propose to his two remaining comrades-in-arms that they try to seize the ship, "if by any devilishness of desperation possible," by running amuck among the crew with mincing knives (MD, 218). It is, of course, a suicidal plan. Instead of letting his hero go through with it, Melville thwarts him by having Steelkilt's two cohorts treacherously fall upon him and deliver him gagged and bound to the captain. Once having hamstrung the rebel with whom he identifies, Melville characteristically glorifies him in defeat. Steelkilt is condemned to be tied overnight in the mizen rigging between his betrayers, like Christ between "the two crucified thieves" (MD, 219), and to be flogged the following morning.

Conversely, the scene of Steelkilt's ensuing flogging, closely paralleling White-Jacket's arraignment at the mast, reveals almost as much resistance on Melville's part to dramatizing his hero's capitulation as to imagining the consummation of his rebellion. Just as White-Jacket is miraculously spared both submitting to his threatened flogging and becoming "a murderer and a suicide" in an attempt to avert it (WJ, 281), so Steelkilt improbably twice forestalls his own flogging—the first time he hisses out "something, inaudible to all but the Captain; who, to the amazement of all hands," backs down; the second time, with "another hiss," he momentarily stays Radney's uplifted arm.

Ultimately, Melville awards Steelkilt a guiltless revenge against Radney, as well as a bloodless triumph over the captain. While Steelkilt is laying plans to murder his persecutor, Moby Dick is suddenly sighted; and in the subsequent chase, Radney alone of the entire boat's crew falls overboard and is seized in the white whale's jaws, to be carried to the bottom of the sea. Melville moralizes: "by a mysterious fatality, Heaven itself seemed to step in to take out of [Steelkilt's] hands into its own the damning thing he would have done" (MD, 221). Soon afterwards, joined by most of the crew, Steelkilt deserts the ship and forces the captain to give the deserters a six-day head start to the nearest port, thereby ensuring their escape.

The outcome of "The Town-Ho's Story" thus exhibits the same tensions we have noticed in *Mardi* and *White-Jacket*—once more Melville's strong fellow-feeling for men he equates with slaves vies with his deep-seated reluctance to defy authority. Yet in "The Town-Ho's Story" Melville comes closer than he ever will again to resolving these tensions in favor of the slave's right to reclaim his manhood, whatever the cost in human bloodshed. Unlike White-Jacket, who contemplates an individual act of rebellion, Steelkilt actually leads a collective mutiny and succeeds in liberating a body of men from an unjust captain. Unlike the "great Philanthropist" Time, whom Melville conjures somehow to right the slave's wrongs without violence in *Mardi*, and unlike the officer who speaks up for White-Jacket, the deus ex machina Melville invokes in "The Town-Ho's Story" does not merely save or vindicate a wronged subaltern, but kills his oppressor in the process. Moreover, the climactic scene in which Moby Dick intervenes in the *Town-Ho*'s civil strife to avenge a slave analogue against his master prefigures both the culmination

of the larger narrative in which "The Town-Ho's Story" appears
and the meaning which at least two other critics have seen in that
culmination—apocalyptic doom for America's slavery-rocked ship
of state.[39]

39. Foster, "Something in Emblems," 33; Heimert, "Moby-Dick and American Political Symbolism," 500–502, 526–34. The most complete apocalyptic interpretation of Moby-Dick (though not linked to slavery) is Michael T. Gilmore's "Melville's Apocalypse: American Millennialism and Moby-Dick," ESQ: A Journal of the American Renaissance, XXI (1975), 154–61, included in his book The Middle Way: Puritanism and Ideology in American Romantic Fiction (New Brunswick, N.J., 1977), 136–51.

THREE   *A* Jonah's Warning
to America in *Moby-Dick*

CENTERING his allegorical indictment of slavery on
the experience of men abused and demeaned beyond the uttermost
limits of human endurance, as Melville did in *White-Jacket* and "The
Town-Ho's Story," inevitably led him to concentrate on the moral
issue of whether men in such circumstances may justifiably resort
to violence to overthrow their oppressors. This literary exploration
in turn confronted Melville with his own unresolved conflict between submitting to and rebelling against repressive authority, be
it parental, societal, religious, or political. Since he envisioned both
alternatives as self-destructive, he seems to have been unable to
sustain the tension of openly identifying with the slave. Instead, he
retreated to the safer emotional vantage point from which, in *Mardi*,
he had first begun exploring the moral problems that slavery posed.
Displacing his personal conflict over defying authority onto the
nation at large, Melville concerned himself increasingly with the
political dilemma of ending slavery in time to avert an interracial
bloodbath, yet in such a way as not to court the destruction of the
Union. This shift of focus also entailed a more global assessment
of slavery as an institution that different peoples had imposed on
each other from time immemorial and that deformed both its per-
petrators and its victims, generating an endless cycle of vengeance.
    The watershed in Melville's approach to slavery occurs in *Moby-
Dick*, where he views the problem of slavery from many angles,
including the metaphysical. As Ishmael muses ironically: "Who aint

a slave? Tell me that. Well, then, however the old sea-captains may order me about—however they may thump and punch me about, I have the satisfaction of knowing that it is all right; that everybody else is one way or other served in much the same way—either in a physical or metaphysical point of view, that is; and so the universal thump is passed round, and all hands should rub each other's shoulder-blades, and be content" (MD, 15).

In *Moby-Dick*, Melville envisages several possible dénouements to the American crisis over slavery, along with various answers to the question of whether individuals (and nations) help to weave their own destiny into the warp of necessity or are entirely caught in the threads of Fate's loom.[1] "The Town-Ho's Story" offers Steelkilt's rebellion and its successful issue as one such dénouement.[2] The main narrative of *Moby-Dick* offers another alternative to Ahab's destructive polity and the retribution it brings on the *Pequod*; for Ishmael, buoyed up by the coffin his friend Queequeg had ordered for himself and subsequently turned into a life buoy for the *Pequod*, miraculously escapes the cataclysm that overtakes his shipmates. As the means of Ishmael's escape betokens, his freely chosen friendship with Queequeg plays a conspicuous part in modifying his destiny, even though "those stage managers, the Fates," may have had the first and last word in sending him on this ill-starred voyage and ordaining its ending.[3] Ishmael's friendship with Queequeg dramatizes the conclusions about racial prejudice that Melville had reached in *Redburn* and suggests that by embracing the Negro as an equal partner, American citizens might still avert the tempest that threatened to engulf their ship of state.

But before we can be sure of these racial implications, we must first determine whether Melville meant to identify Queequeg with

1. *Moby-Dick*, Chaps. 1, 47, 93, 102, 134, epilogue.
2. Heimert, *"Moby-Dick* and American Political Symbolism," 530, suggests that Melville may have originally conceived the tale "as something other than a mere interlude" in a more hopeful political allegory that he did not "imagine . . . as ending in disaster."
3. In Chapter 1, Ishmael asserts that "those stage managers, the Fates," impelled him to go on a whaling voyage while "cajoling me into the delusion that it was a choice resulting from my own unbiased freewill," and he identifies the whale, and specifically the "phantom" of Moby Dick, as one of the chief inducements (MD, 16). In the epilogue, Ishmael is "he whom the Fates ordained to take the place of Ahab's bowsman" and thus to escape going down with the *Pequod*. But as Edgar A. Dryden has shown (*Melville's Thematics of Form*, 104–13), Ishmael also recognizes the possibility of "weaving his own destiny" by telling his tale.

the Negro—a question that has elicited lively debate among critics interested in Melville's racial attitudes. Those who credit Melville with enlightened racial views cite the cannibal as a fully developed and complimentary negroid characterization and emphasize the unprecedented egalitarianism of picturing a white man sharing a bed with a dark-skinned savage. Conversely, those who accuse Melville of racism point out that Queequeg is not an American Negro and theorize that Melville's deeply felt Marquesan experience might have led to a "deification of Polynesians" without affecting his prejudices toward Africans or, for that matter, American Indians.[4] What both sides seem to have missed—despite recognition of the way Queequeg telescopes Polynesian, American Indian, African, Islamic, and even Christian features and customs—is how deliberately Melville has blurred racial lines in portraying the savage, and how explicitly he has related Queequeg's ambiguously perceived racial identity to the issue of anti-Negro prejudice.

The most obvious sign that Melville intended to endow Queequeg with African attributes is the series of allusions that initially provoked the controversy. As critics of both schools have noted, Queequeg, though a native of the South Sea islands, incongruously worships a "little deformed image . . . exactly the color of a three days' old Congo baby," prompting Ishmael to call it his "negro idol" (MD, 30, 51). Furthermore, Queequeg and Ishmael later attract from passersby some of the hostile notice that Redburn imagines his ship's black steward would have received had he walked arm in arm with a white woman in the streets of New York. Since Ishmael and Queequeg are of the same sex, they are not mobbed, but they are greeted with stares and jeers. Ishmael pointedly comments that these taunts are due not to the outlandish figure Queequeg cuts—the citizens of New Bedford being "used to seeing cannibals like him in their streets"—but to the sight of two racially diverse "fellow beings" on such "companionable" terms. Underscoring the parallel with black-white relations in America, he drops the word "cannibal" to moralize outright: "as though a white man

4. In the first camp, see Simpson, "Melville and the Negro," 27–29; Zirker, "Slavery Dilemma in *White-Jacket*," 480; and Grejda, *Common Continent of Men*, 86–97. In the second, see Widmer, *The Ways of Nihilism*, 69–70, n. 11; and James Baird, *Ishmael: A Study of the Symbolic Mode in Primitivism* (New York, 1960), 118–20, 237–40.

were anything more dignified than a whitewashed negro" (MD, 58–60).[5]

Hence it should be clear that Queequeg represents yet another of the composite racial figures that Melville created to undermine racial categories and to inculcate the lessons in racial tolerance and cultural relativism that he himself had learned in Typee. Through Ishmael's encounter with Queequeg, Melville shows how an educated young man of respectable social background learns to overcome his provincial bigotry and racial prejudices, just as he had earlier shown Redburn learning to overcome his anti-Negro feelings. With Ishmael, however, Melville takes the reader further than with Redburn, since he also calls into question for the first time the reality of the racial differences to which prejudice was generally ascribed in his day.

Even before Ishmael actually meets Queequeg, he confronts the problem of whether he "might be cherishing unwarrantable prejudices against this unknown harpooneer," with whom the landlord has proposed that he share the only remaining bed in the inn (MD, 25). The joke is that the well-defined prejudices Ishmael holds do not prevent the racial identity of his bedfellow from eluding him for the better part of a long chapter. Thus when Ishmael learns that the mysterious harpooneer "is actually engaged this blessed Saturday night, or rather Sunday morning, in peddling his head around this town," he does not connect this "cannibal business" with the previous revelation that the harpooneer is "a dark complexioned chap" who "eats nothing but steaks, and likes 'em rare" (MD, 22, 25, 27). Instead, Ishmael expostulates with the landlord, unconsciously basing his claim to sagacity on color: "you'd better stop spinning that yarn to me—I'm not green." Accentuating the racial implications of this pun, the landlord's answering pun—"May be not . . . but I rayther guess you'll be done *brown* if that ere harpooneer hears you a slanderin' his head" (MD, 26)—hints at the first lessons Ishmael will learn on being thrown together with Queequeg: that color prejudice is a two-way street and color itself a treacherous criterion on which to predicate anyone's identity, let alone his worth.

Ishmael's continued obtuseness regarding Queequeg's racial

5. Kaplan, "Melville and the American National Sin," 325, 330–31; Simpson, "Melville and the Negro," 28; Baird, *Ishmael*, 237–40.

identity becomes more significant when the very sight of the cannibal fails to enlighten him. At the first view of Queequeg's "dark, purplish, yellow" face, "here and there stuck over with large, blackish looking squares," Ishmael supposes that "he's been in a fight, got dreadfully cut, and here he is, just from the surgeon" (MD, 28). On perceiving that the black squares on Queequeg's cheeks are not "sticking-plasters," but "stains of some sort or other," Ishmael takes Queequeg for a "white man . . . who, falling among the cannibals, had been tattooed by them" (MD, 29). He moralizes: "And what is it, thought I, after all! It's only his outside; a man can be honest in any sort of skin." Ironically, Ishmael has not meant to articulate a protest against color-consciousness.

Still under the misapprehension that Queequeg is a "white man," Ishmael struggles to explain how a white could have acquired such an "unearthly complexion." Echoing the scientific debates about whether racial features resulted from the influence of climate or from primordial biological differences, he wavers between two theories—that "the sun . . . produced these extraordinary effects upon the skin," or alternatively, that the stranger's distinctive skin color might arise from some deeper cause than climate: "I never heard of a hot sun's tanning a white man into a purplish yellow one." The "bald purplish head" that the stranger reveals on taking off his beaver hat frightens Ishmael more than his discolored tattooed skin, perhaps because it looks "for all the world like a mildewed skull"—just such a mildewed skull, in fact, as American archaeologists and ethnologists were currently disinterring from Indian burial grounds as a means of determining the racial character of America's aboriginal population.[6] Hitherto curious enough to master his alarm, Ishmael now feels ready to bolt from the room. He accounts for his terror by remarking, "Ignorance is the parent of fear, and being completely nonplussed and confounded about the stranger, I confess I was now as much afraid of him as if it was the devil himself" (MD, 29).

Once again, however, this broad-minded interpretation of racial prejudice ironically precedes Ishmael's realization that Queequeg

6. On the scientific debates over race and climate, see Winthrop D. Jordan, *White Over Black: American Attitudes Toward the Negro, 1550–1812* (Baltimore, 1969), 512–41; also Stanton, *The Leopard's Spots*, 1–44, 82–89.

is not a white man gone native, but an "abominable savage" from the South Seas—a fact that only becomes "quite plain" to him after Queequeg has completely undressed, disclosing a body tattooed from head to foot. Not until Queequeg has sprung upon him crying "Who-e debel you?", bringing the landlord to the rescue, does Ishmael belatedly digest the intuitions he has had about how irrelevant a man's skin color is to his character, and why people of different skin color fear each other as devils: "What's all this fuss I have been making about, thought I to myself—the man's a human being just as I am: he has just as much reason to fear me, as I have to be afraid of him" (MD, 31).

Overcoming color prejudice is but the initial stage of the transformation Ishmael undergoes. Once he removes his racial coloring glasses, Ishmael begins to see his savage bedfellow in another light, which in turn affects his perceptions of his white countrymen. The first breakthrough occurs when Ishmael realizes that the cannibal is in fact behaving "in not only a civil but a really kind and charitable way" toward him. By the next morning, Ishmael has also become aware of the unflattering contrast between his own "great rudeness" in staring at Queequeg and "watching all his toilette motions" as if he were an animal in the zoo, and Queequeg's "civility and consideration" in offering to leave the room so that Ishmael can dress in privacy. This leads Ishmael to question the appropriateness of the terms "savage" and "civilized" and to conclude that savages may be more "civilized" in certain respects than so-called "civilized" peoples: "Thinks I, Queequeg . . . this is a very civilized overture; but, the truth is, these savages have an innate sense of delicacy, say what you will; it is marvellous how essentially polite they are" (MD, 34). Although Ishmael proceeds to regale the reader with a description of how Queequeg commences "dressing at top by donning his beaver hat" and then, "minus his trowsers," crushes himself "boots in hand, and hat on—under the bed . . . to be private when putting on his boots," his sense of Queequeg's idiosyncracies soon gives way to a growing appreciation of the savage's human qualities.

On joining the other sailors at breakfast, Ishmael already views the difference between them and Queequeg as one of degree, rather than kind. Whereas earlier he had tried to classify Queequeg as "white" or "savage," he now foregoes these racial categories altogether and distinguishes among the sailors only on the basis of their sun tans:

> This young fellow's healthy cheek is like a sun-toasted pear in hue, and would seem to smell almost as musky; he cannot have been three days landed from his Indian voyage. That man next him looks a few shades lighter; you might say a touch of satin wood is in him. In the complexion of a third still lingers a tropic tawn, but slightly bleached withal; *he* doubtless has tarried whole weeks ashore. But who could show a cheek like Queequeg? which, barred with various tints, seemed like the Andes' western slope, to show forth in one array, contrasting climates, zone by zone. (MD, 36)

Queequeg's uniqueness, in other words, consists not in being "colored," as opposed to white (or purplish yellow, as opposed to another shade), but in being a compendium of the colors produced by various climates (apparently Ishmael has opted for the climatic explanation of racial differences).

Similarly, when Ishmael goes on to compare Queequeg's bearing and manners with those of his compeers, he no longer dwells on "Queequeg's peculiarities here; how he eschewed coffee and hot rolls, and applied his undivided attention to beefsteaks, done rare," serving himself with his harpoon. Instead, what impresses Ishmael is how much more poised Queequeg looks than the American sailors. They, in their native land, sit "at a social breakfast table—all of the same calling, all of kindred tastes—looking round as sheepishly at each other as though they had never been out of sight of some sheepfold among the Green Mountains." Queequeg, twenty thousand miles away from home and amid people whose language he can barely speak, presides "at the head of the table . . . as cool as an icicle" (MD, 36–37).

In the next chapter, where Ishmael confronts the cross section of nations and races thronging the streets of New Bedford, his astonishment "at first catching a glimpse of so outlandish an individual as Queequeg circulating among the polite society of a civilized town" entirely evaporates. He remarks:

> In thoroughfares nigh the docks, any considerable seaport will frequently offer to view the queerest looking nondescripts from foreign parts. Even in Broadway and Chestnut streets, Mediterranean mariners will sometimes jostle the affrighted ladies. Regent street is not

unknown to Lascars and Malays; and at Bombay, in the Apollo
Green, live Yankees have often scared the natives. . . . In New Bedford, actual cannibals stand chatting at street corners; savages outright; many of whom yet carry on their bones unholy flesh. It makes
a stranger stare. (MD, 37)

Lumping Mediterranean mariners and Yankees with Lascars and
Malays, Ishmael jolts us into realizing, as *he* now does, that we are
as anomalous to foreign peoples as they are to us—indeed perhaps
more so, since the Lascars and Malays in London seem to attract
no notice from the British, and the savages in jaded New Bedford
go unheeded except by strangers, whereas in Bombay "live Yankees
have often scared the natives." He also implies that no set of racial
traits is inherently stranger than any other; that the strangeness, in
short, is in the eye of the beholder. Thus a white seaman from Spain
or Italy can seem more fearsome to an American lady who has never
seen one than a cannibal does to a native of New Bedford. Ishmael
delivers the final blow to his countrymen's ethnocentrism and color
consciousness by asserting that what the reader will find "still more
curious, certainly more comical" than all the dark-skinned "Fee-
geeans, Tongatabooans, Erromanggoans, Pannangians, and Bri-
ghggians" he will run across in New Bedford, is the spectacle of
the "green Vermonters and New Hampshire men" who descend on
the town by the score "all athirst for gain and glory" in the untried
career of whaling: "Many are as green as the Green Mountains
whence they come. . . . Look there! that chap strutting round the
corner. He wears a beaver hat and swallow-tailed coat, girdled with
a sailor-belt and sheath-knife. Here comes another with a sou'wester
and a bombazine cloak" (MD, 37–38). The analogy with Queequeg
in his beaver hat is unmistakable, as is the moral, driven home in
the following paragraph, that the South Sea savage who dons his
boots under the bed is intrinsically no more ludicrous than the
homegrown "bumpkin dandy" who mows his native acres "in buck-
skin gloves" during the dog days, "for fear of tanning his hands"
(MD, 38).

The change in Ishmael's perceptions, resulting in this sophisticated cultural relativism, culminates when he is able to discern
the nobility of character underlying Queequeg's bizarre exterior:

Savage though he was, and hideously marred about the face—at least to my taste—his countenance yet had a something in it which was by no means disagreeable. You cannot hide the soul. Through all his unearthly tattooings, I thought I saw the traces of a simple honest heart; and in his large, deep eyes, fiery black and bold, there seemed tokens of a spirit that would dare a thousand devils. And besides all this, there was a certain lofty bearing about the Pagan, which even his uncouthness could not altogether maim. He looked like a man who had never cringed and never had had a creditor. (MD, 51–52)

Not only does Ishmael overlook the disfigurements that had previously repelled him; he has also come to realize that his own distaste for tattooing is as ethnocentric as Queequeg's preference for it. But Ishmael's most radical departure from the racial prejudice that had originally distorted Queequeg into a devil in his eyes consists in ascribing phrenological excellence to Queequeg's negroid cranial conformation, with its retreating forehead and projecting brow, and identifying it with George Washington's: "certain it was his head was phrenologically an excellent one. It may seem ridiculous, but it reminded me of General Washington's head, as seen in the popular busts of him. It had the same long regularly graded retreating slope from above the brows, which were likewise very projecting, like two long promontories thickly wooded on top. Queequeg was George Washington cannibalistically developed" (MD, 52). We need only recall that nineteenth-century Americans placed Washington side by side with Shakespeare at the pinnacle of human evolution—and consigned the African cannibal to its nadir—to measure the distance Ishmael has traveled.[7]

Paralleling Ishmael's intellectual growth is the maturation of his acquaintance with Queequeg into a friendship destined to alter the course of his life. When Ishmael accepts Queequeg as his bedfellow with the famous words, "Better sleep with a sober cannibal than a drunken Christian," he carries the principles of racial tolerance and egalitarianism to what Redburn had recognized as their logical conclusion—vindicating "amalgamation." Ishmael, however, goes a step beyond Redburn; for he actually practices what he preaches and contracts a "marriage" with someone of another race symboli-

7. See "Is Man One or Many?" 5.

cally associated with America's twin pariahs, the Negro and the Indian.

The insistent matrimonial imagery describing Ishmael's budding friendship with his new bedfellow has drawn much comment, both for its homosexual and its racial overtones.[8] Whatever sexual predilections it may indicate in Melville, he knew he could get away with dramatizing a happy interracial marriage by disguising it as a male comradeship which his public would not dare interpret as homosexual. The crucial fact about Melville's imagery, after all, is that it elevates the taboo relationship between a white and a nonwhite to the plane of a legal marriage between equals—and a love marriage at that. Except when Ishmael, under the influence of his "unwarrantable prejudices," worries about having a strange harpooneer "tumble in upon me at midnight" with no way of knowing "from what vile hole he had been coming" (MD, 24), Melville's jokes about the relationship are never merely bawdy. On the contrary, Ishmael and Queequeg consummate their friendship in the landlord's own conjugal bed, where their union issues in a "hatchet-faced baby" (Queequeg's tomahawk-calumet); Queequeg holds Ishmael in a "bridegroom clasp . . . as though naught but death should part us twain" (which indeed proves to be the case); Queequeg pronounces himself "married" to Ishmael, according to "his country's phrase"; Queequeg and Ishmael lie abed chatting in their "hearts' honeymoon" like "some old couples"; and Ishmael at last sees "how elastic our stiff prejudices grow when love once comes to bend them" (MD, 27, 33, 53–55).

Beyond its propagandistic function of vindicating interracial marriage, the narrative significance of Ishmael's friendship with Queequeg lies in symbolizing the commitment that Ishmael makes, through Queequeg, to loving his fellow man and acknowledging the tie that binds him to the rest of humanity. This commitment, which will later protect Ishmael against succumbing entirely to Ahab's hate-driven pursuit of the white whale, initially rescues him

8. On its homosexual overtones, see Arvin, *Herman Melville*, 27–28, 174; Daniel G. Hoffman, *Form and Fable in American Fiction* (New York, 1961), 264–68; Leslie A. Fiedler, *Love and Death in the American Novel* (rev. ed.; New York, 1966), 366–90; and Miller, *Melville*, 200–201. On its racial overtones, see Simpson, "Melville and the Negro," 28–29; Zirker, "Slavery Dilemma in *White-Jacket*," 480; and Grejda, *Common Continent of Men*, 96–97.

from the mood of misanthropic despair that had impelled him to go to sea as an antidote to "methodically knocking people's hats off" and a "substitute for pistol and ball" (MD, 12).[9]

On Ishmael's second day with Queequeg, as he sits in the bedroom watching the savage, he begins "to be sensible of strange feelings": "I felt a melting in me. No more my splintered heart and maddened hand were turned against the wolfish world. This soothing savage had redeemed it. There he sat, his very indifference speaking a nature in which there lurked no civilized hypocrisies and bland deceits" (MD, 53). The scene that follows evokes the historical encounter between white settlers and American Indians and offers a moving alternative to the mutual hostilities that had ensued when whites had seized Indian lands, anathemized the Indians' way of life, and set out to destroy the Indians themselves in wars like the one that had left the Pequots—the "celebrated tribe of Massachusetts Indians" for whom the *Pequod* is named—"extinct as the ancient Medes" (MD, 67). Queequeg responds warmly to Ishmael's overtures, and the two seal their friendship over that hoary Indian symbol, the peace pipe.[10] Thereupon Queequeg embraces Ishmael, declares that they are henceforth "married" and that "he would gladly die for me, if need should be," and divides his belongings equally with Ishmael while Ishmael remonstrates against his generosity. Climaxing this ritual, which suggests an egalitarian marriage of the races on the American continent and their sharing of America's resources in a conjugal spirit, Queequeg invites Ishmael to join him in worshipping his negro idol—a reversal of the traditional roles of white missionary and savage proselyte. Ishmael's acquiescence and his use of the golden rule to justify it represent Melville's crowning affirmation that the essence of religion is a love

9. Among the many critics who have pointed this out are William Ellery Sedgwick, *Herman Melville: The Tragedy of Mind* (Cambridge, Mass., 1944), 119–26, reprinted in the Norton Critical Edition of *Moby-Dick*, 643–48; Arvin, *Herman Melville*, 170–71, 174–82; Baird, *Ishmael*, 233–51; Hoffman, *Form and Fable*, 235, 262–71; William Rosenfeld, "Uncertain Faith: Queequeg's Coffin and Melville's Use of the Bible," *Texas Studies in Literature and Language*, VII (1966), 320–22; Carl F. Strauch, "Ishmael: Time and Personality in *Moby-Dick*," *Studies in the Novel*, I (1969), 468, 476, 480–81; Robert Zoellner, *The Salt-Sea Mastodon: A Reading of "Moby-Dick"* (Berkeley, 1973), Chap. 11; Grejda, *Common Continent of Men*, 95–96.

10. See Hennig Cohen, "Melville's Tomahawk Pipe: Artifact and Symbol," *Studies in the Novel*, I (1969), 397–400.

for one's fellow man that transcends all barriers of race and creed and precludes all forms of intolerance:

I was a good Christian; born and bred in the bosom of the infallible Presbyterian Church. How then could I unite with this wild idolator in worshipping his piece of wood? But what is worship? thought I. Do you suppose now, Ishmael, that the magnanimous God of heaven and earth—pagans and all included—can possibly be jealous of an insignificant bit of black wood? Impossible! But what is worship?—to do the will of God—*that* is worship. And what is the will of God?—to do to my fellow man what I would have my fellow man to do to me—*that* is the will of God. Now, Queequeg is my fellow man. And what do I wish that this Queequeg would do to me? Why, unite with me in my particular Presbyterian form of worship. Consequently, I must then unite with him in his; ergo, I must turn idolator. So I kindled the shavings; helped prop up the innocent little idol; offered him burnt biscuit with Queequeg; salaamed before him twice or thrice; kissed his nose; and that done, we undressed and went to bed, at peace with our own consciences and all the world. (MD, 54)

Ishmael is not simply saying that the true spirit of the golden rule is contrary to the letter of Christianity, or that his "particular Presbyterian form of worship" is intrinsically no more faithful to the religion Jesus preached through the golden rule than Queequeg's idolatry. On the profoundest level, he is asserting that loving one's fellow man means wishing to overcome human separateness by sharing whatever is precious in one's own eyes with one's fellow, and that the union made possible by respecting this wish is more sacred than the most sacred institutions of any culture.

Ishmael's surrender to Queequeg is the first of the quasi-mystical experiences of human solidarity that eventuate in freeing him from Ahab's obsession with the "subtle demonisms of life and thought . . . personified . . . in Moby Dick" (MD, 160). The second experience occurs in the chapter called "The Monkey-Rope," where Ishmael, bound to Queequeg by a rope attached to both their belts during the precarious blubber-stripping operation, so as to ensure that Ishmael will pay with his own life for any failure to guard Queequeg's, has an appalling insight into the "dangerous liabilities" of being "wedded" to his fellow man "for better or for worse":

So strongly and metaphysically did I conceive of my situation then, that while earnestly watching his [Queequeg's] motions, I seemed distinctly to perceive that my own individuality was now merged in a joint stock company of two: that my free will had received a mortal wound; and that another's mistake or misfortune might plunge innocent me into unmerited disaster and death. . . . I saw that this situation of mine was the precise situation of every mortal that breathes; only, in most cases, he, one way or other, has this Siamese connexion with a plurality of other mortals. If your banker breaks, you snap; if your apothecary by mistake sends you poison in your pills, you die. True, you may say that, by exceeding caution, you may possibly escape these and the multitudinous other evil chances of life. But handle Queequeg's monkey-rope heedfully as I would, sometimes he jerked it so, that I came very near sliding overboard. Nor could I possibly forget that, do what I would, I only had the management of one end of it. (MD, 271)

In short, Ishmael apprehends on a metaphysical level the same truth that Melville dramatized through Redburn's subjection to social discrimination in England—that he must indeed be his brother's keeper, since no misfortune befalling his brother is without peril to himself, however innocent he may be of causing it.

Ishmael's third major experience of human solidarity reaffirms the more positive aspect of the "Siamese ligature" binding him to the rest of mankind, which his marriage with Queequeg originally expressed. As Ishmael sits with other sailors at the task of squeezing crystallized lumps of spermacetti back into liquid, he is transported into a state of ecstatic good will toward humanity in which he forgets "all about our horrible oath" to hunt Moby Dick to his death and purges his hands and heart of it:

Squeeze! squeeze! squeeze! all the morning long; I squeezed that sperm till I myself almost melted into it; I squeezed that sperm till a strange sort of insanity came over me; and I found myself unwittingly squeezing my co-laborers' hands in it, mistaking their hands for the gentle globules. Such an abounding, affectionate, friendly, loving feeling did this avocation beget; that at last I was continually squeezing their hands, and looking up into their eyes sentimentally; as much as to say,—Oh! my dear fellow beings, why should we longer cherish any social acerbities, or know the slightest ill-humor or envy! Come; let us squeeze hands all round; nay, let us all squeeze ourselves into each other; let us squeeze ourselves universally into the very milk and sperm of kindness. (MD, 348–49)

Despite the comic homoerotic spirit of this passage,[11] it serves as serious a purpose as the comic account of the friendship with Queequeg that reaches its consummation in the landlord's conjugal bed. Like the earlier episode in which Ishmael discovers "how elastic our stiff prejudices grow when love once comes to bend them" (MD, 55), Ishmael's rhapsodic description of being fused into loving oneness with his compeers calls upon the reader to renounce the "social acerbities" that alienate him from his "fellow beings" and to give himself up instead to the barrier-dissolving power of love.

Two chapters later, in "The Try-Works," Ishmael shows the reader the antithesis of this ideal and invites him to join in choosing once and for all between saving himself and his fellow men by acknowledging the "Siamese ligature" that binds them together, or destroying himself and them by denying their common humanity to pursue a phantasm. Steering the ship while whale blubber is being boiled down into oil, Ishmael finds himself possessed for the last time by Ahab's infernal vision of the world. As Ishmael gazes into the flaming try-works, his friend Queequeg and the other pagan harpooneers, whose task is to pitch the "hissing masses of blubber into the scalding pots" with their "huge pronged poles," begin to look to him like devils stoking the flames of hell. At the same time, the "capricious emblazonings" of the try-works transform the lounging sailors of the night watch, with some of whom Ishmael has been blissfully squeezing sperm only a few hours before, into "tawny," smoke-begrimed barbarians. Interpreting their venial sailor yarns now as "tales of terror" about "unholy adventures," Ishmael fancies that their "uncivilized laughter forked upwards out of them, like the flames from the furnace" (MD, 353). In this state of mind, he perceives the "rushing Pequod, freighted with savages, and laden with fire, and burning a corpse, and plunging into that blackness of darkness," as the "material counterpart of her monomaniac commander's soul" (MD, 354).

The mental aberration Ishmael comes to share with Ahab in "The Try-Works" consists in focusing so exclusively on the dark side of life that he no longer sees anything but evil. As Ishmael explains: "Wrapped, for that interval, in darkness myself, I but the better saw the redness, the madness, the ghastliness of others." The

11. See Fiedler, *Love and Death*, 371–72.

moral price of such an obsession with evil, Ishmael discovers, is that his soul becomes deadened to good until it is perverted into a mirror of the evil he sees in others: "The continual sight of the fiend shapes before me, capering half in smoke and half in fire, these at last begat kindred visions in my soul" (MD, 354). But as Ishmael has already become aware while holding Queequeg by the monkey-rope, no man can endanger himself without the risk of likewise plunging others into "unmerited disaster and death" (MD, 271). Thus Ishmael almost capsizes the ship when, in the midst of his hallucination at the helm, he unwittingly turns his back on the tiller and compass in accordance with his inverted moral perceptions. Unlike Ahab, however, whose ultimate shipwreck he prefigures, Ishmael awakens from his hallucination in time to right the ship and rescue her crew from the consequences of his madness. The moral he draws from this experience marks the parting of his way from Ahab's:

> Look not too long in the face of the fire, O man! Never dream with thy hand on the helm! Turn not thy back to the compass; accept the first hint of the hitching tiller; believe not the artificial fire, when its redness makes all things look ghastly. To-morrow, in the natural sun, the skies will be bright; those who glared like devils in the forking flames, the morn will show in far other, at least gentler, relief; the glorious, golden, glad sun, the only true lamp—all others but liars! (MD, 354)

If Ishmael refuses to credit the hellish view of his fellow men disclosed by firelight, it is not because he would overlook the evil in people; rather, it is because he would not lose sight of their humanity in contemplating their flaws. The natural light of the sun, Ishmael concludes, reveals evil enough to afflict a wise man without his needing to intensify it: "The sun hides not Virginia's Dismal Swamp, nor Rome's accursed Campagna, nor wide Sahara, nor all the millions of miles of deserts and of griefs beneath the moon. The sun hides not the ocean, which is the dark side of this earth, and which is two thirds of this earth. So, therefore, that mortal man who hath more of joy than sorrow in him, that mortal man cannot be true—not true, or undeveloped" (MD, 354–55).

The ultimate difference between Ishmael and Ahab—tested and sealed by the choice Ishmael makes in turning away from the fire to save the ship—is that Ishmael's marriage with Queequeg has made it possible for him to retain his human values and his allegiance to his fellow man in the face of the overwhelming evil and woe he sees in the world. Although Ishmael's commitment to preserving the *Pequod* and her crew cannot prevail against Ahab's monomania, he does survive to warn his compatriots away from the débacle toward which their ship of state is heading, and to seduce them into the marriage with their dark-complexioned fellow man and the consummation of their union with all mankind which, he has learned, constitute their sole hope of changing their disastrous course.

So far we have been considering the alternatives Melville offers in *Moby-Dick* to Ahab's polity and the shipwreck in which it culminates: the mutiny Steelkilt enacts in "The Town-Ho's Story" and the friendship with Queequeg through which Ishmael dissociates himself from Ahab's monomaniacal pursuit of a phantasm. Now we must confront the disaster Ishmael escapes and attempt to define more precisely the political meaning with which Melville invests it.

As early as the second chapter of *Moby-Dick*, Melville hints that the fateful whaling voyage on which Ishmael has set out, scheduled in the "grand programme of Providence" between a *"Grand Contested Election for the Presidency of the United States"* and a "BLOODY BATTLE IN AFFGHANISTAN," symbolizes the apocalpytic judgment that threatens America for her continued enslavement of the Negro. Heading toward the waterfront in quest of cheap lodgings in New Bedford, Ishmael stumbles over the ash-box of a Negro church which he mistakes for an inn and which he forebodingly dubs "the sign of 'The Trap'" (MD, 18). On entering, he is greeted by an assembly of black faces that reminds him of "the great Black Parliament sitting in Tophet," and he hears a Negro preacher, whom he recognizes intuitively for "a black Angel of Doom," warn of "the blackness of darkness, and the weeping and wailing and teeth-gnashing there" (MD, 18). This Negro preacher, whose message Ishmael heeds by backing out muttering, "Wretched entertainment at the sign of 'The Trap!'", is the first of the black characters in *Moby-Dick* who prophesy of the retribution overtaking their white oppressors.

But the next warning Ishmael hears is delivered by a white preacher in a chapel whose black-bordered marble tablets, dedicated

to whalemen killed in the chase, starkly admonish Ishmael that he
has embarked on a deadly career. Father Mapple's sermon, as Charles
H. Foster and Alan Heimert have shown, resounds with the abolitionist rhetoric of the momentous years 1850–1851, when the
Compromise of 1850 and the implementation of its infamous Fugitive Slave Law were polarizing the country.[12] Like the abolitionists, who called upon Americans to obey "a higher law than the
Constitution," Father Mapple promises "Delight,—top-gallant delight . . . to him, who acknowledges no law or lord, but the Lord
his God, and is only a patriot to heaven" (MD, 51). Echoing the
denunciations abolitionists thundered against the two Massachusetts
dignitaries responsible for legislating and executing the Fugitive
Slave Law—Senator Daniel Webster and Melville's own father-in-
law, Judge Lemuel Shaw—Father Mapple also preaches "Woe to
him who seeks to pour oil upon the waters when God has brewed
them into a gale!" and condemns "all sin though he pluck it out
from under the robes of Senators and Judges" (MD, 50–51).

The document Foster cites as bearing the closest resemblance
to Father Mapple's sermon, however, is not an abolitionist tract, but
the celebrated letter Melville wrote to Hawthorne while working
on *Moby-Dick*— the letter in which he complained: "Try to get a
living by the Truth—and go to the Soup Societies. Heavens! Let
any clergyman try to preach the Truth from its very stronghold, the
pulpit, and they would ride him out of his church on his own pulpit
bannister."[13] The association clearly reveals that Melville felt his
own truth-telling mission to be akin to a clergyman's. Indeed, in
the next paragraph of his letter, Melville ruefully confesses to Hawthorne that he has been preaching "an endless sermon." Hence we
can conclude that the "awful lesson which Jonah teaches" Father
Mapple as "an anointed pilot-prophet"—"To preach the Truth to
the face of Falsehood!"—is one that Melville considered equally
applicable to himself and which, in *Moby-Dick*, is addressed specifically to his narrator Ishmael. Ishmael, in fact, will undergo a
near-fatal encounter with a whale analogous to Jonah's and, like
Jonah, will escape to prophesy of the doom that awaits an unre-

12. Foster, "Something in Emblems," 11–20; Heimert, "*Moby-Dick* and American
Political Symbolism," 508–12.
13. Foster, "Something in Emblems," 8–11, 17; Davis and Gilman (eds.), *Letters of
Melville*, 126–31.

pentant people. The very purpose of his narrative, Ishmael implies in the epigraph that prefaces the account of his rescue, is to make the chastising experience he has undergone serve as a warning to his readers: "AND I ONLY AM ESCAPED ALONE *TO TELL THEE*" (italics added).[14] By identifying Ishmael with Jonah, Melville may also have been inviting his readers to learn a lesson from the portion of Jonah's story that Father Mapple does not discuss in his sermon. Just as the citizens of Nineveh, to whom Jonah had been assigned to prophesy the destruction of their city, ultimately repented of their wickedness and thus turned God's wrath into mercy, so the epilogue of *Moby-Dick* suggests that Ishmael's fellow citizens may perhaps avert the apocalyptic doom the *Pequod*'s fate augurs, if they heed his message in time and choose to follow his example rather than Ahab's.[15]

After Father Mapple, Ishmael will hear a number of white voices warn of impending judgment in the fanatical accents of the sectarian millennialists who, concurrently with the abolitionists, were deluging the country with Old and New Testament apocalyptic prophecies, literally applied to the contemporary American scene.[16] The first of these is the mercenary, pharisaical owner of the *Pequod*, Captain Bildad, who presses on Queequeg a tract entitled, "The Latter Day Coming; or No Time to Lose," and admonishes him: "Son of darkness, I must do my duty by thee; I am part owner of this ship, and feel concerned for the souls of all its crew; if thou still clingest to thy Pagan ways, which I sadly fear, I beseech thee, remain not for aye a Belial bondsman. Spurn the idol Bel, and the hideous dragon; turn from the wrath to come" (MD, 85).

In the next chapter, Ishmael and Queequeg are accosted by a second crier of doom, a ragged prophet calling himself Elijah, after the Old Testament prophet who denounced King Ahab's wickedness

---

14. Dryden, *Melville's Thematics of Form*, 105, emphasizes the significance that the epigraph gives to Ishmael's telling of his experience.

15. For interpretations of Father Mapple's sermon antithetical to mine, see Nathalia Wright, *Melville's Use of the Bible* (New York, 1969), 82–84; Hoffman, *Form and Fable*, 236, 257–62; and Zoellner, *Salt-Sea Mastodon*, Chap. 4.

16. Among the sects predicting an imminent fulfillment of apocalyptic prophecy were the Shakers, the Mormons, and the Millerites (followers of William Miller, who had predicted that the end of the world would occur in 1843–1844). I do not agree with Heimert, "*Moby-Dick* and American Political Symbolism," 514–15, that Melville is identifying these enthusiastic sectarians with the abolitionists.

and foretold his downfall, and who, as many millennialists believed, was to return to earth to herald "the great and dreadful day of the LORD" (Mal. 4:5). Although Ishmael dismisses Elijah as "nothing but a humbug, trying to be a bugbear," the stranger's oracular pronouncements correctly warn that in the *Pequod*'s voyage the crew's "souls" are at stake; and his crazy ruminations formulate a philosophical problem central to *Moby-Dick*—that of predetermination versus free will: "Well, well, what's signed, is signed; and what's to be, will be; and then again, perhaps it wont be, after all" (MD, 87–88).

The last of these unlikely augurs of the *Pequod*'s fate is the delirious Shaker prophet aboard the whaler *Jeroboam*, who calls himself the archangel Gabriel and claims to carry in his vest-pocket the terrible "seventh vial" of the Apocalypse. Categorically branded a fanatic whose "measureless self-deception" is only surpassed by "his measureless power of deceiving and bedevilling so many others," Gabriel nevertheless proves right in predicting "speedy doom to the sacrilegious assailants" of Moby Dick and in telling Ahab that he is soon to go the way of the *Jeroboam*'s mate, struck down by Moby Dick in the chase. Further enhancing his prophetic stature, the "crazy sea" itself appears to be "leagued with" Gabriel: waves rock the *Jeroboam*'s whale boat and interrupt her captain's story whenever he attempts to reprimand or discredit the self-styled archangel (MD, 266–68). Although all of these apocalyptic alarmists are stigmatized as zealots or lunatics, the eventual fulfillment of their prognostications forces us to take them more seriously than Ishmael does. Perhaps Melville means to suggest that among the critics of America's polity, even those who represented the lunatic fringe were "bottomed upon the truth, more or less" (as Melville's "endless sermon" to Hawthorne asserts of "Reformers" in general),[17] in sensing that the nation was rushing headlong toward an apocalyptic holocaust.

The chapter in which Melville envisions this holocaust most explicitly as an interracial and fratricidal conflict over slavery is one in which the angels of doom are once again black. Significantly, neither Ishmael nor Queequeg participates in this scene, entitled "Midnight, Forecastle," where the crew's "federated" unity breaks down into local particularisms as sailors from "all the isles of the

---

17. Davis and Gilman (eds.), *Letters of Melville*, 127.

sea, and all the ends of the earth" (MD, 108) riot in their distinctive ways after sealing their commitment to Ahab's feud. Paralleling the onset of a storm at sea, the undercurrent of racial antagonisms expressed through these revels at length erupts in a row between the African harpooner Daggoo and a Spanish sailor. The row is touched off when Daggoo's hypersensitivity to racist slurs makes him bristle at an old Manxman's warning that the "pitch black" sky, shot through with "lurid-like" lightning flashes, presages danger for the ship. "What of that?" parries the African; "Who's afraid of black's afraid of me! I'm quarried out of it!" (MD, 153).

Daggoo, whom Ishmael has earlier described as "a gigantic, coal-black negro-savage, with a lion-like tread—an Ahasuerus to behold" (MD, 107), is the very embodiment of the "erect, lofty-minded African" Melville had imagined in *White-Jacket*. Like Queequeg, whose free spirit he shares, Daggoo has "voluntarily shipped on board of a whaler" and has "retained all his barbaric virtues," never having been exposed to slavery or second-class citizenship. Even more than Queequeg, Daggoo towers over his white shipmates in physique and dignity: "There was a corporeal humility in looking up at him; and a white man standing before him seemed a white flag come to beg truce of a fortress" (MD, 108). Daggoo also resembles that noble white primitive, Steelkilt, in his striking superiority to his commanding officer, the third mate Flask. "Curious to tell," remarks Ishmael, "this imperial negro, Ahasuerus Daggoo, was the Squire of little Flask, who looked like a chess-man beside him"—a contrast that becomes more uncomplimentary to Flask than ever during the chase, when Flask finds himself too "small and short" to satisfy the "large and tall ambition" that he can fulfill only by climbing onto his black harpooner's "lofty shoulders":

> But the sight of little Flask mounted upon gigantic Daggoo was yet more curious; for sustaining himself with a cool, indifferent, easy, unthought of, barbaric majesty, the noble negro to every roll of the sea harmoniously rolled his fine form. On his broad back, flaxen-haired Flask seemed a snow-flake. The bearer looked nobler than the rider. Though, truly, vivacious, tumultuous, ostentatious little Flask would now and then stamp with impatience; but not one added heave did he thereby give to the negro's lordly chest. (MD, 191)

Interestingly, just as Ahasuerus Daggoo corresponds to Charlemagne Steelkilt, the "pugnacious" Flask has equally strong affinities with Steelkilt's mate Radney, likewise a Vineyarder and "full of social quarrel" (MD, 106, 210). Thus Alan Heimert has linked Flask, as well as Radney, with the "'fiery and intractable race' which Melville discovered in the south of Vivenza" and has interpreted the picture of "Flask, perched precariously on Daggoo's shoulders," as an icon of "the southern economy itself," precariously based on the Negro.[18]

Notwithstanding these analogies, the interracial row Melville stages in "Midnight, Forecastle" differs considerably from the paradigmatic slave revolt dramatized in "The Town-Ho's Story." To begin with, the Spanish sailor ranged against Daggoo is not his commanding officer, but a regular seaman who technically ranks below Daggoo in the hierarchy of a whaling crew, where a harpooneer enjoys the status of a petty officer. Daggoo's and the Spaniard's relative positions aboard the Pequod appropriately reflect a period in history when the Spaniards were subjugated by the Moors, an African people who ruled Spain for more than five centuries. Evidently the Spanish sailor remembers this. "Ah!—the old grudge makes me touchy," he mutters on hearing Daggoo flaunt his blackness, and he immediately assumes that the African "wants to bully." His response to fear is the same that elicited Queequeg's cry, "Who-e debel you?" and Ishmael's confession, "I was now as much afraid of [the stranger] as if it was the devil himself" (MD, 29, 31): "Aye, harpooneer," he tells Daggoo, as the Spanish colonists of the New World and their Anglo-Saxon successors told their Indian and African captives, "thy race is the undeniable dark side of mankind— devilish dark at that." He adds, as if to imply that he is merely stating a fact rather than casting an aspersion, "No offence." But Daggoo, whose pride in his African heritage has not been crushed by a white supremacist society, is proof against this attempt to sap his self-esteem by injecting him with his enemy's prejudices. "White skin, white liver!" he retorts in kind, meeting further provocation with his fists. Meanwhile, the Spaniard tries to knife the unarmed Daggoo, prompting the reader to wonder whether the white race,

18. Heimert, "Moby-Dick and American Political Symbolism," 502. See also Kaplan, "Melville and the American National Sin," 24, 327–28; and Simpson, "Melville and the Negro," 29–30, on the antiracist implications of this icon.

rather than the black, might not incarnate the devilish side of mankind.

Once again, however, Melville's obvious sympathy with Daggoo's reaction to the Spaniard's insults does not prevail against his horror of violence, and he brings this racial row to an abortive end. As the threatened storm at last bursts, forestalling the consummation of these racial hatreds and reuniting the crew in the ship's defense, Daggoo cedes his place as a black angel of doom to a less menacing figure—"Black Little Pip," the "poor Alabama boy" who shrinks from his violent shipmates and is "called a coward here," though destined to be "hailed a hero" in heaven (MD, 108). Chorus-like, Pip speaks the last lines in this theatrical chapter, commenting on the scene he has witnessed and the tempest in which it has culminated, and articulating Melville's premonitions about the storm brewing over black slavery on the American continent:

> Jimmini, what a squall! But those chaps there are worse yet—they are your white squalls, they. White squalls? white whale, shirr! shirr! Here have I heard all their chat just now, and the white whale—shirr! shirr!—but spoken of once! and only this evening—it makes me jingle all over like my tambourine—that anaconda of an old man swore 'em in to hunt him! Oh, thou big white God aloft there somewhere in yon darkness, have mercy on this small black boy down here; preserve him from all men that have no bowels to feel fear! (MD, 154–55)

Whatever the metaphysical meaning of Ahab's fiery hunt, the association Pip makes between the white whale and the "white squalls" personified by the crew gives the hunt political connotations and suggests that civil war was one of the consequences Melville apprehended from his nation's pursuit of a white phantasm. Indeed, he seems to imply here that civil war, as a storm that ultimately imperils the whole crew, constitutes a worse danger for his ship of state than even an interracial conflict. At the same time, Melville offers the hope that the very threat of such a cataclysm might somehow serve to bring about a union of expedience, if not a love marriage, among the hostile members of his nation's crew. In this respect, "Midnight, Forecastle" ends more optimistically than Ishmael's narrative. It also ends more optimistically than a later narrative that it foreshadows—"Benito Cereno"—which restages the confrontation between the two parties Melville saw as historical prototypes of the southern slaveholder and his slave: the Spaniards who introduced African slavery into the New World and the full-blooded Africans who embodied the cultural heritage of American blacks and thus impressed Melville as the most fitting vindicators of black pride and black manhood.[19]

Although the way in which Pip's alarm succeeds Daggoo's militancy in "Midnight, Forecastle" expresses Melville's recoil from violent solutions to the slavery problem, it in no sense implies that Melville would ever embrace the stereotype of the happy slave as an alternative to facing America's black nemesis. Pip no less than Daggoo incarnates Melville's conviction that the Negro held the key to America's destiny. Throughout *Moby-Dick*, Melville makes his three principal black characters—Daggoo, Pip, and the ship's cook Fleece—serve as angels of doom, warning the *Pequod* of her fate and sometimes actually lifting up their voices against whites. Of the three, Pip is most explicitly cast as a prophet, especially after an event befalls him "which ended in providing the sometimes madly merry and predestinated craft with a living and ever accompanying prophecy of whatever shattered sequel might prove her own" (MD, 344). This event, which Charles H. Foster and Alan Heimert have likened to the northern abandonment of the Negro betokened by Judge Shaw's remanding of the fugitive slave Thomas Sims, is Stubb's abandonment of Pip when the latter jumps from a whale boat in the midst of the chase.[20] "A whale would sell for thirty times what you would, Pip, in Alabama," Stubb tells Pip in admonishing him not to jump, thereby indirectly hinting, according to Ishmael, "that though man loves his fellow, yet man is a money-making animal, which propensity too often interferes with his benevolence" (MD, 346).

Before his tragic mishap, Pip seems to epitomize the Negro's proverbial gaiety: "Pip, though over tender-hearted, was at bottom very bright, with that pleasant, genial, jolly brightness peculiar to his tribe; a tribe, which ever enjoy all holidays and festivities with

19. Other critics who have noted the relationship between "Midnight, Forecastle" and "Benito Cereno" are Kaplan, "Melville and the American National Sin," 22, n. 21, 329; Simpson, "Melville and the Negro," 30; and Charles Nicol, "The Iconography of Evil and Ideal in 'Benito Cereno,'" in Raymona E. Hull (ed.), *Studies in the Minor and Later Works of Melville* (Hartford, 1970), 28–29.

20. Foster, "Something in Emblems," 25; Heimert, "*Moby-Dick* and American Political Symbolism," 513.

finer, freer relish than any other race. For blacks, the year's calendar should show naught but three hundred and sixty-five Fourth of Julys and New Year's Days" (MD, 345). In asserting that Pip and his fellow blacks are capable of an uninhibited enjoyment of life's pleasures that eludes other races, Melville verges on romantic racialism. Yet he pointedly refrains from claiming that the calendar *does* show "naught but three hundred and sixty-five Fourth of Julys and New Year's Days" for blacks, which would amount to endorsing the popular notion that the Negro was less susceptible to sorrow or pain than other races. On the contrary, he observes, Pip's love of life and "all life's peaceable securities" has made him suffer hardships all the more keenly, "so that the panic-striking business in which he had somehow unaccountably become entrapped, had most sadly blurred his brightness" (MD, 345). Just as the "healthful glow" of a diamond worn on a "blue-veined neck" in the clear light of day acquires an evil blaze when set against a "gloomy ground" and illuminated by "unnatural gases," so, intimates Melville, does the air of joviality the Negro wears turn sinister against the backdrop of slavery, where song and dance function to deaden pain rather than to express happiness. Thus Pip's clouded brightness is "destined to be luridly illumined by strange wild fires" after the injury the "panic-striking business" of whaling inflicts on him.

Left floating for hours in the ocean with no assurance of being rescued, Pip experiences an "intense concentration of self in the middle of such a heartless immensity" that permanently affects his sanity (MD, 347). Thereafter he becomes an oracular voice reproaching his shipmates for their callousness and echoing the heartlessness of a God who allows evil and does not intervene to prevent his creatures from destroying each other and themselves. "Pip! Pip! Pip! One hundred pounds of clay reward for Pip; five feet high— looks cowardly—quickest known by that!" (MD, 427), he calls out, in what Alan Heimert has characterized as a "tragic parody of a fugitive-slave handbill."[21] Pip watches and sums up his shipmates' deluded attempts to decipher the cryptic signs of their destiny engraved on Ahab's doubloon: "I look, you look, he looks; we look, ye look, they look." His chorus-like commentary ends in weird apocalyptic accents:

21. Heimert, "*Moby-Dick* and American Political Symbolism," 513.

Here's the ship's navel, this doubloon here, and they are all on fire to unscrew it. But, unscrew your navel, and what's the consequence? Then again, if it stays here, that is ugly, too, for when aught's nailed to the mast it's a sign that things grow desperate. Ha, ha! old Ahab! the White Whale; he'll nail ye! This is a pine tree. My father, in old Tolland county, cut down a pine tree once, and found a silver ring grown over in it; some old darkey's wedding ring. How did it get there? And so they'll say in the resurrection, when they come to fish up this old mast, and find a doubloon lodged in it, with bedded oysters for the shaggy bark. Oh, the gold! the precious, precious gold!—the green miser'll hoard ye soon! Hish! hish! God goes 'mong the worlds blackberrying. Cook! ho, cook! and cook us! (MD, 363)

Pip's "crazy-witty" language, though as undecipherable as the doubloon, heralds the *Pequod*'s watery end and links it to the fires of hell, the general resurrection to follow, and the casual indifference of a "blackberrying" (black burying?) reaper god, treading the grapes of wrath on a pleasure party. At the same time, Pip's tale of the "old darkey's wedding ring" that his father found embedded in a pine tree seems to hark back obscurely to Ishmael's wedding imagery and the alternative to apocalyptic destruction that it offers the reader.

Indeed, Pip and Ishmael have many affinities with each other, as Edgar A. Dryden has pointed out.[22] Not only does Pip's experience of being a "castaway" prefigure Ishmael's at the end of the book, but it gives Pip insights much like those at which Ishmael arrives in contemplating the whiteness of the whale. Pip perceives in the infinite ocean where he has been abandoned the same "heartless voids and immensities of the universe" that Ishmael apprehends in the "indefiniteness" of whiteness (MD, 169, 347). Similarly, Pip sees "God's foot upon the treadle of the loom" in the "wondrous depths" to which he is transported and feels God's indifference, as Ishmael does when he comes face to face with the world's "weaver-god" in a "wondrous" bower in the Arsacides and finds him so "deafened" by his weaving "that he hears no mortal voice" (MD, 374).

Pip also holds out to Ahab the same promise of redemption through love that Queequeg holds out to Ishmael. He attracts Ahab's attention on the heels of one more ill omen that the monomaniacal

22. Dryden, *Melville's Thematics of Form*, 104–105.

captain has stubbornly refused to heed—the snapping of the log-line. Troubled by Pip's madness, Ahab reproaches the gods for having begotten this helpless black boy only to abandon him. "There can be no hearts above the snow-line," he exclaims (MD, 428). In identifying the "frozen heavens" with the North, as Alan Heimert has noticed, Ahab echoes the southern apologists' "ringing indictment of northern hypocrisy and indifference to the Negro's welfare."[23] Yet when he vows that "Ahab's cabin shall be Pip's home henceforth, while Ahab lives," the captain ironically overlooks the problem of what will happen to Pip afterwards. He thus follows the example of both the gods he denounces and the numerous southern masters whose deaths plunged favorite slaves into the worst horrors of slavery.

Ultimately, of course, Ahab will forsake Pip to pursue the fanatic chase he has never considered giving up. But for the moment, he seems to be feeling the "Siamese ligature" with Pip that Ishmael learns to acknowledge toward all mankind. "Thou touchest my inmost centre, boy; thou art tied to me by cords woven of my heart-strings," he tells Pip. Pip likewise seizes Ahab's hand "as a man-rope; something that weak souls may hold by," recalling the monkey-rope through which Ishmael is "wedded" to Queequeg "for better or for worse." Like Ishmael and Queequeg, Ahab and Pip even contract a symbolic marriage. Claiming that "had poor Pip but felt so kind a thing" as the "velvet shark-skin" of Ahab's hand, he might never have been lost, Pip summons the blacksmith to "rivet these two hands together; the black one with the white, for I will not let this go" (MD, 428). Ahab, on his part, characteristically turns the ritual into a histrionic gesture meant to vindicate his quarrel with God: "Lo! ye believers in gods all goodness, and in man all ill, lo you! see the omniscient gods oblivious of suffering man; and man, though idiotic, and knowing not what he does, yet full of the sweet things of love and gratitude. Come! I feel prouder leading thee by thy black hand, than though I grasped an Emperor's!" (MD, 428). It is no accident, however, that Ahab's union with Pip takes place in the chapter "The Log and Line," where it is framed by the snapping of the log-line and by the old Manxman's complaints that

23. Heimert, "*Moby-Dick* and American Political Symbolism," 513.

the line is too "rotten" to mend. The same is evidently true of the cords woven of Ahab's heart-strings, which prove too fragile to hold him to Pip when he feels Moby Dick's pull. Thus Pip's description of Ahab's hand as "velvet shark-skin" may express a crazy intuition of the irredeemable sharkishness underlying Ahab's kindess towards him. Ahab, unlike Ishmael, is not saved by his marriage with his fellow man, since he does not truly commit himself to it as the alternative to the phantasmic hunt through which he carries his shipmates to their doom.

In his role as a prophet, Pip acts both as a harbinger of doom and as a potential savior. The other two blacks whose voices we hear aboard the *Pequod* speak mainly in the stern accents of the former. Daggoo, besides championing the dignity of blackness and physically attacking a white man who dares to deny it, literally becomes an apocalyptic "angel of doom": on the first day Moby Dick is sighted, he rouses his sleeping shipmates "with such judgment claps that they seemed to exhale from the scuttle, so instantaneously did they appear with their clothes in their hands" (MD, 446).

Still more ominous is the role played by old Fleece, the ship's cook, whose sermon to the sharks (a cynical parody of St. Francis' sermon to the birds)[24] ends on a note that recalls "the blackness of darkness, and the weeping and wailing and teeth-gnashing there," of which the black clergyman encountered by Ishmael in New Bedford had warned. Fleece is the only black character in *Moby-Dick* to speak in dialect and to exhibit the mannerisms of a slave, yet his sullen pretense of following orders is as subversive as Daggoo's militancy and shows how aware Melville was of the artful sabotage that represented the slave's chief weapon against his master.[25] Awakened by Stubb at midnight to cook him a whale steak, Fleece is subsequently charged with the task of exhorting the sharks to

24. Noted by Tyrus Hillway, "In Defense of Melville's 'Fleece,' " *Extracts*, XIX (1974), 10; also Zoellner, *Salt-Sea Mastodon*, 223.
25. Fleece has been the subject of another critical controversy over Melville's racial attitudes. Among those who see him as a racist stereotype are Simpson, "Melville and the Negro," 32; Zoellner, *Salt-Sea Mastodon*, 220; and Edward Stone, "The Whiteness of the Whale," *CLA Journal*, XVIII (1975), 355–59, 362. Among those who see Fleece as a covert rebel are Kaplan, "Melville and the American National Sin," 330; Hillway, "In Defense of 'Fleece,' " 10–11; Grejda, *Common Continent of Men*, 106–107; and Stuart C. Woodruff, "Stubb's Supper," *Emerson Society Quarterly*, XLIII (1966), 46–48.

cease their din over the dead whale's body so that Stubb can enjoy
his whale steak in peace. The parallel between the sharks—"in-
variable outriders," Melville tells us, "of all slave ships crossing the
Atlantic"—and "Massa Stubb," who treats this crippled old black
like a slave, is unmistakable, and Fleece subtly underscores it in the
"benediction" he delivers to the sharks at the conclusion of his
unheeded sermon about "gobern[ing] de shark in you": "Cussed
fellow-critters! Kick up de damndest row as ever you can; fill your
dam' bellies till dey bust—and den die" (MD, 249, 251–52). Stubb
continues to bedevil the old man, criticizing his cooking, making
fun of his religious hopes, and calling him back twice more to order
various other whale delicacies for breakfast and supper, but Fleece
has the last word, and a baleful word it is: "'Wish, by gor! whale
eat him, 'stead of him eat whale. I'm bressed if he ain't more of shark
dan Massa Shark hisself,' muttered the old man, limping away; with
which sage ejaculation he went to his hammock" (MD, 254). Whether
curse or prophecy, Fleece's "sage ejaculation" is destined to be dramatically borne out; for Stubb is indeed eaten by a whale in the
end, though not without Fleece's sharing his fate. As Ishmael has
learned, men cannot escape the "dangerous liabilities," however
unjust, of being bound together, so that like the *Pequod*'s shipwreck,
an apocalyptic shipwreck over slavery would engulf all Americans—
guilty or innocent, white or black, southern or northern. Appropriately, the *Pequod* goes down with that primal American, Tashtego
the Indian, nailing her flag to the mast and capturing in its folds
the bird that symbolized America's expansive ambitions—the sky-
hawk, or eagle.[26]

To end our examination of *Moby-Dick* with the somber judgment
that America's black avenging angels invoke on her would, however,
be untrue to the spirit of Melville's epilogue—an epilogue reaffirming, through Ishmael's miraculous escape on Queequeg's coffin, the
hope of salvation that a love marriage between the races promises.
That hope may appear slight at best—and almost a mockery in view
of Queequeg's own death—until we recall the parallel between
Ishmael and Jonah that redefines Ishmael as not merely the sole

26. This symbolism is discussed by Foster, "Something in Emblems," 33; and Heimert, "*Moby-Dick* and American Political Symbolism," 504, 507–508.

survivor of an apocalyptic cataclysm, but the prophet of a future cataclysm that may yet be averted by timely repentance. Ishmael's role as a Jonah also puts Queequeg's otherwise morally inexplicable death in another light; for shortly after offering to die for Ishmael "if need should be," Queequeg, it will be remembered, sends Ishmael out at the behest of his "negro idol" Yojo to select the ship on which they will both sail, while he himself spends the day—characterized by Ishmael as "some sort of Lent or Ramadan"—closeted with Yojo in "fasting, humiliation, and prayer" (MD, 66), as if to intercede for Ishmael. The fruit of both Queequeg's intercession and Yojo's alleged effort to befriend Ishmael and Queequeg is that Ishmael chooses the *Pequod* in preference to two other ships whose names suggest damnation and the devil's proverbial fondness for "that good dish, man"[27] —the *Devil-Dam* and the *Tit-bit*. In short, it is possible to read *Moby-Dick* as a morality play staged for an American Nineveh, in which Yojo acts as the chastising yet ultimately merciful God who commissions Ishmael/Jonah to prophesy of the retribution overtaking an unregenerate nation, and Queequeg as a Christlike redeemer whose life inculcates the message of love, and whose death propitiates divine justice for the sins of his fellow men.[28]

Yet one feels that such a reading is not altogether honest in the face of the cruel irony of being asked to accept the fate meted out to Ishmael and Queequeg as a mark of Yojo's favor, not to mention the equivocal syntax describing Yojo as "a rather good sort of god, who perhaps meant well enough upon the whole, but in all cases did not succeed in his benevolent designs" (MD, 66)—both typifying Melville's wry vision of the deity. It is symptomatic of the far bleaker view Melville would soon come to take of the slavery dilemma and its probable outcome that the metaphysical implications of *Moby-Dick*, most strikingly embodied in the appalling white whale himself, are nowhere near as hopeful as the political or humanistic implications of Ishmael's friendship with Queequeg. Nor has this paradox failed to trouble other interpreters of the book's political symbol-

27. From Herman Melville, *The Confidence-Man: His Masquerade*, ed. H. Bruce Franklin, 187.
28. For similar interpretations, see Rosenfeld, "Uncertain Faith," 320–22; and Strauch, "Ishmael: Time and Personality," 480. Other critics who stress Yojo's and Queequeg's redemptiveness, though in different terms, are Zoellner, *Salt-Sea Mastodon*, 69–71 and Chap. 11; and Hoffman, *Form and Fable*, 270–71.

ism.[29] As it happens, Melville's greatest statement of the democratic faith that animates all his early works was also his last. No sooner was *Moby-Dick* off his hands than Melville found himself "plunged . . . into certain silly thoughts and wayward speculations," as he wrote to a sympathetic Pittsfield neighbor,[30] that led him to his next book, the desperately cynical *Pierre.*

29. See, for examples, Heimert, *"Moby-Dick* and American Political Symbolism," 532–33; and Milton R. Stern, *"Moby-Dick,* Millennial Attitudes, and Politics," *Emerson Society Quarterly,* LIV (1969), 52–53, 60. The crux of the problem is that if, like the vast majority of critics, one views the white whale as embodying either "the heartless voids and immensities" of a godless natural universe, or a supernatural power capriciously indifferent and perhaps outright inimical to man, one is forced to recognize a certain grandeur in Ahab's defiance of Moby Dick—a grandeur transcending his role as a political demagogue. Joyce Sparer Adler's brilliant reading of *Moby-Dick* in her forthcoming book on Melville's attitude toward war may resolve this seeming contradiction.

30. Davis and Gilman (eds.), *Letters of Melville,* 138.

FOUR

The American Revolution
Reevaluated in *Pierre* and *Israel Potter*

IN *Moby-Dick*, Melville faced the prospect that his
nation's long crisis over slavery was moving toward a violent dénouement, be it an uprising by slaves and free blacks, or a civil war
between antislavery and proslavery partisans. The question he went
on to confront in his later fiction was whether the liberty won
through violent revolution ever proved worth its cost in bloodshed.
To answer this question, he turned to reexamining the best historical
prototype he knew of the impending war over slavery—the American Revolution. As we shall see in the next chapter, the conclusions
Melville reached about the Revolution in *Pierre* (1852) and *Israel
Potter* (1854–1855) would color the view of slave revolt that he
projected in his tales from the same period, several of which present
slave revolt as inevitable, but portray the rebels almost as unsym-
pathetically as their oppressors.

Much of Melville's pessimism can be attributed to the bleak
political atmosphere of the 1850s. Slavery then seemed to be acquiring new impetus under the prosouthern regime of Franklin
Pierce, prompting growing numbers of antislavery partisans to envisage violence as the sole means of containing, let alone overthrowing, slavery. Melville's pessimism can also be partially ascribed to
the inroads that scientific racism and other theories of innate racial
inequality were making among intellectuals during these years,
spelling defeat for his hopes that his fellow Americans could learn

to overcome their "unwarrantable prejudices" (MD, 25).[1] Yet one cannot fully understand the dramatic shift in Melville's outlook from qualified hopefulness to despair, or the corresponding eclipse of sympathetic rebellious characters like Steelkilt, without taking into account two personal factors: first, his increasingly cynical vision of the Deity as an archdeceiver beguiling mankind with equivocal commands and false promises; and second, his intensified anguish over the social isolation and financial ruin he was facing as an author.[2]

Under the ever more oppressive weight of the various powers over his life—God, religious orthodoxy, publishers, editors, reviewers, the reading public with its religious and political sensibilities and literary tastes, the family circle with its demands and its attitude toward his failure to meet those demands—Melville seems to have felt driven in *Pierre* and *Israel Potter* to make herculean but perversely self-defeating efforts to regain social sanction by embracing the conventional wisdom he had been accused of flouting. The result in *Pierre* was a domestic novel à la Catharine Sedgwick, peopled with characters from Melville's own milieu, that could not help burlesquing both itself and them. The result in *Israel Potter* was a Cooperesque historical saga of the Revolution that ran down the heroes of that struggle and accentuated its less glorious aspects.

Setting the tone of both novels are florid dedications that mock the nostalgia for royalty shown by the heirs of the American Revolution and insinuate that the Revolution's egalitarian ideals do not really animate the nation. *Pierre*, reviving a "right noble custom" of prerevolutionary days when "authors were proud of the privilege of dedicating their works to Majesty," is ceremoniously presented on bended knee to Mount "Greylock's Most Excellent Majesty." Melville unmistakably associates this reactionary homage with the triumph of monarchical forces over republican ideals in Europe; for

1. For background on this period, see Filler, *The Crusade Against Slavery*, Chaps. 9–10; and George M. Fredrickson, *The Inner Civil War: Northern Intellectuals and the Crisis of the Union* (New York, 1965), Chap. 3.
2. On the evolution of Melville's religious views, see William Braswell, *Melville's Religious Thought: An Essay in Interpretation* (New York, 1973). Among critics who emphasize Melville's vision of the Deity as an archdeceiver are Lawrance Thompson, *Melville's Quarrel with God* (Princeton, 1952); H. Bruce Franklin, *The Wake of the Gods: Melville's Mythology* (Stanford, 1963); and Dryden, *Melville's Thematics of Form*. On Melville's financial troubles and isolation, see Arvin, *Herman Melville*, 195–215.

he calls the mountain chain to which Greylock belongs "a grand Congress of Vienna of majestical hill-tops." *Israel Potter*, figuratively laid at the feet of the Bunker Hill Monument, obsequiously addresses that towering emblem of the American Revolution and the Republic it inaugurated as "your Highness"—a gesture whose "obscure sarcasm" nettled one of Melville's reviewers.[3] Both *Pierre* and *Israel Potter* spotlight the wrongs in American society that the Revolution had not righted. *Israel Potter* pays tribute to the segment of American society that sacrificed most during the Revolution and benefited least from it—"the anonymous privates . . . who may never have received other requital than the solid reward of [the Bunker Hill Monument's] granite." *Pierre* focuses rather on the class whose aristocratic privileges and inordinate hereditary wealth survived the "Revolutionary flood" (P, 11).

The theme of the Revolution's failure to level the class distinctions and inequalities of monarchical times—epitomized by the continued existence of "mighty lordships in the heart of a republic" (P, 11)—emerges at the beginning of *Pierre* and dominates the chapters set in Saddle Meadows. Immediately after introducing Pierre as the last scion of the "historic line of Glendinning," Melville devotes a whole chapter to dispelling the monarchical world's misconceptions about "demagoguical America" (P, 5, 8). While pretending to defend America against aristocratic detractors by arguing that America can outdo England "in this short little matter of large estates, and long pedigrees" (P, 11), Melville in fact comments on the double irony that America may have sold her democratic birthright for an aristocratic mess of pottage, and that the ingredients constituting that pottage—lineage, title, landed property—are all tainted. Thus Melville cites, as evidence of America's aristocratic claims, the "old and oriental-like English planter families of Virginia and the South; the Randolphs for example," and the "Hindooish" antiquity imbuing the boundless Dutch manors of the North, where "regular armies,

3. Leyda, *Melville Log*, II, 501. See Dryden, *Melville's Thematics of Form*, 142–46, for a fine analysis of these twin dedications. All citations from *Pierre; or, The Ambiguities* will be from the Northwestern-Newberry edition, ed. Harrison Hayford, Hershel Parker, and G. Thomas Tanselle (Evanston, 1971). In the absence of a Northwestern-Newberry edition of *Israel Potter: His Fifty Years of Exile*, all citations will be from the Sagamore Press edition, ed. Lewis Leary (New York, 1957). Page references to both will be given parenthetically in the text.

with staffs of officers, crossing rivers with artillery, and marching through primeval woods, and threading vast rocky defiles, have been sent out to distrain upon three thousand farmer-tenants of one landlord, at a blow" (P, 10–11). At the same time, Melville hints that these very claims (oriental not only in the sense of being hoary, but also of being ultratyrannical and ultimately mythical) represent a betrayal of America's best and truest heritage; for the power the Dutch patroons wield over their empire is "most suggestive two ways; both whereof shall be nameless here," and the implied stricture pertains equally well to the mastery the Randolphs exert over their slave domains. Melville further undermines aristocratic pedigrees per se by recalling their inglorious origins—bastardy in the case of the vast majority of English families deriving their titles from Charles II, "no very fine fountain," and usurpation in the case of the infinitesimal minority descended from the Norman "thief knights" who had wrested the English throne from the Saxons (P, 9–10). The sole aristocracy to which Melville accords any legitimacy is the American Indian aristocracy violently dethroned by the white colonists of the New World. If the Randolphs can boast a lineage superior to the Buccleughs', Melville points out, they owe it not to their untitled English ancestor of "King James' time," but to the Indian Princess Pocahontas whom he married, "in whose blood therefore an underived aboriginal royalty was flowing over two hundred years ago" (P, 10).

As yet innocent of these multiple ironies, Pierre Glendinning, when we first make his acquaintance, takes great pride in a family history, estate, and parentage that vie with many an English nobleman's. But over and over in the opening chapters recurs the litany that "this sort of thing in [Pierre] showed him no sterling Democrat," and that before long, a "maturer and larger interior development . . . should forever deprive these things of their full power of pride in his soul" (P, 6, 13). Among the false values that Pierre learns to reject, the most important for understanding Melville's loss of faith in American democracy is Pierre's glorification of his ancestors' role in American history, which has led him to confuse family pride with patriotism.

Pierre hero-worships his great-grandfather for having given his life in an Indian battle that secured the colony for British settlers and the estate of Saddle Meadows for the Glendinning family. Yet Melville implies that the rightful title to the Glendinning lands does not in fact derive from Pierre's great-grandfather, but from the Indians he defeated: "The Glendinning deeds by which their estate had so long been held, bore the cyphers of three Indian kings, the aboriginal and only conveyancers of those noble woods and plains" (P, 6).[4] Moreover, Melville expressly divests this Glendinning warrior's "soldierly fate" of the mantle of Christian martyrdom which Pierre has placed over it. Although "all alive to the beauty and poesy" of the faith that furnished Pierre's great-grandfather with "Glory's shroud," Pierre, remarks Melville drily, "little foresaw that this world hath a secret deeper than beauty, and Life some burdens heavier than death" (P, 7).

Similarly, Pierre apotheosizes his grandfather as a paragon of the Founding Fathers' virtues, without realizing how his grandfather's life-style belied the ideals in whose name he and his peers had gone to war. Despite the resemblance between General Glendinning and Melville's own grandfather—likewise a Revolutionary War hero who had "for several months defended a rude but all-important stockaded fort, against the repeated combined assaults of Indians, Tories, and Regulars," and captured a British kettle-drum "in fair fight" (P, 6, 12)—Melville's ironic treatment of General Glendinning reveals little of the conventional patriotism and family pride that prompted him to name his second son after the "Hero of Fort Stanwix" even while he was writing Pierre.[5] Instead, Melville denigrates the Revolution as a "vindictive war" and reduces it to a disagreeable interlude in the intercourse of gentlemen by recalling how one of the very enemies against whom Pierre's grandfather had fought so bitterly, "the gentlemanly, but murderous half-breed, Brandt," had "survived

4. The following analysis is an elaboration of Milton R. Stern, *The Fine Hammered Steel of Herman Melville* (Urbana, 1957), 171–72.
5. On the naming of Stanwix, see Davis and Gilman (eds.), *Letters of Melville*, 140–41. For references to General Gansevoort showing Melville's family pride, see *Letters*, 217–18, 234–35; also Leyda, *Melville Log*, I, 52, and II, 771, 774. Melville's use of General Gansevoort as a model for General Glendinning has been most thoroughly documented by Henry A. Murray in his introduction and notes to the Hendricks House edition of *Pierre* (New York, 1949), xxi–xxii, 432–33, 443. Alice P. Kenney, *The Gansevoorts of Albany: Dutch Patricians in the Upper Hudson Valley* (Syracuse, 1969), 139–40, confirms that General Gansevoort indeed owned slaves. In examining his papers at the New York Public Library (Gansevoort-Lansing Collection), I came across several bills of sale for slaves.

to dine with General Glendinning, in the amicable times which followed" (P, 6).[6] Shortly afterwards, Melville makes the moral distinction between the revolutionary hero and his "gentlemanly, but murderous" foe appear as elusive as the political differences that had motivated them to wage war:

> In a night-scuffle in the wilderness before the Revolutionary War, [General Glendinning] had annihilated two Indian savages by making reciprocal bludgeons of their heads. And all this was done by the mildest hearted, and most blue-eyed gentleman in the world, who, according to the patriarchal fashion of those days, was a gentle, white-haired worshiper of all the household gods; the gentlest husband, and the gentlest father; the kindest of masters to his slaves; of the most wonderful unruffledness of temper; a serene smoker of his after-dinner pipe; a forgiver of many injuries; a sweet-hearted, charitable Christian; in fine, a pure, cheerful, childlike, blue-eyed, divine old man; in whose meek, majestic soul, the lion and the lamb embraced—fit image of his God. (P, 29–30)

As this masterly sketch indicates, General Glendinning embodies the chief contradictions of American history: the contradiction between Indian genocide and the Puritans' self-allocated mission of converting the heathen and founding Christ's kingdom in the New World; and the contradiction between black slavery and the revolutionaries' professed doctrine that all men were created equal and entitled to life, liberty, and the pursuit of happiness.

Conceiving of his religion as a mere "silken sash" to gird "the complete polished steel of the gentleman" (P, 7), General Glendinning, unlike Melville, finds no difficulty in reconciling warfare with "docile homage" to an ethic that preaches turning the other cheek and returning good for evil.[7] Nor, initially, does Pierre, who incongruously sees the "fine *military* portrait" of his grandfather as "a glorious *gospel* framed and hung upon the wall, and declaring to all people, *as from the Mount*, that man is a noble, god-like being, full of choicest juices; made up of strength and beauty" (P, 30; italics added). The note of burlesque in the phrase "choicest juices"

---

6. Stern, *Fine Hammered Steel of Melville*, 172, interprets this similarly.
7. Cf. Melville's harsh criticism of the Christianity preached aboard a man-of-war: "How can it be expected that the religion of peace should flourish in an oaken castle of war? How can it be expected that the clergyman, whose pulpit is a forty-two pounder, should convert sinners to a faith that enjoins them to turn the right cheek when the left is smitten?" (WJ, 157).

demarcates the distance between the narrative viewpoint and Pierre's. It also prepares us for the moment when, in the midst of his first great moral crisis, Pierre violently repudiates the Reverend Mr. Falsgrave, who reincarnates his grandfather's accommodating faith with its worldly marriage of the lion and the lamb, the serpent and the dove, and whom Pierre has been taught to regard as "a splendid example of the polishing and gentlemanizing influences of Christianity upon the mind and manners" (P, 98).

Melville's satire on General Glendinning's brand of Christianity has escaped few modern critics. Yet in notable contrast, his characterization of General Glendinning as a kind slaveholder, interwoven with that satire, has often been taken at face value as evidence that Melville realized "the slaveholder could be kindhearted and genial," and that Melville shared the racial attitudes of "the Delano who loved Negroes as he might his Newfoundland dogs."[8] There is, indeed, some similarity between the narrative tone of "Benito Cereno" and that of the Saddle Meadows chapters in *Pierre*, and it is no coincidence that both have made some critics uncomfortable and have suggested to others a satiric intent.[9] The passages on General Glendinning's relationship with his slaves deserve close scrutiny; for they provide the first example of the mock-serious style, alternating between cliché and burlesque and often permeated with sexual innuendo, to which Melville frequently resorted in the mid-1850s, and which became his favorite mode of attacking his readers' racial prejudices, as we shall see in "Benito Cereno," "The 'Gees," and *The Confidence-Man*.

Significantly, the key passage begins immediately after the ironic

8. Floan, *The South in Northern Eyes*, 138; Kaplan, "Melville and the American National Sin," 29.

9. For a summary of the debate over whether Melville intended *Pierre* as a popular domestic novel or as parody, see the "Historical Note" by Leon Howard and Hershel Parker in the Northwestern-Newberry edition of *Pierre*, 365–410. For persuasive analyses of the Saddle Meadows chapters as parody, see William Braswell, "The Satirical Temper of Melville's *Pierre*," *American Literature*, VII (1936), 424–38, and "The Early Love Scenes in Melville's *Pierre*," *American Literature*, XXII (1950), 283–89; also Joseph Flibbert, *Melville and the Art of Burlesque* (Amsterdam, 1974), Chap. 6. On "Benito Cereno," see Guy Cardwell, "Melville's Gray Story: Symbols and Meaning in 'Benito Cereno,'" and Allen Guttmann, "The Enduring Innocence of Captain Amasa Delano," both reprinted in Runden (ed.), *Melville's "Benito Cereno,"* 133–42, 179–88. Cardwell attempts to see "plain good sense" in what Melville's rhetoric invites us to experience as a "foolish stereotype" (p. 138), while Guttmann argues that Melville is satirizing Delano's perceptions.

equation of General Glendinning's military portrait with the Gospel and Sermon on the Mount:

> Now, this grand old Pierre Glendinning was a great lover of horses; but not in the modern sense, for he was no jockey;—one of his most intimate friends of the masculine gender was a huge, proud, gray horse, of a surprising reserve of manner, his saddle-beast; he had his horses' mangers carved like old trenchers, out of solid maple logs; the key of the corn-bin hung in his library; and no one grained his steeds, but himself; unless his absence from home promoted Moyar, an incorruptible and most punctual old black, to that honorable office. He said that no man loved his horses, unless his own hands grained them. Every Christmas he gave them brimming measures. "I keep Christmas with my horses," said grand old Pierre. This grand old Pierre always rose at sunrise; washed his face and chest in the open air; and then, returning to his closet, and being completely arrayed at last, stepped forth to make a ceremonious call at his stables, to bid his very honorable friends there a very good and joyful morning. Woe to Cranz, Kit, Douw, or any other of his stable slaves, if grand old Pierre found one horse unblanketed, or one weed among the hay that filled their rack. Not that he ever had Cranz, Kit, Douw, or any of them flogged—a thing unknown in that patriarchal time and country—but he would refuse to say his wonted pleasant word to them; and that was very bitter to them, for Cranz, Kit, Douw, and all of them, loved grand old Pierre, as his shepherds loved old Abraham. (P, 30)

Stylistically, this passage opens on a humorous note, with the gratuitous assertion that "grand old Pierre," whose robust girth has just been graphically described, "was no jockey," followed by the high-sounding phrases, "most intimate friends of the masculine gender" and "surprising reserve of manner," which, applied to a horse, cannot but strike the reader as ludicrous. Although Melville immediately shifts into an apparently straightforward version of the literary genre he has been parodying (nostalgic evocation of the old-fashioned country squire's life, which the southern plantation romancers had adapted from Irving and his English antecedents), his rhetoric continually relapses into satire and burlesque. Witness, for example, the comic device of repeating "grand old Pierre" and "Cranz, Kit, Douw, or any of them" ad nauseam, not to mention the jarring juxtaposition of "a very good and joyful morning" (addressed to the horses) with "Woe to Cranz, Kit, Douw, or any other of his stable slaves."[10]

Crowning Melville's overdrawn picture of this old-time patriarch is a comparison between the love his slaves bear him and the love "old Abraham" supposedly inspired in his shepherds—a comparison that subtly identifies the real object of Melville's satire. It is, of course, the very notion that one can be a true Christian, as General Glendinning believes himself to be, and still hold slaves. The ideal of the Christian slaveholder was passionately defended by proslavery writers, who capitalized on the example of Abraham and the other slaveowning Old Testament patriarchs in arguing that Christianity and the Bible, far from disallowing slavery, actually ordained it. In the words of one apologist, "A beautiful example and illustration . . . is found in the . . . Patriarch Abraham. His wives and his children, his men servants and his maid servants, his camels and his cattle, were all equally his property. He could sacrifice Isaac or a ram, just as he pleased. He loved and protected all, and all shared, if not equally, at least fairly, in the products of their light labor. Who would not desire to have been a slave of that old Patriarch, stern and despotic as he was?"[11] Melville satirizes the ideal of the Christian slaveholder most effectively—and this is the whole point of the passage—by showing that grand old Pierre's horses obviously take precedence over his slaves in his affections. While grand old Pierre promotes his horses to the status of special friends and goes so far as to "keep Christmas" with them, it does not occur to him to show such consideration to his "stable slaves." A mere "pleasant word" suffices to greet *them*, in contrast to the courtly salutations lavished on the horses, and that, too, is contingent on how satisfactory grand old Pierre finds their care of the horses. Catching "one weed" in his

10. See Taylor, *Cavalier and Yankee*, 178–88, on the derivation of the plantation romance from the English manor genre. Braswell, "Satirical Temper of *Pierre*," 434, points out other instances where the "device of repetition is . . . used in a comical way." Frederick Douglass' *Narrative of the Life of Frederick Douglass, an American Slave. Written by Himself* (1845; rpt. Garden City, N.Y., 1963), 18–19, offers a remarkable parallel to this passage in *Pierre*: "in nothing was Colonel Lloyd more particular than in the management of his horses. . . . If a horse did not move fast enough, or hold his head high enough, it was owing to some fault of his keepers. . . . 'This horse . . . has not been sufficiently rubbed and curried, or he has not been properly fed . . . he had too much hay, and not enough of grain; or he had too much grain, and not enough of hay.'"

11. George Fitzhugh, *Sociology for the South, or The Failure of Free Society* (1854; rpt. New York, n.d.), 297.

steeds' hay is reason enough for him to cold shoulder his slaves. Grand old Pierre's vaunted "kindness," it is to be supposed, consists primarily in not having his slaves flogged for such derelictions of duty. Certainly he does not seem to concern himself unduly with the quality or quantity of *their* food, at Christmas or otherwise. Thus even on the most straightforward level, a passage that has been interpreted as a tribute to the slaveholder at his best proves to be a devastating indictment of the good conscience with which "the kindest of masters" can rank human beings below horses.

On another level, an undercurrent of sexual innuendo, which provokes much the same malaise in the reader as the language articulating Delano's view of the Negro in "Benito Cereno," suggests that there may be something libidinous in grand old Pierre's attachment to his horses. Reinforcing this suggestion is an earlier chapter in which the Glendinning horses seem to stand for slaves. In Saddle Meadows, where "man and horse are both hereditary," the descendants of General Glendinning's horses are "a sort of family cousins to Pierre" (P, 21, 32)—like the illegitimate mulatto children fathered by slaveholders. "The same fountain that by one branch supplied the stables with water, by another supplied Pierre's pitcher." Remembering Melville's disparagement of Charles II, we can guess that it is "no very fine fountain" (P, 9). As if to confirm the innuendo, Melville adds that the Glendinning horses are well aware of being "but an inferior and subordinate branch of the Glendinnings, bound in perpetual feudal fealty to its headmost representative" (P, 21). These hints that General Glendinning may have been more than "kind" to his slaves of the feminine gender, besides echoing the charges of sexual exploitation that abolitionists leveled at slaveholders, anticipate Melville's development of this theme in later writings as a means of symbolizing how totally slavery violates the slave and perverts the master. Within the narrative framework of *Pierre*, moreover, the insinuations of illicit sexuality that tarnish General Glendinning's character are far from gratuitous. On the contrary, they are directly related to the tragedy of Pierre, which turns on his discovery that his father, whom he has hitherto worshiped as the "personification of perfect human goodness and virtue" (P, 68), has sired an illegitimate daughter (is it out of place to recall that she is olive-skinned and dark-haired?) who is living in poverty and ignominy while he, Pierre, is enjoying wealth and social prestige.

I do not, of course, mean to imply that *Pierre* is a novel about slavery, except insofar as the failure of General Glendinning's generation to include slaves in their struggle for liberty enters into Melville's reevaluation of the legend his forefathers helped engender and of the polity they bequeathed to the nation. But *Pierre* is very much a novel about how a patriotic and sensitive young American, born to the social position the Melville family had inherited, comes to recognize the disparity between the democratic and religious ideals his peers and mentors profess and the poverty, exploitation, and injustice they sanction. Even more, *Pierre* is a novel about the entrapment of a young American who, unlike Ishmael, cannot transcend his discredited world view by finding a meaningful way of acting on his new perceptions and affirming his solidarity with downtrodden humanity.

Whereas in *Pierre* Melville debunked the American aristocracy's version of the Revolution, in *Israel Potter* he reconstructed the Revolution from the perspective of the forgotten common man. The seeming futility of General Glendinning's revolutionary exploits, which result only in a restoration of the prewar status quo, becomes glaringly evident in Israel Potter's disjointed military career, which symbolically culminates in lifelong exile under the very regime he fought to overthrow. Although Israel participates in two of the Revolution's most famous military engagements—the Battle of Bunker Hill and the sea fight between the *Bonhomme Richard* and the *Serapis*—and comes into close contact with three of its most celebrated leaders—Benjamin Franklin, John Paul Jones, and Ethan Allen—neither his own valiant deeds nor the historic events he helps mold lead to freedom for the yeoman class he represents. Instead, Israel ends up as a pauperized industrial slave, his unsung heroism having served but to consolidate the power of the rising mercantile class that Franklin epitomizes, and to win "loud fame" for Jones, who incarnates what "America is, or may yet be": "intrepid, unprincipled, reckless, predatory, with boundless ambition, civilized in externals but a savage at heart" (IP, 161, 170).

Through the eyes of a "private of Bunker Hill" whose "faithful services" have "promoted [him] to a still deeper privacy under the ground" (IP, v), the Revolution looks entirely different from the providential drama written and directed by the Benjamin Franklins, John Paul Joneses, and General Glendinnings.[12] Israel's Revolution takes the form of bungled military operations, abortive daredevil feats that never seem to yield any worthwhile results, shocking butchery, successive imprisonments, promises of liberation repeatedly broken, perpetual flight, and at last the realization that "whether as an Englishman, or whether as an American," he is "equally subject to enslavement," be it as an impressed seaman, a prisoner of war, or an industrial worker: "He whom love of country made a hater of her foes—the foreigners among whom he now was thrown—he who, as soldier and sailor, had joined to kill, burn and destroy both them and theirs—here he was . . . serving that very people as a slave, [and] . . . helping, with all his strength, to extend the walls of the Thebes of the oppressor" (IP, 217, 224).

For Israel, the vaunted aims of the Revolution are practically indefinable. True, he sees the act of "throwing off the yoke of his king" as analogous to emancipating himself from his "unreasonable and oppressive" father, and like a stanch democrat, he cannot bring himself to address an English knight by his title (IP, 7, 34–35). Yet in a revealing episode where Israel actually encounters the king, he is dazzled by the "cheap and easy magnanimity, which in private belongs to most kings," and concludes, contrary to his former belief, that "it could not be the warm heart of the King, but the cold heads of his lords in council, that persuaded him so tyrannically to persecute America" (IP, 42). It is "the peculiar disinterested fidelity" of his "patriotism," rather than any clear sense of what he is fighting for, that makes him refuse the king's invitation to enlist in the British army. But for that patriotism, adds Melville ironically, we would

12. I am indebted for this formulation to H. Bruce Franklin's incisive comments on the original version of this chapter; see his brief but trenchant analysis of *Israel Potter* in *The Victim as Criminal and Artist*, 62–63. Other critics I have found helpful are Arnold Rampersad, *Melville's Israel Potter: A Pilgrimage and Progress* (Bowling Green, 1969); Alexander Keyssar, *Melville's Israel Potter: Reflections on the American Dream* (Cambridge, Mass., 1969); Harry B. Henderson III, *Versions of the Past: The Historical Imagination in American Fiction* (New York, 1974); Wayne Charles Miller, *An Armed America: Its Face in Fiction: A History of the American Military Novel* (New York, 1970), 29–32; and above all, Gilmore, *The Middle Way*, 151–65.

not "have had to follow him . . . through long, long years of obscure and penurious wandering."

Even more revealing is the completeness with which Israel and the reader lose sight of the War after Israel joins the ranks of the English proletariat. The questions of national identity and patriotism that loomed so large at the outset appear utterly irrelevant in the face of the desperate plight Israel shares with the English working class. Hence the cessation of hostilities between America and England occurs as a mere parenthesis in Israel's long exile, precipitating his descent "from the gutter . . . to the sewer" (IP, 231). Nothing in Melville's narrative reminds us that the Revolution ended in an American victory and the establishment of a democratic republic that purported to guarantee all men the rights to life, liberty, and the pursuit of happiness. All that matters is that Israel reaps no rewards from this victory. Still symbolically banished from the fabled land of freedom and opportunity, he finds himself driven out of employment in England, where "hordes of disbanded soldiers" now compete for scarce jobs, thousands of them choosing, "rather than starve, or turn highwaymen," to "work for such a pittance as to bring down the wages of all the laboring classes" (IP, 231).

But the final and bitterest irony is reserved for Israel's homecoming after a fifty-year exile, only to have his own countrymen exclude him from the rights for which he has fought. Arriving in Boston on a Fourth of July, Israel finds himself an invisible intruder in a celebration of the independence whose fruits he has never enjoyed. His very presence ignored by the celebrants, giving the lie as it does to the legend they are honoring, Israel is "hustled by the riotous crowd near Faneuil Hall," and narrowly escapes "being run over by a patriotic triumphal car in the procession, flying a broidered banner, inscribed with gilt letters: "'BUNKER-HILL 1775. GLORY TO THE HEROES THAT FOUGHT!'" (IP, 238). As this tableau foreshadows, Israel is destined to be "repulsed in efforts after a pension by certain caprices of law" and to die as he has lived, unrecompensed for the hardships he has endured on his country's behalf, except by a stone monument (IP, 241).

If Israel's fate seems to brand the Revolution as a cruel joke on the class that bore the brunt of it, that verdict does not merely demythicize America's past. It also expresses Melville's foreboding that a war against black slavery might cement the oppression of the working class with their own blood and rivet the shackles of wage slavery more firmly than ever.

Nowhere is it more apparent that Melville is viewing the Revolution as "a type, a parallel, and a prophecy" of the impending civil war than in his account of the great naval battle between the *Bonhomme Richard* and the *Serapis*; for Melville pictures the two ships as entangled in what "seemed more an intestine feud, than a fight between strangers . . . as if the Siamese Twins, oblivious of their fraternal bond, should rage in unnatural fight" (IP, 170, 178). This is, of course, the same imagery of fratricidal strife that would later cling to the Civil War. Even when Melville shifts the conceit—comparing the embattled ships to "two houses, through whose party-wall doors have been cut; one family (the Guelphs) occupying the whole lower story; another family (the Ghibellines) the whole upper story" (IP, 180–81)—he falls irresistibly into the rhetoric inspired by the Civil War, anticipating both Lincoln's metaphor of the "House Divided" and the haunting question he himself would ask in his postmortem of the War: "Were the Unionists and Secessionists but as Guelphs and Ghibellines?"[13]

Melville's description of the battle graphically illustrates what he meant by his premonition that America might become "the Paul Jones of nations" (IP, 170). It is a battle in which "neither party could be victor" and "mutual obliteration from the face of the waters" seems the sole outcome possible. Only by refusing to admit defeat, whatever the cost in human life, does Jones succeed in "winning" this "unparalleled death-lock" (IP, 169, 185). In the process, he emerges as a diabolical madman, hiding the attributes of a savage under the accoutrements of a gentleman: "His Parisian coat, with its gold-laced sleeve laid aside, disclosed to the full the blue tattooing on his arm, which sometimes in fierce gestures streamed in the haze of the cannonade, cabalistically terrific as the charmed standard of Satan. . . . his frenzied manner was . . . intended to inspirit and madden his men" (IP, 181). Melville dwells relentlessly on the stag-

13. Cf. Lincoln's "House Divided" speech, delivered in 1858, in Roy P. Basler (ed.) *The Collected Works of Abraham Lincoln* (8 vols.; New Brunswick, N.J., 1953), II, 461–69; and Melville's Supplement to *Battle-Pieces and Aspects of the War*, ed. Sidney Kaplan (Amherst, 1972), 272.

gering toll in dead and wounded on both sides—"one-half of the total number of those engaged" (IP, 186). That Jones's British adversary chose to surrender rather than prolong such carnage, Melville says, is "honor to him as a man, and not reproach to him as an officer" (IP, 185). Capitalizing on the irony of a "victory" in which the victorious ship, as if in retribution for her bloodlust, sinks "gorged with slaughter . . . and blasted by tornadoes of sulphur . . . like Gomorrah," Melville asks: "What separates the enlightened man from the savage? Is civilization a thing distinct, or is it an advanced stage of barbarism?" (IP, 186). Few but committed pacifists would have raised this question in connection with the Revolutionary War. Indeed, the political stance it most resembles is that of the pacifist Garrisonian abolitionists, who likewise opposed resorting to violence to overthrow slavery, but held that violent rebellion would be no more reprehensible in black slaves than in America's revolutionary forefathers.[14]

Despite the evident revulsion with which Melville was contemplating the prospect of civil war, he no longer saw any alternative. By the time he wrote *Israel Potter*, the hope he had cherished in *Moby-Dick*—that his compatriots would find a "prudent" way out of their dilemma by embracing blacks as equal partners in America's destiny—had clearly failed him. Poignantly attesting its extinction is an inverted replay of Ishmael's encounter with Queequeg. This time, Israel offers to share his bed with John Paul Jones, and Jones refuses: "'When, before the mast, I first sailed out of Whitehaven to Norway,' said Paul, coolly, 'I had for hammock-mate a full-blooded Congo. We had a white blanket spread in our hammock. Every time I turned in I found the Congo's black wool worked in with the white worsted. By the end of the voyage the blanket was of a pepper-and-salt look, like an old man's turning head. So it's not because I am notional at all, but because I don't care to, my lad'" (IP, 86). Compounding the ironies of this inversion, Jones turns out to be exactly what Ishmael had first taken Queequeg for—a white man

14. For a succinct statement of the Garrisonian position, see the "Declaration of Sentiments of the American Anti-Slavery Convention," in *Selections from the Writings and Speeches of William Lloyd Garrison* (1852; rpt. New York, 1968), 66–67. Also relevant are the selections from the *Liberator* on slave violence, reprinted in Nelson (ed.), *Documents of Upheaval*, 4–31. For a fine historical analysis, see Demos, "The Antislavery Movement and Violent 'Means,'" 501–26.

gone savage. Unlike Queequeg, Jones is totally incapable of love; unlike Ishmael, he remains as prejudiced as ever after sleeping with a dark-skinned shipmate. Jones seems to represent an America impermeable to human fellowship. He may also specifically embody the spirit of the South. As Michael Gilmore has pointed out: "He thinks of war in terms of the *code duello* . . . and announces that he lives entirely for the sake of honor and glory. He looks, according to Melville, 'like one who never had been, and never would be, a subordinate.' . . . he apparently once flogged a man to death for disobeying orders, and he revels in the idea of kidnaping kings and taking royalty captive: 'the nobleman, Lord Selkirk, shall have a bodily price pinned on his tail-coat, like any slave up at auction in Charleston.'"[15]

In contradistinction to Jones, Israel apparently stands for America's slaves, both black and white. Once again exemplifying Melville's unsegregated sympathy with the oppressed, Israel's experience suggests many parallels with the Negro's. When Israel is subjected to "such extremities of harassment . . . [by] incessant pursuit" that he almost decides "in a fit of despair" to "surrender himself, and submit to his fate" (IP, 43), we think of how fugitive slaves reacted to the same ordeal, particularly during the dragnet authorized by the Fugitive Slave Law of 1850.[16] When Israel, in one of his most nightmarish adventures, seeks to "blend himself" with the enemy crew among whom he has fallen but is "blackballed out of every club" he tries to join, from the prestigious topmen to the despised waisters, "the vilest caste of an armed ship's company" (IP, 193–94), we can hardly avoid recalling the Negro's history as a pariah in a hostile white man's country. When Israel shows up as a living negation of the Fourth of July, we are irresistibly reminded of Frederick Douglass' thunderous indictment: "What to the American slave is your Fourth of July? I answer, a day that reveals to him, more than all other days in the year, the gross injustice and cruelty to which he is the constant victim. To him, your celebration

15. Gilmore, *The Middle Way,* 157–58.
16. Martineau, *Society in America,* II, 321–23, cites cases of fugitive slaves unconsciously exposing themselves to reenslavement under the stress of such harassment. Gilmore, *The Middle Way,* 157, also notices Israel's resemblance to a fugitive slave and conjectures that "Melville intended a criticism of the Compromise of 1850 in his treatment of Franklin and Jones."

is a sham . . . your denunciation of tyrants, brass-fronted impudence; your shouts of liberty and equality, hollow mockery . . . your religious parade and solemnity, are to him mere bombast, fraud, deception, impiety, and hypocrisy—a thin veil to cover up crimes which would disgrace a nation of savages."[17] In *Israel Potter*, however, the function of these parallels is not to bring the issue of black slavery to the forefront, as in *White-Jacket* and "The Town-Ho's Story." Instead, it is to make manifest what Melville had by now come to see as the chief outcome of the American Revolution—the enslavement of the white working class to the native American overlords who had replaced the British.

17. Douglass, "What to the Slave is the Fourth of July?", extract from an oration of July 5, 1852, reprinted in *My Bondage and My Freedom*, 445.

FIVE   *D*arkening Shadows of Doom
in "The Encantadas," "Benito Cereno,"
and "The Bell-Tower"

HOWEVER pessimistic the view *Pierre* and *Israel Potter* present of the American Revolution as a type of the impending war over slavery, Melville's other works of this period squarely confront the factors that made a violent overthrow of slavery seem necessary, as well as inevitable. "The Encantadas," which precedes the first installment of *Israel Potter* in *Putnam's Monthly* by four months, unflinchingly exposes the ugliness of slavery and the brutality of the master class. "Benito Cereno" and "The Bell-Tower," both submitted to *Putnam's* within two months of the last installment, dramatize the obdurate blindness of the master class in the face of slave revolt. All three warn that the perpetuation of slavery spells apocalyptic destruction for America.[1]

In "The Encantadas," Melville fuses the critique of slavery and racism that occupied such a conspicuous place in his earlier works with the reevaluation of America's colonial and revolutionary history offered by *Pierre* and *Israel Potter*. A descriptive account of the Galapagos Islands, including among its ten sketches two complementary pictures of miniature slave dominions, "The Encantadas" exhibits a land in which slavery has taken root as suffering from an irremediable moral blight.

The apocalyptic doom that the *Pequod's* fate augurs for an unrepentant America seems already to have overtaken the Encantadas: "A group rather of extinct volcanoes than of isles; looking much as

1. Leyda, *Melville Log*, I, 484–89, II, 498–501.

the world at large might, after a penal conflagration."[2] As a "type of all-forsaken overthrow," the Encantadas surpass "weedy Babylon"; disowned even by the jackals to which Scripture had consigned that fallen city, these desolate islands are inhabited almost exclusively by reptiles, most notably the giant tortoises that have given the Encantadas their better-known name, Galapagos. The "strangely self-condemned . . . appearance of these creatures," with their expression of "lasting sorrow and penal hopelessness," has inspired among mariners the superstition that they are reincarnations of "wicked sea-officers, more especially commodores and captains . . . at death (and, in some cases, before death) transformed into tortoises" and thenceforth condemned to dwell upon "these hot aridities, sole solitary lords of Asphaltum" (E, 102). Grotesque though this fantasy may be, it expresses the insight that the ultimate punishment for tyrants is to be translated into what they are: creatures imprisoned in their own armor, isolated in their self-elected hell of command, and morally debased below human status. It may also serve to remind America's captains and commodores that "as in the days that were before the flood they were eating and drinking, marrying and giving in marriage, until the day that Noe entered into the ark, And knew not until the flood came and took them all away" (Matt. 24:38–39), so would the day of reckoning burst upon their revels. At least that is what Melville seems to hint when he confesses to being haunted amid "scenes of social merriment," particularly when "held by candle-light in old-fashioned mansions" (one thinks of the Glendinning manor, and of the southern plantation mansion), by the "ghost of a gigantic tortoise, with 'Memento * * * * *' burning in live letters upon his back" (E, 102–103).

Besides the portentous tortoises, the Encantadas harbor all sorts of derelicts in human form, some of whom have fled the tyranny of life at sea or on other shores to become petty tyrants in their turn over self-allocated island domains, and others of whom have "too

<hr/>

2. In the absence of a Northwestern-Newberry edition of *The Piazza Tales* and Melville's other stories of the 1850s, all citations from them ("Benito Cereno" partially excepted) will be from the complete, readily available paperback collection by Warner Berthoff (ed.), *Great Short Works of Herman Melville*. Page references will be given parenthetically in the text, keyed to abbreviations for the individual stories in this collection.

sadly experience[d] the fact, that flight from tyranny does not of itself insure a safe asylum, far less a happy home" (E, 148). Both Charles's Isle and Hood's Isle have been colonized by such "refugees," and their histories furnish contrasting lessons in the degradation to which men can sink when their passions for absolute domination and unbounded license are given free play.

The history of Charles's Isle, which raises some of the same questions *Pierre* and *Israel Potter* do about the ideals invoked to justify America's violent colonization and Revolution, illustrates how the twin perversions of autocracy and "*Riotocracy*" beset revolutions waged in the name of liberty. The cycle starts with Peru's war for independence against Spain, when a Creole adventurer who has fought for Peru and advanced to "high rank in the patriot army" demands Charles's Isle as his recompense, stipulating that it must henceforth be deeded solely to him and declared "forever free of Peru, even as Peru of Spain" (E, 122). Having established himself as "Supreme Lord of the Island, one of the princes of the powers of the earth," the Creole heads a colonizing party of eighty "pilgrims" (E, 123), men and women, in a voyage to the "promised land" (E, 122) that proves to be a satanic travesty of the first expeditions to Massachusetts and Virginia. Almost before it begins, the pilgrimage turns into a nightmare evoking the dark side of America's colonization: the introduction of slavery, the Indian wars, the feuds among unprincipled fortune seekers in colonies like Virginia, Mexico, and Peru.

The Creole sets out on the voyage surrounded by a bodyguard of "large grim dogs," recalling the bloodhounds used to track down runaway slaves. The tyranny that he proceeds to institute on Charles's Isle, where he directs the building of a capital city complete with a "lava-palace" for himself, smacks of a slave regime. "The disorders incident to settling all primitive regions, in the present case . . . heightened by the peculiarly untoward character of many of the pilgrims," allegedly compel "His Majesty" to impose martial law (E, 123). This not only entails conscripting his more reliable human subjects into a bodyguard subordinate to the "canine janizaries, whose terrific bayings prove quite as serviceable as bayonets in keeping down the surgings of revolt." It also involves His Majesty's hunting and shooting "with his own hand" subjects whom he suspects of rebellious intentions. As under even the worst forms of tyranny and slavery, however, the threat of depopulation acts as a check on excessive application of the death penalty. Since "the state of politics in this unhappy nation" is such that all except members of the bodyguard are "downright plotters and malignant traitors," His Majesty's depredations are halted "owing to the timely thought, that were strict sportsman's justice to be dispensed among such subjects, ere long the Nimrod King would have little or no remaining game to shoot" (E, 123).

Meanwhile, the "census" of the colony has diminished so alarmingly that the Creole must resort to recruiting new subjects from among the crews of visiting whalers. Although he gives the "renegado strangers" special privileges to ensure their loyalty, this policy proves no more successful in cementing the Creole's rule than his original policy of terrorization. Before long, like the "foreign-born Praetorians, unwisely introduced into the Roman state, and still more unwisely made favorites of the Emperors"—and like the indulged "house servants" revealed in the annals of southern slave conspiracies as "the most likely to revolt" [3] —the "petted" outsiders join the rest of the populace in overthrowing the king and proclaiming a republic.

Savagely though Melville caricatures the state of slavery in this parable about a misbegotten promised land, his picture of the regime the ex-slaves establish in its place, perhaps reflecting proslavery writers' descriptions of Haiti,[4] almost rivals it in gloom. The pendulum now swings from despotism to anarchy, as the insurgents confederate themselves into a "democracy neither Grecian, Roman, nor American," but rather a "permanent *Riotocracy*, which gloried in having no law but lawlessness" (E, 124–25). Declared "the asylum of the oppressed of all navies," the republic welcomes deserters and hails "each runaway tar . . . as a martyr in the cause of freedom." But such a regime hardly evinces itself more satisfying to the human

3. William W. Freehling, *Prelude to Civil War: The Nullification Controversy in South Carolina, 1816–1836* (New York, 1968), 56.
4. See the widely quoted report on conditions in Haiti made by Robert Walsh, in his capacity as official representative of the U.S. in Haiti, to Daniel Webster, then secretary of state, cited in Jenkins, *Pro-Slavery Thought*, 245–46.

spirit than the one it replaces. If the insurgents never pronounce their republic a failure or recall their former king from exile, contrary to his fond expectations, neither do they choose to continue forever a life of unrestrained debauchery. "Sated with the life of the isle, numbers from time to time" seek passage back to the outside world and its once despised discipline (E, 125). Possibly Melville means us to interpret this as a sign that the anarchy following a revolution may be but a passing phase. Gainsaying such an interpretation, nevertheless, Charles's Isle remains a "Riotocracy."

The sardonic presentation of both master and slaves in this sketch of Charles's Isle testifies to how far Melville has come from the empathy with the slave rebel shown in *White-Jacket* and *Moby-Dick*. Unlike the narratives of White-Jacket's and Steelkilt's confrontations with their domineering officers, the tale of "Charles's Isle and the Dog-King" has no heroes. The improbably painless resolutions of the conflict between unjust authority and unlawful rebellion in these former tales has given way to a violent enactment of the conflict, issuing in no viable alternative to the abuse of authority. Yet even if the sketch itself did not leave one—as I believe it does—with the impression that the Nimrod King's capricious reign of terror is more intolerable than the lawlessness that succeeds it, Melville's subsequent account of a tyrant on neighboring Hood's Isle, still more depraved than the Dog-King of Charles's Isle, indicates that slavery continued to strike him as the greater of the two evils.

The sketch of "Hood's Isle and the Hermit Oberlus" parallels that of "Charles's Isle and the Dog-King" in many ways. Both of these island despots are styled "kings," a title that evokes the royal masters the American colonists had cast off. In the latter sketch, Melville actually compares the Dog-King with Oberlus, ostensibly to differentiate the self-protective severity of the first from the unprovoked malevolence of the second. Left-handedly vindicating the Dog-King from being considered any worse than other founders of colonies, Melville allows that "the unfortunate Creole" might have been "in some degree influenced by not unworthy motives; such as prompt other adventurous spirits to lead colonists into distant regions and assume political pre-eminence over them" (E, 141). He also claims to find the Dog-King's recourse to "summary execution" of rebellious subjects "pardonable, considering the desperate characters he had to deal with." For the hermit Oberlus, on the other hand, Melville asserts that "no shade of palliation can be given," since "he acted out of mere delight in tyranny and cruelty," a propensity inherited from his wicked mother (E, 141). In a sly footnote at the end of the Oberlus sketch, however, Melville cites conflicting testimony as to whether Oberlus in fact lived on Hood's Isle or on Charles's Isle (E, 146)—a confusion that seems to nullify his earlier distinction between the two tyrants, inviting the reader to view Oberlus rather as an extension of the allegedly less vicious Dog-King.

Although the story of Charles's Isle has some bearing on the colonization of the New World and the form that slavery took in the American South, without being reducible to political allegory, the Oberlus sketch proclaims itself almost at the outset as an allegorical history of slavery in the New World: a history that presents the antiface of the European myth in which the white man civilizes the wilderness and overcomes its inhabitants' savagery by virtue of cultural and religious superiority. As Leo Marx has shown, this myth is reflected in "Shakespeare's American Fable," *The Tempest*.[5] Thus it is not surprising that allusions to *The Tempest* permeate the opening pages of the Oberlus sketch.

Described as "a wild white creature . . . in the person of a European bringing into this savage region qualities more diabolical than are to be found among any of the surrounding cannibals" (E, 139), the hermit Oberlus enacts the role of Shakespeare's Prospero, who epitomizes the European as bringer of civilization, while embodying the characteristics of Prospero's slave Caliban, the primitive creature whose deformity, gross sexuality, irreclaimable savagery, and symbolic name (an anagram for cannibal), all associate him with the early European conception of primitive man in general and the African in particular.[6] Like Prospero, Oberlus has made himself the master of a desert island, but his spiteful and malicious sway is the antithesis of the benevolent despotism Prospero exercises through superior wisdom and magic lore. The traits that account

5. Leo Marx, *The Machine in the Garden: Technology and the Pastoral Ideal in America* (New York, 1964), Chap. 2.
6. *Ibid.*, 54–56. See also Jordan, *White Over Black*, 28, 32–37.

for Oberlus' domination constitute a debased version of Prospero's faculties. Low cunning stands Oberlus in lieu of Prospero's intellect. Corresponding to Prospero's learning, a letter evincing "a certain clerkliness," as well as a "tristful eloquence," proves Oberlus "an accomplished writer, and no mere boor" (E, 145–46). Oberlus' equivalent for Prospero's magic powers is a "nameless witchery peculiar to some of the ugliest animals" (E, 146).

Physically, however, Oberlus, who claims his island "by Sycorax my mother," is modeled after the sole indigenous inhabitant Prospero finds on the island when he arrives—the monster Caliban, son of the evil witch Sycorax who ruled the island until her death: "His appearance, from all accounts, was that of the victim of some malignant sorceress; he seemed to have drunk of Circe's cup; beast-like; rags insufficient to hide his nakedness; his befreckled skin blistered by continual exposure to the sun; nose flat; countenance contorted, heavy, earthy; hair and beard unshorn, profuse, and of fiery red. He struck strangers much as if he were a volcanic creature thrown up by the same convulsion which exploded into sight the isle" (E, 139).

At the same time that this description identifies Oberlus with Caliban, it inescapably evokes the Negro, likewise said to be the victim of a curse. (The Negro's blackness was commonly explained as part of the curse of perpetual servitude that Noah had inflicted on his son Ham and all his progeny, in retribution for the sexual transgression Ham had committed in looking on his father's nakedness.)[7] Like Shakespeare's Caliban, Oberlus exhibits certain negroid features, hideously distorted by the European imagination into a phantasm of the earthy, bestial sexuality European man feared in himself. Yet ironically, while Oberlus' "volcanic" aura may suggest the blackness of lava, his most hideous features are in fact typically Caucasian: skin befreckled and blistered, rather than uniformly darkened by the sun, and profuse hair and beard of fiery red. Immediately succeeding this physical description, the picture of Oberlus "hidden under his shocking old black tarpaulin hat, hoeing potatoes among the lava" with a hoe "elbowed more like a savage's war-sickle than a civilized hoe-handle," reinforces Oberlus' affinities

7. Jordan, *White Over Black*, 17–19. Gen. 9:18–27.

with the Negro, conjuring up both the black slave hoeing in his master's fields and the savage that many proslavery writers discerned in him.[8]

As in character and physiognomy, so in the lust for dominion that his name may express, Oberlus telescopes the antipodal images of the powerful European conqueror and the degraded savage whom the European was theoretically predestined to subjugate. When Oberlus assumes proprietorship, in the name of Sycorax, of the island he has discovered, he follows in the footsteps not of his literary prototype Caliban, who was native to the island he claimed, but of the early European voyagers who took over new territories in the name of their royal patrons. Like them, he displays the innate drive for mastery and conquest that supposedly distinguished the Caucasian from other races and attested to his expansive intellect.[9] Oberlus, however, testifies rather to Melville's conviction that "the love of rule for its own sake, far from being the peculiar infirmity of noble minds," is a mere animal instinct, furthest developed in "beings which have no mind at all" (E, 140).

Having introduced Oberlus as a fusion of Prospero and Caliban, European type and savage countertype, Melville begins his own fable about the historical relationship between the two with a reference to the technological event that triggered the era of colonization by establishing European primacy over other peoples—the development of firearms. Thus it is the acquisition of "an old musket, with a few charges of powder and ball," that stimulates Oberlus "to enterprise, as a tiger that first feels the coming of its claws" (E, 140), and that incites him to extend his sway over human beings, as well as virgin lands: "Armed now with that shocking blunderbuss, strong in the thought of being master of that horrid isle, he panted for a chance to prove his potency upon the first specimen of humanity which should fall unbefriended into his hands" (E, 141).

Significantly, Oberlus' first victim, a sailor from a boat's crew that has landed on the island to gather wood, turns out to be a Negro. The ensuing account of Oberlus' attempts to capture the

8. Fredrickson, Black Image in the White Mind, 54; Jenkins, Pro-Slavery Thought, 245–46.
9. Fredrickson, Black Image in the White Mind, 100.

Negro by feigning amity and, when treachery fails, by resorting to threats and at last to violence, closely parallels narratives of how Europeans embarked on the African slave trade in the sixteenth century.[10] Yet it counters the notion that blacks were peculiarly susceptible to enslavement. Seeing through Oberlus' wiles, the Negro resists his bullying and surrenders only when Oberlus actually fires at him. Moreover, undismayed at being exultantly informed that "henceforth he is to work for [Oberlus], and be his slave, and that his treatment would entirely depend on his future conduct," the Negro avails himself of a chance to retaliate as soon as Oberlus "slackens his vigilance." Throwing Oberlus to the ground and tying his hands "with the monster's own cord," the Negro turns him over to the ship's crew, who beat and rob the hermit, even "destroying his hut and garden" (E, 142). Hence Melville shows that slavery necessarily generates violent reprisals, and that oppressors are destined to be caught in the toils they have laid for their victims.

Oberlus eventually escapes, his slaveholding ambitions undaunted. To capture and enslave stray seamen, he now enlists a subtler weapon Europeans had used to subjugate primitive peoples (although Oberlus' subsequent victims are all white)—alcohol. When sailors visit his island, he "makes up to them like a free-and-easy comrade," plies them with drink, rendering them insensible, and then ties them hand and foot until their ship leaves, upon which he reveals his true colors: "finding themselves entirely dependent upon Oberlus, alarmed at his changed demeanor, his savage threats, and above all, that shocking blunderbuss, they willingly enlist under him, becoming his humble slaves, and Oberlus the most incredible of tyrants. So much so, that two or three perish beneath his initiating process" (E, 143).

At this point, Melville's allegorical history of slavery in the New World enters the phase that followed the acquisition of slaves—that

10. See, for example, the narrative cited in St. George Tucker, *A Dissertation on Slavery: with A Proposal for the Gradual Abolition of it, in the State of Virginia* (1796; rpt. Westport, Conn., 1970), 24–28, note h. Melville would have found similar accounts in the works of the old voyagers, such as Richard Hakluyt and Samuel Purchas, of which he was so fond.

of "breaking in" the new captives by driving them mercilessly and punishing them continually until they no longer have the will to resist.[11] Oberlus' "initiating process" consists in setting his slaves at backbreaking tasks, keeping them on "roughest fare," and flourishing his blunderbuss "at the slightest sign of insurrection." Once he has converted them "in all respects . . . into reptiles at his feet," there is no action, "however at first abhorrent to them," that Oberlus cannot cajole or coerce them into performing. The moral price these men pay for adjusting to slavery is far higher than that paid by a Guinea or a Landless. Even the riotocracy of the Dog-King's ex-subjects seems preferable to the acquiescence of Oberlus' slaves in his evil designs. Like the Dog-King's subjects, nevertheless, they are too degraded to inspire sympathy. Morally created of the same stuff as Landless ("without shame, without a soul, so dead to the least dignity of manhood that he could hardly be called a man"), these hapless sailors have been almost predisposed to yield to Oberlus' impress: "indeed, prepared for almost any eventual evil by their previous lawless life, as a sort of ranging Cow-Boys of the sea, which had dissolved within them the whole moral man, so that they were ready to concrete in the first offered mold of baseness now; rotted down from manhood by their hopeless misery on the isle; wonted to cringe in all things to their lord, himself the worst of slaves; these wretches were now become wholly corrupted to his hands. He used them as creatures of an inferior race" (E, 143). It is as though Melville were trying to show us what happens when a "happy Jack" falls into the hands of a Simon Legree. While once again offering a white analogue to the brute pictured in proslavery writings and suggesting that the subhuman slave is made and not born, Melville's view of the psychic injury that the average man sustains under such conditions leaves little hope that the majority of American slaves—the products of generations of Simon Legrees— will be able to make better use of freedom, in the short run, than the debauched freedmen of Charles's Isle.

Despite this departure from Melville's earlier championship of slave rebels, the sketch of "Hood's Isle and the Hermit Oberlus" constitutes a devastating refutation of the proslavery argument. By

11. For a description of the initiating process, see Stampp, *The Peculiar Institution*, 144–48.

fusing in Oberlus the roles of slavetrader, overseer, and slaveowner, Melville symbolizes the historical and moral continuity of these aspects of slavery, making it impossible to separate the glamorous gentleman planter from his sordid ancestors and accomplices. Behind every slaveholder, however kindhearted, Melville seems to be saying, looms the shadow of an Oberlus. The sketch also dispels the myth that slaves elect to remain with their masters out of affection, loyalty, or innate dependency.[12] True, Oberlus' slaves "willingly enlist under him," but only because they find themselves entirely at his mercy; they are impelled by terror of his "savage threats" and, "above all," by his musket, rather than by the prospect of comfort or protection, as proslavery apologists maintained. Likewise answering the apologists' boast that southerners would dare even to arm their slaves in the South's defense, without fear of treachery or insurrection, Melville points out that Oberlus can afford to discount the possibility of "servile war," since the weapons he has entrusted to his slaves—mere "rusty cutlasses" and "sad old scythes"—are no match for the blunderbuss he reserves for himself, "which by its blind scatterings of all sorts of boulders, clinkers, and other scoria would annihilate all four mutineers, like four pigeons, at one shot" (E, 143–44). Southerners might claim that they did not hesitate to sleep unarmed in unlocked bedrooms, but Melville knows better than to believe that any slaveholder would put his life in the hands of creatures he rules, ultimately, by brute force, broken-spirited though they be. In contrast, Melville describes Oberlus as either hiding from his slaves at night, or binding them hand and foot, concealing their cutlasses, and sleeping outside the door of their improvised cell with "blunderbuss in hand" (E, 144). Thus vivifying his assertion that Oberlus is "himself the worst of slaves," Melville shows that the tyrant pays almost as extreme a price for his mastery as his slaves do for being spared their wretched lives in exchange for serving him—a point abolitionists often made about slaveholders, with reference to the coercive laws southerners imposed on themselves for the sake of protecting the slave system.[13] Besides discrediting the patriarchal image of slavery projected by the pro-

12. Formulations of the proslavery arguments mentioned below can be found in *The Pro-Slavery Argument*, 81, 112, 221.
13. Martineau, *Society in America*, II, 343–52.

slavery apologists and plantation romancers, Melville hints at the expansionism of the slavocracy; for he conjectures that Oberlus, "not content with daily parading over a cindery solitude at the head of his fine army," may have conceived the design of commandeering "some passing ship touching at his dominions," massacring her crew, and sailing away with his slaves to greener pastures (E, 144).

Melville's finest stroke, however, is to let Oberlus speak in his own defense through a letter supposedly discovered in the hermit's cave. Both outrageous and pitiful, this letter is "full of the strangest satiric effrontery" (E, 146). It brilliantly illuminates the mind of a man who, to all appearances, sees his brutal tenure on Hood's Isle as an endeavor "by hard labor and much solitary suffering, to accumulate something to make myself comfortable in a virtuous though unhappy old age," and who genuinely believes himself to be "the most unfortunate ill-treated gentleman that lives" (E, 145). Melville later applied similar insight into the slaveholder's desperate self-deception in developing his subtle characterization of Benito Cereno, another master who complains, seemingly with greater plausibility, of having been taken for a "monster," though "not only an innocent man, but the most pitiable of all men."[14]

As examples of inhuman tyranny, riotous rebellion, and abject submission that complement and counterpoint each other, the sketches of the Dog-King and the hermit Oberlus foreshadow the relationship we will find between "Benito Cereno" and "The Bell-Tower," which likewise hold up complementary pictures of slave societies and dramatize versions of slave revolt that seem to redefine each other. Before attempting to interpret these twin tales, however, we should take note of three magazine pieces that bridge the chronological gap between "The Encantadas" and "Benito Cereno" and furnish external evidence that Melville may have conceived "The Bell-Tower" as a companion-piece to "Benito Cereno." Actually presented in diptych format, "The Two Temples," "Poor Man's Pudding and Rich Man's Crumbs," and "The Paradise of Bachelors and The

14. From John P. Runden (ed.), *Melville's "Benito Cereno": A Text for Guided Research* (Lexington, Mass., 1965), 74. Unless otherwise indicated, all citations from "Benito Cereno" will be from this edition, and page references will be given parenthetically in the text.

Tartarus of Maids" all indicate that Melville was experimenting with paired sketches during this period as a means of providing a dual perspective on moral problems.[15] Although the problem these diptychs explore is not slavery but poverty, they contrast the worlds of wealth and poverty and expose the complacency with which the wealthy view poverty from within their barricaded sanctuaries, in a manner that sheds much light on Melville's intentions in "Benito Cereno" and "The Bell-Tower."

"The Paradise of Bachelors and The Tartarus of Maids," in particular, prepares us in several respects for "Benito Cereno" and "The Bell-Tower."[16] First, "The Paradise of Bachelors" is much akin to "Benito Cereno" in style, with its perplexing vacillations of tone between straightforward social description and Melvillean burlesque; with its sexual innuendoes, continually belying and belied by the narrator's insistence on the perfect decorum the bachelors maintain; and with its reliance on a narrator who, like Captain Delano, the obtuse central intelligence through whom "Benito Cereno" is narrated, is less aware of the implications of his language and perceptions than the author manipulating him. Second, "The Tartarus of Maids" is equally close to "The Bell-Tower" in theme, dramatizing as it does the deadly subjection of human beings to the machines they enlist in their service, and also highlighting a form of exploitation that was often compared to slavery and even referred to as "wage slavery."[17] Third, the relationship between the two halves of this diptych, with the latter half spelling out the latent

15. Two recent critics who discuss Melville's experimentation with paired sketches are Marvin Fisher, *Going Under*, 35, who sees it foreshadowed in "The Encantadas" (though not specifically in the Oberlus and Dog-King episodes); and William B. Dillingham, *Melville's Short Fiction, 1853–1856* (Athens, Ga., 1977), 8–9, 104, 208–209, who links "Benito Cereno" with "The Bell-Tower," but reaches a conclusion opposite to mine about how this link modifies our understanding of both.

16. My analysis of the sexual allegory and "psycho-sociological" implications of this diptych, and of the relationship between its two halves, will be based on three excellent studies: Beryl Rowland's "Melville's Bachelors and Maids: Interpretation through Symbol and Metaphor," *American Literature*, XLI (1969), 389–405; Fisher, *Going Under*, 70–94; and Franklin, *The Victim As Criminal and Artist*, 52–56. The comparisons with "Benito Cereno" and "The Bell-Tower" are my own.

17. See the comparisons between northern and British workers and southern slaves in *The Pro-Slavery Argument*, 47–56, 135–40; and in Fitzhugh, *Sociology for the South*, 66–72, 84–86, 92–93, 161–68. For a summary of these arguments, see Wilfred Carsel, "The Slaveholders' Indictment of Northern Wage Slavery," *Journal of Southern History*, VI (1940), 504–20. Wage slavery is also a basic Marxist concept.

moral indictment of the former half, constitutes a striking precedent for the way "The Bell-Tower" seems to redefine "Benito Cereno." Finally, the extended sexual allegory of "The Paradise of Bachelors and The Tartarus of Maids," which so clearly links tabooed and deviant sexuality with systems of economic exploitation, illuminates the function of the sexual perversions hinted at in "Benito Cereno" and "The Bell-Tower": to suggest that slavery is by definition an institution that licenses sado-masochistic impulses.

Hardly does the narrator introduce the convivial bachelor lawyers known as Templars, into whose "paradise" he has led the reader, than he pointedly recalls the legacy they inherit—a society based, like the contemporary South, on systematic exploitation of an outcast people, often taking a literally sexual as well as economic form: "Templar? That's a romantic name. Let me see. Brian de Bois-Guilbert was a Templar, I believe" (PBTM, 203). Brian de Bois-Guilbert, of course, was familiar to the average reader, acquainted with the Knights-Templars through Scott's *Ivanhoe*, as the ruthless monk-knight who abducted a Jewess, in defiance of both his order's sexual code and his society's ostracism of the Jews, and who then sought to save his honor by letting her be accused of witchcraft.[18] The allusion thus evokes two kinds of sexual exploitation as relevant to the plantation as to the medieval world of the Knights-Templars: on the one hand the direct violation of the slave's person, in flagrant breach of the religious ideals by which the master class rationalized its own prerogatives and the slave's status as a pariah; on the other hand the projection of the master class's sexual guilt onto its victims. Later, through an incongruous pun on bachelorhood, the narrator specifically conjures up the southern plantation idyll, with its images of carefree hosts, hospitable mansions, and convivial gatherings, when his memories of the "genial hospitalities" he has enjoyed beneath the Templars' "time-honored roofs" inspire him to sing "Carry me back to old Virginny!" (PBTM, 205).[19] Besides relating old England to "old Virginny," this pun points toward one of the central questions the sketch raises: whether the modern "Brethren

18. Rowland, "Melville's Bachelors and Maids," 395.
19. Fisher, *Going Under*, 76, interprets this as a pun undercutting the "narrator's celebration of celibacy" and referring to the "virgin state" and the "more vital and virgin New World."

of the Order of Celibacy" lead lives any more virgin than their historical namesakes, on whom, as the narrator tells us immediately after referring to Brian de Bois-Guilbert, history has rendered a still harsher verdict than fiction: "We know indeed—sad history recounts it—that a moral blight tainted at last this sacred Brotherhood. Though no sworded foe might outskill them in the fence, yet the worm of luxury crawled beneath their guard, gnawing the core of knightly troth, nibbling the monastic vow, till at last the monk's austerity relaxed to wassailing, and the sworn knights-bachelors grew to be but hypocrites and rakes" (PBTM, 203). In "The Paradise of Bachelors," as later in "Benito Cereno," where the reader must view the master-slave relationship through Delano's avid eyes in order to feel the moral degradation it involves, Melville makes it impossible either to answer the question of the Templars' chasteness or to judge the world the narrator recalls so nostalgically without participating in his covert sexual fantasies about it.

This sketch does not, like the previous year's "Poor Man's Pudding and Rich Man's Crumbs," remind the reader of the "mass of lean, famished, ferocious creatures, struggling and fighting" for the scraps of just such a feast as the Templars are gorging themselves on (PMP, 174). Instead, it encourages us to abandon ourselves to the matchless pleasures of "good living, good drinking, good feeling, and good talk" that this bachelors' haven offers (PBTM, 209). Even more subversively, it seduces us into relishing the suggestiveness of the courses that "inaugurated the affair" (oxtail soup of "a rich russet hue" and turbot "just gelatinous enough, not too turtleish in its unctuousness" [PBTM, 206–207]); reading hints of masturbation into the bachelors' reluctance to be "seen taking a lonely, unparticipated glass"—an act held "indelicate, selfish, and unfraternal" (PBTM, 208); probing for intimations of homosexuality in the "tender concern" the bachelors display for each other's "entire well-being and lasting hygiene," a concern they express "in flowing wine" (PBTM, 207); fantasizing about the "choice experiences in their private lives" that they bring out, "like choice brands of Moselle or Rhenish, only kept for particular company," as their spirits rise "to perfect genialness and unconstraint" under the influence of wine (PBTM, 208); fleshing out their "spicy anecdotes" of student life at Oxford among "most frank-hearted noble lords" and "liberal com-

panions," and of "the private life of the Iron Duke," about whom
one bachelor recounts an incident "never printed, and never before
announced in any public or private company"; and dwelling on the
phallic significance of the peculiarly shaped "mull of snuff" that
crowns the occasion: "an immense convolved horn, a regular Jericho
horn, mounted with polished silver," whose embellishments include
"two life-like goats' heads, with four more horns of solid silver,
projecting from opposite sides of the mouth of the noble main horn"
(PBTM, 209).

Ironically, we sophisticated modern readers lose ourselves as readily in ferreting out the sexual connotations of this meal as the contemporary public to whom the sketch is addressed would have in
vicariously sharing the bachelors' gluttony.[20] Thus we fail to register
the apocalyptic warning that the Jericho horn conveys to the de-
cadent ruling class of Temple Bar. Furthermore, by concentrating
on the bachelors' unhealthy sexuality, and whether it consists in
regressing to "a haven of oral nurture" or anal pleasure, or in titillating latent homosexual fancies, or in performing overt homosexual
acts,[21] we all too easily miss the point of the sketch—that the voluptuous life of this privileged elite is made possible solely by the
unremitting labor, "twelve hours to the day, day after day, through
the three hundred and sixty-five days, excepting Sundays, Thanks-
giving, and Fast-days" (PBTM, 222), of a working populace denied
any life at all; that the serenity of such an elite depends on not merely
ignoring, but actively deadening itself against the "grindstone experience of the practical misery and infamy of poverty" that Melville
dramatized so vividly in "Poor Man's Pudding and Rich Man's
Crumbs" (PMP, 172): "How could men of liberal sense, ripe scholarship in the world, and capacious philosophical and convivial un-
derstandings—how could they suffer themselves to be imposed upon
by such monkish fables? Pain! Trouble! As well talk of Catholic
miracles. No such thing.—Pass the sherry, sir.—Pooh, pooh! Can't
be!—The port, sir, if you please" (PBTM, 209). This moral, as
implicit throughout "The Paradise of Bachelors" as the condem-

20. Leyda, *Melville Log*, II, 579, cites an account of a dinner Judge Shaw gave in
Melville's honor which testifies to contemporary gluttony.
21. See the various interpretations suggested by Fisher, *Going Under*, 75–76; Franklin,
The Victim as Criminal and Artist, 55; and Rowland, "Melville's Bachelors and Maids,"
396–98.

nation of the master class's mentality is in "Benito Cereno," becomes unmistakable in "The Tartarus of Maids," which confronts us directly with a world that is "the very counterpart of the Paradise of Bachelors, but snowed upon, and frost-painted to a sepulchre" (PBTM, 214).

The sexual and "psycho-sociological" implications of the "Tartarus" have been too thoroughly analyzed by critics like Beryl Rowland, Marvin Fisher, and H. Bruce Franklin to need reiteration here. Suffice it to say that what we see in the "Tartarus" is the obverse of the barren, passively homoerotic male sexuality of the bachelor Templars; that it is, to quote Franklin, an aggressive "male sexuality entering a woman's genitals in the quest for dollars" and perverting the female sexuality it enslaves "to produce nothing but blank paper and profits"; and that "combined with the first half of the diptych," as Marvin Fisher puts it, "the 'Tartarus' ironically spells out a cruel paradox; for while the womb of the New World is far more productive than the tradition-laden refuge of the Old World, it is in human terms far more destructive and deadly."[22]

In contrast to the ruddy, portly convivialists of Temple Bar, the "girls" who labor in the hell into which the narrator next leads us— the Devil's Dungeon paper mill, whose proprietor turns out to be an old bachelor—are "pale with work, and blue with cold," their eyes "supernatural with unrelated misery," their brows prematurely "ruled and wrinkled" with care, their bodies "consumptive," their lungs ridden with "fine, poisonous particles" from the rags they convert into lint in the papermaking process (PBTM, 214–15, 217–18). Serving their inflexible iron master, the machine, "mutely and cringingly as the slave serves the Sultan," these violated women, like all exploited workers, have been forced by the system that oppresses them to become "their own executioners; themselves whetting the very swords that slay them" (PBTM, 216, 218).

Although the slavery delineated here is the wage slavery of the New England factory system, rather than the chattel slavery of the plantation, the sketch consistently invites us to notice how the features of each system are replicated in the other. When the narrator asks why, "in most factories, female operatives, of whatever age, are

22. Franklin, *The Victim as Criminal and Artist*, 52–53; Fisher, *Going Under*, 77, 79

indiscriminately called girls, never women" (PBTM, 222), he is drawing attention to a denial of the subjugated class's adulthood that is common to all slave systems, and whose counterpart in the southern plantation system, under which slaves never graduated from the status of "boys" and "girls" to that of men and women, may have been even more familiar to some of Melville's readers.[23] At the outset of the sketch, moreover, an allusion to the narrator's business connections with the South tells us that the two slave systems are not only analogous, but actually leagued with each other. This allusion, which reminds us that in the first half of the diptych, the narrator had sighed nostalgically for "old Virginny" and old England in the same breath, occurs as a parenthesis in his explanation of what takes him to the Devil's Dungeon paper mill:

> Having embarked on a large scale in the seedsman's business (so extensively and broadcast, indeed, that at length my seeds were distributed through all the Eastern and Northern States, and even fell into the far soil of Missouri and the Carolinas), the demand for paper at my place became so great, that the expenditure soon amounted to a most important item in the general account. . . . For economy's sake, and partly for the adventure of the trip, I now resolved to cross the mountains, some sixty miles, and order my future paper at the Devil's Dungeon paper-mill. (PBTM, 211–12)

As a businessman selling seeds to be planted by chattel slave labor and buying paper produced by wage slave labor, the narrator reveals himself to be an accomplice in two forms of exploitation that, as Frederick Douglass said of the southern form, reduce "man to a mere machine."[24] "The Tartarus of Maids" thus includes the slave system in its indictment of a factory system that Melville exhibits as transforming women into "mere cogs to the wheels" of a gigantic machinery that has usurped even their procreativity in its total assault on their humanity.

It is this double-barreled indictment that relates "The Tartarus" so closely to "The Bell-Tower," in which we find the same pattern of elaborate and sometimes fanciful verbal parallels linking it to a companion-piece situated as far from it, geographically speaking, as the London men's club of the "Paradise" from the New England

23. Stampp, *The Peculiar Institution*, 328.
24. From "The Nature of Slavery," a lecture given in Rochester on December 1, 1850, reprinted in Douglass, *My Bondage and My Freedom*, 431.

paper mill of the "Tartarus." Both of these sketches equate (wo)man dominated by machinery with (wo)man reduced to a machine. Both use sexual allegory to vivify how utterly such exploitation violates the personalities of its victims, robbing them of everything that makes them human, and how terrifyingly it licenses the master class's lust for domination. Both sketches dramatize this kind of exploitation through the metaphor of a machinery that obviates human reproduction, in the "Tartarus" by simulating the process, and in "The Bell-Tower" by replacing the product. Both make this diabolical machinery the attribute of a man who has banished female sexuality from his life: in the "Tartarus," it is the property of the satanic factory owner "Old Bach," in "The Bell-Tower," the creation of the vulcanic inventor Bannadonna. Both stories represent women as incorporated into an inexorable mechanical system that alienates them from each other and destroys all their human ties; the "pallid girls" in the "Tartarus" are as "menially" subject to their factory owner's "iron animal" as the harem slave to the sultan, and the "gay girls" chiseled on the face of Bannadonna's clock are subordinated by him to the mechanical bell ringer he has invented, who severs their clasped hands with a blow of his mailed fist. Both, finally, rely on inverted color symbolism—in the "Tartarus" the enslavement of "sheet-white" maids to a "dark-complexioned" master, in "The Bell-Tower" the destruction of the white inventor at the hands of his black robot—to show that no race is immune to either the degradations of enslavement or the temptations of mastery, and to prophesy a day when America's black slaves will avenge themselves against their white oppressors and overturn the hierarchy of white over black under which they have so long been crushed, perhaps to become oppressors in their turn.

Having familiarized ourselves with the features of "The Paradise of Bachelors and The Tartarus of Maids" that most closely anticipate "Benito Cereno" and "The Bell-Tower"—the use of an obtuse narrator, the stylistic mixture of seriousness and burlesque, the sexual allegory, the color symbolism, the diptych structure, and the dual indictment of the master class—we are ready to tackle the thorny problems of interpretation that the first of these tales, in particular, poses. I would like to postpone taking up the issue on which critics have deadlocked in interpreting "Benito Cereno"—whether Melville champions or condemns the rebels. In the first place, I do not believe Melville formulates the problem of slavery in these terms, either in "Benito Cereno" or elsewhere. As his other fiction indicates, Melville was so ambivalent about his own rebellious feelings that he could only champion rebels in suicidal situations, and when it came to dramatizing successful slave revolts, he regularly found himself torn between recognizing the justice, as well as the probable inevitability, of slave revolt, and dreading such an outcome as a tragic waste of human potential, perhaps more productive of evil than of good. In the second place, I do not believe that "Benito Cereno" is primarily a dramatization of slave revolt, let alone a psychological study of the slave rebel, but rather an exploration of the white racist mind and how it reacts in the face of a slave insurrection. As such, it appears to me to be less a response to the immediate danger of a slave revolt than to the menacing gains racism was making under the aegis of science at the time Melville wrote "Benito Cereno," and I find it more rewarding to approach the story from this angle.

We may recall that in 1854, only one year prior to the publication of "Benito Cereno," the southern ethnologist Josiah C. Nott and his English collaborator, the famous Egyptologist George R. Gliddon, had published their influential compendium of current scientific thinking on race, *Types of Mankind*, whose principal thesis, defended with much erudition, was that the human races were entirely separate species, endowed with vastly different physical, intellectual, and temperamental characteristics and ranked hierarchically on a biological scale ranging from the lowest type of Negro to the highest type of Caucasian, the Anglo-Saxon.[25] Melville had almost certainly seen the lengthy review of this work, reluctantly endorsing its scientific findings, that had appeared in the same issue of *Putnam's* as the first installment of *Israel Potter*.[26] It must have been immediately obvious to him, from such a journal's capitulation to racist propaganda, that the "scientific" demonstration of Negro inferiority threatened to deflect the issue of the Negro's rightful status in American society and to lull the American public into supposing that the Negro would bear his chains indefinitely.

25. See Chap. One, pp. 21–25 herein.
26. "Is Man One or Many?" *Putnam's Monthly Magazine*, IV (July, 1854), 1–14.

Melville eventually devoted one of his last magazine sketches, "The 'Gees," specifically to refuting these pernicious theories. In "Benito Cereno," however, he reacted to their ascendancy by plumbing the mentality of the men who embraced them; by limiting the reader to their myopic view of slavery, the Negro, and the problems of race relations; by graphically illustrating the perils of regarding one's fellow men as tractable children, domestic animals, or fiends; by bitterly dissipating the hope that such minds can ever be enlightened, even by violence; and by prophesying the ultimate triumph of the intelligent will to freedom over the blind forces of oppression.

Because "Benito Cereno" relies on the device of presenting all incidents, both concurrently and in retrospect, through the eyes of obtuse observers, the central critical problem the story poses is that of distinguishing between Melville's interpretation of the events that transpire on board the *San Dominick* and the interpretations he ascribes to his chief protagonists, the Yankee captain Amasa Delano and the Spaniard Benito Cereno; between Melville's attitudes toward slavery and the Negro, and theirs. Broadly speaking, we can identify the body of the narrative as Captain Delano's version of the *San Dominick*'s ordeal, the deposition as Benito Cereno's, and the few pages of narrative at the end that set these versions against each other and focus for the first time on the slave ringleader Babo as Melville's.[27]

Since the finale representing Melville's viewpoint consists chiefly in a tribute to the mind of the "black—whose brain, not body, had schemed and led the revolt, with the plot" (BC, 75), we can most profitably begin by comparing this assessment of the Negro's intelligence with the estimate that emerges from Delano's comments on the Negro in general and Babo in particular. While Delano repeatedly praises Babo as "uncommonly intelligent" (BC, 47), he seems to mean uncommonly so for a Negro. In the famous shaving scene, where he notices that Babo has selected the flag of Spain as

27. Allen Guttmann was the first critic to differentiate Melville's viewpoint from "*Captain Delano's thoughts*" and "*Don Benito's testimony*," in his seminal 1961 article, "The Enduring Innocence of Captain Amasa Delano," reprinted in Runden (ed.), *Melville's "Benito Cereno*," 179–88 (citations are from 182, 185–86). See also Joyce Sparer Adler, "Melville's *Benito Cereno*: Slavery and Violence in the Americas," *Science & Society*, XXXVIII (1974), 19–48, for a similar reading based on a tripartite division of the tale. Dillingham, *Melville's Short Fiction*, 243, contends that there are four narrative perspectives: "repertorial, official (the deposition), authorial, and individual (Delano)."

a bib for the Spanish captain, Delano implicitly acknowledges the seditious meaning of this gesture in his words to Benito Cereno, to whom he confides, "It's well it's only I, and not the King, that sees this." Yet unable to credit the Negro with having intended such a sardonic piece of effrontery, Delano condescendingly twits Babo with the words "'it's all one, I suppose, so the colors be gay;' which playful remark did not fail somewhat to tickle the negro" (BC, 42). Earlier, in attempting to fathom the disquieting symptoms on board the *San Dominick*, Delano dismissed the fleetingly entertained suspicion of Benito Cereno's "complicity with the blacks" on the grounds that the blacks "were too stupid." Moreover, he instinctively attributed any conceivable plot to Don Benito, rather than to Babo, assuming that "the whites . . . by nature, were the shrewder race." And he rejected the notion of collusion between the two, in language revealing his susceptibility to the racist ethnology that was gaining currency in the mid-1850s: "Besides, who ever heard of a white so far a renegade as to apostatize from his very *species* almost, by leaguing in against it with negroes?" (BC, 32; italics added).[28]

Not only does the entirety of "Benito Cereno" give the lie to Delano's complacent reliance on the Negro's intellectual inferiority, but as some critics have recognized, Melville's portrayal of Babo as an almost disembodied brain—"his slight frame, inadequate to that which it held"—reverses the conventional racist stereotype of the Negro as all brawn and no brain.[29] More subversively, perhaps, it also reverses the conventional appraisal of the black and white races' respective fortes; for Babo yields only to the "superior *muscular* strength of his captor," and at a moment when the "long-benighted mind" of that captor, who happens to be Delano himself, has not even grasped what is going on (BC, 57, 75; italics added).

Having seen, then, that Melville and Delano utterly differ on at least one crucial point—whether the Negro's innate intelligence equaled that of whites—we may be better prepared to approach the pivotal passage, set almost at dead center of the tale, where Melville invites the reader to participate in Delano's fantasies about the Ne-

28. Another reference to Nott's theory that the human races were distinct species is Delano's interest in the "hybrid" complexion and character of the mulatto Francesco (BC, 46). Nott, *Types of Mankind*, Chap. 12, contended that mulattoes were a hybrid species, sharing characteristics of such animal hybrids as mules.

29. *E.g.*, Nicol, "Iconography in 'Benito Cereno,'" 28.

gro's "peculiar" fitness for "avocations about one's person" (BC, 40).
This passage must surely have made every reader from Melville's
day on uncomfortable. Very much in the manner that the larger
narrative cyclically lulls the reader, then alarms him, at length re-
assures him, yet hardly allows his trepidations to subside before
arousing them anew, the tone of Melville's prose constantly vacillates
here between cliché and burlesque. Ostensibly straightforward ob-
servations about the Negro in his most familiar nineteenth-century
capacity slide imperceptibly into innuendoes about the tastes to
which a dextrous Negro body servant can cater—only to relapse
into platitudes that seemingly let the reader off the hook until a
jarring note of burlesque again stirs in the reader an obscure suspicion that he is being made a fool of:

> There is something in the negro which, in a peculiar way, fits him
> for avocations about one's person. Most negroes are natural valets
> and hair-dressers; taking to the comb and brush congenially as to
> the castinets, and flourishing them apparently with almost equal
> satisfaction. There is, too, a smooth tact about them in this em-
> ployment, with a marvelous, noiseless, gliding briskness, not un-
> graceful in its way, singularly pleasing to behold, and *still more so
> to be the manipulated subject of*. And above all is the great gift of
> good-humor. Not the mere grin or laugh is here meant. Those were
> unsuitable. But a certain easy cheerfulness, harmonious in every
> glance and gesture; *as though God had set the whole negro to some
> pleasant tune.* (BC, 40–41; italics added)

The unique power of Melville's rhetoric—the way it has of getting
under our skin and making us squirm—perhaps reflects his awareness that in sounding the depths of Delano's mind, he was exorcising
something of Delano's unhealthy attitude toward blacks from his
own mind and participating in the discomfiture he was inflicting
on the reader. In a society where most blacks are restricted to menial
employment, there is always a fine line between admiring the native
physical grace of a people as yet uncramped by a sedentary, top-
heavy existence—as Melville had admired the grace of the Typees—
and projecting onto them the uninhibited sexuality tabooed in the
ruling class's value system; between appreciating the joie de vivre
of a people who, as Melville wrote in *Moby-Dick*, "ever enjoy all
holidays and festivities with finer, freer relish than any other race"
(MD, 345), and deducing from it an immunity to sorrow that makes

them ideal whipping posts for the ruling class—as Melville carefully avoided doing in his description of Pip, amidst which that racial generalization occurs.

Having himself trod this fine line separating legitimate anthropological observation from romantic racialism and outright racism, Melville surely knew what he was doing by repeatedly forcing the reader to cross it, as cross it we must when we witness through Delano's uncomprehending and guiltily envious eyes the morbid dependence of the "hypochondriac Benito Cereno" on his body servant. But the reader who unwittingly joins Delano in fantasizing about the Negro's peculiar aptitude for gratifying white men's forbidden cravings finds himself willy-nilly embracing an ideology that justifies imprisoning the Negro in that role. Accordingly, Delano falls into the language of the southern apologists of slavery as soon as he begins to rationalize these fantasies:[30] "When to this is added the *docility arising from the unaspiring contentment of a limited mind*, and that susceptibility of blind attachment sometime inhering in *indisputable inferiors*, one readily perceives why those hypochondriacs, Johnson and Byron—it may be, something like the hypochondriac Benito Cereno—took to their hearts, almost to the exclusion of the entire white race, their serving men, the negroes, Barber and Fletcher" (BC, 41; italics added).

The sentence following this literary mantrap announces with a confusing shift in point of view that we are moving from Delano's fantasies about the titillating relationship men like Don Benito enjoy with their body servants into Melville's analysis of Delano's attraction toward Negroes—an attraction that Melville significantly pronounces *not* philanthropical, though many a reader has doubtless misread him:

> But if there be that in the negro which exempts him from the inflicted sourness of the morbid or cynical mind, how, in his most prepossessing aspects, must he appear to a benevolent one? When at ease

30. As this language reveals, Delano's stereotype of the Negro puts too much emphasis on contentment and intellectual inferiority to be identified with the abolitionists' views, contrary to the assertions of critics like Simpson, "Melville and the Negro," 36–37. See Taylor, *Cavalier and Yankee*, Chap. 9, and Fredrickson, *Black Image in the White Mind*, Chap. 4, on the origins of this stereotype with the proslavery apologists and plantation novelists, who used it to romanticize the master-slave relationship and to show that blacks were content to remain slaves and incapable of staging a successful revolt.

with respect to exterior things, Captain Delano's nature was not only benign, but familiarly and humorously so. At home, he had often taken rare satisfaction in sitting in his door, watching some free man of color at his work or play. If on a voyage he chanced to have a black sailor, invariably he was on chatty and half-gamesome terms with him. In fact, like most men of a good, blithe heart, Captain Delano took to negroes, not philanthropically, but genially, just as other men to Newfoundland dogs.

Hitherto, the circumstances in which he found the San Dominick had *repressed the tendency*. But in the cuddy, *relieved* from his former uneasiness, and, for various reasons, more sociably inclined than at any previous period of the day, and seeing the colored servant, napkin on arm, *so debonair about his master, in a business so familiar* as that of shaving, too, all *his old weakness for negroes* returned. (BC, 41; italics added)

Delano finds the Negro "in his most prepossessing aspects" as a docile subordinate. Continually dismayed by "the noisy indocility of the blacks in general" aboard the *San Dominick*, Delano takes "humane satisfaction" in the "steady good conduct of Babo," whose "affectionate zeal" in waiting on his master "transmutes into something filial or fraternal acts in themselves but menial" (BC, 7–8, 27). Not only does Delano revel in "the beauty of that relationship which could present such a spectacle of fidelity on the one hand and confidence on the other"; he even approves of the "contrast in dress, denoting their relative positions" (BC, 13), that gives the slave coarse, patched trousers and a bare torso and the master an ornate toilet (one thinks of Frederick Douglass' bitter description of the slave's position: "he is clad in coarse and tattered raiment that another may be arrayed in purple and fine linen").[31] Though Delano "impulsively" pays tribute to the "royal spirit" of the intransigent slave Atufal (using the meaningful exclamation, "upon my conscience"), he is "annoyed" the next instant by Babo's "conversational familiarities," when the black implies something less than contentment at having been "only a poor slave" all his life (BC, 18–19). As for Delano's "benign" temperament, it is later cheered and reassured by the sight of a black man in chains (ironically, it is this same Atufal), which Delano takes as part of Nature's "benign aspect,"

31. From Douglass' "The Nature of Slavery," reprinted in *My Bondage and My Freedom*, 430.

testifying to an "ever-watchful Providence above" (BC, 54–55). Since at heart he so obviously acquiesces in slavery, even while cherishing illusions of moral superiority to slaveholders like Don Benito, it is not surprising that he offers, only half in jest, to buy Babo (BC, 27).

Yet underlying Delano's preference for the Negro in chains is an unmistakable sexual attraction toward the "naked nature" he thinks he sees in the Negro, whether embodied in the "colossal form" of Atufal or in a "slumbering negress . . . lying, with youthful limbs carelessly disposed" and nursing a "stark naked" baby at her "lapped breasts" (BC, 18, 29–30). The thought that the enslaved Negresses of the *San Dominick* might be "some of the very women whom Ledyard saw in Africa, and gave such a noble account of" does not sadden Delano, because he can safely admire them only in captivity. They incarnate the animal in himself—an animal that must at all costs be domesticated, but that, once domesticated, can be indulged with impunity. This is why the unruly circumstances in which he has found the blacks on the *San Dominick* have "repressed" his tendency to sport with them, whereas the spectacle of a black tame enough to be entrusted with the intimate task of shaving his master has restored "all his old weakness for negroes."

If, then, as should now be clear, Melville does not share Delano's view of the Negro, but exposes it as a projection of the white man's tabooed sexuality, what of Benito Cereno's view and the deposition that codifies it? As many critics have noted, Melville considerably rewrote the deposition he found in his source for "Benito Cereno," on the one hand accentuating the ferocity of the black rebels and hinting at an act so barbarous that "the deponent . . . so long as reason is left him, can never divulge" it (BC, 70), on the other hand toning down the account of the Spanish survivors' sanguinary vengeance by introducing palliating factors and whitewashing the Spanish captain.[32] Consequently, critics like Sidney Kaplan have accused Melville of pandering to current fears of the Negro as a bloodthirsty savage and substituting a far more pernicious racist stereotype for the one he discredits in Delano. But Melville's aim in making the

32. Kaplan, "Herman Melville and the American National Sin," 19–22; Widmer, *The Ways of Nihilism*, 70–71; Feltenstein, "Melville's 'Benito Cereno'" (reprinted in Runden [ed.], *Melville's "Benito Cereno,"* 126).

legal version of the slave revolt look so one-sided is surely to highlight the inherent one-sidedness of the original court records.[33] Though appearing more objective on the surface, the historical deposition, like Melville's fictional travesty of it, deals only with the secondary results of the slave revolt and shows a total failure to confront its primary cause. Admitting any other motive in the mutineers than sheer savagery bursting out of control would entail facing the unwelcome truth that no amount of freedom to "range within given bounds," as the San Dominick's slaves were allowed to do (BC, 12), would ever reconcile men to enslavement, nor any amount of force suffice permanently to keep them in chains. This in turn would mean acknowledging that justice necessarily takes the form of a charade when a society reposing on brute force tries and convicts those who defy it. Hence, far from serving to vindicate Benito Cereno and his fellow Spaniards as innocent victims of unmotivated brutality, the obviously biased testimony Melville ascribes to the Spanish captain reveals Don Benito as attempting to justify the status quo his slaves have disrupted and to canonize himself at their expense as a martyr whose kindliness and trust they have cruelly betrayed.

Consistently mistaking Don Benito's self-image for Melville's view of him, critics have almost unanimously seen Benito Cereno as "the good man, the religious man," reading "the blessed serenity of the Benedictine" into his name, imputing his destruction to his "good intentions," which have placed him " 'at cross-purposes in a world of . . . horrible and inscrutable inhumanities,' " and even identifying his agony, explicitly or implicitly, with Christ's.[34] While Don Benito does indeed wrap himself in the mantle of the New Testament, as did many of his fellow slaveholders in the American South when they sought to justify slavery,[35] the character type on

33. Guttmann, "Enduring Innocence of Delano," 186, argues similarly that Melville meant to discredit the deposition's "legalistic pretensions of objectivity" and subvert the "official and attested view of the matter." See also Dryden, Melville's Thematics of Form, 199–216, for an illuminating comparison of the deposition with the more obviously distorted official report at the end of Billy Budd.

34. Kaplan, "Melville and the American National Sin," 19–20; Max Putzel, "The Source and the Symbols of Melville's 'Benito Cereno,' " and Feltenstein, "Melville's 'Benito Cereno,' " both reprinted in Runden (ed.), Melville's "Benito Cereno," 161, 165, 130–31; and Franklin, The Wake of the Gods, 146–50.

35. Proslavery apologists contended, in the words of James H. Hammond, that "American slavery is not only not a sin, but especially commanded by God through Moses, and

which Melville models him is to be found neither in the Gospels nor in the *Lives of the Saints*, but in the contemporary plantation myth; for Don Benito corresponds in almost every respect to the literary stereotype of the southern gentleman dubbed by William R. Taylor "the Southern Hamlet."[36] "Introspective, given to brooding—one in whom the springs of action have become somehow impaired," this mythical figure, according to Taylor, traced his ancestry to a historical southerner, the Virginian John Randolph, who "set the pattern for the doomed Southerner in the same way that [Benjamin] Franklin had earlier set the pattern for the emergent Yankee." Like Don Benito, Randolph looked consumptive, suffered from ill health during much of his life, inclined towards "hypochondria" and "fits of madness," and sported a soldierly attire and "arrogant aristocratic manner" belied by sexual impotence. While Randolph, unlike Don Benito, did not die young, "he never matured physically" and retained a boyish appearance and "rich soprano voice" until his death of tuberculosis. Melville actually mentions the "chivalric Virginian, John Randolph" in *White-Jacket* (wj, 141), but he did not need to resort to any biography for his own version of the haunted southerner. As Taylor points out, Randolph's death in 1833 had "closely coincided with [the] first outburst of fiction about the plantation," and by 1855 the image he had helped spawn of the morbid southern gentleman was widely disseminated in northern as well as southern novels. Ambivalently incarnating the South's ideal of the sophisticated culture made possible by slavery, and its uneasy sense of that culture's flaws, the "Southern Hamlet" also expressed both the parvenu North's nostalgia for Old World gentility and its complacent sense of its own superior vigor. The former

---

approved by Christ through his apostles" (*The Pro-Slavery Argument*, 108). Nearly all the allusions that have been interpreted as identifying Don Benito with Christ are specifically Don Benito's, not Melville's. The exceptions are: (1) Don Benito's age, twentynine, which Melville retained from his source and reported in two contexts, the first (Delano's speculations about whether Don Benito is a bona fide gentleman) having nothing to do with Christ, the second (the end of the deposition), again representing Don Benito's self-description; (2) the allusion to Babo's hand on the table (bc, 47–48), which seems to recall Judas at the Last Supper until Melville explicitly compares it with the hand "on the wall" that had interrupted Belshazzar's feast to write out the doom of a kingdom "weighed in the balances, and . . . found wanting" (Dan. 5)—a symbol far more relevant to a tale of slave revolt; (3) Don Benito's death in a monastery on Mount Agonia, which suggests agony, but hardly Christian martyrdom or the crucifixion.

36. The following passage draws on Taylor, *Cavalier and Yankee*, 157–60.

aspect of the "Southern Hamlet" corresponds to Benito Cereno's self-image, the latter to the fantasies that Delano, long recognized among critics as the archetypal Yankee, projects onto his aristocratic interlocutor when he puzzles over whether Don Benito is a bona fide gentleman (BC, 20).

Granted that Melville intended his pitiable Spaniard to evoke the doomed southerner rather than the Man of Sorrows, we have yet to resolve the question: does Melville, like those of his fellow northerners who hankered after the southern cavalier, in any way endorse the cavalier's hopeless acquiescence in Negro slavery? More precisely, does he present Benito Cereno's view of the Negro as in any way more realistic than Delano's? The answer, I believe, lies in Benito Cereno's response to the slave ringleader who held him captive while masquerading as his "officious servant": "During the passage, Don Benito did not visit" Babo (by then safely chained in the hold). "Nor then, nor at any time after, would he look at him. Before the tribunal he refused. When pressed by the judges he fainted" (BC, 75). Benito Cereno, in short, proves incapable of facing the murderous rage that seethes beneath the Negro's apparent submission to enslavement and that threatens to erupt again and again in furious revolt as long as he remains a slave.

In Don Benito—averting his eyes from the Negro and repressing the memory of the symbolic castration he has undergone in being forced by his African captor to don the garb of the all-powerful slaveholder he no longer is, complete with a silver-mounted sword that is only an empty, "artificially stiffened" scabbard—Melville has created a trenchant symbol of the consistently escapist attitude southerners took toward all slave violence, whether individual or collective. Epitomized in the words "the negro" that comprise Benito Cereno's sole reply to the question Delano asks him after his rescue— "what has cast such a shadow upon you?"—the phantasm of the bloodthirsty black savage that had emerged from the Santo Domingo uprising haunted the southern mind only as an abstraction, paid lip service in such clichés as "the horrors of Santo Domingo." Whenever cases of arson, poisoning, physical retaliation, or insurrection vivified the phantasm, southerners responded with silence, denial, or externalization. Newspapers censored their accounts of many incidents and failed to report others. Liberal southerners like the

Charleston judge William Johnson, who condemned the excesses of the tribunal that executed thirty-five slaves for participating in the Denmark Vesey conspiracy, minimized or simply refused to believe evidence that favorite body servants could actually have plotted to murder their masters. The mass of slaveholders habitually treated outbreaks like the Nat Turner revolt as aberrations and blamed them on individual "fanatics" or the machinations of abolitionists.[37]

Although Benito Cereno manifests all three tendencies, externalization is the course he favors when he and Delano recapitulate the lessons of the San Dominick's tragedy:

> "You were with me all day; stood with me, sat with me, talked with me, looked at me, ate with me, drank with me; and yet, your last act was to clutch for a monster, not only an innocent man, but the most pitiable of all men. To such degree may malign machinations and deceptions impose. So far may even the best man err, in judging the conduct of one with the recesses of whose condition he is not acquainted. But you were forced to it; and you were in time undeceived. Would that, in both respects, it was so ever, and with all men." (BC, 74)

In other words, Benito Cereno's "moralizing" on the experience of enslavement to which he has been subjected constitutes nothing more than a self-pitying claim to being the innocent victim of a malign conspiracy, and a self-righteous warning against an outsider's capacity to judge him fairly. (One hears in his voice the paranoid accents of the antebellum slaveholder fending off northern criticism, as well as the sentimental accents of the postbellum plantation romancers and historians who represented the southern cavalier as the most tragic victim of slavery.) Meanwhile, the chief lesson Benito Cereno should have learned from his initiation into the feelings of a man who finds himself totally at the mercy of another man's will— that slavery is an intolerable condition—has completely eluded him. "The negro" has cast his shadow over Don Benito's spirit, but has left his mind as obtuse as ever.

37. See Freehling, Prelude to Civil War, Chap. 3, on South Carolinians' reactions to several important insurrection panics and to prospects of openly discussing slavery. Judge Johnson's and other representative southern and northern views are cited in Robert S. Starobin (ed.), Denmark Vesey: The Slave Conspiracy of 1822 (Englewood Cliffs, N.J., 1970), 67–91.

Revealingly, our generation has found it harder to see how little Benito Cereno has learned than to realize that Delano has learned nothing. We have pitted Delano's inability to "indulge in personal alarms, any way involving the imputation of malign evil in man" (BC, 1), against the disabused Don Benito's paranoid vision of evil centering in the Negro, and have pronounced him inferior to the Spaniard in insight. Embracing the Spaniard's paralyzing despair as the antidote to the Yankee's bland optimism, and the slaveholder's horror of Negro savagery as the answer to the Yankee's misplaced confidence in Negro docility and stupidity, we have forgotten that not Delano, but Don Benito and his friend Aranda, have acted on the fatal delusion that their slaves were tractable—just as historically it was not abolitionists or Yankees of Delano's ilk, but southern slaveholders, who proved the worst dupes of the myths they disseminated about the Negro.

Besides overrating Benito Cereno's discernment in relation to Delano's, we have faulted Delano for the wrong reasons. We have not charged him with shrugging off the universe's appalling indifference to the wrongs that engender such death struggles among its creatures. Instead, we have judged him naïve to dismiss the suffering on board the San Dominick that had originally aroused his sympathy as "more apparent than real," and to dissolve the horror of Don Benito's experience in the cheering sunlight of nature (BC, 74). Furthermore, the suffering we have most often reproached him for minimizing has been merely that of the master overmastered by his slaves, and the dark side we have chided him for overlooking in nature has been but the evil that Benito Cereno projects onto the Negro.[38]

If Melville ultimately discredits both captains' interpretations of the events in which they have participated and endorses neither's view of the Negro, what kind of statement about the outcome of black slavery in America does he then make in this grim tale of a thwarted slave revolt, and what view of the Negro does he project? The final vision of Babo's impaled head looming over the citadel of his moribund subjugator and meeting "unabashed, the gaze of the

38. Simpson, "Melville and the Negro," 33–35, states this indictment of Delano most explicitly, but many other critics have drawn a similar moral from the tale. See, for example, Widmer, The Ways of Nihilism, 86–87; Kaplan, "Melville and the American National Sin," 16–19, 25–26; and Putzel, "Source and Symbols of Melville's 'Benito Cereno,'" 166.

whites," certainly suggests that the Yankee and the slaveholder allied
against him have won but a hollow victory, and slavery but a temporary reprieve. More specifically, this ominous ending may also
expose the "compromise" the North had recently made with slavery,
by reaffirming her commitment to suppressing insurrections and
recapturing fugitives, as a futile attempt to postpone the day of
reckoning. The message it conveys might be paraphrased something
like this: "Even if we succeed in putting down more revolts of this
kind—and there are bound to be more—sooner or later we will
succumb to our own inner rot, and a Babo will preside over our
destruction."

As for the image of the Negro that emerges from the story's
emblematic culmination, only by remaining ambiguous, perhaps,
can it conform to the spirit of a narrative that forces the reader to
view the black man through racist lenses. What we think Melville
sees in Babo depends in the last analysis on what we ourselves see
in Babo's present-day avatars. Personally, I find Babo on the whole
a favorable portrayal of a black rebel, despite the fearsomeness with
which he is tinged in his role as white America's nemesis. In characterizing him, Melville counteracts most of the baneful stereotypes
his contemporaries propagated of the Negro. No mindless brute,
"the black—whose brain, not body, had schemed and led the revolt"
(BC, 75) stands out as by far the most intelligent character in "Benito
Cereno." Even as he enacts the part of Don Benito's symbolic executioner in the terrible shaving scene, Babo shows an artistry that
recalls an African heritage of civilization, rather than of barbarism;
for he seems "a Nubian sculptor finishing off a white statue-head"
(BC, 45).[39] Evoking another African civilization cited by abolitionists as proof that blacks had evolved high cultures in the past and
were capable of doing so in the future, Babo's "right hand man"
Atufal, the slave-king whose elaborate masquerade is Babo's handiwork, appears "monumentally fixed at the threshold, like one of

39. It is revealing of our white racist fantasies of black savagery that many critics have
responded only to the sinister overtones of the words "finishing off" (which reflect Delano's
state of mind), but have utterly missed the significance of portraying Babo as a traditional
African artist, rather than a savage. E.g., Kaplan, "Melville and the American National
Sin," 25.

those sculptured porters of black marble guarding the porches of Egyptian tombs" (BC, 49, 68).[40] Although Babo's guileful plotting and "voiceless end" have been said to cast him as a black Iago,[41] he surely does not share Iago's motiveless malevolence, since he avenges a wrong originally inflicted on him and seeks his enemy's ruin as the necessary means to his own freedom. As one recent critic has pointed out, "Babo's silence . . . expresses not only the intransigence of Negro rebels and voiceless black experience, but the status of black slaves in America," legally deprived of the right to make themselves heard, even in the courtroom.[42] One is reminded again of Frederick Douglass' poignant characterization of the slave's plight: "ask the slave what is his condition—what his state of mind—what he thinks of enslavement? and you had as well address your inquiries to the *silent dead*. There comes no *voice* from the enslaved."[43]

Some readers may argue that neither the emphasis on Babo's subtle intelligence nor the tributes to African culture keep Babo from striking an unsympathetic figure throughout the story. Granted the truth of this objection, the irony is, nevertheless, that most of our negative impressions of him are based either on the misconceptions of Delano or the distortions of Benito Cereno. On the one hand, the fawning servility Babo manifests turns out to be a masquerade adapted to Delano's expectations. On the other hand, Babo's cruelty—to the extent that it strikes us as peculiarly savage—is never actually visible to us, except possibly in the shaving scene, where it takes the form of psychological torture rather than physical brutality. (An irony of this scene that seems to have escaped many readers is that the man we see cringing under his slave's razor is

40. The Egyptians, described by Herodotus as woolly-haired and black, were the focal point of both abolitionist efforts to vindicate the Negro's claims to a civilized past, and of proslavery ethnologists' efforts to discredit them by establishing the Egyptians as a nonnegroid race (the debate also extended to the Nubians and other African peoples known to have achieved high civilizations). See Stanton, *The Leopard's Spots*, 50–51, 99; Frederickson, *Black Image in the White Mind*, 13–15, 74–82; Nott and Gliddon, *Types of Mankind*, Chaps. 5–8.
41. See Kaplan, "Melville and the American National Sin," 20; Nicol, "Iconography in 'Benito Cereno,'" 29; and Gilmore, *The Middle Way*, 167.
42. Jean Fagan Yellin, "Black Masks: Melville's 'Benito Cereno,'" *American Quarterly*, XXII (1970), 687–88.
43. From "The Nature of Slavery," in Douglass, *My Bondage and My Freedom*, 434.

merely undergoing ministrations that must have been part of his daily routine as a slaveholder, except that he, and not his slave, is now tasting their humiliations and feeling their threat to his manhood.) Our vivid sense of Babo's savagery derives only from Benito Cereno's allegation that Babo had the skeleton of Aranda prepared "in a way the negroes afterwards told the deponent, but which he, so long as reason is left him, can never divulge"—an innuendo which we are left to flesh out in accordance with our own primitive fears and fantasies. The sole objective glimpse Melville allows us of Babo discloses him surrendering with dignity to superior force of arms, continuing unshaken in his silent resistance, going to his death with the stoic resolution Melville most admired, and looking "unabashed" at the overlords who have burned his body to ashes without subduing his spirit.[44]

Moving as I find this glimpse, I do not believe one can honestly deduce from it an unequivocal endorsement of revolutionary violence as a means of ending slavery (to return to the issue I sidestepped at the outset). For one thing, it is characteristic of Melville that he cannot identify with Babo until he has met defeat. For another thing, whatever else Babo represents, he is clearly Melville's most powerful personification of the Negro as America's "black Angel of Doom."[45] The horror with which so many readers have reacted to this personification and to the ruthlessness of his vengeance cannot be wholly subjective; for Melville himself, as all the works we have so far examined patently indicate, had to contend with lifelong inhibitions against overthrowing the tyrannies and authorities he felt to be so repressive—inhibitions deep enough to make him vent his revulsion against the carnage of warfare even in the saga of the American Revolution that he had undertaken as a potboiler. The point is that Melville found himself as unable to countenance violence in a White-Jacket or a Steelkilt as in a Daggoo or a Babo, and that like the

44. As Melville wrote in *Redburn*, 291: "in every being's ideas of death, and his behavior when it suddenly menaces him, lies the best index to his life and his faith." Similar passages bespeaking the importance Melville attached to meeting death with "a firm lip" and "practical resolution" occur in *Mardi*, 585, and *Moby-Dick*, 284.

45. Cf. Daggoo, Fleece, and the "black Angel of Doom" Ishmael encounters in the Negro church in New Bedford; also Melville's Civil War poem "The Swamp Angel," which I discuss in Chap. 8, p. 264 herein.

Garrisonian abolitionists, he judged his forefathers' war for independence by the same standards as he did an attempt by black slaves to win their liberty. Hence while disputing the claim of some critics, that Melville champions the cause of slave revolt in "Benito Cereno," one can nevertheless exonerate him from the charges of racism that others have leveled at him for having exhibited slave revolt in such an appalling light.

This said, we cannot but recognize that Melville's qualms about resorting to arms to cut the Gordian knot of slavery left him as tragically paralyzed as most of his contemporaries in the face of the nation's most pressing moral and political dilemma. Though by 1855 the resolution toward which Melville had once urged his countrymen to aspire—the love marriage between America's Ishmaels and Queequegs that would spare the nation from paying the price of its sin—must have seemed more remote than ever, he still quailed at the conclusion he would reach after the Civil War: that "only through agonized violence could so mighty a result" as the abolition of slavery be accomplished.[46]

Before pronouncing a final judgment on the attitude toward slave revolt expressed in "Benito Cereno," we must realize that the story represents only half of a statement about the probable outcome of slavery in the New World. The other half, which Melville submitted to *Putnam's* four to six weeks later,[47] is contained in "The Bell-Tower."

The three epigraphs that preface "The Bell-Tower" announce its relationship to "Benito Cereno":

Like negroes, these powers own man sullenly; mindful of their higher master; while serving, plot revenge.

The world is apoplectic with high-living of ambition; and apoplexy has its fall.

Seeking to conquer a larger liberty, man but extends the empire of necessity.

The interplay between the two tales that these suggestive aphorisms

46. Herman Melville, *Battle-Pieces and Aspects of the War*, 268.
47. Leyda, *Melville Log*, II, 500–501.

lead us to expect begins right in the opening scene, which introduces a set of images that immediately remind us of the execution in which "Benito Cereno" culminates.[48] In place of the black head "fixed on a pole in the Plaza" (BC, 315), we find the base of a ruined tower that stands "central in a plain" and "at distance, seems the black mossed stump of some immeasurable pine" (BT, 223). The tower's fallen superstructure, looking like the "last-flung shadow of the [pine's] perished trunk," recalls both the shadow the Negro has cast over the dying Benito Cereno and the shadow Babo's gibbeted head casts over the churches of Lima. The dazzlingly white South American viceregal city that seals Babo's fate at the scaffold has given way to a "once frescoed capital" in the south of Europe, "now with dank mould cankering its bloom." Both the unnamed Italian capital, "enriched through commerce with the Levant" (BT, 224), and the dilapidated San Dominick, with its "Venetian-looking water-balconies" and its apparent relics of "superannuated Italian palaces" (BC, 241, 268), evoke Venice, a city Melville had explicitly compared to Lima in Moby-Dick (" 'Corrupt as Lima.' So, too, Venice" [MD, 215]). And the association with Venice, of course, places both "Benito Cereno" and "The Bell-Tower" against the backdrop of a more famous racial tragedy set in Venice—Shakespeare's Othello, which a number of critics have already linked with "Benito Cereno."[49]

These allusive parallels between the two stories continue to crop up from beginning to end in eerie detail. The ruined Italian tower is foreshadowed in a "castellated forecastle" on the San Dominick that "seemed some ancient turret . . . left to decay" (BC, 241). The bell tower's "metallic aviary," from which "birded chimes of silver throats had rung" (BT, 223), takes the unlikely form in "Benito Cereno" of an octagonal network overhanging the San Dominick's mainmasts "like three ruinous aviaries, in one of which was seen perched, on a ratlin, a white noddy" (BT, 241). As incongruously,

48. Kaplan, "Melville and the American National Sin," 30–31, was the first to point this out. To facilitate comparisons between "Benito Cereno" and "The Bell-Tower," all citations from both stories will hereafter be from Berthoff (ed.), Great Short Works of Herman Melville, and page references will be given parenthetically in the text.

49. Kaplan, "Melville and the American National Sin," 20; Nicol, "Iconography in 'Benito Cereno,'" 29; Gilmore, The Middle Way, 167. I am indebted to Nicol for the citation from Moby-Dick.

the spectators thronging the site of Bannadonna's mounting edifice cling to the scaffolding "like sailors on yards" (BT, 224), and the belfry, like a ship's hold, is entered through a "scuttle" (BT, 228). Bannadonna's state bell is "dented with mythological devices" (BT, 225), just as the shield-like stern piece of the *San Dominick* is "medallioned about by groups of mythological or symbolical devices" (BC, 241). His mysterious "domino"—calling to mind both the "throngs of dark cowls" peering over the *San Dominick*'s bulwarks and the role of "old dominies" played by the ship's black oakum-pickers (BC, 240, 253)—is hoisted into the belfry "wrapped in a dark sack or cloak" and later further concealed by a "coarse sheet of workman's canvas" (BT, 226–27), just as the skeletal figurehead of the *San Dominick* is hidden by "canvas wrapped about that part" of the ship (BC, 241). Even the "corroded and partly encrusted" earthen cup Bannadonna allegedly uses to "test the condition of metals in fusion" (BT, 226) finds a weird echo in the once gilt letters of the *San Dominick*'s name, now "streakingly corroded with tricklings of copper-spike rust" (BC, 241–42).

Although some of these verbal associations seem almost fanciful, the more significant ones thematically relate the major emblems of "The Bell-Tower" to the deceptive regime of "despotic command" aboard the *San Dominick*. These emblems are Bannadonna's state bell, fatally weakened "where man's blood had flawed it" (BT, 237), and the semihuman black robot he creates to ring it by "issuing from the sentry-box each sixty minutes; sliding along a grooved way, like a railway; advancing to the clock-bell, with uplifted manacles; striking it at one of the twelve junctions of the four-and-twenty hands; then wheeling, circling the bell and retiring to its post, there to bide for another sixty minutes" (BT, 235). The corresponding emblems in "Benito Cereno" are the *San Dominick*'s forecastle bell, with its "dreary grave-yard toll, betokening a flaw"—a bell rung by one of the ship's slaves—and the human version of Bannadonna's robot which the bell calls forth every two hours: the chained black slave Atufal whom Delano jokingly calls Benito Cereno's "tall man and time-piece," because he is "stationed" like a "sentry" to "abide" his master's coming, at which time, "slowly advancing towards the elevated poop," he enacts the ritual of "slowly raising both arms, let[ting] them lifelessly fall, his links clanking, his head bowed; as much as to say, ' . . . I am content'" (BC, 255–56, 289, 292).[50]

These parallels have several important functions, and analyzing them will take us straight to the fundamental questions that "The Bell-Tower" raises, in conjunction with "Benito Cereno," about the moral onus falling on each of the parties to a slave revolt, whether individual or collective: the slave rebel himself, the master against whom he retaliates, the slaveholding society that punishes him, and the state whose representatives aid and abet the master class in putting down revolts. First, the role played by the flawed bell and programmed man/timepiece in each tale serves to amplify and shed light on its meaning in the other. Thus the unexplained, yet strangely ominous flaw in the *San Dominick*'s forecastle bell finds elucidation in the human blood that mars Bannadonna's state bell when he kills a frightened worker in the process of casting it; conversely, the sound the *San Dominick*'s bell emits, "as of the tolling for execution in some jail-yard" (BC, 291), reverberates ironically through the casting of the great state bell that is to grace the "noblest Bell-Tower in Italy"—"deemed no small triumph" for Bannadonna and "one, too, in which the state might not scorn to share" (BT, 224–25). Similarly, the living slave who acts as a timepiece in "Benito Cereno" reinforces the implication that Bannadonna's vaunted automaton may be a human being reduced to robot condition by slavery. At the same time, the relationship between Bannadonna and the mechanical creature that kills him by being "true to its creation, and true to its heedful winding up" (BT, 236), only to be in turn destroyed by the state's magistrates, redefines the multiple levels of the masquerade Atufal stages to decoy Delano into thinking Benito Cereno controls the *San Dominick*'s slaves. Belying the black's pose as a slave, chained by his master to break his spirit, is his actual status as a rebel leader, ready to drop his assumed chains in a flash; yet that ephemeral mastery is itself poignantly belied by the ultimate truth his masquerade conveys—that he is in fact still a slave, destined to be crushed by the master class he has sought to overthrow.

A second function served by the complementary symbolism of "Benito Cereno" and "The Bell-Tower" is to redress the moral

---

50. Nicol, "Iconography in 'Benito Cereno,'" 26, was the first to point out the continuity of these emblems from "Benito Cereno" to "The Bell-Tower."

imbalance many readers have felt the earlier tale creates by focusing on a savage slave revolt without dramatizing the day-to-day brutality of slavery itself.[51] Whereas in "Benito Cereno" Melville chooses to show us slavery only through the distorting media of Delano's stereotypes, the Spanish court's one-sided judgment, and Don Benito's self-pity, in "The Bell-Tower" he confronts us directly with a slave society's naked contempt for human values. We see Bannadonna strike a terrified worker in cold blood without even turning aside from his work long enough to notice that his blow has killed the man. We see him disdain to acknowledge the bloodguilt that has stained his tribute to the republic, except by attempting to conceal the "blemish." We see judge, priest, and public opinion unite in overlooking his homicide, indeed in romanticizing it as an act of "esthetic passion" attesting the spirit of a noble—"a kick from an Arabian charger; not sign of vice, but blood." We see the republic sanctioning his crime in the name of its glory by "honoring the tower and its builder with another holiday" (BT, 225).

Such incidents form a pattern in "The Bell-Tower" that reveals them to be characteristic of this society. After completing the tower, Bannadonna withdraws into "more than usual solitude" to perfect its belfry. Although this seclusion arouses suspicions that his work must involve something sinister—suspicions quite warranted by Bannadonna's previous record—no one interferes until it is presumably too late to undo the damage. Only when a mysterious piece of statuary, which a "shrewd old blacksmith" surmises to be "but a living man" (BT, 226), is publicly lifted up to the belfry and seems "almost of itself to step into" it, do the authorities take it upon themselves to investigate their architect's activities. Even then, the inquiry seems doomed before it begins, relegated as it is to "the chief-magistrate of the town, with an associate"—men who have a stake in vindicating the architect they have commissioned and already once exonerated, and who, to boot, are "both elderly men" (BT, 226), as Melville pointedly tells us, leaving us to infer that they must be none too keen-sighted. How timidly these worthies undertake their probe, "not without demur from Bannadonna." How easily they repress the misgivings occasioned by all the omens that

51. See, for example, Matthiessen, *American Renaissance*, 508; Kaplan, "Melville and the American National Sin," 20; and Widmer, *The Ways of Nihilism*, 72–73.

humanity is again being sacrificed to Bannadonna's art and the state's glory: the impression the cloaked statue gives them of changing its position; the unraveled look of the cloth covering the top of the statue, as if to provide ventilation near its head; Bannadonna's "equivocal reference to the object" as "him," quickly amended to "*it*"; and the mysterious noises they and others hear of footfalls and "half-suppressed screams and plainings" in the belfry (BT, 226–30).[52] The magistrates all but admit that the state's "interest" in Bannadonna's "success" at immortalizing it overrides any moral scruples they might have about the means he uses (BT, 227–28).

That "interest" likewise prevents the magistrates from reexamining the state's commitment to what Bannadonna has stood for after he has failed. Making much the same point abolitionists did about the corrosive effect slavery had on the morals of both the nation that tolerated it and the society that practised it,[53] Melville shows how thoroughly the callous disregard for justice that has allowed the state's highest officers to gloss over Bannadonna's trespasses pervades their republic. Thus when a "dull, mangled sound" greets the multitude assembled for the first ringing of the state bell, and the magistrates discover Bannadonna "prostrate and bleeding" at its base, with his automatic bell ringer "impending over him, like Jael over nailed Sisera" (BT, 231), their first impulse is not to inquire into the causes of the débacle, but to cover up the vulnerability Bannadonna's defeat has revealed in their society. They might avail themselves of an opportunity to verify at last their impression that Bannadonna has somehow violated the republic's laws, perhaps by passing off a human being as an automaton; they might seek to learn how and why this ambiguous automaton has felled its creator, and whether it has done so accidentally or in deliberate retaliation for something to which Bannadonna has subjected it. Instead, the magistrates destroy Bannadonna's invention on the spot and bury it at sea—"Nor to any after urgency, even in free convivial hours, would [they] ever disclose the full secrets of the belfry" (BT, 232).

In short, the magistrates behave very much as we have seen the

---

52. See Fisher, *Going Under*, 100–101, and Dillingham, *Melville's Short Fiction*, 217–18, for similar interpretations of this evidence that Haman may be either "a machine with human attributes, or a human viewed in a mechanistic, subhuman way" (Fisher's words).

53. See, for examples, Barnes and Dumond (eds.), *Weld-Grimké Letters*, I, 244, 367–68; and Martineau, *Society in America*, II, 320–36.

Spanish court in "Benito Cereno" behave when it tries and executes the rebels without ever raising the question of what motivates slaves to make such desperate, murderous attempts to throw off their masters' yokes. They also exhibit the same escapist tendency Benito Cereno does after his rescue in refusing ever again to lay eyes on Babo or to speak of the emasculation he has endured at Babo's hands. What both the magistrates and Benito Cereno are unable to face is the mocking specter of the retribution impending over their society, forever belying its self-idealization as an earthly paradise of benevolent masters and contented slaves, forever warning that the days of its hegemony are numbered.

The magistrates, however, are guilty of more than moral cowardice; for they also reenact Bannadonna's crime in the effort to conceal it. Apparently one of the secrets of the belfry is the evidence they have suppressed that Bannadonna's mechanical slave may indeed be animate. Intimately associated with the fate of the automaton is a spaniel that has followed the magistrates into the belfry "unbeknown to them" (BT, 231). An age-old byword for the cowering, abject slave,[54] the spaniel seems to merge with its mechanical counterpart in death. Some aver, Melville reports, that the shot the crowd hears fired in the belfry was aimed not at the mysterious automaton but at "the spaniel, gone mad by fear" (BT, 232). Whatever the case, the spaniel is never seen again and "for some unknown reason" shares the burial of the automaton. The relationship Melville establishes between spaniel and automaton suggests that rather than merely destroying a robot, the magistrates may be taking revenge on a living slave, or engaging in such reprisals as often victimized innocent slaves in the wake of insurrection panics.[55] The joint burial of spaniel and automaton also hints darkly at a national effort to expunge the traces of an unsuccessful state-sponsored robotization of man by eliminating its victims—perhaps a metaphor for the recurrent American fantasy of doing away with the Negro along with slavery.[56]

54. OED; Melville uses the word in this sense in Redburn, 59: "They all . . . cringed and fawned about him like so many spaniels."
55. An example is the indiscriminate "'slaughter of many blacks without trial and under circumstances of great barbarity'" in the midst of the Nat Turner panic, cited by Herbert Aptheker, American Negro Slave Revolts (New York, 1969), 301.
56. For penetrating analyses of two forms this fantasy took, see Jordan, White Over Black, 567, on the colonization scheme, and Fredrickson, Black Image in the White Mind,

As the sequel reveals, the state has learned so little from the portent of Bannadonna's fate that, having shrouded his fiasco in secrecy, it sanctions his crimes anew, thereby dooming itself to share in his downfall. Just as the republic earlier honored its architect with a national holiday after absolving him of homicide, so it now decrees Bannadonna a "stately funeral," "not unmindful of [his] rare genius" (BT, 236). But the "powerful peasant" the state hires to toll Bannadonna's bell proves as recalcitrant as his mechanical prototype, bringing the great bell crashing to the ground with "one concentrate jerk" of the rope. This final omen of something fundamentally amiss in the edifice commissioned as the national emblem goes unheeded. The state has the bell recast without investigating the source of its weakness, which turns out, of course, to be the spot "where man's blood had flawed it" (BT, 237). Appropriately, the nation reaps the consequences "on the first anniversary of the tower's completion," when an earthquake destroys bell and belfry alike (BT, 236–37). Never will the blighted republic recover the lost promise of that "high hour of renovated earth" when it had offered mankind the hope of a new beginning (BT, 224).

So far we have seen how the picture "The Bell-Tower" provides of a society that supports slavery redefines Benito Cereno's and the Spanish court's reactions to the slave revolt on board the *San Dominick*. It is above all through Bannadonna, however, who exhibits the slaveowner's ruthless power lust stripped of its glamorous, courtly veneer, that "The Bell-Tower" counterpoises the benign image of the gentleman slaveowner seemingly projected by "Benito Cereno." Significantly, Bannadonna does not boast the aristocratic lineage that is apparently Don Benito's birthright. Instead, he is a "foundling" (BT, 223), uncannily fitting William R. Taylor's description of the "effective characters" that plantation novelists contrasted with the refined, but feckless, cavalier: characters "apt to be 'orphans' . . . or men of mixed, unknown or unspecified ancestry."[57] As a foundling promoted to the status of a gentleman, Bannadonna also reminds us that all noble lineages arise from humble and sometimes ignoble origins—an irony on which Melville had

---

Chap. 5, on nineteenth-century theories about how "the free operation of 'natural laws' might lead to the extinction of the Negro" in North America.

57. Taylor, *Cavalier and Yankee*, 154.

expatiated in *Pierre*,[58] and which gives another twist to Delano's suspicion that Don Benito might not, after all, be a "Castilian Rothschild," but a "low-born adventurer," "playing a part above his real level" (BC, 258).

Bannadonna acts as a foil to Don Benito in other respects as well. With his arrogance and "sudden transports of . . . passion," he recalls the "Southern Hothead," the literary antithesis, and often the double, according to Taylor, of the languid, brooding, morbid southern Hamlet, to whom Don Benito corresponds.[59] He also embodies the opposite extreme of Don Benito's impotent, effeminate sexuality, symbolized by the empty, "artificially stiffened" scabbard the Spaniard has been compelled by his African captor to sport in lieu of a sword. Accordingly, the emblem of Bannadonna's sexuality is the tower that has "soar[ed] into Shinar aspirations" and borne the consequences, and his name, as Marvin Fisher has suggested, implies that he "dispenses with woman."[60] In Bannadonna, the normal instinct of procreation has been perverted into the ambition to "rival" nature by inventing a substitute for her highest creature, to "outstrip her" by reproducing himself independently, "asking no favors from any element or any being," and ultimately to "rule her" by "stocking the earth with a new serf" totally amenable to his will—an "all-accomplished Helot" combining the contradictory "excellences" of all nature's creatures, without any of their drawbacks: "more useful than the ox, swifter than the dolphin, stronger than the lion, more cunning than the ape, for industry an ant, more fiery than serpents, and yet, in patience, another ass" (BT, 233–34).

Bannadonna's phallic fixation on bell towers has directly engendered this ambition.[61] He has been in the habit of gazing up at old-fashioned belfries and observing the way their "exposed" bells are rung by "stalwart watchmen," the chief fascination of the scene

58. *Pierre*, Bk. I, Chap. 3, discussed in Chap. Four, 94–95 herein.
59. Taylor, *Cavalier and Yankee*, 159.
60. Fisher, *Going Under*, 101.
61. My understanding of the psychosexual symbolism of "The Bell-Tower" is based on H. Bruce Franklin's provocative essay in *Future Perfect: American Science Fiction of the Nineteenth Century* (New York, 1966), 141–50. For a different psychoanalytic interpretation, see Jacqueline A. Costello and Robert J. Kloss, "The Psychological Depths of Melville's 'The Bell-Tower,'" *ESQ: A Journal of the American Renaissance*, XIX (1973), 254–61.

being the "purely Punchinello aspect" the watchmen acquire through the distortions of perspective: "Perched on a great mast or spire, the human figure, viewed from below, undergoes such a reduction in its apparent size, as to obliterate its intelligent features. It evinces no personality. Instead of bespeaking volition, its gestures rather resemble the automatic ones of the arms of a telegraph" (BT, 233). In short, Bannadonna finds himself attracted to the sight of man robbed of everything that makes him human, man transformed into a laughable puppet. This is what inspires him to "devise some metallic agent" to usurp the living watchman's function and "strike the hour, with its mechanic hand, with even greater precision than the vital one." Not content with reproducing the "Punchinello" of his fantasies, however, Bannadonna wishes to complete his triumph over nature by restoring to his puppet "the appearance, at least, of intelligence and will" (BT, 233); for to dominate a creature seemingly capable of resisting is infinitely more satisfying than to control a mere machine.

Thus Bannadonna enacts the sadistic counterpart of the passive homosexual fantasies which the sight of the "hypochondriac Benito Cereno" being shaved by his slave prompts in Delano. Through Bannadonna, as through Delano and Don Benito, Melville associates slavery with sexual perversion and hints that it is the systematic fulfillment of an urge to debase and exploit other human beings.

As Bannadonna's preferred form of sexual exploitation differs from the form Delano unconsciously fancies—which has ironically entrapped Don Benito—so, too, does the proslavery ideology in terms of which Bannadonna conceives his "iron slave" differ from the romanticized image of the master-slave relationship, derived from plantation fiction, that colors Delano's perceptions of Don Benito and Babo. Representing the Negro as a quasi-indestructible beast of burden, in contrast to the affectionate and tractable child that plantation romancers limned, this hard-nosed proslavery ideology took its cue from the "science" more apt to attract a "practical materialist" like Bannadonna—ethnology. Its chief spokesman was Samuel Cartwright, who had made it his mission to "prove" that certain alleged "peculiarities" of mind and body, which he insinuated made the Negro appear to be an intermediary species between man and ape, especially adapted him to slavery and disqualified him for any other status.[62]

The "experimental automaton" Bannadonna determines to design neither "after the human pattern, nor any animal one, nor after the ideals . . . of ancient fable" (BT, 234–35) serves the same purpose as the phantasmal Negro that Cartwright and his ilk fashioned to meet their needs as slaveowners and reflects a kindred "utilitarian ambition collaterally extended" (BT, 234). Accordingly, Bannadonna confines his creature in manacles like a slave and equips it with a skin that appears as impervious to hard usage as some proslavery apologists claimed the Negro's to be:[63] "a scaly mail, lustrous as a dragon-beetle's" (BT, 231–32). Outdoing his ideological counterparts in their negation of the Negro's humanity, he goes so far as to deny that his automaton is even animate. When the investigating magistrates think they hear human footfalls in the belfry, Bannadonna identifies the sound as mortar that has fallen out of "its place" in the tower's stone-work—an explanation blatantly affirming that a slave's life serves but to uphold the edifice of the state.[64] To allay the magistrates' scruples, he further assures them they hear "no soul"—another implication of proslavery ideology to which Melville had earlier objected in *Mardi*, as Marvin Fisher has pointed out. The very name that Bannadonna assigns his creature—"Haman"— conveys his idea of it as no more than a "half-man," to quote Fisher again, and clearly associates that idea with the Negro, generally considered a descendant of the biblical Ham. It also applies to Bannadonna the lesson of the biblical Haman's downfall—that oppressors end up on the gallows they prepare for their victims, becoming in every sense the soulless creatures to which they have tried to reduce others.[65]

62. Paraphrased from Cartwright's "How to Save the Republic, and the Position of the South in the Union," *De Bow's Review*, XI (August, 1851), 186.

63. See, for examples, Cartwright, *Essays*, 15–16, 18–20; Estes, *Defence of Negro Slavery*, 63, 135; and *The Pro-Slavery Argument*, 128–29.

64. This notion reached its most explicit formulation in the notorious Senate speech of March 4, 1858, in which James H. Hammond propounded the necessity of a menial class as the "very mud-sill of society"; cited in Jenkins, *Pro-Slavery Thought*, 286–87.

65. Fisher, *Going Under*, 99–101. Abolitionists cited Haman as typifying the slaveholder's "lust of power" and determination to crush opposition to his will. See, for example, Theodore Dwight Weld, *American Slavery As It Is: Testimony of a Thousand Witnesses* (1839; rpt. New York, 1969), 111.

Bannadonna further illustrates another lesson abolitionists drew from slavery—that "arbitrary power . . . wrought . . . its mystery of iniquity" in all who exercised it, inflaming the tempers of slave-holders and making them as unable to brook criticism from their peers as from their slaves.[66] Hence Bannadonna's whole attitude toward life is permeated by the contempt for human dignity and the passion for total mastery that have driven him to fashion a creature destined solely to execute his will. We have already noticed how Bannadonna's conception of his slave pertains to the workers he treats so callously. More subtly revealing is his reaction to the magistrates' observation that the face of Una, the first of the "gay girls" personifying the hours on his clock-bell, does not look joyous, as he had intended, but strangely fateful (BT, 228–29). Although Bannadonna retorts by paying lip service to the "law in art" that defies complete realization of the artist's intentions, he subsequently betrays that he cannot tolerate the thought of losing control over his creations, any more than he can bear having other people perceive them differently from the way he wants them perceived. Far from prompting him to heed the warning he has unconsciously registered through his art, the magistrates' criticism only exacerbates Bannadonna's need to impose his own version of reality on the world. And this need proves his downfall: while he is trying to "abate that strange look of Una" by retouching her features, his automatic bell ringer has "left its post precisely at the given moment; along its well-oiled route, slid noiselessly toward its mark; and, aiming at the hand of Una, to ring one clangorous note, dully smote the intervening brain of Bannadonna" (BT, 235–36).

As the dupe of the untroubled picture he insists on projecting of his society, and the victim of a monster he himself has created and integrated into that picture, Bannadonna redefines Don Benito's and his friend Aranda's belief that their slaves are tractable. We now see that this belief is a denial of their society's oppressiveness, rather than a denial of the Negro's capacity for malevolence, and that like Bannadonna, and like the southern apologists of slavery who loom behind them all, Don Benito and Aranda have fallen prey to a myth they have evolved to mask from themselves, as well as from outsiders,

66. Weld, *Slavery As It Is*, 185, 210.

the evil of reducing men to puppets. If the tormented Don Benito, unlike the overbearing Bannadonna, remains pitiable in our eyes, Bannadonna's personification of a more sinister type of southern slaveholder nevertheless reminds us that the slave system did not take its keynote from the southern Hamlet's pathetic qualms, but from the stern dictates of practical materialists.

Similarly, Bannadonna's mechanistic concept of the "iron slave" that ultimately destroys him redefines the Negro Benito Cereno would have us see as an incarnate fiend. The cumulative effect of the rhetoric by which Bannadonna dehumanizes his creature is ironically to absolve it of all responsibility for its master's death. In contrast to Babo, the ambiguous "Haman" emerges as neither devil nor hero, but as impersonal agent. The long account of how this automaton has been programmed to work—an account which directly precedes the horrific tableau of the creature "impending over Bannadonna, as if whispering some post-mortem terror," and which rationally explains how the catastrophe occurred (BT, 235-36)— tends to transmute the slave's revenge into a mechanical process invested with an almost Marxian inevitability. Consequently, the trauma of slave revolt that dominates "Benito Cereno" recedes into the background in "The Bell-Tower," and with it the anguish of the overpowered master class. Instead, the latter tale focuses on the ineluctable manner in which the master class brings about its own downfall.

This leads us to the final purpose served by the complementary symbolism associating the fate of the once ornate *San Dominick* with that of the "once frescoed" South European capital fallen into decay since the collapse of the tower embodying its "Shinar aspirations"— the purpose of completing the cycle of retribution temporarily arrested at the end of "Benito Cereno," when the Spanish master class reasserts its ascendancy over the defeated black rebels. "The Bell-Tower," in effect, begins where "Benito Cereno" leaves off, fulfilling the doom Babo's "unabashed" gaze portends for the society that has cemented its dominion with his blood. As we have seen, the first of the cardinal emblems linking the two stories—the manacled "tall man and time-piece" who seconds the thwarted revolt in "Benito Cereno" and becomes the instrument of his master's destruction in "The Bell-Tower"—symbolically carries out the doom of the slaveholding class itself. The second of these emblems, however, extends that doom beyond the southern capitals of slavery to the republic whose fictional Yankee representative in "Benito Cereno," like his historical counterparts of the 1850s, has demonstrated his commitment to supporting slavery by crushing a slave insurrection and pursuing fugitive slaves; for the flawed bell betokening the *San Dominick*'s hidden weakness becomes in "The Bell-Tower" an "icon" which, as several critics have noted, poignantly recalls that northern voice of America's pristine credo, the Liberty Bell.[67]

Like Bannadonna's mammoth handiwork, to which the "public spirit" of the leading citizens has contributed, the Liberty Bell, commissioned for the Philadelphia statehouse and first rung to celebrate the Declaration of Independence, was defectively cast from the start and continued to be plagued with fractures in spite of being recast three times. Its two most memorable fractures likewise occurred on solemn national occasions commemorating great statesmen who happened to be slaveholders. Just as the state bell, of which Bannadonna is persistently called "the founder," cracks when tolled for his own funeral and is irretrievably damaged "on the first anniversary" of his edifice's completion, so the Liberty Bell had cracked once while tolling for the death of the eminent jurist who had forged the basis for American constitutional law, Chief Justice John Marshall of Virginia, and had fissured beyond repair on the birthday of America's Founding Father, George Washington. But the crowning parallel between Bannadonna's state bell and the Liberty Bell was the broken moral promise the Liberty Bell's flaw bespoke. After all, the Liberty Bell had once boldly heralded the declaration of all men's equal and inalienable rights to life, liberty, and the pursuit of happiness. Moreover, it bore a biblical inscription which, as abolitionists pointed out, specifically enjoined the freeing of slaves: "Proclaim liberty throughout all the land unto all the inhabitants thereof."[68] Yet America's Founding Fathers had not seen

67. Franklin, *Future Perfect*, 149; Fisher, *Going Under*, 102; Adler, "Melville's *Benito Cereno*," 45.

68. Theodore Dwight Weld, *The Bible Against Slavery* . . . (New York, 1837), 57–58, explained that this command applied to the semicentennial Jubilee festival, on which occasion the Hebrews were to free all their slaves. As the U.S. approached its second Jubilee, a post–Civil War historian of the Liberty Bell rejoiced that the "Divine Command" inscribed on the bell "is about now to be obeyed to the letter," making the nation's first

fit to apply either the political or the religious precept to their own slaves. A mind imbued, as Melville's was, with the Puritan habit of reading sermons in stones could not but have drawn a moral from the perpetual muteness to which the Liberty Bell had been condemned, could not but have construed it as divine retribution for the sin of perverting God's word. Hence in "The Bell-Tower," Melville held up the fate of the Liberty Bell as an omen both of the hidden vulnerability that would prove the slave system's undoing and of the extinction that threatened the American republic if it failed to repair its moral flaw and make good its pledge of freedom to all mankind.

Now that we have examined the evidence for reading "The Bell-Tower" as a companion-piece to "Benito Cereno," and ascertained how such a reading modifies and enhances our understanding of both, we must nevertheless confront the fact that Melville chose not to publish these twin tales as a diptych. Although written later, "The Bell-Tower" appeared two months earlier than the first installment of "Benito Cereno" in *Putnam's Monthly*; and when Melville brought out an anthology of his magazine sketches the following year, he sandwiched two other stories between "Benito Cereno" and "The Bell-Tower," as if to disavow the connection between them, and even suppressed the epigraphs that had so clearly invited the reader to interpret the magazine version of "The Bell-Tower" as a parable about slave revolt.[69]

Given the marked preference we have noticed in Melville's mature fiction for subverting rather than offending the reader's prejudices, it would be easy to explain his subsequent effort to divorce the two tales he had so painstakingly interwoven as merely another instance of his covertness in dealing with controversial subjects. Such an explanation, however, skirts the question raised by the striking disequilibrium in length and quality that, in the last analysis, militates against putting "The Bell-Tower" on a par with "Benito Cereno," as the second half of a true diptych. Despite its ambitious

centennial truly a "'Jubilee' unto us and unto all men." See Frank M. Etting, "The Old Liberty Bell," *American Historical Record*, II (1873), 13.

69. Herman Melville, *The Piazza Tales* (New York, 1856). See also Melville's correspondence with his publishers about the proposed order of the stories in the collection, which he originally wanted to entitle *Benito Cereno & Other Sketches* (although even at this stage he apparently did not contemplate placing "The Bell-Tower" right after "Benito Cereno"), in Davis and Gilman (eds.), *Letters of Melville*, 177–79.

conception, "The Bell-Tower" conspicuously fails to match the sustained development of a companion-piece five times as long, and its stiff and artificial prose, the bane of many a reader,[70] falls sadly short of the supple, suggestive rhetoric that makes "Benito Cereno" so compelling. Epitomizing this disparity, the conclusion of "The Bell-Tower," which reduces its penetrating insights to a pat set of adages, seems uncomfortably anticlimactic beside the portentous final tableau of Babo's execution and his master's death. Nor is the contrived, Hawthornesque vagueness and ambiguity with which Melville surrounds the magistrates' demolition of Bannadonna's robot nearly so effective as the insinuations of unspeakable atrocities that vivify Babo's reign of terror aboard the *San Dominick*.

These telling symptoms may mean that the emotional sources of Melville's imagination could not fully uphold the verdict his conscience apparently delivered when it impelled him to counterbalance the forbidding picture of slave revolt he had drawn in "Benito Cereno" with a dispassionate historical justification of it. Whether or not "The Bell-Tower" proves to be an artistically adequate companion-piece, however, it does spell out the warning Melville had left implicit in "Benito Cereno"—that unless slavery were abolished, the irreconcilable conflict between a white master class blinded with racism and a black slave population seething with hatred would culminate in the ruin of the flawed republic he loved.

If Melville's tales of the 1850s refrain from glorifying the violent overthrow of slavery they present as inevitable, and portray rebels far less attractively than the preceding novels, their racial message remains as radically egalitarian. The characters Melville created in these tales—Oberlus, the Dog-King, and their slaves; the bachelors of Old and New England and the "sheet-white" girls they exploit; Don Benito and Delano, Babo and Atufal; Bannadonna, the magistrates who support him, and the robot who destroys him—all contradict the baneful stereotypes of master and slave, white and black, that were blinding Melville's contemporaries to the apocalyptic retribution they were bringing on themselves. All expose the master class's racial categories and hierarchies as arbitrary fictions

70. George William Curtis, who reviewed "The Bell-Tower" for *Putnam's*, nearly turned it down on the grounds of style (Leyda, *Melville Log*, II, 502). See also Berthoff's prefatory note to "The Bell-Tower" in *Great Short Works*, 223. Nevertheless, "The Bell-Tower" was popular enough with Melville's contemporaries to be his most reprinted story.

that do more violence to human nature than the vengeful passions destined to obliterate them. Whatever the pessimism with which Melville regarded his compatriots, white and black alike, he never wavered in his commitment to a unitary view of the human race. Indeed, he reaffirmed that commitment more militantly than ever in a sketch published a week after *The Piazza Tales* went to the printer's with the ominous link between "Benito Cereno" and "The Bell-Tower" edited out of it—a savage parody of scientific racist writings called "The 'Gees."

SIX ╱𝒜 Stranger Need Have a Sharp Eye to Know a 'Gee: A Riposte to Scientific Racism

OF ALL Melville's works, "The 'Gees" has received least attention, even from critics interested in his racial views.[1] Yet this deceptively flippant sketch, covering a mere two and a half pages in fine print of the March, 1856, issue of *Harper's Monthly*, furnishes one of the best keys to the radical beliefs Melville held about race and to his distinctive mode of inculcating those beliefs in his readers.[2] It encapsulates Melville's technique of creating fictional analogues for the Negro and illustrates more clearly than any other work his use of caricature, burlesque, and parody to jolt

---

1. To date, there have been only four published discussions of "The 'Gees," besides my article "Melville's 'The 'Gees': A Forgotten Satire on Scientific Racism," *American Quarterly*, XXVII (1975), 421–42, of which this chapter is a slightly expanded version. They are: Kaplan, "Melville and the American National Sin," 31–32, which takes the sketch literally as a "tasteless" slur on the Cape Verdeans; Berthoff's prefatory note to "The 'Gees" in *Great Short Works of Herman Melville*, 355, which suggests its relevance to the exploitation of workers and slaves; R. Bruce Bickley, Jr., *The Method of Melville's Short Fiction* (Durham, 1975), 56–58, which argues that the "rhetorical focus of the sketch" is on the narrator's bigotry; and Dillingham, *Melville's Short Fiction*, 357–59, which contends that "the sketch is in reality a veiled depiction of the rudementary [*sic*] average man," for whom the 'Gee is a "metaphor." Page references for all citations from "The 'Gees" will be to the Berthoff text.

2. According to Merton M. Sealts, Jr., "Melville's Short Fiction," *ESQ: A Journal of the American Renaissance*, XXV (1st Qt., 1979), 57, note 19, "The 'Gees" was submitted to *Harper's* in September, 1854. If so, Melville must have been referring to "The 'Gees" in his letter of September 18 [1854?], which informs the editors of *Harper's* that he has sent them "a brace of fowl—wild fowl," and comments, "Hope you will like the flavor."("A brace" fits Melville's mention of "*The two 'Gees*" early in the sketch, while "the flavor" seems to allude to the 'Gees' "wild, marine, gamy savor.") See Davis and Gilman (eds.), *Letters of Melville*, 172.

readers into recognizing the grotesque distortions inherent in their racist stereotypes. Challenging readers to distinguish a possibly mythical creature from other human beings on the basis of slippery physical and behavioral criteria, "The 'Gees" is also a miniature dress rehearsal for the far more ambitious work Melville published the following year: *The Confidence-Man: His Masquerade.*

First and foremost, however, "The 'Gees" is a response to the growing popularity of the racial theories embodied in Josiah C. Nott's and George R. Gliddon's *Types of Mankind*, which by 1856 had already gone through seven editions.[3] In "The 'Gees," Melville parodies the format and style of the ethnologists' treatises on the Negro, while purporting to describe a curious race he has encountered in his "sea-goings." Inhabiting the Portuguese colony of Fogo, one of the Cape Verde Islands, off the West African coast, this race constitutes an almost exact counterpart of the American Negro in ethnic origin and social status. At the same time, Melville's version of its history fuses the Negro with his foil in ethnological studies, the American Indian, whose fortunes had been intertwined with the Negro's ever since the Spaniards had begun importing African slaves into their American colonies to replenish the stock of Indian laborers they had so rapidly depleted.[4]

Melville characterizes the natives of Fogo as the product of three centuries' amalgamation between "an aboriginal race of negroes" and a group of Portuguese convicts resettled in their midst. Known among seamen as " 'Gees," these islanders, Melville informs us, have

3. Joseph Sabin's *Bibliotheca Americana: A Dictionary of Books Relating to America, from Its Discovery to the Present Time* (29 vols.; New York, 1868–1936), XIII, 441, lists seven editions by 1855—a prodigious number for such an expensive volume.
4. Melville's history of the 'Gees may be based partially on an eighteenth-century travelogue attributed to Daniel Defoe: *The Four Years Voyages of Capt. George Roberts . . . With a . . . Description and Draught of the Cape de Verd Islands . . .* (London, 1726). This is the only informative source I have found to which he might have had access (I have canvassed all books on the Cape Verdes catalogued at the Library of Congress, and their bibliographies, as well as all articles listed in Poole's *Index to Periodical Literature* through 1856). Melville's fondness for old travel literature, his habit of consulting factual works for background material, and his adoption of the same misspelling, "Cape de Verd," make it likely that he knew this work. A comparison of Melville's account of the 'Gees' origins with Defoe's (see pp. 151, 159–63, 386–89, 415–17) and other works I have consulted on the Cape Verdes, however, reveals some interesting discrepancies suggesting that Melville chose to substitute certain fictional parallels with American Indians for actual parallels with American Negroes. For example, no aboriginal race was displaced by the Portuguese settlers of the Cape Verdes, then uninhabited. Instead, African slaves were imported from the mainland to work the settlers' estates.

derived their name from a contemptuous "abbreviation, by seamen, of *Portuguee*, the corrupt form of *Portuguese*" (G, 355). Like the analogous racial epithet "nigger," which it calls to mind—similarly an insulting corruption of the Portuguese word "Negro"—the word " 'Gee," according to Melville, expresses "pure contumely; the degree of which may be partially inferred from this, that with [seamen] the primitive word Portuguee itself is a reproach" (G, 356). The "curtailment" of the 'Gees' name, remarks Melville, reflects the decimation they have undergone as a race; for the present-day inhabitants of Fogo comprise but the "melancholy remainder" of a populace whose flower was long ago "drafted off as food for powder" (G, 355–56).

If American ethnology, with its slant toward providing a scientific rationale for the enslavement of the Negro and the extermination of the American Indian, determined the formal structure of "The 'Gees," several other factors seem to have influenced Melville's choice of Cape Verdean sailors as analogues for black slaves through whom he could telescope the problems of racism, economic exploitation, and slavery. Sailors, of course, had always been Melville's readiest analogues for slaves, since the tyranny and drudgery to which they were subjected were the closest approximation to slavery in Melville's experience. Although Cape Verdeans were sufficiently exotic to offer a convenient pretext for a bogus ethnological memorandum, Melville had in fact known many in his stints aboard the *Acushnet*, the *Lucy Ann*, and the *United States*. None of Melville's references to Cape Verdeans in *Omoo*, *White-Jacket*, or *Moby-Dick* [5] indicates that they were looked down upon by their shipmates or reputed to be "inferior tar[s]," as Melville alleges in "The 'Gees." Nevertheless, these islanders did face certain forms of exploitation that made them peculiarly apt analogues for American blacks. For one thing, as Melville implies, their native Fogo, a volcanic island cursed with a "soil . . . such as may be found of a dusty day on a road newly Macadamized" (G, 356), was so barren that they could be hired on

5. Melville's list of his shipmates on board the *Acushnet* includes three "Portuguese" (Leyda, *Melville Log*, I, 399–400). A Cape Verdean named Antone is mentioned among Melville's fellow mutineers in *Omoo*, 45, 77. References to Cape Verdeans occur in *White-Jacket*, 48, 102–103, 137. A sailor from St. Jago, another of the Cape Verde Islands, appears in "Midnight, Forecastle" (MD, 153). The spelling St. Jago, which Charles Feidelson, Jr., has footnoted as "unusual" in his annotated edition of *Moby-Dick* (Indianapolis, 1964), 237, is also to be found in Defoe's travelogue.

terms most other sailors would disdain. This was why "certain masters of our Nantucket ships" had formed the habit of "touching at Fogo, on the outward passage, there to fill up vacancies among their crews arising from the short supply of men at home" (G, 357). The menace of starvation in Fogo and the lure of food aboard ship were enough to attract 'Gee sailors by the score: "Any day one may go to their isle, and on the showing of a coin of biscuit over the rail, may load down to the water's edge with them" (G, 358). Thus both the economic exploitation to which Cape Verdeans lent themselves and its effects on their white competitors in America dramatized the plight of northern blacks under capitalist "wage slavery." In addition, the Cape Verdeans' condition often corresponded literally to that of southern chattel slaves, since "unsophisticated 'Gee[s]" would contract to work for biscuit in lieu of wages, not knowing "what other wages mean, unless cuffs and buffets be wages" (G, 357).[6]

Perhaps the timeliest factor behind Melville's choice of Portuguese-African sailors as vehicles for challenging the racial theories that justified relegating American blacks to de jure or de facto slavery, however, was a controversy that had recently arisen over a Portuguese sailor of mixed blood (though not a Cape Verdean) who had narrowly escaped being enslaved under the "Colored Seamen Laws" of South Carolina and Georgia. These laws, which decreed that any sailor of African extraction entering the ports of either state was to be imprisoned for the duration of the ship's call, at the ship's expense, or else be sold into slavery to cover the cost of jail fees, aroused vigorous protest in the mid–1850s, after several cases had come to public attention. The case of the Portuguese seaman Manuel Pereira would have particularly interested Melville, for it inspired a polemical novel that tried somewhat confusedly to show that a sailor need not be a "nigger" to be arrested as such under the Colored Seamen Laws.[7] Demonstrating scientifically that a "nigger"

6. A modern traveler's account of the Cape Verdes which confirms Melville's description of their poverty and barrenness, and his insinuation that Cape Verdeans sold themselves into slavery aboard passing ships in times of famine, is Archibald Lyall's *Black and White Make Brown: An Account of a Journey to the Cape Verde Islands and Portuguese Guinea* (London, 1938), 33.
7. Francis Colburn Adams, *Manuel Pereira; or, The Sovereign Rule of South Carolina; with Views of Southern Laws, Life, and Hospitality* (Washington, D.C., 1853), 46–50, 100–101, 195, 281–82 n. See also the British and Foreign Anti-Slavery Society tract

could be readily differentiated from a man of any other race was, of course, one of the prime goals of ethnologists like Josiah Nott and his popularizer Samuel Cartwright, both of whom had oriented their study of race chiefly toward proving that the Negro was dis- tinguished by inferior intellect and a physical affinity to the lower animals, and that his place at the bottom of the American socio- economic ladder corresponded to the position he occupied in the biological hierarchy of human races.

To discredit these theories in "The 'Gees," Melville relies pri- marily on satire as a means of exposing their absurdity. He achieves his effects through the use of two main literary techniques. The first of these—the puns and word-plays that continually satirize the way ethnologists prostituted science, history, and even linguistics to the end of establishing the Negro as less than a man—emerges in the title itself, especially as Melville explains it.

A complex pun identifying the 'Gees as analogues for American Negroes, and initiating the animal imagery used to describe the 'Gees in Melville's sketch and the Negroes in ethnological studies, the word " 'Gee" calls forth at least five associations. In its plural form, " 'Gees" sounds almost exactly like "Geez" or, to adopt Nott's spelling, "Gheez," the ancient language of Abyssinia in which the Ethiopic version of the Scriptures was written. Through this eso- teric pun, the title relates the negroid people discussed in the sketch to an advanced African civilization and refers generally to the study of the African past, one of the disciplines ethnologists had preempted for the sake of demeaning the Negro more systematically.[8] " 'Gees" also reminds us of geese, animals reputed for stupidity and un- gainliness, and perhaps as such giving rise to another contemptuous epithet applied to the Portuguese which may have been in use in Melville's time: "Geese." Melville later reinforces this association by comparing the 'Gee's "wild, marine, gamy savor" to that of "the sea-bird called haglet," a type of gull (G, 357).[9]

Imprisonment of Coloured Seamen under the Law of South Carolina: A Tract Containing the Cases of Manuel Pereira and Reuben Roberts; and of John Glasgow, A Free British Subject Who Was Sold into Slavery in Georgia (London, 1854).

8. Nott and Gliddon, *Types of Mankind*, 195–96.

9. Maurice H. Weseen (ed.), *Dictionary of American Slang* (New York, 1934), Chap. 21: "General Slang," entry "Geese." The gull, of course, is another bird proverbial for foolishness and credulity (*gull*ibility).

We have already noticed the analogy with the better-known epithet "nigger." As an epithet, "'Gee" in fact has a still closer correspondent in "Geechee," a derogatory word for a southern Negro derived from the creolized Gullah and Geechee dialects of Georgia and Carolina slaves.[10] Finally, the most common usage of the word "'Gee" is as an equivalent of "giddy-up," an imperative directed at a horse, which Melville even spells conformably when he marvels at the "prolongation of taunt into which [an angry sailor] will spin out the one little exclamatory monosyllable Ge-e-e-e-e!" (G, 356). This association must have something to do with the equine imagery that pervades Melville's description of the 'Gees.

Another elaborate series of puns connects the derisive abridgment of the name 'Gee with the near-annihilation of the race, whose surviving remnant Melville dubs a "caput mortuum" (G, 355–56). Literally translated as "death's-head," the phrase evokes both the Latin titles of the ethnologist Samuel G. Morton's twin treatises, based on the study of skulls—Crania Americana and Crania Aegyptiaca—and the formidable collection of skulls that lined Morton's laboratory, which his colleagues had christened the "American Golgotha."[11] The technical meaning of caput mortuum in chemical usage, however, is the residuum remaining after distillation of a substance (OED). Melville puns on this meaning, too, when he calls the 'Gees a "residuum" and characterizes the contraction "'Gee" as a "subtle distillation" from the "primitive word Portuguee," standing "in point of relative intensity to it, as attar of roses does to rosewater" (G, 356). Through this chemical conceit, Melville suggests the violence that science perpetrates on its human subjects under a cloak of euphemistic jargon. Just as ethnologists glossed over the massacre of the Indians by ascribing it to an "intrinsic race-character" that doomed the Indians to "fade away before the onward march of the frontier-man,"[12] so Melville disguises the human

10. Harold Wentworth and Stuart Berg Flexner (eds.), Dictionary of American Slang (New York, 1967). See also Lawrence W. Levine, Black Culture and Black Consciousness: Afro-American Folk Thought from Slavery to Freedom (New York: Oxford University Press, 1977), 146. This analogy was pointed out to me by Professor Simone Vauthier of the Université de Strasbourg. Professor Vauthier's monumental doctoral thesis on the image of the Negro in nineteenth-century American literature (Université de Paris, 1977), and her numerous articles in the Bulletin de la Faculté des Lettres de Strasbourg, and in Recherches anglaises et américaines, deserve to be better known to American scholars.
11. Stanton, The Leopard's Spots, 103.
12. Nott and Gliddon, Types of Mankind, xxxiii.

tragedy of the 'Gees' decimation by enveloping it in the terminology of a chemical experiment. Reflecting the cold-blooded spirit in which ethnologists collected human skulls for their laboratories and consigned to "ultimate extinction" the species of their fellow creatures whose crania they found wanting (a spirit that prompted their collaborators to ransack burying grounds and morgues for fresh contributions to science),[13] Melville's chemical puns force the reader to ask who is actually civilized and who savage.

The opening paragraph of "The 'Gees" inaugurates a third wordplay central to Melville's *reductio ad absurdum* of racist ethnology. Immediately after introducing the 'Gees as a "singular people," Melville refers to them, in a manner professedly "quite natural and easy," as a people much like better-known national groups: "I have said *The two 'Gees* just as another would say *The two Dutchmen*, or *The two Indians*" (G, 355). What initially strikes the reader is the incongruity of asserting the 'Gees to be unique and, in the same breath, putting them on a footing with such familiar peoples as the Dutch and the Indians. Prefiguring an intricate pattern of antitheses throughout the sketch, this contradiction mirrors the organic inconsistencies of the proslavery argument underlying ethnology—inconsistencies that all the ethnologists' sophistry failed to dissimulate. On the one hand, the implication that the 'Gees may not, after all, be so exceptional as to warrant an ethnological account, calls into question the very purpose of ethnology as a science concerned with the peculiarities that allegedly distinguished races from each other in general and the Negro from "superior" races in particular. On the other hand, in the context of the ethnological memorandum Melville leads us to expect, the three peoples he mentions naturally bring to mind the conventional tripartite division of mankind into black, white, and brownish yellow races—a division that the contemporary public Melville was addressing would doubtless have traced to the Bible, as did some ethnologists, and identified with Ham, Japheth, and Shem respectively.[14] Yet the very sentence that

13. It was considered a tribute to one of Morton's collaborators, for example, to state that "*without any particular scientific interest*," he risked his life "robbing an Indian burial-place" and carrying "his *spoils*" through hostile territories "in a highly *unsavory* condition" (*ibid.*, xxix; italics added).
14. *E.g.*, Cartwright, *Essays*, 8–11. See also Nott and Gliddon, *Types of Mankind*, 83–85.

evokes this convention simultaneously flouts it. Not only has Melville pointedly substituted particular peoples for the broad racial categories of Negro, Caucasian, and Mongol; he has also blurred the polemical lines within the racial triad by designating uncontroversial or imprecise examples of each race. He has replaced the Negro with an unfamiliar people (whose negroid ancestry, in fact, is not divulged until the next paragraph); he has overlooked the Anglo-Saxon in favor of a less-celebrated representative of the white race; he has neglected to specify whether he means the East Indian (technically registered as Caucasian) or his American namesake (usually grouped with the Mongol family). Moreover, as the following paragraph makes clear, the black ethnic group Melville proposes to introduce to ethnologists is an "amalgamated" group, "hybrid" in appearance, whose very existence impeaches the ethnologists' racial classifications and whose survival after three centuries of inbreeding on a remote island patently contradicts Nott's predication that mulattoes, as the "hybrid" progeny of crossbreeding between incompatible human species, were "the shortest-lived of any class of the human race" and so unprolific as to "die off" after a few generations.[15] (Significantly, the 'Gees have dwindled to a "melancholy remainder" through the hazards of war, rather than the laws of genetics.)

A final anomaly that this deceptively innocuous sentence presents—all the more glaring on the heels of the phrase "a singular people"—is the seeming gratuitousness of citing examples by two's: two 'Gees, two Dutchmen, two Indians. Since the ethnologists' convention was to postulate a single norm for each race and to dismiss all instances belying that norm as mere aberrations or symptoms of degeneracy (as Cartwright, for example, adjudged the lighter skin color of the Hottentots and Bushmen, whom he consequently declared "inferior in mind and body to the typical [jet-black] African of Guinea and the Niger"[16]), Melville's departure from this practice points up its deficiency. Perhaps Melville means to suggest the need for dual poles of reference in generalizing about national character. Certainly he emphasizes throughout the sketch that individually there are two sides to every 'Gee, while collectively 'Gees come in two varieties—"green" and "ripe"—and symbolically

15. Nott and Gliddon, *Types of Mankind*, 373, 399, 402.
16. Cartwright, "Slavery in the Light of Ethnology," 708–709.

'Gees stand for both American Negroes and American Indians. Similar dualities might also pertain to Indians and Dutchmen, though Melville does not spell them out here. In the case of Indians, for example, one thinks not only of the historical confusion between the Indians of Asia and the American aborigines, but also of the white man's dichotomous view of American Indian character—a subject Melville would enlarge on in *The Confidence-Man*, completed four or five months after publication of "The 'Gees."[17] As for Dutchmen (a term equally subject to confusion, having traditionally encompassed both Hollanders and Germans), Melville, being of Dutch origin, may have known that they sustained a dual relationship to the Negro as the first slave traders to sell Africans to the British colonists of Virginia, in 1620, and among the first colonists in North America to remonstrate against slavery and the slave trade, in 1688.[18] (The latter group of Dutchmen were Quakers, and in "The 'Gees" it is the Nantucket Quakers who exemplify this moral duality in their treatment of 'Gees, the objects at once of their rapacity as whaling captains and their philanthropy as sponsors of a pilot project in 'Gee education.) The verbal tension established at the outset between singularity and duality thus foreshadows the pivotal irony of Melville's mock ethnological memorandum: that the disparity between the 'Gees' "private nature" and "public coat" (G, 358), not to mention the diversity of aspects they assume—greenness and ripeness, docility and recalcitrance, hardiness and infirmity, simplicity and sophistication—defies the experts' generalizations and constantly undercuts Melville's own formal pretense of describing a typical 'Gee.

Puns, in sum, function as a leading vehicle of Melville's satire on ethnology. They encompass the various subsidiary disciplines that fortified ethnology, from the classification of crania to the research into Egyptian, biblical, and American Indian antiquities. They expose the "niggerology" that masqueraded as disinterested investigation of racial differences and relate the habit of anatomizing

17. See *The Confidence-Man*, Chaps. 25–28. Melville had probably completed the book by late July, 1856 (Leyda, *Melville Log*, II, 517–18).
18. The Dutch ship that carried the first shipment of slaves to Virginia was regularly mentioned by proslavery apologists (*e.g.*, *The Pro-Slavery Argument*, 353). On the antislavery remonstrance written by the Dutch, German, and Swiss colonists of Germantown, Pennsylvania, see Thomas E. Drake, *Quakers and Slavery in America* (Gloucester, Mass., 1965), 11–14.

men as if they were animals to the system of working them as beasts of burden. Exploiting the sinister overtones of the crudest ethnological writings, Melville's puns equate the procurement of crania with headhunting, the comparative analysis of human organs with cannibalism. Ultimately, they highlight the fundamental contradictions and fallacies that discredited ethnology as a science.

Melville's second literary weapon against scientific racism—devastating parody of ethnological convention and jargon, often lapsing into sheer burlesque—accomplishes similar purposes, but to more radical effect; for it subverts the ethnologists' theories by preempting the very techniques that elevated the study of race to scientific status.

In conformance with the major tasks Nott had prescribed for ethnologists—those of ascertaining the "primitive organic structure" and "moral and psychical character" of every race, studying the modifications that "time and moral and physical causes" may have wrought on the races, and determining "what position in the social scale Providence has assigned to each type of man"[19] — Melville opens his description of the 'Gees by defining their racial ancestry and gauging the level of civilization, physique, and morality attained by the "aboriginal race of negroes" from whom the 'Gees spring. While following the ethnologists' procedure and mimicking their pompous tone, however, Melville pointedly replaces their precise formulas with loose approximations that bespeak the subjective basis of their science. The primitive inhabitants of Fogo, he judges flippantly, were a people "ranking pretty high in incivility, but rather low in stature and morals" (G, 355).

Having classified the 'Gees, Melville enters into the detailed discussion of the race's anatomy and psychology that served, in the standard ethnological account of the Negro, to illustrate the compatibility of the black race's genetic makeup with its servile station in life. Here Melville's parody of ethnological convention dovetails into parody of the proslavery argument, just as ethnology historically merged with proslavery apologetics in the writings of Samuel Cartwright.

Besides confirming the common view that "strong muscles, hardy frames," and resistance to sunstroke qualified blacks for the kind

19. Nott and Gliddon, *Types of Mankind*, 49.

of drudgery under a burning sun thought fatal to whites, Cartwright claimed to have discovered various genetic traits that immunized the Negro against the "ills . . . otherwise . . . incident to a state of slavery" and therefore made it impossible to overwork him. Among these was an instinct "assimilating the negro to the mule" in causing him to balk at unreasonable demands. A proslavery writer para-phrasing Cartwright called the result "a certain hardihood of constitution, which, as in the case of the mule, gives great power of endurance."[20]

Melville clearly draws on such fantasies about the Negro as a well-nigh inexhaustible beast of burden when he presents the 'Gee, "in his best estate," as "hardy; capable of enduring extreme hard work, hard fare, or hard usage, as the case may be" (G, 356). In taking a "scientific view" and inferring from his alleged hardiness a possible "natural adaptability in the 'Gee to hard times generally," Melville adopts the same circular reasoning that ethnologists used to establish the Negro's biological adaptedness to slavery. The syllogism by which Nott and Cartwright argued that the Negro's history of enslavement testified to his having been predestined for slavery leads Melville to find the 'Gee's hypothetical fitness for hard times "not uncorroborated by his experiences."[21] Melville also duplicates Cartwright's vertiginous induction that the "wise provision of Providence," in endowing the Negro with an anatomy appropriate to his condition, proved that God had designed the Negro for the condition best suited to his "peculiar organization."[22] The "kindly care of Nature" in accoutering the 'Gee for hardship, surmises Melville, attests the 'Gee's "natural" attunement to it. Embroidering on the protective virtues ethnologists imputed to the Negro's skin, Melville intimates that the 'Gee's skin appears to be as effective in inuring him against the "cuffs and buffets" he habitually receives as a "tough leather suit from top to toe," like the one Melville imagines the Quaker George Fox to have donned to equip himself for "his hard rubs with a hardened world." According to proslavery

20. Cartwright, "Slavery in the Light of Ethnology," 718, 723, and *Essays*, 14–15; Estes, *Defence of Negro Slavery*, 79–80.
21. Cartwright, *Essays*, 16; Nott, "Statistics of Southern Slave Population. With Especial Reference to Life Insurance," *De Bow's Review*, IV (1847), 280; Nott and Gliddon, *Types of Mankind*, 252–56, 461–62.
22. Cartwright, *Essays*, 13–16.

apologists, the Negro's emotional insensitivity to the "infamy . . . of the lash" more than matched his physical callousness.[23] Similarly, the 'Gee, as Melville euphemistically renders this fancy, "is by no means of that exquisitely delicate sensibility expressed by the figurative adjective thin-skinned" (G, 356).

The brutish picture Melville proceeds to sketch of the 'Gee obviously caricatures the ethnologists' manner, carried to grotesque extremes by Cartwright, of portraying the Negro as a creature of underdeveloped brain and overgrown "animal appetites . . . approaching the simiadiae [monkeys] but stopping short of their beastiality" [sic]. Cartwright, comparing the "prognathous species of mankind" with the Caucasian, had remarked of the Negro: "All the senses are more acute, but less delicate and discriminating, than the white man's. He has a good ear for melody but not for harmony, a keen taste and relish for food but less discriminating between the different kinds of esculent substances than the Caucasian."[24] Melville, in phrases uncannily close to Cartwright's, contrasts the 'Gee's "physicals and spirituals" and observes: "The 'Gee has a great appetite, but little imagination; a large eyeball, but small insight. Biscuit he crunches, but sentiment he eschews" (G, 356).

However, Melville's formulation of this hackneyed racial slur punningly undercuts the antithesis between the 'Gee's handling of physical and of spiritual nutriment, by counterpointing "crunches" with "eschews," which looks and sounds very much like "chews," a synonym rather than an antonym of "crunches." Moreover, the 'Gee's anatomy, as Melville describes it, differs considerably from the ethnologists' presentation of the Negro's, in that it conspicuously fails to exemplify the alleged disparity between his sensual and intellectual faculties. Unlike the "peculiarly small eyes" ethnologists attributed to the Negro,[25] the 'Gee's "large eyeball" does not seem to convey little in-sight. Nor does the 'Gee's stomach—incommensurate, in Melville's opinion, with a "mouth disproportionally large" (G, 357)—indicate a "great appetite"; indeed the disproportion rather gives the impression that the 'Gee is underfed. The feature

23. *The Pro-Slavery Argument*, 34, 51, 59, 128–29; also Estes, *Defence of Negro Slavery*, 135.
24. Cartwright, "Slavery in the Light of Ethnology," 710.
25. Nott and Gliddon, *Types of Mankind*, 416.

172 SHADOW OVER THE PROMISED LAND

embodying Melville's most crucial departure from the ethnologists' version of the Negro's anatomy is the 'Gee's head, whose distinctive shape and size—which ethnologists belittled as ill-formed, small, and symptomatic of deficient intellect in the Negro[26] —Melville commends as "round" (the most perfect of geometrical shapes), "compact" (concentrating much brain in its limited space), and "betokening a solid understanding" in the 'Gee (G, 357).

Complementing the ethnologists' emphasis on the Negro's supposed animal propensities was a concerted denigration of his intellect, which Nott, for example, pronounced as "dark" as his skin and ascribed to "a cephalic conformation that renders all expectance of [the Negro's] . . . future melioration an Utopian dream, philanthropical, but somewhat senile."[27] Accordingly, Melville complements his own account of the 'Gee's anatomy with an assessment of the race's intellectual potential that parodies the ethnologists' arguments against educating the Negro.

Melville broaches this controversial subject with a double entendre that immediately lays bare the fallacy of evaluating the intellect of a servile class. "The intellect of the 'Gee," he notes wryly, has so far been "little cultivated" (G, 360). Reflecting the ethnologists' inconsistencies in alternately ignoring pioneering ventures in black education altogether or dismissing them as chimerical,[28] Melville at first denies that any "well-attested educational experiment" has ever been made on the 'Gee; he then brushes aside the reported precedent, "in the last century," of a young 'Gee sent to Salamanca University by a "visionary Portuguese naval officer" and pointedly fails to record the outcome of that experiment. In the same vein, he subtly discredits a current proposal to enroll "five comely 'Gees, aged sixteen," at Dartmouth College, by presenting it as nebulous "talk" and ascribing it to the Nantucket Quakers, members of a sect notorious for its literally visionary beginnings and its subsequent antislavery zeal.

Ethnologists also sought to impugn the feasibility of educating blacks by showing that previous crusades for Christianizing and civilizing the Indians had ominously foundered on an "intrinsic race-

26. *Ibid.*, 182, 185, 430.
27. *Ibid.*, 185.
28. *Ibid.*, 456.

character" inimical to all edifying influences.[29] Hence Melville recalls how the "venerable institution" slated to uplift the Quakers'
Cape Verdean protégés had originally been "founded partly with
the object of finishing off wild Indians in the classics and higher
mathematics" (G, 360). The phrase "finishing off," which suggests
extermination, evokes the ethnologists' characterization of the Indian
as "an untamable, carnivorous animal," destined for extinction. Like
the ethnologists, who contrasted the irreclaimable red savage with
the "naturally mild and docile" Negro, an animal capable of being
"domesticated," Melville implicitly differentiates the "wild" Indian,
done in by a classical education, from the tractable 'Gee, whose
"docility . . . excellent memory, and still more excellent credulity"
furnish a "hopeful basis for his intellectual training."[30] Once again,
however, Melville turns the tables on ethnologists: the "qualities"
he commends in the 'Gee as conducive to intellectual advancement
equate intelligence with the ability to follow instructions and parrot
facts. For the man who had hailed a whale-ship as "my Yale College
and my Harvard,"[31] this unflattering assessment of American education and of the intellectual level requisite to qualify for it was a
fitting protest against the criteria ethnologists used to deny the
Negro's educability.

Misrepresenting the Negro's anatomy and disparaging his intellect were twin spearheads of the ethnologists' strategy of identifying the Negro as a link between man and brute.[32] A more blatant
method of degrading blacks to bestial status, which Melville subverts by a like combination of caricature and travesty, was to adopt
the jargon of the horse farm in analyzing the Negro's behavior and
in speculating about the results of crossbreeding him with other

29. *Ibid.*, xxxiii, 461. See also *The Pro-Slavery Argument*, 276–85, where William
Gilmore Simms cites an unsuccessful experiment in educating an Indian boy at a northern
college and argues that "our Indians" would have been more effectively civilized if "we
had conquered and subjected them." This is reprinted from Simms's *The Wigwam and the
Cabin* (1845).
30. Nott, "Statistics of Southern Slave Population," 280. Professor Vauthier has suggested to me that Melville's reference to the classics and higher mathematics in connection
with educational experiments of "the last century" might be an esoteric allusion to the
eighteenth century's two most famous educated blacks, the poet and classicist Phillis
Wheatley and the astronomer-mathematician Benjamin Banneker.
31. In *Moby-Dick*, Chap. 24 ("The Advocate"), 101.
32. Nott and Gliddon, *Types of Mankind*, 457–60; Cartwright, "Slavery in the Light
of Ethnology," 707–708.

races. Thus, corresponding to the mulish traits Cartwright ascribed to the Negro, Melville singles out a number of equine features in the 'Gee, including "what are called butter-teeth, strong, durable, square, and yellow," and a "serviceably hard heel" (G, 357), reminiscent of a hoof. He diverges from Cartwright, however, in comparing the 'Gee not to the domesticated, if stubborn, mule, but to the untamed zebra, significantly a native African equine species. Furthermore, whereas Cartwright attributed the shape of the Negro's foot to a congenitally flexed knee emblemizing the "servile type of his mind,"[33] Melville construes the 'Gee's heel to evince his capacity for refractoriness. A kick from the 'Gee, Melville warns, "is by the judicious held almost as dangerous as one from a wild zebra" (G, 357). As the mettlesome, bounding zebra symbolizes a spirit alien to the plodding mule's, it also bodies forth a concept of hybridity countering the principles Nott applied to the intermixture of blacks and whites;[34] for unlike the crossbred animals with which Nott compared the mulatto, the zebra is hybrid only in appearance. With its black and white stripes answering to the 'Gee's "hybrid" complexion, it illustrates a union of black and white strains in a single species—and an attractive one at that.

Even more subversively, Melville substitutes culinary locutions for the ethnologists' veterinary terms, and edible game for the domestic beasts of burden to which ethnologists assimilated the Negro. Where Cartwright, for example, lucubrated on the Negro's "strong odor,"[35] Melville descants on the 'Gee's "wild, marine, gamy savor," which he explicitly distinguishes from the "peculiar savor" of the Negro and likens instead to that of "the sea-bird called haglet." Perhaps with such gross prototypes in mind as Cartwright's estimate that the "difference in the flesh of the white and black man, in regard to color," equaled the difference between "the flesh of the rabbit and the hare,"[36] Melville extends his savory metaphor into actual cannibalism by reporting the 'Gee's flesh to be "like venison . . . firm

33. Cartwright, "Slavery in the Light of Ethnology," 710–11, and *Essays*, 8; also Estes, *Defence of Negro Slavery*, 63.
34. Nott and Gliddon, *Types of Mankind*, Chap. 12 ("Hybridity of Animals, Viewed in Connection with the Natural History of Mankind").
35. Cartwright, "Slavery in the Light of Ethnology," 714.
36. Cartwright, "Diseases of the Negro," 65.

but lean" (G, 357). Ironically, cannibalism was one of the barbarities associated with the Negro's savage state in Africa, from which pro-slavery apologists claimed the slave trade had "rescued" him. Yet Melville, who had ten years earlier defended the Typees as more "humane and virtuous," despite their cannibalism, than "the polished communities of Europe," now reverses the traditional notions of barbarism and civilization altogether, hinting that the latest refinement of European civilization—the science of probing racial differences—involves connoisseurship in human flesh (T, 203–205).[37]

Beyond burlesquing the ethnologists' convention of treating the Negro as a species of animal, Melville expressly questions the scientific value of seeking to explain racial traits as products of a cosmic scheme. Considerable pedantry, Melville instances, has been expended by "captains at a loss for better discourse during dull, rainy weather in the horse-latitudes," on whether the 'Gee's distinctive teeth are "intended for carnivorous or herbivorous purposes, or both conjoined." But as Melville points out, on the barren island of Fogo "the 'Gee eats neither flesh nor grass," so that "this inquiry would seem superfluous" (G, 357), at least from a scientific perspective.

When Melville goes on to supplement his account of the 'Gee's physical and temperamental peculiarities with practical advice on how to select and manage 'Gees as sailors, he mirrors the way ethnologists like Nott and Cartwright addressed themselves to the operational concerns of slaveholders, as well as to their ideology.[38] Ironically, it was precisely where the scientific view of the Negro as a creature innately predisposed toward slavery intersected with the mundane problem of exacting service from him that irreconcilable contradictions emerged in the ethnological case for Negro slavery. Thus the theory that the Negro's greater physical resistance and lower intelligence made him perform better than other races as a slave jarred with the provoking realities, implicitly acknowledged by Cartwright, of high mortality, rampant disease, and fre-

37. *The Pro-Slavery Argument*, 273–74, 299–300; Fitzhugh, *Sociology for the South*, 84–88, 278.
38. Cartwright, *Essays*, 18–22, and "Diseases of the Negro," *passim*; Nott, "Statistics of Southern Slave Population," *passim*, and "Nature and Destiny of the Negro," *De Bow's Review*, X (1851), 329–32.

quent fatalities among black slaves on the one hand, and their inclination on the other to "break, waste, [and] destroy [property], idle their time, feign sickness, run away, and do all manner of acts to vex and torment" their masters.[39] At the same time, the contention that the Negro's brain was too inadequate to allow even for satisfying his animal wants independently,[40] let alone achieving the least degree of civilization, raised the question of how so incorrigibly inferior a creature could accomplish any task well enough to prove so indispensable as a slave.

Capitalizing on this conflict between the need to fantasize an ideal slave, born only to serve, and the necessity of facing and circumventing the drawbacks of a slave who shared the recalcitrance of ordinary human beings, Melville embodies the same discrepancies in the 'Gees. "Though of an aquatic nature" and "expert" at catching fish for themselves, the 'Gees, reports Melville, lack the "higher qualifications" of good seamanship (G, 356). In fact, "green 'Gees are wont, in no inconsiderable numbers, to fall overboard the first dark, squally night" (G, 358)—a tendency that evokes both the suicides and deaths of African slaves during the "Middle Passage,"[41] and the frequent escapes responsible for the Fugitive Slave Law.

The 'Gees' assets, Melville claims, are not skills, but rather the biological stamina and docility ethnologists pronounced characteristic of the Negro and a convenient preference for biscuit in lieu of wages, paralleling the Negro's supposed preference for the comforts of chattel slavery over the distresses of wage slavery.[42] On these grounds, Melville notes, giving the proslavery argument a sly twist, "some captains will go the length of maintaining that 'Gee sailors are preferable, indeed every way, physically and intellectually, superior to American sailors—such captains complaining, and justly, that American sailors, if not decently treated, are apt to give serious trouble" (G, 357).

Yet 'Gees, too, it transpires, can prove troublesome, their very virtues becoming a bane. Offsetting the profits of employing 'Gees

39. Cartwright, *Essays*, 21, and "Diseases of the Negro," 333–34.
40. Cartwright, "Slavery in the Light of Ethnology," 702, 718–19, 727, and "Diseases of the Negro," 66, 334.
41. Another debt to Professor Vauthier. See Melville's graphic description of the *"middle-passage"* on "Portuguese slavers . . . off Cape Verde" in *Redburn*, 57.
42. Cartwright, "Slavery in the Light of Ethnology," 718–19; Fitzhugh, *Sociology for the South*, 85–87, 166–68, 274, 289–90.

are many of the disadvantages southerners lamented in their slaves. Hence Melville cautions that the naïveté making 'Gees so docile and exploitable when green also makes them even more bungling and slow-witted than other green sailors, necessitating the hiring of "twice as many 'Gees" as a captain would need of American sailors "to provide for all contingencies" (G, 358). This drawback recalls the notorious inefficiency of slaves, which some slaveholders imputed to the Negroes' constitutional inability "as a race" either to "do as much work [or] continue at it as long as . . . whites."[43] When ripe, 'Gees lose in submissiveness what they gain in proficiency and become more ungovernable than American sailors. Just as southerners chafed at the "rascality" their "smart" slaves manifested in sabotaging and shirking work, so Melville warns against the wiles of "knowing" 'Gees. "Discreet captains," he avers, always opt for green 'Gees.

The captain's dilemma of choosing between the shortcomings of green 'Gees and ripe 'Gees is no more easily resolved than the slaveholder's dilemma of choosing between the obtuse brute he could master and the potentially dangerous thinking human being he could teach to do his work. Confronted with the day-to-day exigencies of managing slaves, slaveholders found themselves obliged to evolve criteria for evaluating and differentiating among their chattels that automatically entailed a more realistic view of the Negro's nature. They had to select slaves with sufficient mettle and intelligence to perform the tasks for which they were needed, which meant looking for qualities the Negro theoretically lacked. They had to restrain their slaves and forestall innumerable acts of resistance, which meant recognizing a rebellious propensity supposedly alien to the Negro. In order to make their slaves work efficiently, slaveholders had to provide incentives and to alternate sternness with kindness, thus taking into consideration human feelings the Negro theoretically did not harbor. As Cartwright discovered, "the empire of the white man's will over the prognathous race is not absolute," and the simple use of force beyond a certain point only

---

43. "The Negro," De Bow's Review, III (1847), 419. See Stampp, The Peculiar Institution, Chap. 3, for an excellent analysis of the slave as "A Troublesome Property." One of the sources Stampp draws on is Olmsted's Journey in the Seaboard Slave States, whose view of the contradictions in the proslavery argument and of the quandary of the docile, but stupid, versus the intelligent, but recalcitrant slave is remarkably similar to Melville's (see Seaboard Slave States, 58–59, 84, 91, 199–200, 591).

resulted in driving blacks "into a state of impassivity, in which they are more plague than profit."[44]

The directions Melville gives for testing 'Gees prior to hiring them, and the pitfalls against which he admonishes "inexperienced captains" in distinguishing between the 'Gee's "public coat" and "private nature" dramatize these contradictions. They also conjure up the slave market scenes described by so many visitors to the South. Observers often remarked on the resemblance of slave markets to horse markets and likened the "transactions in buying and selling slaves" to the "spirit of jockeying."[45] Melville accordingly comments that becoming a "sound judge of 'Gees" requires much the same study as becoming a "judge of horses," and advises that tyros consult a " 'Gee jockey," meaning "a man well versed in 'Gees," as a preliminary to hiring a crew in Fogo. Furthermore, he recommends a procedure for inspecting the 'Gee that smacks of putting a horse through its points: "Get square before him, at, say three paces, so that the eye, like a shot, may rake the 'Gee fore and aft, at one glance taking in his whole make and build—how he looks about the head, whether he carry it well; his ears, are they over-lengthy? How fares it in the withers? His legs, does the 'Gee stand strongly on them? His knees, any Belshazzar symptoms there? How stands it in the region of the brisket? etc., etc." (G, 358). Assessing the 'Gee as if he were a blooded race horse, Melville calls for a spirited, proud-stepping carriage diametrically contrary to the broken, downtrodden demeanor said to qualify the Negro for slavery. Whereas the Negro was identified with the mule or scrub horse, Melville mentions as undesirable in the 'Gee such characteristics of the mule as "over-lengthy" ears (irrelevant in a human being). He even discountenances in the 'Gee the very trait that, according to Cartwright, marked the Negro as a "*self-submissive knee bender*": inability to "walk flat on his feet," due to "the legs and thighs being arched outwards and the knees bent."[46] Not only does Melville emphasize that the 'Gee's legs should be strong and his knees steady; he subsequently displays as unfit for labor of any kind a 'Gee corresponding exactly to Cartwright's version of the Negro: "forlornly

44. Cartwright, "Slavery in the Light of Ethnology," 722–23.
45. Theodore Dwight Weld, *American Slavery As It Is*, 110, 167.
46. Cartwright, "Slavery in the Light of Ethnology," 710, and *Essays*, 8 and *passim*.

adroop as upon crutches, his legs looking as if broken at the *cart-wheel*" (G, 359; italics added).[47]

The next step Melville specifies in the hiring process parallels another slave market practice that reminded northerners of horse-buying: examining a slave's person for whip scars and similar indices of "bad character."[48] Melville's version of this test, however, reminds the reader that such stigmas betray the character of the master who has inflicted them, as well as of the slave who bears them: "draw close to, and put the centre of the pupil of your eye—put it, as it were, right into the 'Gee's eye; even as an eye-stone, gently, but firmly slip it in there, and then note what speck or beam of vicious-ness, if any, will be floated out" (G, 358–59). Recalling the biblical injunction against descrying the mote in a neighbor's eye rather than attending to the beam in one's own (Matt. 7:3), the experiment leaves ambiguous whether the symptom of "viciousness" to emerge from such sadistic inspection will derive from the 'Gee's eye or from his scrutinizer's.

Ultimately, Melville concedes, none of these precautions is fool-proof, and "the best judge may be deceived" by a 'Gee who knows "what things to hide and what to display, to hit the skipper's fancy" (G, 359). The instance Melville cites perfectly illustrates the absurd contradictions the skipper's (or slaveholder's) fancy embraces, and the impasse to which they lead. A 'Gee who stands "straight and stout, in a flowing pair of man-of-war's-man's trowsers, uncommonly well filled out," and whose "diffidence" presumably indicates a be-coming submissiveness, is promptly hired, but turns out to be par-alyzed by elephantiasis—a fitting ailment for the phantasm Melville had described as an "elephantine Helot" in his earlier tale of an ill-fated attempt to create an ideal slave.[49] Simultaneously satirizing the Colored Seamen Laws and parodying the argument that slavery, unlike free labor, insured sick and disabled workers against loss of employment benefits, Melville goes on to tell of how, though "useless as so much lumber," this "elephantine 'Gee" had been "at every port prohibited from being dumped ashore," obliging the captain who hired him to trundle him "round the globe" for "three weary years,"

47. Surely a punning allusion to Cartwright.
48. Weld, *Slavery As It Is*, 110; Stampp, *The Peculiar Institution*, 260.
49. "The Bell-Tower," 233–34. Olmsted, *Seaboard Slave States*, 388, also describes slaves as sluggish and "elephantine."

during which the 'Gee had never stopped "crunching biscuit" (G, 359).

The moral of this story and of "several similar experiences" has apparently escaped "old Captain Hosea Kean of Nantucket." Instead of renouncing his vain pursuit of a 'Gee uniting the spirit and energy of a race horse with the dumb endurance of a mule, Captain Kean has resorted to a new strategy of recruiting such 'Gees that strongly suggests the African slave trade (then reaching its highest level of activity since its legal abolition):[50]

> He lands at Fogo in the night; by secret means gains information where the likeliest 'Gee wanting to ship lodges; whereupon with a strong party he surprises all the friends and acquaintances of that 'Gee; putting them under guard with pistols at their heads; then creeps cautiously toward the 'Gee, now lying wholly at unawares in his hut, quite relaxed from all possibility of displaying aught deceptive in his appearance. Thus silently, thus suddenly, thus unannounced, Captain Kean bursts upon his 'Gee, so to speak, in the very bosom of his family. (G, 359)

But far from thereby finding 'Gees who better approximate his fantasies, Captain Kean only happens on examples more glaring than ever of the disparity between the 'Gees' "public coat" and their "private nature": "A 'Gee, noised abroad for a Hercules in strength and an Apollo Belvidere for beauty" (notice the subversiveness of comparing the 'Gee to the ethnologists' favorite symbol of Caucasian beauty) "of a sudden is discovered all in a wretched heap" (G, 359).

The captains hiring 'Gees are not alone in having to discriminate between the image of the 'Gee that fulfills their psychological needs and the actuality of the 'Gees who man their ships. The mates charged with supervising 'Gees after they have been hired, reports Melville, have likewise found that when there is "hard work to be done, and the 'Gees stand round in sulks," it is expedient to refrain from acting on the conviction that the 'Gee is a species of monkey: "However this may be, there is no call to which the 'Gee will with more alacrity respond than the word 'Man!'" In short, to induce the 'Gees to work as men, nothing suffices but to treat them as men:

50. See W. E. B. Du Bois, *The Suppression of the African Slave-Trade to the United States of America, 1638–1870* (1896; rpt. New York, 1970), Chap. 11; also Ronald T. Takaki, *A Pro-Slavery Crusade: The Agitation to Reopen the African Slave Trade* (New York, 1971), Chap. 9.

"'Here, my men!' cries the mate. How they jump. But ten to one when the work is done, it is plain 'Gee again. . . . In fact, it is not unsurmised, that only when extraordinary stimulus is needed, only when an extra strain is to be got out of them, are these hapless 'Gees ennobled with the human name" (G, 360). Appealing to the 'Gee's sense of manhood may be but a ploy, resorted to in extreme emergencies, and then only for the duration of the crisis; nevertheless, Melville implies, the 'Gee's inalienable humanity, like that of all slaves, triumphs over the dehumanizing prejudice of the master class by compelling this minimal acknowledgment.

The outcome of this digression, which Melville introduces into his ethnological account of the 'Gee for the sake of adapting science to the pragmatic needs of sea captains dependent on the 'Gee's cheap and docile services, reflects the predicament of ethnology as a discipline bound to a doomed racial slave system and committed to rationalizing the insuperable fallacies of the proslavery argument. The prostitution of science to the object of furthering what Melville would later call "the systematic degradation of man"[51] eventuates on the one hand in reducing science to absurdity, and on the other hand in duping the oppressor who relies on such a science into misjudging the creature he exploits.

Compromised though ethnology was by its bond with a proslavery ideology that most northerners repudiated, the influence of scientific racism in America, as Melville appears to have foreseen, was destined to outlive by far the legal enslavement of the Negro. It was no mere rhetorical flourish on Nott's part to quote the fiery abolitionist Theodore Parker in propounding the thesis that the Caucasian—"master of the other races—never their slave"—had fathered the aggregate achievements of mankind. The concept of racial "gradations"—stretching from the "lowest and most beastly specimens" of the Negro race (the Hottentot and Bushman) and culminating in the pinnacle of Caucasian civilization (the Anglo-Saxon)—this premise of scientific racism actuated the North as thoroughly as the proslavery view of the Negro did the South.[52]

Thus in challenging scientific racism, Melville could not content

51. In the prose Supplement to *Battle-Pieces*, 261.
52. Nott and Gliddon, *Types of Mankind*, 97, 182, 209–10, 462.

himself with punning on the ethnologists' etymological inferences, parodying their degrading jargon, travestying their sophistic pedantry, burlesquing their portrayal of the Negro, or enmeshing their study of the Negro in the toils of the proslavery argument. Ultimately, Melville undertook nothing less than to undermine the very basis of ethnology as a science classifying human beings according to observable criteria. In its place, he advanced a unitary view of mankind, highlighting the almost infinite variety of human "types" and the corresponding range of variation within each "type" that made all criteria used to draw lines of demarcation purely arbitrary.

Among these criteria, the most arbitrary, as Melville had indicated by ranking the 'Gees "pretty high in incivility, but rather low in stature and morals," were those that determined a race's status in the scale of being, and hence its rightful station in society. Having unmasked the ethnocentric value judgments that passed for science, Melville now tackles the phenomenon of racial prejudice itself, which ethnologists rationalized as an innate instinct based on objective differences between races.

"Of all men seamen have strong prejudices, particularly in the matter of race," Melville tells us, adding bluntly, "They are bigots here" (G, 356). Their bigotry consists in espousing the very view of the 'Gee that ethnologists were promulgating of the Negro: they despise him as "a creature of inferior race." Melville shows, however, that these seamen have no clear grounds for differentiating themselves from the fellow crew members they consider "inferior tar[s]." Neither occupational status nor color provides an infallible distinction, since "regularly bred seamen" and 'Gees perform the same low-grade tasks and blacken their hands in the same substance that has given all sailors the sobriquet "tars." Skill, which Melville associates with color by playing on the word "green," proves an equally elusive distinction. When 'Gees "chance to be . . . green hands," asserts Melville, they are the most lubberly of sailors, "a green 'Gee being of all green things the greenest" (G, 358). Yet this is a difference in degree, rather than kind. A tar doesn't have to be a 'Gee to be green, and of course any green tar, 'Gee or otherwise, is an "inferior tar," in the sense of being inept at discharging his duties. Moreover, not all 'Gees are necessarily green; like other tars, the 'Gee sheds his greenness with practice and eventually becomes "sophisticated," in which case he is no longer an "inferior tar." In the end, the main distinction between 'Gees and other sailors turns out to be an economic factor: "The 'Gees undersell them, working for biscuit where the sailors demand dollars" (G, 360). This, says Melville, gives an "added edge" to the supposedly "innate disdain of regularly bred seamen toward 'Gees." He thus replaces the ethnologists' instinctual theory of racial prejudice with a strikingly modern concept of racism as a smoke screen for economic exploitation, victimizing "regularly bred seamen" along with 'Gees, and setting these exploited classes against each other, instead of uniting them against their common oppressors. Even more subversively, Melville points out that the sailors' economic investment in calumniating their competitors from Fogo tends to discredit "any thing said by sailors to the prejudice of 'Gees"; and the particular aspersion Melville singles out—the sailors' insinuation that the 'Gee is a species of monkey—unmistakably extends this insight to southern ethnologists like Nott and Cartwright, with their investment in keeping the Negro a slave.

Just as the sketch opens with a twofold racial triad that likens "that singular people the 'Gees" (G, 355) to familiar, though ambiguously identified, Old and New World peoples, so it closes with another that challenges ethnologists to distinguish the "sophisticated" 'Gee frequenting American seaports from his fellow immigrants to the New World: "The above account may, perhaps, among the ethnologists, raise some curiosity to see a 'Gee. But to see a 'Gee there is no need to go all the way to Fogo, no more than to see a Chinaman to go all the way to China" (G, 360). (Or, one might add, to see a Negro to go all the way to Africa.) Like the ethnologists of the American school, Melville hails the New World as a kind of human zoo harboring specimens from all over the globe. Ethnologists, however, had exulted in the ideal laboratory America afforded for exploring racial differences.[53] Melville, on the contrary, holds that the immigration of so many different races to America signals the end of ethnology, as their ethnic diversity dissolves under the rays of the American sun: " 'Gees are occasionally to be encountered in our sea-ports. . . . But these 'Gees are not the 'Gees of Fogo.

53. *Ibid.*, xxxii–xxxiii.

That is, they are no longer green 'Gees. They are sophisticated 'Gees, and hence liable to be taken for naturalized citizens badly sunburnt" (G, 360).

In intimating that a deep sunburn is enough to turn a naturalized citizen into the image of a 'Gee, Melville is obviously reverting to the preethnological theory that attributed racial traits to climatic conditions. As he no doubt realized, this theory lay at the root of the Greek word "Ethiopians," an ancient name for blacks meaning simply, "sunburnt faces" (OED).[54] As for Melville's "sophisticated 'Gees," they incarnate the second main factor blurring the line between 'Gees and other citizens; for the word "sophisticated," which signifies "adulterated," as well as "knowing," reminds us that the 'Gees, like American Negroes, are an "amalgamated" people, and that as such, they cover a wide range of colors attesting many degrees of black and white parentage. In short, Melville is affirming that racial intermixture has not been the exception, but the rule, in human history—a fact that invalidates classifications based on permanent physical differences among the races.

Characteristically, Melville's use of the term "naturalized citizens," and his comparison of the 'Gees with the Chinese, whose large-scale immigration as coolie laborers was currently arousing great consternation among nativists, also serve an ulterior purpose: to link the problem of racial prejudice with the timely issue of citizenship rights for nonwhite immigrants. Deftly fusing his refutation of ethnology itself with a riposte to a recent nativist poem "On a Chinaman in Broadway," Melville counters the ideal of an Anglo-Saxon America that had inspired the poem with his own radical version of the melting pot ideal he had earlier championed in *Redburn*.[55] Whereas the poet dwelled on how incongruous a Chinaman looked in New York, and touchingly exhorted the "poor native of Cathay" to "speed . . . home" to the rice fields where he belonged, Melville suggests that on arriving in America, foreign nationals, be they 'Gees or Chinamen, put off their racial features along with their native costumes and join the mainstream of American life, becoming indistinguishable from other citizens: "Many a China-

54. See also *ibid.*, 253.
55. "On a Chinaman in Broadway," *United States Magazine and Democratic Review*, n.s. IV (1855), 411–12; *Redburn*, 168–69, 292–93.

man, in new coat and pantaloons, his long queue coiled out of sight in one of Genin's hats, has promenaded Broadway, and been taken merely for an eccentric Georgia planter. The same with 'Gees; a stranger need have a sharp eye to know a 'Gee, even if he see him" (G, 360–61). In contrast, then, to both the lily-white society nativists advocated, which had no place for other races, and the racist society ethnologists took for granted, where the white man exterminated the Indian and "managed" the Negro and the Chinese coolie, Melville envisions a multiracial society where the symbolic concourse of Broadway offers room enough for all comers to promenade on an equal footing, and opportunities enough for all to fulfill the American dream.

Were anything needed to make Melville's egalitarian message more radical than to proclaim racial differences as extrinsic as clothing, it would be his assertion that the treacherous racial categories on which white Americans have staked their supremacy have already failed them; already, without realizing it, they have "taken"—not "mistaken," because that would implicitly validate their racial classifications—many a Chinaman, and doubtless many a Negro "passing" among them, for one of themselves. No wonder, then, that Melville refers the baffled reader seeking "further and fuller information" on the 'Gee to that "sharp-witted American whaling captain . . . Hosea Kean, of Nantucket, whose address at present is 'Pacific Ocean'" (G, 361)—for where else could a reader sharing Captain Kean's notions of race be, if not at sea?

SEVEN   *The* Devil is Never So Black
As He Is Painted: The Confidence-Man's
Joke on America

The Confidence-Man: His Masquerade sums up many
of the themes explored in Melville's previous works: the reevaluation
of American history (*Pierre*, *Israel Potter*, "The Encantadas"), the
double-barreled broadside against southern chattel and northern
wage slavery ("The Paradise of Bachelors and The Tartarus of
Maids," "The Bell-Tower"), the exposé of racial categories as in-
tangible and delusive (*Moby-Dick*, "The 'Gees"), and the threat of
apocalyptic retribution for the sin of slavery (*Moby-Dick*, "The Encantadas," "Benito Cereno," "The Bell-Tower"). Our study of this
novel should begin with the theme of apocalyptic judgment, since
it shapes the allegorical context in which we must place *The Confidence-Man's* indictment of slavery, and explains the leading role of
the character who most obviously incarnates America's "black Angel
of Doom"—Black Guinea.

The *Confidence-Man* dramatizes an apocalyptic judgment overtaking America in her slaveholding territorial hub, just as Americans fancy themselves overtaking the millennium. Symbolizing this
irony, the steamer *Fidèle*, which has succeeded the *Pequod* as America's
allegorical ship of state, is headed not for the New Jerusalem, but
for New Orleans, the financial capital of slavery and of the cotton
kingdom that underpins northern industry. The biblical prophecies
The Confidence-Man enacts are the very ones on which contemporary
Americans based their expectations of a glorious national future.
Yet belying those expectations, they foretell a fearful day of reckon-

ing when Christ will return to earth "in such an hour as ye think not" (Matt. 24:44), to test his followers and to destroy the evil world forever, along with all who prove false to him, before gathering the faithful into the heavenly kingdom he will establish on a new earth.[1]

The very first sentence of *The Confidence-Man* describes the dawning of that day "at sunrise on a first of April"—the unexpected hour par excellence—and announces the "advent" of a mysterious stranger in cream-colors who has appeared "suddenly as Manco Capac," the Peruvian sun god.[2] "His hair flaxen, his hat a white fur one, with a long fleecy nap," the stranger, as several critics have noted, recalls the vision of Christ in the Book of Revelation: "His head and his hairs were white like wool, as white as snow" (Rev. 1:14).[3] Illumined by the rising sun, the stranger may also exhibit the "countenance . . . as the sun shineth in his strength" that further characterizes the apocalyptic Christ (Rev. 1:16).

Many other details correspond to biblical prophecy. The apocalyptic advent of Christ was to be "as the lightning cometh out of the east, and shineth even unto the west" (Matt. 24:27). The stranger's advent has been equally sudden and effulgent, and he is linked to "a mysterious impostor, supposed to have recently arrived from the East" (CM, 4). The parable of the talents compares the coming of Christ's kingdom to "a man travelling into a far country" and returning after a long absence to reckon with the servants to whom he had delegated his goods (Matt. 25:14–30). The stranger seems, from the "tossed look, almost linty," of his cream-colored

1. The best recent history of American millennialism is Ernest Lee Tuveson's *Redeemer Nation: The Idea of America's Millennial Role* (Chicago, 1968). On the Puritan and eighteenth-century background of millennialism, see Sacvan Bercovitch, *The Puritan Origins of the American Self* (New Haven, 1975); and Alan Heimert, *Religion and the American Mind, from the Great Awakening to the Revolution* (Cambridge, Mass., 1966). The basic New Testament apocalyptic texts are Matthew 24 and 25, I and II Thessalonians, I and II Peter, and Revelation. The theologian whose interpretations I have found most helpful in making historical sense out of these enigmatic and often contradictory prophecies is Albert Schweitzer. See especially his *The Mystery of the Kingdom of God: The Secret of Jesus' Messiahship and Passion* (New York, 1964); and *The Quest of the Historical Jesus: A Critical Study of Its Progress from Reimarus to Wrede* (New York, 1968).
2. All page references will be to *The Confidence-Man: His Masquerade*, ed. H. Bruce Franklin, the best annotated edition of the book.
3. Elizabeth S. Foster was the first critic to point this out in her annotated edition of *The Confidence-Man*, 290, note 1.7. See also R. W. B. Lewis, *Trials of the Word: Essays in American Literature and the Humanistic Tradition* (New Haven, 1965), 210; and Franklin (ed.), *The Confidence-Man*, 3, note 5.

suit, to have been "traveling night and day from some far country beyond the prairies" (CM, 9). (Both the financial conceit of this parable and its harsh moral—"unto everyone that hath shall be given . . . abundance; but from him that hath not shall be taken away even that which he hath"—will prove singularly relevant to the Confidence-Man's chief mode of testing the passengers of the *Fidèle*: requesting money from them.) In a number of parables about the perils the advent holds for the unwary, Christ warns: "I will come on thee as a thief, and thou shalt not know what hour I will come upon thee" (Rev. 3:3). The man in cream-colors reminds a fellow passenger of an "escaped convict, worn out with dodging" (CM, 11). Christ's prime role on his apocalyptic return is to awaken the dead for the Last Judgment (John 5:27–29). Perhaps sensing the stranger's supernatural aura, another passenger suspects him for a "spirit-rapper"—someone who summons and interrogates the spirits of the dead through the raps he elicits from them.[4]

Although most Americans anticipated a "spiritual," rather than a physical advent, they located that event on American soil, and sometimes in the Mississippi Valley, the very site of the man in cream-colors' advent.[5] One contemporary sect, the Mormons, incorporated this belief into a new Bible that specifically envisioned Christ as coming in person to inaugurate the millenium in America. The Mormon prophet Joseph Smith, who went to his death "as a lamb to the slaughter" when a mob routed the Mormons out of Nauvoo, their New Jerusalem on the Mississippi, claimed to be Christ's forerunner.[6] That may be why still another passenger

4. Franklin (ed.), *The Confidence-Man*, 10–11, note 4. I have discussed Melville's satire of the contemporary spiritualist movement in "Spiritualism and Philanthropy in Brownson's *The Spirit-Rapper* and Melville's *The Confidence-Man*," *ESQ: A Journal of the American Renaissance*, XXV (1st Qt., 1979), 26–36.
5. For the Puritan sources of this belief, see Alan Heimert, "Puritanism, the Wilderness, and the Frontier," *New England Quarterly*, XXVI (1953), 361–82; and Bercovitch, *Puritan Origins*, 50–71. The most famous and influential prophecies of a millennium in America were Jonathan Edwards' *Some Thoughts Concerning the Present Revival of Religion in New England*, in *The Great Awakening*, ed. C. C. Goen (New Haven, 1972), Vol. IV of *The Works of Jonathan Edwards* (5 vols.; New Haven, 1957–77), 353–58; and Lyman Beecher's *A Plea for the West* (1835; rpt. New York, 1977), 9–10.
6. One of the most complete nonsectarian accounts of the early Mormons by a contemporary is Henry Mayhew's *The Religious, Social, and Political History of the Mormons, or Latter-day Saints . . .* , ed. Samuel M. Smucker (New York, 1856). The quotation is from p. 175.

guesses the "lamb-like" stranger in cream-colors to be a "green prophet from Utah," the Mormons' new home (CM, 10).

Hinting at the outset that the masquerade this Christlike stranger initiates is intended to test the ideals of the passengers aboard the *Fidèle*—and those of the reader—these apocalyptic portents recur as the Confidence-Man (of whom I take the man in cream-colors to be the first incarnation) assumes different guises throughout the book. One of his avatars, for example, the man in gray, declares ominously, "I am for doing good to the world once for all and having done with it" (CM, 58). Citing the precedent of another long-delayed fulfillment of prophecy, Sarah's conception of Isaac in old age, he asks rhetorically: "And is the age of wonders passed? Is the world too old?" (CM, 59). Shortly afterwards, the man in gray stages his own fulfillment of prophecy. "Mindful of the millennial promise"— "And it shall come to pass afterward, that I will pour out my spirit upon all flesh" (Joel 2:28)—he reveals a "spirit of benevolence which . . . had gone abroad over all the countries of the globe" (CM, 59–60). Since this latter-day outpouring of the spirit was supposed to have been prefigured at Pentecost, when tongues of fire descended on the apostles and empowered them to speak in foreign tongues (Acts 2:1–20), the man in gray appropriately manifests "a not un-silvery tongue, too . . . with gestures that were a Pentecost of added ones" (CM, 60).

In his next incarnation as the president and transfer-agent of the Black Rapids Coal Company, the Confidence-Man offers a chance to invest either in his own infernal-sounding business, or in the New Jerusalem, "the new and thriving city, so called, in northern Minnesota . . . originally founded by certain fugitive Mormons" (CM, 70). Later, echoing the parable of the talents and similar promises of material reward to those who invest in the kingdom of heaven (*e.g.*, Matt. 6:33), the Black Rapids man explains the "mystery" of his business in these terms: "All I have to do with you is to receive your confidence" (symbolized, as in the parable of the talents, by cash), "and all you have to do with me is, in due time, to receive it back, thrice paid in trebling profits" (CM, 102–103). His "humble profession," as his successor the herb-doctor spells out, is to make "people's fortunes for them—their everlasting fortunes" (CM, 141).

The herb-doctor, urging a sick man to "retain or reject" his cure, invokes the classic apocalyptic incentive: "time is short." In declining to specify when the cure can be expected—"not in a day, nor a week, nor perhaps a month, but sooner or later; I say not exactly when, for I am neither prophet nor charlatan" (CM, 113)—he borrows the language of Christ's second advent prophecies: "But of that day and hour knoweth no man, no, not the angels of heaven, but my Father only" (Matt. 24:36).

Of all the lamb-like man's avatars, the cosmopolitan plays the most explicitly apocalyptic role. As the lamb-like man corresponds to the image of Christ with which the Book of Revelation opens, the cosmopolitan, who brings the Confidence-Man's masquerade to a close, fittingly corresponds to the image of Christ as the Word of God, in which St. John's apocalyptic vision culminates. Indeed, he first reveals himself *verbally*, as a "voice, sweet as a seraph's," speaking out of a "spicy volume of tobacco-smoke," like the voice of God issuing from the clouds of smoke on Mt. Sinai (CM, 183). The Word of God is "clothed with a vesture dipped in blood" (Rev. 19:13). The cosmopolitan's equivalent for this is a "vesture barred with various hues, that of the cochineal predominating" (CM, 184). Cochineal is a red dye made from the dried bodies of insects, and its Italian root literally means "scarlet vesture" (*OED*). Reinforcing the blood symbolism, the "various hues" of the cosmopolitan's garment recall Joseph's "coat of many colors," which was dipped in blood by his brothers, making Joseph a "type" of Christ. (The parallel with Joseph is as relevant to *The Confidence-Man*'s indictment of slavery as to its apocalyptic allegory; for Joseph, sold into slavery by his brothers, was the subject of a famous antislavery tract: Samuel Sewall's *The Selling of Joseph*.)[7] Analogous to the "many crowns" worn by the Word of God, signifying that he is King of Kings (Rev. 19:12, 16), the cosmopolitan, "king of traveled goodfellows, evidently," is "crowned . . . off at top" by a "jaunty smoking-cap of regal purple" (CM, 185). He also holds in his hand a symbolic orb: "a Nuremburgh pipe in blast, its great porcelain bowl painted in miniature with linked crests and arms of interlinked nations." The Word of God treads the winepress of the wrath of God (Rev.

7. Samuel Sewall, *The Selling of Joseph: A Memorial*, ed. Sidney Kaplan (1700; rpt. Amherst, 1969).

19:15). The cosmopolitan, a lover of wine to whom a eulogy of the winepress is later addressed, describes himself as "a sort of London-Dock-Vault connoisseur, going about from Teheran to Natchitoches, a taster of races; in all his vintages, smacking my lips over this racy creature, man, continually" (CM, 187, 238–39). The Word of God acts as commander-in-chief of the armies of heaven (Rev. 19:14). The cosmopolitan's apparel, "in style participating of a Highland plaid, Emir's robe, and French blouse," trebly qualifies him for that role: the plaid is native to the warlike Highland Scots (while Highland may connote heaven); *emir* is the Arabic word for *commander* and the root of the English word *admiral* (OED); the "French blouse" probably refers to the "well-known blue blouse of the French workman" (OED), and hence, by implication, to the French Revolutions of 1789 and 1848.

Few critics have missed the apocalyptic overtones of the last scene over which the cosmopolitan presides: a scene taking place after midnight in a cabin lit by a solar lamp, the "last survivor of many" (CM, 333).[8] The cosmopolitan makes his advent in this scene exactly according to prophecy. Having just bilked the ship's barber of a shave (at least in the barber's opinion), he literally comes "as a thief." Like the delayed bridegroom in the parable of the wise and foolish virgins (Matt. 25:1–13), he arrives "as any bridegroom tripping to the bridal chamber might come" (CM, 334), but only after nearly everyone in the marriage party has fallen asleep. "Seeming to dispense a sort of morning through the night," he recalls both the sun, "which is as a bridegroom coming out of his chamber," in the words of the Psalmist (Ps. 19:5), and the "bright and morning star" with which Christ identifies himself in one of the last verses of Revelation (22:16). But it is mourning, rather than morning, that the cosmopolitan will dispense.

At the sound of the cosmopolitan's voice, a "dreamy" passenger begins to talk in his sleep. "He's seeing visions now, ain't he?" comments the cosmopolitan, as the disturbed sleeper calls out, "What's that about the Apocalypse?" (CM, 336–37). Despite the

8. See, for examples, Foster (ed.), *The Confidence-Man*, lxxxiv–lxxxv; John W. Shroeder, "Sources and Symbols for Melville's *Confidence-Man*," reprinted in the Norton Critical Edition of *The Confidence-Man*, ed. Hershel Parker (New York, 1971), 309–12; Hoffman, *Form and Fable*, 307–10; Lewis, *Trials of the Word*, 75, 210; Dryden, *Melville's Thematics of Form*, 184–88; and Franklin (ed.), *The Confidence-Man*, xxv–xxvii.

cosmopolitan's repeated promptings, the lone passenger who remains awake does not recognize the fulfillment of the prophecy: "your sons and your daughters shall prophesy, your old men shall dream dreams, your young men shall see visions" (Joel 2:28). Instead, he is taken as unawares by the apocalypse as the rich man in the parable who let his house be broken into because he did not know in what watch the thief was coming (Matt. 24:43). Ironically, this passenger even tries to buy protection against thieves from a "juvenile peddler . . . of travelers' conveniences" (CM, 339–43). Nor does he heed the portent in the red and yellow rags that flame about the young peddler "like the painted flames in the robes of a victim in *auto-da-fé*"—symbolizing both the "fiery trial" that was to test Christ's followers (I Pet. 4:12), and the final conflagration "in the which the heavens shall pass away with a great noise, and . . . the earth also and the works that are therein shall be burned up" (II Pet. 3:10).

By the time the cosmopolitan offers to read the old man a chapter from the Bible that is "not amiss," it is too late. The solar lamp has begun to dim and sputter, and the cosmopolitan must extinguish it "for the good of all lungs" (CM, 348–50). The lamp he snuffs out represents the Old and New Testaments, as the alternating images on its ground-glass shade indicate: "a horned altar, from which flames rose," emblemizes the Old Testament sacrificial altar; "the figure of a robed man, his head encircled by a halo," emblemizes Christ, the "altar" of the New Testament (Heb. 13:10; CM, 332).[9] Hence this lamp is the "sure word of prophecy" to which Christians are exhorted to "take heed, as unto a light that shineth in a dark place, until the day dawn, and the day star arise in your hearts" (II Pet. 1:19). By extinguishing it, the cosmopolitan signifies that he is the day star whose dawning supersedes the light of prophecy and climaxes the apocalyptic drama. For America, however, the cosmopolitan brings not light, but darkness. It is as if Melville were answering his country's presumptuous millennial expectations in the spirit of the prophet Amos: "Woe unto you that desire the day of the Lord! to what end is it for you? . . . Shall not the day of the

9. Among the critics who have contributed to explaining the symbolism of the solar lamp are Foster (ed.), *The Confidence-Man*, 363, note 272.3; Shroeder, "Sources and Symbols," 310; Hoffman, *Form and Fable*, 309; and Franklin (ed.), *The Confidence-Man*, 332, note 2. The references to Heb. 13:10 and II Pet. 1:19 are my own contribution.

Lord be darkness, and not light? even very dark, and no brightness in it?" (Amos 5:18–20).

In *The Confidence-Man*, as in *Moby-Dick*, "The Encantadas," "Benito Cereno," and "The Bell-Tower," Melville attributes this apocalyptic judgment on America specifically to slavery, which he had described early in his career as a "sin . . . foul as the crater-pool of hell" (M, 534), and which he had long viewed as epitomizing America's betrayal of her national creed. The issue of slavery is inescapable in *The Confidence-Man*. It dominates the book's very geography. The *Fidèle's* twelve-hundred-mile voyage through America's heartland begins and ends in slave territory. Its point of departure, St. Louis, Missouri, was the scene of two political confrontations over slavery. The admission of Missouri to the Union as a slave state in 1821 had occasioned the first major crisis over slavery, signaling the institution's entrenchment and sounding the "fire-bell" of sectional strife. Fifteen years later, the city of St. Louis publicized itself by lynching and burning a black man. A few miles upriver from St. Louis, on the opposite bank of the Mississippi, stood its partner in guilt, Alton, Illinois, where the abolitionist editor Elijah Lovejoy, hounded out of St. Louis for denouncing this crime, met his death at the hands of another mob.[10] *The Confidence-Man* repeatedly calls attention to its historical and geographical setting. At the center of the book, a "Missouri bachelor" and an agent of an Alton employment office argue about slavery and comment on the political status of their respective abodes as slave or "free" states. The narrator pointedly tells us that the *Fidèle* carries among her passengers "slaves, black, mulatto, quadroon" (CM, 14)—a fact we will find doubly sinister when we remember the slave's proverbial dread of being sold "down South." The *Fidèle's* final destination is New Orleans, the nation's most flourishing slave market. From the auction blocks of New Orleans, most of the *Fidèle's* slaves will probably be sold to the outlying cotton and sugar plantations, where it was reputedly more profitable to work slaves to death during the peak seasons than to prolong their lives through "good treatment" at the risk of lowering the output of these lucrative crops. New Orleans

10. Filler, *The Crusade Against Slavery*, 12, 78–81. See also Edward Beecher's eyewitness *Narrative of Riots at Alton* (1838; rpt. New York, 1965).

had other uses, however, for attractive mulatto and quadroon women: the city was famous for its light-skinned slave concubines.[11]

Slavery also casts its shadow over *The Confidence-Man*'s immediate setting, the soot-streaked steamer *Fidèle*, which "might at distance have been taken by strangers for some whitewashed fort on a floating isle" (CM, 12, 51). From afar, this steamer, like the New World transfigured by legend, history, and physical remoteness, suggests a religious or political haven, a New Atlantis. Yet a closer view reveals the blackened decks—the quarters, Melville informs us, reserved for the humblest passengers (CM, 9)—that belie her immaculate aspect, defy her whitewash, and metaphorically recall both the slaves she transports and the slavery that has sullied America. The *Fidèle* thus symbolizes at once the shining City upon a Hill that America's Puritan fathers sought to establish in the New World, and the tarnished City of Destruction they bequeathed to their posterity. Her name calls to mind the millennial faith that guided the pilgrims toward their promised land and presided over the theocracies they founded. Indeed, the *Fidèle*'s passengers, too, are pilgrims: a "piebald" (literally, black-and-white) "parliament, an Anacharsis Cloots congress of all kinds of that multiform pilgrim species, man" (CM, 14). Some of them, however—notably the slaves and "moccasined squaws," the "grinning negroes, and Sioux chiefs solemn as high-priests," the Lazaruses (diseased beggars) and "clay-eaters" (people suffering from an acute form of malnutrition particularly prevalent in the South)—have been unwillingly conscripted on this misdirected pilgrimage. That is why one of them, a "grinning negro" beggar, will play a major role in exposing the cant of his fellow pilgrims' millennial aspirations.

Reflecting the primacy Melville accords slavery in provoking the Confidence-Man's apocalyptic visitation, the first guise the lamb-like harbinger assumes on launching his latter-day assizes is that of an American Negro named for the Guinea Coast slave trade that brought his people to the New World. Black Guinea's appearance unmistakably evokes the condition to which slavery has reduced his race. He is clad in "tow-cloth" (CM, 15), one of the coarse, cheap

11. Weld, *Slavery As It Is*, 39; Martineau, *Society in America*, II, 326–27; Stampp, *The Peculiar Institution*, 259.

materials, vulgarly known as "Negro cloth," used to make slave clothing.[12] Like many of his brethren who, as Melville had noted in *Redburn*, "almost always form a considerable portion of the destitute" in the cities of the "'free states' of America" (R, 201–202), he is beggared and houseless. Socially, as well as physically, he is crippled—"in effect, cut down to the stature of a Newfoundland dog" (CM, 15)—for in America his color cripples him, and race prejudice relegates him to subhuman status, whether he be slave or free.

We cannot fully understand Black Guinea's role in *The Confidence-Man*, however, without realizing that he embodies the enslaved black man not merely as America's chief victim, but also as her apocalyptic nemesis, like Babo and the robot Haman: hence the allusion to the Spanish Inquisition in a later chapter, hinting that Guinea, like Babo, is a victim-turned-inquisitor.[13] Whereas Babo represents the inquisitor as torturer, Guinea represents rather the inquisitor as judge, or witness for the prosecution. He fulfills much the same function as the "juvenile peddler" in the last chapter, whose red and yellow attire makes him look like a "victim in *auto-da-fé*" (the death by fire imposed on Moors and other infidels during the Spanish Inquisition). In fact, several critics have noticed the resemblance between Guinea and the grimy-faced, homeless peddler, both of whom are called "Caffre[s]" (a pejorative term for African, derived from the Arabic word *kaffir*, or infidel).[14] Just as the peddler materializes at the instant the old man affirms his faith in man and God, to try this faith and prove it wanting, Guinea similarly tests the religious and humanitarian ideals his fellow Americans profess. The central issue of the chapter in which Guinea plays the role of a crippled black beggar is whether the passengers—and the readers— who encounter him evidence any fellow feeling for the Negro. This issue is equally central to the succeeding chapters in which, under

12. Weld, *Slavery As It Is*, 42; Stampp, *The Peculiar Institution*, 290.
13. See Chap. 11 (80–81), where the Black Rapids man asserts that "no one ever heard of a native-born African . . . Torquemada" (organizer of the Spanish Inquisition). Babo, of course, is a native-born African, and he symbolically reenacts the Inquisition.
14. See, for example, Franklin, *The Wake of the Gods*, 156–57; and Dominique Arnaud-Marçais, "*The Confidence-Man: His Masquerade* et le problème noir," in Viola Sachs (ed.), *Le Blanc et le Noir chez Melville et Faulkner* (Paris, 1974), 63.

the guises of the man with the weed, the man in gray, and the Black Rapids man, "Guinea" follows up the passengers who have seemingly befriended him and unmasks their racism.

Ironically, if the body of criticism *The Confidence-Man* has elicited is any indication (and I am speaking as one who has long shared its premises), those of us who think we fathom the Confidence-Man's masquerade may come off worse than any of the *Fidèle*'s passengers in the tests Guinea devises to expose the racist attitudes that condition white Americans' responses to someone they take for a Negro. Precisely because we see a nihilistic religious allegory lurking beneath the tableau of a world governed by money relationships, and because we think we recognize in the Confidence-Man a diabolical being whose every word and gesture we must reconnoiter for some suspected metaphysical ambush, we uncritically accept the racist literary conventions Melville is actually satirizing.[15] We thus find ourselves gulled again and again into making the racist assumptions that deliver the passengers of the *Fidèle* into the Confidence-Man's clutches. One such assumption is that skin color and other "racial" traits define a person's identity and provide a valid means of differentiating one human being from another. This leads us to overlook the radical statement Melville is making about race in having the Confidence-Man masquerade at will as a white or as a black, and to conclude instead that these shifts of racial identity mark the Confidence-Man as a supernatural being. A more pernicious error consists in taking for granted the traditional European association of blackness with evil and of the black man with the Devil (the "Black Man"), with the result that we see Black Guinea only as an incarnate fiend, deserving no human sympathy in his miserable plight.[16]

15. A great many critics, for example, have accepted the story of the Indian-hater at face value and have maintained that Melville was using Indians as symbols of evil, and the Indian-hater as a symbol of the heroic man who resists evil. See Shroeder, "Sources and Symbols," 312–15; also his "Indian-hating: An Ultimate Note on *The Confidence-Man*," *Books at Brown*, XXIV (1971), 1–5; also Merlin Bowen, "Tactics of Indirection in Melville's *The Confidence-Man*," *Studies in the Novel*, I (1969), 413–16. For a brilliant analysis of the Indian-hater episode as, on the contrary, a burlesque of racist attitudes toward Indians, see Adler, "Melville on the White Man's War Against the American Indian," 417–42.

16. Foster (ed.), *The Confidence-Man*, lii–liii, is fairly representative of the way critics have viewed Black Guinea: "The crippled Negro with his 'black fleece,' coming immediately after the lamblike man with his white, fleecy vesture, suggests a deliberate contrast between

Fittingly, the first passenger whose attitude toward the Negro Black Guinea will expose on this day of reckoning turns out to be a proslavery apologist. A "purple-faced drover," this man betrays the slaveowner's habit of confounding slaves with cattle, as soon as he accosts Guinea with the words: "What is your name, old boy?"; for he puts "his large purple hand on the cripple's bushy wool, as if it were the curled forehead of a black steer" (CM, 15). He may indeed be a slave driver, rather than a cattle drover. As abolitionists frequently pointed out, "the same terms are applied to slaves that are given to cattle. . . . When moved from one part of the country to another, they are herded in droves like cattle, and like them urged on by drivers."[17] The drover's next question reveals that he considers slavery the norm for blacks: "And who is your master, Guinea?"

Guinea's answer invites the drover to expatiate on the merits of slavery. "Oh sar," he says as if asking for pity, "I am der dog widout massa." The drover falls right into the trap: "Well, on your account, I'm sorry for that, Guinea. Dogs without masters fare hard" (CM, 16). Both Guinea and the drover are echoing a hackneyed proslavery argument: that the industrial workers of "free" society were but "slaves without masters" who would gladly exchange their "liberty" to be turned out of employment at a moment's notice for the lifelong job security enjoyed by the southern slave.[18]

Having drawn the drover onto the ground where a proslavery

the pure ideal of Christianity and the black use made of it by the powers of evil, or the white ideal and the black perversion wrought by man. . . . It seems that Melville carried over from 'Benito Cereno' the dog-like black man as a symbol for the black, deceitful, universal malice masquerading as fidelity and love. (Melville's use of both Negroes and Indians as symbols, it ought to be made clear, has no relation to his humanitarian attitudes, expressed elsewhere, to them as people.)" Two recent critics who have questioned this interpretation and drawn attention to the critique of racism Melville is making through Guinea are Grejda, *Common Continent of Men*, 125–29; and Arnaud-Marçais, *"The Confidence-Man* et le problème noir," 47–64.

17. Weld, *Slavery As It Is*, 110. The drover's purple face also suggests the drunkenness traditionally associated with slave traders and overseers. Eugene D. Genovese, *Roll, Jordan, Roll: The World the Slaves Made* (New York, 1976), 372, confirms that the terms slave driver and slave trader were often used interchangeably. Although slave drivers, in the narrow sense of the word, were black slaves, Melville habitually uses the word in the broader sense implied here ("slave-driving planter," WJ, 385).

18. See *The Pro-Slavery Argument*, 53; also George Fitzhugh, *Cannibals All! or, Slaves Without Masters* (1857; rpt. Cambridge, Mass., 1960). As C. Vann Woodward points out in his introduction to *Cannibals All!*, xiv, the phrase "slaves without masters" was borrowed by southern apologists from Thomas Carlyle's essay "The Present Age," which attacks British abolitionists and West Indian emancipation.

apologist is most vulnerable—the vindication of slavery as "nature's mutual insurance society" that "never fails, and covers all losses and all misfortunes"[19] —Guinea blandly turns the tables on him and knocks the bottom out of this proslavery philanthropy. "So dey do, sar; so dey do," he agrees. Then, with quiet but deadly irony, he explains why he is "free": "But you see, sar, dese here legs? What ge'mman want to own dese here legs?"[20] In other words, he, a cripple, has been condemned to fend for himself by the very gentlemen who claim to enslave his able-bodied brethren to guarantee them against penury. A living refutation of the myth that American slaves, unlike European paupers, were "never seen . . . imploring alms and exhibiting their ailings and their wants," Guinea instead confirms the abolitionists' charges that slaves "no longer able to work for their 'owners,' were . . . inhumanly cast out in their sickness and old age."[21]

The drover, however, interprets Guinea differently. Apparently he regards a free black merely as an unclaimed slave, and hence fair game. Whether because he himself has use for Guinea, or because the idea that any black might prefer freedom to slavery poses a threat to the proslavery argument, the drover tries so pertinaciously to make Guinea say he would be better off as a slave that he almost gives the impression of being about to relieve Guinea of the burden of freedom.[22] "Where do you sleep . . . of nights?" he asks. When Guinea answers, "On der floor of der good baker's oven, sar," the drover is quick to retort that the oven of white society has no room for black charity cases: "What baker . . . bakes such black bread in his oven, alongside of his nice white rolls, too. Who is that too

19. Fitzhugh, *Sociology for the South*, 168.

20. A striking parallel to this bit of dialogue occurs in Adams, *Manuel Pereira*, 222–23, where an old black, asked if he is a slave, answers: "Ole Simon a'n't no massa what say I his fo' bacon. . . . When Simon young . . . den massa say Simon his; woff touzan' dollars. . . . Now I woff nosin', no corn and bacon."

21. Spiller, "Cooper's Defense of Slave-Owning America," 580; Weld, *Slavery As It Is*, 44, 54. See also Douglass, *Narrative*, 57; Stampp, *The Peculiar Institution*, 128; and Ira Berlin, *Slaves without Masters: The Free Negro in the Antebellum South* (New York, 1976), 152–53.

22. Fitzhugh, *Sociology for the South*, 274, reports having tried unsuccessfully to persuade a free black couple to sell themselves back into slavery for the sake of greater security. See also Stampp, *The Peculiar Institution*, 58, 216–17, 258, on the uses of partially disabled slaves, legal attempts to reenslave the free black population, and slave kidnaping. Melville mentions the slave kidnaper Murrell in *The Confidence-Man*, 5. See Franklin (ed.), *The Confidence-Man*, 5, note 16.

charitable baker, pray?" Evidently he has been influenced by the ethnologists' theories that blacks and whites have been created out of different dough and baked separately.

Once again, Guinea shows himself more than a match for racist arguments in favor of slavery. "With a broad grin lifting his tambourine high over his head," he points to the sun that shines indiscriminately over blacks and whites, testifying to their equality in the sight of the great baker who looms beyond. Appropriately, the drover does not acknowledge the latter, since he worships the "atheistical iniquity" of slavery, as Melville would later call it.[23] "The sun is the baker, eh?" he asks. "Yes sar," Guinea affirms; "in der city dat good baker warms der stones for dis ole darkie when he sleeps out on der pabements o' nights."

Although Guinea succeeds in refuting the proslavery argument on every count, the homeless condition to which he has been reduced as a free black, and the scant comfort the "good baker" offers him, hardly evidence the superiority of "free" society in providing for the Negro. On the contrary, the drover's parting shaft—"How about winter, when the cold Cossacks come clattering and jingling? How about winter, old boy?"—reminds us that, throughout the country, winter has overtaken the "higher law" of the "good baker" and has licensed slave catchers, of whom the drover may be one, to deprive the Negro of even his right to take refuge from slavery on the North's pavements. From this bald assertion of the slave power's rule, Guinea takes his cue to retire: "'Den dis poor old darkie shakes werry bad, I tell you, sar. Oh, sar, oh! don't speak ob der winter,' he added, with a reminiscent shiver, shuffling off into the thickest of the crowd, like a half-frozen black sheep nudging itself a cozy berth in the heart of the white flock" (CM, 16).[24]

Significantly, Black Guinea's first encounter has involved no appeal for charity. None has been needed to expose a proslavery apologist's lack of fellow feeling for the Negro. Yet as proslavery apologists and abolitionists alike emphasized, most northerners did not treat blacks any better; in fact, anti-Negro discrimination in the North, which denied blacks all but the meanest jobs, constituted one of

23. In his prose Supplement to *Battle-Pieces*, 268.
24. This bit of dialogue may also refer ironically to the theory that the Negro was only suited to hot climates and would die out in cold climates. See Fredrickson, *Black Image in the White Mind*, Chap. 5, *passim*.

southerners' strongest arguments against emancipation—that "custom or prejudice . . . would degrade [free blacks] to the condition of slaves; and soon should we see, that 'it is happened unto them, according to the true proverb, the dog is turned to his own vomit again.'"[25] Thus on escaping the drover, Black Guinea will test whether, as a "free dog," he is still a dog in the eyes of his fellow passengers.

He meets them in the grotesque guise that America has imposed on the Negro. Grinning, shuffling, beating his tambourine, Guinea exudes the native jollity that white Americans want to see in the Negro as the compensation for his lowly status. Generating mirth "out of his very deformity, indigence, and houselessness, so cheerily endured," he reinforces the more prosperous passengers in their complacent illusion that he is happier with his lot than they, "whose own purses, hearths, hearts, all their possessions, sound limbs included, could not make gay" (CM, 15). Rubbing "his knotted black fleece and good-natured, honest black face . . . against the upper part of people's thighs . . . making music, such as it was, and raising a smile even from the gravest," he indulges the sexual fantasies these respectable whites project on the Negro, and titillates their repressed lusts.

The role of the happy slave, however, does not earn Guinea "very many pennies." Once the passengers "get their fill of him as a curious object," Guinea can attract their "charity" only by resorting to a literally dehumanizing "expedient"—one that puts him "on a canine footing" still "more than his crippled limbs"—catching pennies in his mouth (CM, 17). That is, having tried his fellow passengers' sympathy for the free black's desperate straits at the bottom of American society, and found it wanting, Guinea now lures them into reenacting on the day of reckoning their historic crimes toward the Negro. The passengers quickly succumb: "as in appearance he seemed a dog, so now, in a merry way, like a dog he began to be treated." Meanwhile, Guinea plays the menial's part to the hilt. "Whatever his secret emotions" at receiving mere crumbs from the masters' table, he contrives to "appear cheerfully grateful under the

25. *The Pro-Slavery Argument*, 213, 435–36; Barnes and Dumond (eds.), *Weld-Grimké Letters*, I, 263, 270–76, 368–69; Lydia Maria Child, *An Appeal in Favor of [That Class of] Americans Called Africans* (1833; rpt. New York, 1968), 195–216; Garrison, *Selections from the Writings*, 2–44.

trial" and to swallow his pride "while still retaining each copper this side the oesophagus." Even when "playful almoners" throw him buttons rather than pennies, and aim for his teeth, he keeps up his perpetual grin.

Black Guinea's "game of charity" enters a new phase with the intervention of a "limping, gimlet-eyed, sour-faced person" who starts to "croak out something about [the Negro's] deformity being a sham, got up for financial purposes" (CM, 17). The ensuing confrontation between Black Guinea and the newcomer, who "may be some discharged custom-house officer . . . suddenly stripped of convenient means of support," dramatizes the murderous struggle among society's outcasts for "some mysterious precedency" in gleaning her scraps, which Melville had described so powerfully in "Poor Man's Pudding and Rich Man's Crumbs" and the closing chapters of *Israel Potter*.[26] The most salient fact about the newcomer, as the narrator pointedly comments, is that he, too, is a cripple. Yet it does not seem to occur to anyone in the crowd that "cripples, above all men should be companionable, or, at least, refrain from picking a fellow-limper to pieces, in short, should have a little sympathy in common misfortune" (CM, 17–18). Nor does anyone suspect that a man who "himself on a wooden leg went halt," and who likewise appears destitute, might have ulterior motives for casting aspersions on a rival beggar.

The wooden-legged man, however, makes no bones about his rivalry with Guinea, who, he claims, can not only "walk fast enough when he tries, a good deal faster than I," but "can lie yet faster" (CM, 20)—an accusation suggesting that he, too, is lying and shamming deformity. In a later scene, the wooden-legged man all but gives himself away: asked how Guinea, "if not a cripple," could "twist his limbs so," he answers, "How do other hypocritical beggars twist theirs?" (CM, 47). The "horrible screw of his gimlet" eye that accompanies this retort tells us that he is one of the hypocrites Christ exhorted to "cast out the beam" in his own eye before attending to the "mote" in his brother's (Matt. 7:3–5).

Racism adds an ironic twist to this rivalry. On the one hand, the wooden-legged man tries to discredit Guinea's claims to charity by

26. The quotation is from "Poor Man's Pudding and Rich Man's Crumbs," in *Great Short Works*, 174. See also *Israel Potter*, Chaps. 23–25.

alleging that he is "some white operator, betwisted and painted up for a decoy" (CM, 20)—in other words, that Guinea, being neither black nor crippled, is no worse off than himself. On the other hand, even while the wooden-legged man is implicitly denying the reliability of racial appearances, he is capitalizing on the greater credibility of his own racial appearance as a white man. He thus exemplifies the poor white's historic entrapment into exchanging the birthright of economic and social equality for the pottage of white supremacy.

Guinea's almoners, for their part, are easily decoyed by their own racism. Consumed with anxiety lest a black man should have cheated them out of their pennies, they utterly miss the radical implications of the charge that a white man can successfully masquerade as a black, and even ignore the possibility that Black Guinea may not be black. Instead, they take Guinea for "some sort of black Jeremy Diddler," continue to refer to him by the racist epithets "Ebony" and "darkie" (CM, 24–25), and apply to him the provisions of the slave codes under which southern blacks had to show free papers or travel passes, or else find white guarantors.[27] "Putting the negro fairly and discreetly to the question," the crowd asks Guinea, "had he any documentary proof, any plain paper about him, attesting that his case was not a spurious one" (CM, 19)—a highly unrealistic and unjust demand to make of a black who may have been informally "freed" because his deformity makes him of no use to his master.

Black Guinea reacts to the crowd's suspicions in the only way the slave codes left open to a black: "So far abased beneath its proper physical level, that Newfoundland-dog face turned in passively hopeless appeal, as if instinct told it that the right or the wrong might not have overmuch to do with whatever wayward mood superior intelligences might yield to" (CM, 18). He knows that the law does not allow him to testify in his own defense, nor presume him innocent until proven guilty, nor require that the charges against him be suitably verified. He knows, too, that his white judges will not base their verdict on "the right or the wrong" of a black man's case. If they find him guilty of begging under false pretenses, they will not inquire whether he had any alternative, nor will they weigh his

27. Stampp, *The Peculiar Institution*, Chap. 5; William Goodell, *The American Slave Code in Theory and Practice: Its Distinctive Features Shown by Its Statutes, Judicial Decisions, and Illustrative Facts* (1853; rpt. New York, 1968), especially 295–304, 355–71, on the laws of Missouri; and Berlin, *Slaves without Masters*, 96.

bilking of "a few paltry coppers" against their own extortion of a lifetime of unpaid labor from millions of Guinea's fellow blacks. Ultimately, whatever course they take toward him will depend only on a "wayward mood" that they will mistake for "reason" or "improved judgment," and ascribe to their superior intelligence.

What Guinea is facing, the narrator hints, is a kind of lynching, by a "crowd suddenly come to be all justiciaries . . . as in Arkansas once, a man proved guilty, by law, of murder, but whose condemnation was deemed unjust by the people, so that they rescued him to try him themselves; whereupon, they, as it turned out, found him even guiltier than the court had done, and forthwith proceeded to execution; so that the gallows presented the truly warning spectacle of a man hanged by his friends" (CM, 19). This example reminds the reader of the violence to which many a black in Guinea's position fell victim. Guinea's judges, however, do not go to "such extremities, or anything like them." At least "for the time," they remain content with "sitting in judgment upon one in a box, as surely this unfortunate negro now was."

At length, three passengers seem to rally to Guinea's defense. The first two are clergymen—historically the first champions of the slave. An Episcopal clergyman "with a clear face and blue eye; innocence, tenderness, and good sense triumvirate in his air," takes the lead by asking: "But is there not some one who can speak a good word for you?" His "kindly word[s]" thaw Guinea's memory of a number of "good, kind, honest ge'mmen . . . aboard what knows me and will speak for me, God bress 'em." The gentlemen Guinea describes, all of whom allegedly know him "as well as dis poor old darkie knows hisself" (CM, 20), are those whose guises he will assume on returning to test the extent of his seeming benefactors' fellow feeling for the Negro.

The Episcopal clergyman's charity already looks dubious enough. It conforms to the pattern his church has long since set in the South.[28] Just as the Episcopal church had never fundamentally questioned slavery, but had confined itself to such token efforts on the slaves' behalf as baptizing them and enjoining slaves and masters

28. Jordan, *White Over Black*, 179–215, discusses the various churches' positions on slavery. See also James Thayer Addison, *The Episcopal Church in the United States, 1789–1931* (New York, 1951), 192–98.

to fulfill their respective Christian duties of obedience and paternal care, so the Episcopal clergyman neither challenges the inquisition to which Guinea is subjected nor personally gives him alms, but lamely offers to seek out one of the (white) witnesses Guinea calls on to vouch for his being an authentic charity case. Even this timid gesture almost proves too much for the clergyman; for he falters when another bystander, "whose natural good-feeling had been made at least cautious by the unnatural ill-feeling" of the wooden-legged man, wonders out loud: "But how are we to find all these people in this great crowd?" (CM, 20).

The next passenger to take up Guinea's defense is a Methodist minister, "a tall, muscular, martial-looking man, a Tennessean by birth, who in the Mexican war had been volunteer chaplain to a volunteer rifle-regiment" (CM, 20–21). His southern origins and aggressive support for a war instigated by proslavery expansionists signal at the outset that his charity toward the Negro will be no more reliable. Arriving in the wake of the Episcopalian's departure, as Methodist evangelicalism had historically emerged in protest against the Episcopal church's torpor, he likewise mirrors his church's shifting policy on slavery.[29] In the spirit of the early Methodists who, following the lead of George Whitefield during the Great Awakening of 1740, had fervently censured slavery and preached the spiritual equality of blacks and whites, the Methodist initially acts as Guinea's "impassioned intercessor" (CM, 25). He steps forward in response to the wooden-legged man's charge that Guinea is a white impostor and that "his friends are all humbugs" (CM, 20). "Have you no charity, friend?" he counters "in self-subdued tones, singularly contrasted with his unsubdued person." When his pleas for putting "as charitable a construction as one can upon the poor fellow" meet with jeers, he resorts to the abusive language in which Methodist circuit riders denounced sinners, and violently castigates the wooden-legged man as a "godless reprobate" (CM, 22). Reflecting the brand of Christianity the Methodists had stood for in their heyday, when they stormed the citadel of the New

29. Jordan, *White Over Black*, 212–15, 418–19; Berlin, *Slaves without Masters*, 83–84; and Charles Baumer Swaney, *Episcopal Methodism and Slavery, with Sidelights on Ecclesiastical Politics* (New York, 1969), *passim*. The historical significance of the order in which the Episcopal and Methodist clergymen appear was first pointed out by Franklin, *The Wake of the Gods*, 166.

Jerusalem, the Methodist minister explicitly rejects the idea that a Christian must be a "non-combatant" and physically attacks the wooden-legged man, for which he is hailed as the "church militant" incarnate. Like his historical prototypes, however, who soon went the way of other sects and abandoned the slaves to their fate, the Methodist minister, after routing the wooden-legged man, surrenders to doubts about Guinea's merits: "A change had come over that before impassioned intercessor. With an irresolute and troubled air, he mutely eyed the suppliant; against whom, somehow, by what seemed instinctive influences, the distrusts first set on foot were now generally reviving, and, if anything, with added severity" (CM, 25).

The last passenger to befriend Guinea, and the sole to give him alms after the wooden-legged man has discredited the beggar, is a country merchant from Wheeling, Pennsylvania—the man who has previously questioned whether Guinea's friends can be traced in such a large crowd. Apparently Guinea's desperate appeal, "no confidence in dis poor ole darkie"—an appeal "coming so piteously on the heel of pitilessness"—has touched the merchant's humane feelings. "Yes, my poor fellow, I have confidence in you," he exclaims. "And here, here is some proof of my trust. . . . Here, here, my poor fellow" (CM, 25). The half dollar the merchant hands Guinea is a generous contribution to a beggar, even by today's standards. Nevertheless, the merchant's ostentatious way of proclaiming his charity suggests that his motive may not be entirely disinterested. In taking his purse out of his pocket, the merchant "accidentally" (so the narrator assures us) brings forth a business card "along with it" and chances (or contrives) to drop it on the deck, thereby (perhaps) availing himself of an opportunity to advertise his forwarding business through the donation. Besides, what is a contribution to a beggar but a salve for the guilty conscience of the class responsible for the existence of beggars?

Thus all three of Black Guinea's benefactors give him some reason to suspect their charity and to test their motives in befriending him. And all three, as we shall see, will ultimately negate their seeming benevolence toward the Negro by betraying a racism as thoroughgoing as that of the passengers who have spurned Guinea.

Before following Black Guinea's masquerade into this next stage, however, let us sum up what his "game of charity" as a crippled black beggar tells us about the part Melville perceived the Negro to be playing on America's historical stage. First of all, on the level of individual behavior, Black Guinea acts out the dual role assumed by every slave, as a victim of oppression who in turn victimizes his white oppressors by dissimulating his vengefulness under the grinning mask they want him to wear. This facet of slavery, also dramatized in "Benito Cereno," had been widely discussed both in the southern commercial press, which continually published complaints about the Negro's mendacity, thievery, artful sabotage of work, and occasional treachery, and in abolitionist writings, including slave narratives, which emphasized that "cunning and deception" were indispensable means of survival under slavery.[30] Second, on the collective level, Black Guinea represents the apocalyptic retribution that Melville expected America's four million slave victims to wreak upon her, whether by rising in insurrection, as does Babo, or by permanently blighting the republic built on their blood, as Melville had suggested in "The Bell-Tower." Third, on the level of Melville's racial discourse, Black Guinea, who may after all be only a white masquerading as a black, incarnates the Confidence-Man's joke on America: that the phantasm of race, in whose name Americans had refused to extricate themselves from the slave system that was destroying them, may not exist except in the white mind. Even more subversively, Guinea's masquerade indicates that there is no way of ascertaining whether he is black or white—hence no way of being sure that the treatment American society has reserved for him as a black may not have been "mistakenly" inflicted on a white.

The implication that a person need not be black to fall victim to a society that enslaves blacks is reinforced by many parallels linking Guinea to other characters in the book who also play the slave's dual role as victim and con man.[31] The most poignant example

30. Stampp, *The Peculiar Institution*, Chap. 3, is a useful compendium of slaveowners' complaints about their "Troublesome Property." See also Cartwright, "Diseases of the Negro," 333–34; Olmsted, *Seaboard Slave States*, 117, 145, 187, 480–81, 719–20; Stowe, *Uncle Tom's Cabin*, 219, 417; Douglass, *Narrative*, 36–37.

31. For example, the lamb-like deaf-mute, who is jeered at, pushed, jostled, and punched by the crowd to whom he exhibits his message of charity, and nearly thrown off his feet by "two porters carrying a large trunk" that they "accidentally or otherwise" swing against him; the man in gray, who is treated with "touchy disgust" as another of "these begging fellows," by a "well-to-do gentleman"; the herb-doctor, who, like the lamb-like man, is "all but felled" by a "sudden side-blow" (CM, 7–9, 42–43, 122).

is the crippled "soldier of fortune" Thomas Fry, described by the herb-doctor as "much such a case as the negro's" (CM, 138), although Fry's "interwoven paralyzed legs, stiff as icicles, suspended between rude crutches" (CM, 129), bear no physical resemblance to the "leather stump[s]" that cut Guinea "down to the stature of a New-foundland dog" (CM, 15, 25). Wearing a "grimy old regimental coat" and passing himself off as a casualty of the Mexican War (fought to extend slavery into the southwest), Thomas Fry may in fact be Guinea himself in the guise of the "ge'mman as is a sodjer" he cites among the friends who know him "as well as dis poor old darkie knows hisself" (CM, 20).[32] Certainly the nickname he has gone by, "Happy Tom," conferred on him "because I was so good-natured and laughing all the time" (CM, 132), relates him to the Negro, reverberating as it does with ironic echoes of Uncle Tom, the submissive Christian slave beloved by his masters, and Happy Jack, the dancing and singing sailor beloved by his officers, and presented by Melville as the black slave Guinea's white counterpart (WJ, 378–85). Both of the stories the cripple tells about how he lost the use of his limbs drive home the lesson that American society oppresses whites in many of the same ways it does blacks, and forces them, too, to delude their oppressors by feigning cheerful acqui-escence in the social system that beggars them.

The story Thomas Fry uses to beg for alms while "stumping among the passengers . . . with a jovial kind of air"—that he has been "crippled in both pins at glorious Contreras" (CM, 135)—conjures up the fate of the common soldier. Victimized by his nation's social and racial discrimination at home; recruited in the name of fraudulent ideals of democracy and baneful myths of national glory and aggrandizement; coerced into personally enacting his nation's crimes abroad by brandishing racist slogans, preying on the poor and helpless, bullying, raping, and looting the civilian population, desolating the land, torturing and killing his fellow victims on the opposite side—only to be mutilated, if not killed, himself—the sol-dier is reduced to earning a pittance by perpetuating the illusions about the glories of war that entrapped him in the first place.

32. Foster (ed.), *The Confidence-Man*, lxx–lxxi, argues that Fry "hardly seems an appropriate inclusion in the Negro's list," since "he is a victim rather than an accomplice of the herb-doctor," even though "he qualifies perhaps as a confidence man when he collects money under slightly false pretenses."

The story he relates to the herb-doctor (CM, 132–35) is even more suggestive (particularly in the light of what we have learned about our criminal justice system in recent years). During a political meeting he happened to attend in the park, Thomas Fry saw a drunken "gentleman" push a sober workingman out of the way and kill him when the worker "tried to maintain his rights." Along with the gentleman, he and other witnesses were taken to the Tombs, where the gentleman and his party gave bail, but Fry, because he "hadn't no friends"—"a worse crime than murder"—was locked up in a wet cell until the trial. (This detail adds a new dimension to the derisive question that the wooden-legged man, whose cynicism Thomas Fry recalls, had earlier asked about Black Guinea: "Did ever beggar have such heaps of fine friends?" [CM, 20].) In prison, due to "the wet and the damp," Thomas Fry contracted a paralyzing ailment. At the trial, he testified against the gentleman, but to no avail; thanks to his "friends" (and his money), the gentleman was acquitted. Meanwhile, Thomas Fry had become crippled for life. No wonder that he now airs "unhandsome notions . . . about 'free Ameriky,' as he sarcastically called his country" (CM, 136). The crowning irony, however, is that no one believes his true story because, as the herb-doctor puts it, "it so jars with all, is so incompatible with all" the accepted notions of "the system of things" (CM, 135). That is why Thomas Fry has been obliged to pose as a patriotic Mexican War veteran in order to attract almoners. He thus vivifies what Black Guinea's masquerade symbolizes: that the racial distinctions on which the slave system has based itself are purely illusory and provide no security against oppression for whites in "free Ameriky."

In his guise as Black Guinea, the Confidence-Man has tested how his fellow passengers react to a man they perceive as a Negro. In his three subsequent guises as the man with the weed, the man in gray, and the president and transfer-agent of the Black Rapids Coal Company, he will test whether the same passengers behave any differently toward someone they perceive as white.

The first passenger to come up for review is the good merchant, whose business card, "accidentally" dropped in the act of almsgiving, Black Guinea had "as unconsciously" covered with his "leather stump" (CM, 25). (The narrator's language forces us to view both acts in the same light as equally unconscious or equally intentional. If we nevertheless distinguish between the two men's motives and suppose the merchant to be innocent of any dubious purpose, but Guinea to be guilty of perfidy, we fall into a Melvillean trap laid to expose our own racist attitudes and assumptions.)

Reappearing as "a man in mourning" with "a long weed on his hat," "Guinea" accosts the merchant "with the familiarity of an old acquaintance" (CM, 27). Having appropriated the merchant's business card, he knows the merchant by name. He also recognizes the merchant's face, of course, and seeks to ascertain whether the merchant will recognize his underneath the superficial difference in skin color. Prodding the merchant to notice the resemblance between the black beggar he has just befriended and the black-clad white man who now addresses him, the man with the weed says: "Is it possible, my dear sir . . . that you do not recall my countenance? why yours I recall distinctly as if but half an hour, instead of half an age, had passed since I saw you." Three times he appeals to the merchant to acknowledge his identity with his black predecessor, and by extension their common humanity. Three times the merchant demurs, despite having heard Guinea accused of being a white man masquerading as a black:

> "Don't you know me?"
> "No, certainly."
>
> . . . .
>
> "Don't you recall me, now? Look harder."
> "In my conscience—truly—I protest . . . bless my soul, sir, I don't know you—really, really."
>
> . . . .
>
> "Still you don't recall my countenance?"
> "Still does truth compel me to say that I cannot, despite my best efforts." (CM, 27–28)

The echoes of Peter's denial of Christ, intensified by the exclamations "in my conscience" and "bless my soul," warn that failure to recognize Christ's image in the least of his brethren is being judged on the Last Day as equivalent to denying Christ himself (Matt. 25:31–46, 26:70–74).

"Can I be so changed?" insists the man with the weed. He then hints that the same moral blindness that prevents the merchant from looking beneath the skin of his fellow man also prevents him from looking into his own heart and examining the motive that led him to contribute so ostentatiously to Guinea: "Look at me. Or is it I who am mistaken?—Are you not, sir, Henry Roberts, forwarding merchant, of Wheeling, Pennsylvania? Pray, now, *if you use the advertisement of business cards*, and happen to have one with you, just look at it, and see whether you are not the man I take you for" (CM, 28; italics added). The merchant, then, has probably dropped his business card in the act of almsgiving as a means of advertising his forwarding company. No wonder the man with the weed admonishes him that "self-knowledge is thought by some not so easy," when the merchant tries to say that he does not need to consult his business card in order to know himself.

Having vainly tried to make the merchant recognize him as the "Negro" he has actually encountered, the man with the weed proceeds to invent an account of a former meeting with the merchant, to see whether the merchant will "recognize" him better as a fictitious racial and social peer: "I met you, now some six years back, at Brade Brothers & Co.'s office, I think. I was traveling for a Philadelphia house. The senior Brade introduced us, you remember; some business-chat followed, then you forced me home with you to a family tea, and a family time we had." Although the merchant obviously cannot remember such a meeting, he takes the man with the weed's word for it more readily than he identifies the man with the weed's countenance with Guinea's, yielding to the suggestion that a brain injury may have impaired his memory. (How credible would he have found this suggestion, coming from a ragged black pauper who claimed prior acquaintance with him?) He thus shows that he acknowledges the bonds of race and class, rather than those of human brotherhood. Even more telling is the plea that once and for all allays the merchant's scruples: that the man with the weed is a fellow mason, a "brother" within a still narrower and more artificial peer group.

In this light, the contrast between the merchant's attitude toward Black Guinea and toward the man with the weed becomes singularly instructive. Not only does the merchant find it easier to befriend a respectable white businessman in delicate straits than a crippled, homeless black beggar. He is also more moved by a *tale* "involving calamities against which no integrity, no forethought, no energy, no genius, no piety, could guard" (CM, 32), than by a living example of precisely such a case before his very eyes, in the person of a black who graphically illustrates the undeserved calamities visited on an entire people. Whereas the merchant has relegated a mere coin to Guinea, he reserves a banknote for the man with the weed, which he exchanges for a larger one "at some still more unhappy revelation." The man with the weed's story arouses in the merchant "no sentimental pity," such as Black Guinea has inspired, but "commiseration," the emotion proper to an equal. Correspondingly, its narrator's needs evoke no condescending words, like "here, here, my poor fellow" (CM, 25), but an "air studiously disclamatory of alms-giving" (CM, 32). Nor is the merchant offended that the man with the weed, instead of looking "cheerfully grateful under the trial" (CM, 17), as Guinea would be expected to, should pocket the money "with an air studiously disclamatory of alms-taking," "as if misery, however burdensome, could not break down self-respect, nor gratitude, however deep, humiliate a gentleman" (CM, 32).

Thus throughout his encounter with the man with the weed, the best-intentioned and most generous of the Negro's benefactors has betrayed a racism so deep-seated that it determines his every response to other human beings according to whether he perceives them as black or white. Once we realize that it is not the merchant's charity, but his fellow feeling for the Negro, that Black Guinea's first avatar has tried and found wanting, we can see why the man with the weed now requites the merchant by setting him up for an incriminating investment in the Black Rapids Coal Company.[33]

Even before hearing the man with the weed describe its vicissitudes, we can guess that an investment in the Black Rapids Coal Company is in every sense an investment in hell. As many critics have pointed out, the name Black Rapids Coal Company has diabolical connotations. The Company also, I submit, represents the

33. Because Sidney Kaplan has overlooked the racism betrayed by the merchant and the Episcopal clergyman, he has misinterpreted *The Confidence-Man* as "an indictment of all friends of the Negro, a fatalistic assessment of all anti-slavery efforts" ("Melville and the American National Sin," 33). Neither the merchant nor the clergyman, of course, shows any evidence of "anti-slavery efforts."

industrial analogue of the southern slave system.[34] The coal mining industry remains much akin to slavery today. To fuel the American economy, it relies on a near-captive labor force spanning both North and South, like the business of the seedsman in "The Tartarus of Maids," and requires extracting a black natural resource from the earth under extremely hazardous conditions which blacken the laborers inside and out, making blacks and whites literally indistinguishable. During the antebellum period, moreover, the two biggest mining states, Kentucky and Virginia, were slave states, nearly all of whose miners were black slaves, either owned directly by the mining companies, or hired out to them by their owners.[35] Far from contradicting each other, the religious and socioeconomic connotations of the Black Rapids Coal Company in fact dovetail. Not only had abolitionists long been proclaiming that "the slave-system is one of the strongholds of the devil—perhaps the strongest,"[36] but Melville himself had denounced both chattel and wage slavery in the same idiom, identifying the one with the "crater-pool of hell" (M, 534), the other with "Tartarus" (PBTM).

The very errand that, according to the man with the weed, brings the president and transfer-agent of the Black Rapids Coal Company aboard this southbound Mississippi steamer subtly links him with slavery. "Having been subpoenaed as witness in a stock case on the docket in Kentucky" (both a coal-mining and a slave state), he has set out from his office in St. Louis (also slave territory) and is headed for the courtroom with his transfer-book. The account of Black Rapids stock that immediately follows this disclosure suggests further connections with slavery:

> A month since, in a panic contrived by artful alarmists, some credulous stock-holders sold out; but, to frustrate the aim of the alarmists, the Company, previously advised of their scheme, so managed it as to get into its own hands those sacrificed shares, resolved that, since a spurious panic must be, the panic-makers should be no gainers by it. The Company, I hear, is now ready, but not anxious, to redispose

34. I am indebted for this formulation to H. Bruce Franklin's comments on the original version of my chapter on *The Confidence-Man*.
35. Stampp, *The Peculiar Institution*, 71; Robert S. Starobin, *Industrial Slavery in the Old South* (New York, 1970), 22–23, mentions a Black Heath Coal Company (of Virginia) as having spent $11,345 for Negroes in one year.
36. Garrison, *Selections from the Writings*, 130.

of those shares; and having obtained them at their depressed value, will now sell them at par, though, prior to the panic, they were held at a handsome figure above. That the readiness of the Company to do this is not generally known, is shown by the fact that the stock still stands on the transfer-book in the Company's name, offering to one in funds a rare chance for investment. For, the panic subsiding more and more every day, it will daily be seen how it originated; confidence will be more than restored; there will be a reaction; from the stock's descent its rise will be higher than from no fall, the holders trusting themselves to fear no second fate. (CM, 32–33)

The Company's fluctuations parallel those of the American economy in general, and of the slave system to which that economy was tied in particular. After the disastrous nationwide panic of 1837 (which had bankrupted the Melville family for the second time), the slave system's fortunes, too, had seemed to ebb—only to make a spectacular recovery during the "prosperous fifties," when slave prices skyrocketed to "record highs" under prosouthern administrations.[37] The "artful alarmists" responsible for shaking confidence in the Company's stock and inducing "some credulous stock-holders" to sell out might stand for all contemporary critics of America, among whom abolitionists were most prominent. Besides warning southerners to "sell out" of slavery and northerners to abjure union with slaveholders, on pain of provoking God's judgment on America, abolitionists had greeted the effects of the panic as "warnings, reproofs, and the foreshadows of coming retribution."[38] Like the "gloomy philosophers" later castigated by the Black Rapids man (CM, 68), they had also touched on "stocks, politics, bread-stuffs" (many abolitionists adhered to the whole-wheat vegetarian diet of health reformer Sylvester Graham[39]), "morals, metaphysics, religion" in their sweeping critique of slavery, which they saw as permeating all aspects of American society. Abolitionists had also been accused, like the "theological bear[s]" who cry down Black Rapids stock, of disturbing the "naturally-quiet brightness" of slavery by trumping up such "black panics" as the Nat Turner revolt, and of

37. Stampp, The Peculiar Institution, 415.
38. Barnes and Dumond (eds.), Weld-Grimké Letters, II, 911–12; Garrison, Selections from the Writings, 58–59; Nelson (ed.), Documents of Upheaval, 202–206.
39. Filler, The Crusade Against Slavery, 118; Thomas H. Le Duc, "Grahamites and Garrisonites," New York History, XX (1939), 189–91; Barnes and Dumond (eds.), Weld-Grimké Letters, 531, 753–54.

rejoicing over "the gains got by their pretended sore heads" at the hands of angry mobs. They, too, had been called "hypocrites in the simulation of things dark instead of bright; souls that thrive, less upon depression, than the fiction of depression; professors of the wicked art of manufacturing depressions; spurious Jeremiahs; sham Heraclituses" (CM, 67–68, 72).

We need not allegorize the Black Rapids Coal Company and its depreciators, however, to infer from the man with the weed's account that the Company is under investigation for complicity in shady stock market dealings—or ought to be, if it isn't. Hence the merchant's eagerness to avail himself of this opportunity to invest in Black Rapids stock hardly reflects well on his business ethics.

Lest we miss the point, one last clue alerts us to the moral compunctions and conscientious discourses with which the merchant will subsequently gloss over his surrender to greed. Just before the merchant encounters the Black Rapids man (six chapters after taking leave of the man with the weed), a less scrupulous customer, likewise emerging from a bout with the man with the weed, engages in the same transaction. Earlier described as a pensive, effeminate-looking college sophomore, carrying a volume of Tacitus, this young man not only seems agog to invest in Black Rapids stock, but also evinces a surprising familiarity with the Company's circumstances. The collegian fastens "without the least embarrassment" on the Black Rapids man's casual reference to the Company (CM, 66), although he had previously shown "an ever-increasing embarrassment" at the overtures of the impecunious man with the weed (CM, 41). Resisting the Black Rapids man's pretended efforts to divert his attention from the business of investing to the duty of succoring the man with the weed, the sophomore asks for a statement of the Company's condition. He apparently does not need the information the statement contains, however, for he observes that it fails to mention the recent fluctuations of Black Rapids stock, to which he seems independently privy: "Your statement . . . tells a very fine story; but pray, was not your stock a little heavy a while ago? downward tendency? Sort of low spirits among holders on the subject of that stock?" (CM, 67). The significance of both his knowledge and his predilection for Black Rapids stock ultimately becomes clear when the sophomore applauds the Black Rapids man for imputing the depression to the machinations of "gloomy philosophers": "'I rather like that,' knowingly drawled the youth. 'I fancy these gloomy souls as little as the next one. Sitting on my sofa after a champagne dinner, smoking my plantation cigar, if a gloomy fellow come to me—what a bore!'" (CM, 68). The drawl, the champagne dinner, the plantation cigar—all add up to an aristocratic southern identity that reconciles the seeming opposites of the youth's languid manner, his effeminate dress, his pensive air, and his penchant for the classics, on the one hand,[40] and his businesslike bent, his worldliness, his social callousness, and his preference for pragmatic and "comfortable" philosophies on the other. The crowning touch is the yawn with which the sophomore turns down an opportunity to invest in the New Jerusalem—"the new and thriving city, so called . . . founded by certain fugitive Mormons" (CM, 70–71)—thereby revealing the southerner's notorious disdain for the active millennialist faith and multitudinous "Isms" of the North.[41]

This episode with the sophomore forewarns us that by purchasing Black Rapids stock, the merchant will be aligning himself with the slaveholding class whose cynicism the sophomore epitomizes. It also spells out the moral that to invest in any form of human slavery is to abjure the millennial hope.

Now that we understand how the merchant's false philanthropy toward the Negro, and the racism and cupidity it masks, have delivered him into the power of the Black Rapids man, we are ready to analyze the episode that completes his downfall. It begins with overtones of apocalyptic judgment, when the Black Rapids man enters the cabin "in due time, book under arm," to convict those whose "distrust in man" he has "unwillingly inferred from repeated repulses, in disinterested endeavors to procure . . . confidence," as the "handbill" announcing his advent has it (CM, 73–74). The Black Rapids man's aim is to obtain final proof of the merchant's guilt by eliciting from him a financial investment in the human slavery he at heart condones, and by winning his assent to the ideology that all ruling classes have traditionally invoked to justify the comfortable life they enjoy at the expense of those they exploit.

40. See Taylor, *Cavalier and Yankee*, 160–61, on the "Southern Hamlet."
41. On southerners' repudiation of northern millennialism, see *The Pro-Slavery Argument*, 104–105, 116–17; also Jenkins, *Pro-Slavery Thought*, 299–301.

Almost as soon as the Black Rapids man approaches the merchant, he starts pressing on him the attitude toward life revealed by the bachelors of Temple Bar as they pass the sherry and pooh-pooh "the thing called pain, the bugbear styled trouble" (PBTM, 209). "'Come, come,'" he admonishes the merchant, "luxuriously laying himself back . . . 'fares all paid; digestion sound; care, toil, penury, grief, unknown; lounging on this sofa, with waistband relaxed, why not be cheerfully resigned to one's fate, nor peevishly pick holes in the blessed fate of the world?'" (CM, 76). Ironically, it will take longer to bring the merchant round to this philosophy than to make him commit the act that identifies him with the class it serves. So eager is the merchant to invest in Black Rapids stock that, once his attention has been attracted to the transfer-book through the ruse of "forgetting" it on the settee, he needs no urging from the Black Rapids man. Indeed, the Black Rapids man acts as standoffish with the merchant as with the collegian. Giving the merchant a last chance to recognize him, he remarks: "doubtless, there are plenty who know our Company, whom our Company does not know; in the same way that one may know an individual, yet be unknown to him" (CM, 78). When the merchant reiterates his inquiry about the Company stock, the Black Rapids man chides: "'Dear me, you don't think of doing any business with me, do you? In my official capacity I have not been authenticated to you. This transfer-book, now,' holding it up so as to bring the lettering in sight, 'how do you know that it may not be a bogus one? And I, being personally a stranger to you, how can you have confidence in me?'" These questions invite the merchant—and the reader—to compare the confidence the merchant displays in the Black Rapids man with the mistrust he initially shows toward the man with the weed, not to mention Black Guinea. Clearly his confidence in man increases proportionately to his acquaintance's financial and social status, and the huge sum he is prepared to invest for his own benefit, without the slightest hesitation, contrasts strikingly with the paltry sum he contributes to Guinea after much hemming and hawing about whether the Negro is an authentic charity case. Even the Black Rapids man's pointed warning—"But you have not examined my book. . . . You had better. It might suggest doubts"—does not give the merchant pause. Invest he must, and invest he does.

After the transaction, the Black Rapids man renews his attempt to make the merchant own the callous social and racial views that guide his conduct. A statement by the narrator sets the proper tone for the Black Rapids man's ensuing discussion with a man vaguely aware of having acted against the dictates of his conscience. Interpreting the "sympathetic silence" that temporarily prevails between the two businessmen as a sign of friendliness, the narrator comments: "[It is] a kind of social superstition, to suppose that to be truly friendly one must be saying friendly words all the time, any more than be doing friendly deeds continually. True friendliness, like true religion, being in a sort independent of works" (CM, 79).

The doctrine of salvation by faith rather than works, which the narrator here parodies, was of course held in its most extreme form by Calvinists, who maintained that man's innate depravity made him incapable of saving himself and cast him utterly on the mercy of divine grace. Although it had once gone hand in hand with Puritan revolutionary zeal and millenarian aspirations, by the mid-nineteenth century Calvinist theology had become the refuge of conservatives opposed to social reform. It thus continued to dominate the slaveholding South long after most northern churches had abandoned it. Calvinist clergymen were among the South's most influential exponents of the idea that slavery was "part of the curse which sin [had] introduced into the world," and hence was destined to abide until God himself abolished it with the millennium.[42] Similarly, Calvinist theologians from the northern outposts of "Old School" dogma at Andover and Princeton were the South's stanchest supporters on the issue that divided many churches in the 1830s: whether it was sinful to hold slaves.[43] Just as nineteenth-century Calvinism served to justify slavery by fostering the sense that human beings were impotent to cure the evils springing from "the nature of man as sinful, and the nature of society as disordered,"[44] so the narrator's assertion that "true friendliness, like true religion," is "independent of works" serves to exonerate the merchant's investment in slave labor by taking charity out of the realm

42. Jenkins, *Pro-Slavery Thought*, 215–17.
43. C. Bruce Staiger, "Abolitionism and the Presbyterian Schism of 1837–1838," *Mississippi Valley Historical Review*, XXXVI (1949), 391–414; Filler, *The Crusade Against Slavery*, 122–26.
44. Jenkins, *Pro-Slavery Thought*, 215.

of concrete deeds and refining it into a mere "luxury of unaffected good feeling" (CM, 79).

When the merchant at length breaks the silence, it is to cite cases of human suffering in "other quarters" of the *Fidèle* that prevent him from fully savoring the pleasures of his comfortable cabin. His first example is an invalid miser he has seen in the emigrants' quarters, "eagerly clinging to life and lucre, though the one was gasping for outlet, and about the other he was in torment lest death, or some other unprincipled cut-purse should be the means of his losing it; by like feeble tenure holding lungs and pouch, and yet knowing and desiring nothing beyond them." Perhaps the merchant obscurely recognizes in this grotesque, dehumanized creature—who has "no trust in anything, not even in his parchment bonds," which he has "sealed up, like brandy peaches" to preserve them from the "tooth of time"—a mirror image of what he himself is going to become, now that he, too, has succumbed to greed and invested in treasures that moth and rust corrupt (Matt. 6:19–21). But because the merchant has persisted in his damning course after receiving such an admonition, and because he apparently has no intention of giving up his investment, his pangs of guilt are useless. That is why the Black Rapids man taxes him with "evincing . . . a somewhat jaundiced sentimentality" and urges him to adopt a philosophy more in harmony with his actions—one which, like Emerson's, and like the wealthy Blandmour's of "Poor Man's Pudding," finds "compensatory considerations" in other people's suffering (CM, 80).[45]

Unconvinced by the Black Rapids man's reasoning, the merchant then cites the case of Black Guinea as a second example of unmerited misery. Now that he has denied his fellowship with the Negro and acquired a stake in human slavery, however, it is too late for the merchant to indulge in pitying the likes of Guinea. Against the phony qualms of conscience that allowed northerners of the merchant's ilk to feel superior to slaveholders, the Black Rapids man arrays all the arguments proslavery apologists used to counter sympathy for the slaves: that racial differences made it necessary to judge the feelings of whites and blacks by different standards; that

45. See Melville's parody of Emerson's essay "Compensation" in "Poor Man's Pudding," where Blandmour philosophizes on how "the poor, out of their very poverty, extract comfort" (*Great Short Works*, 165–67).

the Negro's nervous system deadened him to physical pain; that an innate cheerfulness immunized him against grief; that consciousness of mental inferiority reconciled the Negro to lowly status; that the rise of an African nemesis need not be feared, vindictiveness being foreign to the African temperament; that in his own way, the black menial was as happy as the most privileged white, and perhaps even happier:[46]

> [The merchant's] companion suggested whether the alleged hardships of that alleged unfortunate might not exist more in the pity of the observer than the experience of the observed. He knew nothing about the cripple, nor had seen him, but ventured to surmise that, could one but get at the real state of his heart, he would be found about as happy as most men, if not, in fact, full as happy as the speaker himself. He added that negroes were by nature a singularly cheerful race; no one ever heard of a native-born African Zimmermann or Torquemada; that even from religion they dismissed all gloom; in their hilarious rituals they danced, so to speak, and, as it were, cut pigeon-wings. It was improbable, therefore, that a negro, however reduced to his stumps by fortune, could be ever thrown off the legs of a laughing philosophy. (CM, 80–81)

The merchant's contrasting treatment of the man with the weed and Black Guinea, and his inability to recognize them as the same being, have shown to what degree he differentiates between whites and blacks in practice. Thus he is already prepared to accept the theory that rationalizes such discrimination. Finding the insinuation that a white cannot "get at the real state of [a black's] heart" unanswerable, and seeing no contradiction between that view and its white proponent's assurance that "negroes were by nature a singularly cheerful race," he is simply "foiled"—at least as regards the propriety of citing Guinea, or any black, as an example of human suffering.

Ironically, his third and last example of human suffering is the man with the weed, whose story he now repeats to the Black Rapids

46. See *The Pro-Slavery Argument*, 24–27, 32–34, 48, 56, 74–77, 81, 128–33. The first citation (24–27) provides a particularly apt analogue: "We can estimate but very, very imperfectly the good and evil of individual condition. . . . Some unexpected solace arises to alleviate the severest calamity. Wonderful is the power of custom, in making the hardest condition tolerable; the most generally wretched life has circumstances of mitigation, and moments of vivid enjoyment, of which the more seemingly happy can scarcely conceive. . . . If we could perfectly analyze the enjoyments and sufferings of the most happy, and the most miserable man, we should perhaps be startled to find the difference so much less than our previous impressions had led us to conceive."

man, its author in another guise. This time, appropriately, he refuses to be "foiled" by arguments that the man with the weed is happier than he looks. Instead, he once again betrays that the slightest misfortune he hears of in a white is more real to him than the most appalling misery he sees in a black.

We need not follow the merchant to the end of his colloquy with the Black Rapids man. Suffice it that he leaves "sobered, shamed, all but confounded," upon realizing that "truth will *not* be comforted" (CM, 92–93). We can surmise that "truth" in this case refers to the significance of the transaction he has completed.

It might seem that we modern critics ought to resist the Confidence-Man's wiles better than the merchant. Yet too many of us have fallen into the same errors in spite of, or even because of our superior insight. The vast majority of us, for example, have knowingly pounced on the double entendre "full as happy as the speaker himself," identifying the Black Rapids man with Black Guinea, but deduced from it that Guinea's afflictions are not to be pitied—which is exactly what the Black Rapids man's racist arguments have forced the merchant to conclude. Like the merchant, most of us have also taken the man with the weed's tale of woe more seriously than the spectacle of woe Black Guinea presents, notwithstanding the many hints that the story is a total concoction illustrating how libels are fabricated.[47] Very few of us have understood how the riddle of the Confidence-Man's racial identity subverts the racist fallacies through which he decoys the passengers of the *Fidèle*.

What is the riddle of his racial identity? Is the Black Rapids man a white man who earlier masqueraded as a black, or a black man now masquerading as a white? There is no way of knowing, and that is precisely the point. Nothing could more radically discredit the concept of race. Nevertheless, the implications of the racist theories he mouths differ considerably, depending on whether he speaks

47. The title of the story invites us to judge "whether or no [the unfortunate man] has been justly so entitled." Many of the man with the weed's aspersions on Goneril are qualified by phrases like "so at least they said," and "so he averred" (CM, 84, 86). There are also innuendoes that the husband has projected his own sexual perversions onto his wife (homosexual leanings, an Oedipal attachment to his daughter, of whom he accuses his wife of being jealous, etc.). See Franklin (ed.), *The Confidence-Man*, 86, note 6. Foster (ed.), *The Confidence-Man*, 314, is representative of the prevailing interpretation: "Melville's story of Goneril, I take it, was invented as a symbol to connote, even more than to dramatize, the kind of anomalous viciousness that one finds in *King Lear*. . . . Therefore . . . he gives it the hideous connotations of 'Goneril.'"

as a white or as a black. If a white, the Black Rapids man is generalizing about the Negro on the basis of a Negro stereotype he himself has impersonated—thus exemplifying the manner in which ethnologists and proslavery apologists were generalizing about the Negro on the basis of a stereotype the white master class had created through slavery, diffused through literature serving its aims, and even impersonated on the stage in the minstrel shows that Guinea's tambourine patently evokes.[48] If a black, he is adding a deadly new twist to the slave's traditional means of conning the master: instead of merely acting the part of the stupid, tractable, contented menial the master wants to believe in, as Babo does, he is authoritatively confirming the dangerous delusions that will bring about the doom of men like the merchant, and of the slaveowners with whom they ally themselves, both at the hands of temporal Torquemadas like Babo, and at the hands of a Grand Inquisitor whose Judgment will be far more terrible.

The merchant being now accounted for, let us return to Guinea's other seeming benefactors, the Episcopal clergyman and the Methodist minister. The "young clergyman, before introduced," whom we find in the chapter "At the outset of which certain passengers prove deaf to the call of charity"—a title that points back to the scene with Black Guinea—appears at first to be the Episcopal clergyman. In the course of his discussion with Guinea's second avatar, the man in gray, however, it becomes clear, as H. Bruce Franklin has shown, that the two clerics have merged into one,[49] perhaps symbolizing the essential unanimity the Episcopal and Methodist churches had reached on slavery and the Negro's status by the 1850s.

"Catching a chance sight" of the man in gray, the young clergyman seems "suddenly struck by some recollection," and "after a moment's pause," accosts him with the words: "Your pardon, but shortly since I was all over looking for you" (CM, 43). The recollection and pause suggest that he may not have performed his errand of searching out Guinea's friends very faithfully, and is feeling guilty. He pursues: "Do you know anything about the negro, apparently

48. Grejda, *Common Continent of Men*, 128, makes the same point. On the Negro minstrels, see Alexander Saxton, "Blackface Minstrelsy and Jacksonian Ideology," *American Quarterly*, XXVII (1975), 3–28.

49. Franklin, *The Wake of the Gods*, 166–68.

a cripple, aboard here? Is he, or is he not, what he seems to be?" As phrased, this inquiry takes for granted Guinea's identity as a Negro and merely attempts to verify whether he is a genuine cripple. The man in gray's reply, however, raises the issue of race by appealing to "nature" to authenticate Guinea's identity: "Ah, poor Guinea! have you, too, been distrusted? you, upon whom nature has placarded the evidence of your claims?" The force of this appeal consists in its premise that a Negro must always be what he seems, for otherwise the whole edifice of white supremacy would totter. That may be why the clergyman understands it to mean that Guinea is "quite worthy" of charity.

Having beguiled the clergyman into revealing his racist preconceptions in the very act of doing the Negro a good turn, the man in gray leads his unwary interlocutor step by step into betraying himself as a false friend of the Negro. When the clergyman proposes, with cautious vagueness, that they seek out Guinea to "see what can be done," the man in gray laments "another instance that confidence may come too late." He himself, he claims, "assisted the cripple ashore. No time to talk, only to help" (CM, 43). By contrasting his own impulsive deed of charity with the wordy impotence of the church's official representative, he invites a confession.[50] Nor does it tarry: "Really, I regret his going without my seeing him again. . . . You see, shortly after leaving St. Louis, he was on the forecastle, and there, with many others, I saw him, and put trust in him; so much so, that, to convince those who did not, I, at his entreaty, went in search of you, you being one of several individuals he mentioned, and whose personal appearance he more or less described, individuals who he said would willingly speak for him. But, after diligent search, not finding you, and catching no glimpse of any of the others he had enumerated, doubts were at last suggested" (CM, 43–44). The clergyman's account not only falsifies the crowd's attitude toward Black Guinea and glosses over the lynch law with which the Negro is almost threatened, but entirely suppresses the one fact essential to understanding the fuss about Guinea's authenticity—that he has been begging for alms. (The omission permits the clergyman to avoid mentioning that he himself

50. The man in gray is masquerading as a revival preacher (see this work, 226–27). Revivalists berated regularly ordained clergymen for their coldness and formalism.

has not shown trust by giving alms.) Crowning this disingenuous confession, the clergyman blames his ensuing distrust on "prior distrust unfeelingly proclaimed by another" (the wooden-legged man). If he is the Episcopal clergyman who went off to look for Guinea's friends, however, he could not possibly have heard the wooden-legged man attack Guinea as an impostor, since he had already left on his errand by then. Only the Methodist was present when the wooden-legged man accused Guinea of being "some white operator, betwisted and painted up for a decoy" (CM, 20). But the Methodist minister has even less to boast about than the Episcopalian, where putting trust in the Negro is concerned.

Almost as if conjured up by the man in gray to expose the clergyman, the wooden-legged man suddenly appears on the heels of the cleric's last words, which he greets with "a sort of laugh more like a groan than a laugh; and yet, somehow . . . intended for a laugh"(CM, 44). The clergyman hereupon compounds his self-betrayal by identifying the wooden-legged man as "the person to whom I ascribe the origin of my own distrust," and quoting the "very words" that had brought the Methodist to the fore after the Episcopalian's departure (CM, 45–46).

Having unmasked the clergyman, and thereby exhibited the glaring hypocrisy of the church's pose as the Negro's benefactor, the man in gray reverts to the question of Black Guinea's true character. "Would you tell me now," he asks the wooden-legged man, "whether you were not merely joking in the notion you threw out about the negro" (CM, 46). Once again, it is the man in gray who insists on stressing the issue of racial identity that everyone else has ignored. When the wooden-legged man replies curtly, "Well, he's just what I said he was," the man in gray reformulates the charge of imposture, pointedly deleting the reference to shamming deformity, and focusing exclusively on whether Guinea is "a white masquerading as a black?"

The irony, of course, is that the very skeptic who claims to see through Black Guinea's alleged disguise is no more able to recognize Guinea and the man in gray as the same person than the merchant, taking Guinea for a genuine Negro, was able to discern a resemblance between Guinea's countenance and the man with the weed's. Although the wooden-legged man thinks he knows the difference between black paint and black pigmentation, he, too, believes in fixed racial distinctions unmistakably identifying one human being as a Negro and another as a white. Such a concept of race leaves no room for the gray attire of Guinea's avatar, which graphically suggests the infinite variety of nuances between blackness and whiteness reducing these categories to absurdity. Playing on this irony, the man in gray pretends to marvel at the "singular credulity" required (if one assumes that racial traits furnish infallible criteria for differentiating blacks from whites) to suppose that "a white could look the negro so" (CM, 47). Logically, he implies, the wooden-legged man ought either to accept Guinea at face value, or admit that there is no means of finding out whether anyone is what he seems to be. "Does all the world act?" asks the man in gray. "Am *I*, for instance, an actor? Is my reverend friend here, too, a performer?" Despite these loud hints, the cynic does not see through either the man in gray's or the clergyman's masquerade. All he can come up with, as evidence that a white can successfully impersonate a black (while leaving racial categories safely intact), is the "negro-minstrels." The man in gray rightly points out that their black paint is at least as phony-looking as the wooden-legged man says Guinea's is: "they are apt to overdo the ebony; exemplifying the old saying, not more just than charitable, that 'the devil is never so black as he is painted.'" In other words, the man in gray is hinting that the Negro's blackness, whether as minstrel-show stereotype or as Black Man, is a figment of the white imagination.

Significantly, whereas the wooden-legged man cannot further spell out how to tell a "real" Negro from a fake one, he has no trouble answering the man in gray's next question: "But his limbs, if not a cripple, how could he twist his limbs so?" His reply, as we have seen, indicates that he may be guilty of the imposture he imputes to Guinea: "How do other hypocritical beggars twist theirs? Easy enough to see how they are hoisted up" (CM, 47). But it is the wooden-legged man's reaction to the proposal that they go find Guinea, to refute "this injurious hypothesis" in person, that most blatantly reveals the contradictions into which racism has led him: "I'm just in the humor now for having him found, and leaving the streaks of these fingers on his paint, as the lion leaves the streaks of his nails on a caffre." Even while contending that Guinea is only painted black, the wooden-legged man still perceives him as a "caffre," or African, on whom to wreak his hatred.

The final irony is that the wooden-legged man, despite his worldly-wise suspicion that a diabolical purpose, rather than mere financial chicanery, lies behind Black Guinea's masquerade ("Money, you think, is the sole motive to pains and hazard, deception and deviltry, in this world. How much money did the devil make by gulling Eve?"), does not realize what purpose it has actually served—to judge Americans on the day of reckoning by whether they recognize Christ's image in the Negro.

Upon the wooden-legged man's retreat, the man in gray turns back to the clergyman, who now proffers him a "mite" to pass on to Guinea, saying, "it comes from one who has full belief in his honesty, and is sincerely sorry for having indulged, however transiently, in a contrary thought" (CM, 49). But the clergyman is not to be let off the hook so easily, after having shown how little he is prepared to do for the Negro. The man in gray wants to prove that the clergyman has abdicated his moral responsibility toward other victims of America besides slaves. He thus asks if, being of "this truly charitable nature," the clergyman will also answer an "appeal in behalf of the Seminole Widow and Orphan Asylum." The clergyman responds with the same hesitation he exhibited in befriending Guinea, first pleading not to have "heard of that charity," then "irresolutely putting his hand in his pocket," only to stop midway, his distrust aroused "by something in his companion's expression," and at last contributing a "drop," but in the same breath asking to see the asylum's "papers." Needless to surmise, he will miss the bitter irony in the man in gray's account of the "providential way" in which the Seminole Widow and Orphan Asylum "was started": presumably by massacring the Seminole husbands and fathers in the bloody war the American government had recently waged for their Florida territory.[51] This little episode, which consummates the discomfiture of Black Guinea's clerical benefactors, links the Negro and Indian victims of American racism as clearly as Melville had in "The 'Gees," and foreshadows the latter half of the book, where Melville shifts the focus from slavery to Indian-hating.

51. Foster (ed.), *The Confidence-Man*, lv, also points out this irony.

When the man in gray interrupts his narration of the Asylum's founding to leave the clergyman for "one who I know will contribute, and largely" (CM, 50; a final barbed comment on the cleric's stinginess), it is to initiate a dialectic between the northern and southern variants of America's millennial creed—a dialectic that reveals slavery as the underlying fraud vitiating both northern and southern dreams of paradise. In this dialectic, the man in gray plays the role of the quintessential Yankee busybody, advocating the active millennialism that generated northern "benevolent enterprises" like the Missionary, Tract, and Bible Societies. His interlocutor, a "gentleman with gold sleeve-buttons," who identifies himself as a southern gentleman by the "negro body-servant" he conspicuously trails in his wake,[52] speaks for the South, expressing "pleasant incredulity" as to the efficacy of Yankee enthusiasm and offering in its place an aristocrat's urbane sophistication and generosity.

The man in gray displays many hallmarks of the nineteenth-century revivalist preacher. He describes himself in a subsequent chapter as a "brother" of the church and claims to "prefer the company . . . of a brother or sister in good standing" to that of "the people of the world" (CM, 62). His countenance, "upon a cursory view," reveals enough of grief for an uncharitable passenger to accuse him of wearing "a face as long as my arm," though the narrator asserts that "on a closer observation," the reader will find "little of sorrow," but "much of sanctity" in the man in gray's expression (CM, 42–43). It is the countenance revivalists recommended for turning the careless laughter of sinners into mourning—that of a Christian whose anxiety for his fellows' souls "makes him look and act as if he had a load on his mind."[53] The man in gray's "not unsilvery tongue . . . with gestures that were a Pentecost of added ones and persuasiveness before which granite hearts might crumble into gravel" (CM, 60), recall the flamboyant pulpit oratory and theatrical gesticulations of revivalists like Charles Grandison Finney, famous for a "voice of great compass and melody" that he would modulate from shouts to "abject groanings," whipping entire congregations into frenzies as he berated them for their sins, exhorted them to get

52. Hennig Cohen (ed.), *The Confidence-Man* (New York, 1964), xvi, was the first to recognize this gentleman as a southerner.

53. Charles Grandison Finney, *Lectures on Revivals of Religion*, ed. William G. McLoughlin (1835; rpt. Cambridge, Mass., 1960), 18, 30.

"down into the dust before God," and dazzled them with "a new foretaste of heaven."[54] The man in gray also manifests the revivalists' belief that "the spirit of revivals and the spirit of public charity are hereafter to go hand in hand; the one being sustained and cherished in a great degree by the other, until the earth shall be filled with the Redeemer's glory."[55] He intends, he says, to do away with poverty and heathenism by "magnifying and energizing" extant charities and missions and fusing them into a worldwide philanthropical society (CM, 55–58). "Mindful of the millennial promise," his "spirit of benevolence" has "gone abroad over all the countries of the globe" (CM, 60). It is through his shameless commercialization of religion, however, that the man in gray most obviously caricatures the professional soul-winners who had made the mass conversion of sinners a matter of "human calculation, by the arithmetic of faith in God's engagements," as one revivalist put it.[56] Burlesquing what another revivalist called the "free unembarrassed application of physical effort and pecuniary and moral power to evangelize the world,"[57] the man in gray calls for quickening missions with "the Wall street spirit," by inviting competitive bidding for contracts to convert the heathen: "So much by bid for converting India, so much for Borneo, so much for Africa" (CM, 57–58). Like Finney, who had maintained that God depended as much on human agency to produce revivals and convert sinners as to grow a crop of grain, the man in gray argues that "if, confessedly, certain spiritual ends are to be gained but through the auxiliary agency of worldly means, then, to the surer gaining of such spiritual ends, the example of wordly policy in worldly projects should not by spiritual projectors be slighted" (CM, 57–58).[58]

The man in gray's foil, the gentleman with gold sleeve-buttons, fulfills almost perfectly the function that, according to William R. Taylor, literary convention had assigned to the southern cavalier:

54. *Ibid.*, 16. Finney, according to a contemporary observer, preached in "an unclerical suit of gray." See the descriptions in Robert S. Fletcher, *A History of Oberlin College* (2 vols.; Oberlin, 1943), I, 16–18; also William G. McLoughlin, *Modern Revivalism: Charles Grandison Finney to Billy Graham* (New York, 1959), 17.

55. William B. Sprague, *Lectures on Revivals of Religion* (New York, 1833), 217.

56. Calvin Colton, *History and Character of American Revivals of Religion* (London, 1832), 6.

57. Lyman Beecher, *A Plea for the West*, 10.

58. Finney, *Lectures*, 13–14.

to embody a moral alternative to the "strident materialism" many Americans had come to associate with the Yankee. Occupying the pedestal the Puritan divine had forfeited in the popular mind by degenerating into a greedy, canting bigot, the "gay, pleasure-loving and generous-hearted Southerner," as Taylor points out, stood for all the qualities the bustling North seemed to lack. With his "ample estates, his spacious style of life," his time-honored traditions, and his inimitable decorum, he was "immune to acquisitiveness, indifferent to social ambition and hostile to commercial life, cities and secular progress."[59] In conformity with this stereotype, the gentleman with gold sleeve-buttons sports an "ample pocketbook in the good old capacious style" and is generous to the point of prodigality: "To him, he said, charity was in one sense not an effort, but a luxury; against too great indulgence in which his steward, a humorist, had sometimes admonished him" (CM, 53). (One thinks of William Gilmore Simms's Porgy, chided by his overseer for improvidence and excessive indulgence of his slaves.)[60] In dress, the gentleman's "strangely festive finish and elegance," so "inappropriate" for the "time and place, not to hint of his years" (CM, 51), bring to mind the southerner's celebrated dandyism. His manner bespeaks a born aristocrat: he waves the "canopy of his goodness" over the man in gray, "his inferior, apparently, not more in the social scale than in stature," and treats this fund-solicitor not with "conceited condescension, but with that even amenity of true majesty, which can be kind to any one without stooping to it" (CM, 53). His most salient feature is an expression of "goodness" that makes him "look like a kind of foreigner, among the crowd" (CM, 50).

The confrontation of values represented by these opposing regional archetypes seems patly defined by the title Melville originally planned for this chapter: "A righteous man encounters a good man, and an enthusiast a gentleman [a man of common sense]."[61] But embedded in another early title draft, which reads, "A gentleman in fine linen & with gold sleeve-buttons," is a biblical allusion sug-

59. Taylor, *Cavalier and Yankee*, 21, 334–35.

60. *Ibid.*, 152–57; William Gilmore Simms, *Woodcraft; or, Hawks about the Dovecote. A Story of the South at the Close of the Revolution* (1854; rpt. New York, 1961), Chaps. 30, 35, 41, 42, 48.

61. Brackets added. Foster (ed.), *The Confidence-Man*, 305, note 39.2. I have also consulted the manuscript fragments in the Houghton Library at Harvard.

gesting that the distinction between righteous man and good man, enthusiast and gentleman of common sense, may be illusory. The words "in fine linen," which Melville inserted above the line, refer to the "fine linen, clean and white," attiring the incarnate New Jerusalem in the Book of Revelation, and symbolizing the *"righteousness* of saints" who inherit the millennial kingdom and partake of the "marriage supper of the Lamb" (Rev. 19:7–9; italics added). The good man thus turns out to be another form of the righteous man, the man of common sense another enthusiast wrapping himself in the mantle of the saints.

Although Melville ended up dropping the allusion from the title, he kept it in his description of the gentleman with gold sleeve-buttons' toilet: "The inner-side of his coatskirts was of *white satin*, which might have looked especially inappropriate, had it not seemed less a bit of mere tailoring than something of an emblem, as it were; an involuntary emblem, let us say, that what seemed so good about him was not all outside; no, the fine covering had a still *finer lining*" (CM, 51; italics added). The description conveys an irony that would have been sabotaged by the literalism of the original allusion. The gentleman with gold sleeve-buttons' fine white satin lining is not the garb of the saints, but an approximation of it. His destination is not the marriage supper of the Lamb, to which many are called but only those clad in the proper wedding garment chosen to attend (Matt. 22:2–14). (The gentleman's apparel may be "inappropriate" in this sense as well.) Instead, he is on his way to his niece's wedding (CM, 53)—a travesty of the millennial consummation.

The narrative analysis of the gentleman with gold sleeve-buttons' alleged goodness further undermines the flattering contrast the cavalier supposedly presented to the Yankee. So pronounced is the gentleman's expression of goodness, comments the narrator, that "to some it may make him appear more or less unreal in this portraiture" (CM, 50). He pursues: "Such goodness seemed his, allied with such fortune, that, so far as his own personal experience could have gone, scarcely could he have known ill, physical or moral; and as for knowing or suspecting the latter in any serious degree (supposing such degree of it to be), by observation or philosophy; for that, probably, his nature, by its opposition, was imperfectly qualified, or from it wholly exempted" (CM, 50–51). Contrary, then, to the legendary southern cavalier, who lived amidst a decaying splendor and declining prosperity that heightened his thriftlessness, romanticized his bounty, and implicitly rebuked the tightfisted materialism of the Yankee parvenu, the gentleman with gold sleeve-buttons exhibits the kind of goodness allied (and perhaps alloyed) with fabulous wealth. Far from demonstrating that the paternalistic southern planter had to forego the profits of the northern wage system, the gentleman with gold sleeve-buttons testifies to the unwelcome truth that slaveholding was as profitable as any sordid Yankee enterprise.[62]

Another literary convention reversed here is that of attributing to the southern aristocrat a worldliness and sophistication that theoretically made him more cognizant of human evil than the naïvely sanguine Yankee. Instead, financial security and social status have fostered in Melville's southern gentleman the same sort of "good-nature" that shelters the Yankee Delano against "personal alarms, any way involving the imputation of malign evil in man" (BC, 1). Like the bachelors of Temple Bar, he concludes from his own "personal experience" that pain and trouble do not exist for others. The limited moral vision the narrator ascribes to him drastically undercuts the pose of knowing skepticism that the gentleman will later assume vis-à-vis the man in gray; it forewarns us that his naysaying is based not on philosophical acumen, but on class bias.

The most important reversal, however, concerns the bearing that the gentleman with gold sleeve-buttons' "negro body-servant" has on his alleged goodness. In differentiating this goodness from the "righteousness" produced, according to evangelical doctrine, by a "total change and conversion," the narrator pointedly remarks of the gentleman: "*Not* that he looked as if he were a kind of Wilberforce at all; that superior merit, probably, was not his" (CM, 52; italics added). William Wilberforce, of course, was the British abolitionist whose name had become synonymous with emancipation in the British West Indies, and whose example had influenced the American abolitionist movement. Hence the narrator means that the gentleman's goodness would not consist in favoring abolition. Whether, in that case, the gentleman could be considered good at all, by

62. Taylor, *Cavalier and Yankee*, 152–57, 334–35; *The Pro-Slavery Argument*, 26–27.

Christian standards, was one of the controversies that raged between abolitionists and conservatives. Abolitionists held that a person could not be a sincere Christian and remain a slaveholder. Although some liberal and evangelical clergymen supported this view, most churchmen sided with southerners and northern conservatives in contending that slaveholding did not debar anyone from receiving the spirit of Christ, but instead afforded special opportunities for displaying Christian virtues.[63] The narrator ostensibly takes a conservative stand on this issue. While professing to defend the gentleman with gold sleeve-buttons against "severe censors," however, he subverts both the doctrinal and the practical grounds on which the slaveholder's goodness was commonly vindicated.

In the doctrinal sphere, the narrator burlesques the pedantic sophistry of proslavery theologians by quoting a verse from St. Paul (Rom. 5:7) to establish the apostle's preference for goodness over righteousness: "I say, since St. Paul has so meaningly said, that, 'scarcely for a righteous man will one die, yet peradventure for a good man some would even dare to die;' therefore, when we repeat of this gentleman, that he was only a good man, whatever else by severe censors may be objected to him, it is still to be hoped that his goodness will not at least be considered criminal in him" (CM, 52). As Melville was surely aware, the context of this verse gives it a meaning completely at odds with the narrator's interpretation: St. Paul argues that "Christ died for the ungodly" (Rom. 5:6), and not for righteous men, who, by definition, would not have needed his intervention to be saved (Rom. 3, 4, 5, *passim*). The discrepancy thus exemplifies the way southern clergymen twisted the scriptures to justify slavery.

In the practical sphere, the narrator satirizes the notion that slavery fostered the Christian character of the master by impelling him to assume moral responsibility for his slave's physical and spiritual welfare. In contrast, the narrator implies that the gentleman with gold sleeve-buttons keeps himself spiritually, as well as physically, immaculate at the expense of his slave. Parodying the proslavery argument that "nature" had especially equipped the Negro

63. McLoughlin, *Modern Revivalism*, 108–12; Filler, *The Crusade Against Slavery*, 109; Calvin Colton, *A Voice from America to England* (London, 1839), 138–44; Staiger, "Abolitionism and the Presbyterian Schism," 398; James Fenimore Cooper, *The American Democrat* (1838; rpt. Baltimore, 1969), 220–21.

for "sordid, servile, and laborious offices," and had signified her intentions through the "infallible marks" of race,[64] he observes that the gentleman with gold sleeve-buttons retains the spotlessness of his hands aboard the sooty *Fidèle* by relying on his "negro body-servant, whose hands nature had dyed black, perhaps with the same purpose that millers wear white"—"this negro servant's hands did most of his master's handling for him; having to do with dirt on his account, but not to his prejudices" (CM, 51). The narrator then translates this argument into moral terms by comparing the gentleman's clean hands with those of Pontius Pilate and wondering whether, "with the same undefiledness of consequences to himself, a gentleman could also sin by deputy." Although he pretends to dismiss such a contingency as too shocking to be permitted, he adds, "even if it were, no judicious moralist would make proclamation of it" (CM, 51). He doubtless means for us to apply the same analysis to the myth of the kind master, maintained by blaming all the abuses of the slave system on the brutish overseer and low-born slavetrader, and by projecting onto the slave the vices the master could not acknowledge in himself.

Ultimately, the best the narrator can say in favor of the gentleman with gold sleeve-buttons is that "not even a righteous man, would think it quite right to commit this gentleman to prison for the crime" of goodness; "more especially, as, until everything could be known, there would be some chance that the gentleman might after all be quite as innocent of it as he himself" (CM, 52). In goodness, as in wealth and moral awareness, the mythical southern gentleman turns out to be the alter ego, rather than the alternative, to the Yankee whose unbecoming zeal, materialism, and naïve optimism he counterpoints in the popular mind.

Nevertheless, the two regional archetypes represent conflicting ideologies. The man in gray wants to program the millennium into existence through benevolent enterprises, the gentleman with gold sleeve-buttons to retreat to a plantation Eden for invited guests.[65] These differences emerge from their "general talk . . . relative to organized modes of doing good" (CM, 53), which begins right after

64. *The Pro-Slavery Argument*, 51.
65. The polarity corresponds uncannily to the contrast Bercovitch draws between Puritan and southern images of America, in *Puritan Origins*, 137–39.

the gentleman with gold sleeve-buttons gives the man in gray three "virgin bills" in response to the plea for Seminole widows and orphans, apologizing for the "smallness of the contribution" by explaining that he is "bound but a short run down the river, to attend, in a festive grove, the afternoon wedding of his niece: so did not carry much money with him" (CM, 53). In the discussion that ensues, the gentleman with gold sleeve-buttons skeptically disparages all the charitable schemes of the Yankee evangelicals for whom the man in gray speaks, yet continues to donate to them "with a look half humor, half pity" (CM, 60).

Whereas evangelicals hailed the proliferation of benevolent societies throughout the land as "the glory of the present age," preeminently symptomatizing the revitalization of Christianity that was to usher in the millennium,[66] the gentleman with gold sleeve-buttons deplores it as inefficient. Why, he asks, should not all these benevolent societies, "here and there isolated in the land . . . act in concert by coming together, in the way that already in each society the individuals composing it had done, which would result, he thought, in like advantages upon a larger scale" (CM, 53). The idea had, in fact, been proposed some years earlier by a northern leader of the benevolent movement,[67] which may be why the man in gray excitedly claims to have anticipated it in a project he calls the "World's Charity"—"a society whose members shall comprise deputies from every charity and mission extant; the one object of the society to be the methodization of the world's benevolence" (CM, 54–55). But the gentleman with gold sleeve-buttons does not really have any more faith in this solution for the world's ills than in any other. "Such a confederation," he opines with urbane cynicism, "might, perhaps, be attended with as happy results as politically attended that of the states" (CM, 53). As a southern slaveholder, he is, of course, well aware that the confederation of the states has long been threatened by the bitter dispute over slavery, soon to erupt into civil war.

The objections he raises to the Yankee evangelicals' means dissimulate his more fundamental objection to the optimistic millennialism that had inspired those means. The hope of "doing good

66. William Cogswell, *The Harbinger of the Millennium* (Boston, 1833), iv.
67. *Ibid.*, iv, 255–57.

to the world once for all and having done with it," as the man in gray puts it, strikes the gentleman with gold sleeve-buttons as "too enthusiastic," and he criticizes the man in gray for being "over-confident" (CM, 58–59). Such projects as "converting the Chinese *en masse* within six months" by "sending ten thousand missionaries in a body," and eliminating "hunger for one while among the poor of London" by "voting to them twenty thousand bullocks and one hundred thousand barrels of flour," he demurs, are "rather examples of wonders that were to be wished, than wonders that will happen," as is the concept of the World's Charity itself. Unschooled in the revivals out of which the northern benevolent movement had emerged, he discerns no sign of a dawning "age of wonders"—unlike the man in gray (who is probably going to perform wonders quite different from those expected by the evangelicals he caricatures). Instead, the gentleman with gold sleeve-buttons identifies himself with "Abraham reviling the angel" who announces Sarah's conception (Gen. 17:17). Since he is not supposed to be righteous, but "only good," he appropriately does not remember that St. Paul cites Abraham, in the same passage earlier misinterpreted by the narrator, as an instance of justification by faith: "For what saith the scripture? Abraham believed God, and it was counted unto him for righteousness" (Rom. 4:3). Even the argument Finney had called "the reasonableness and utility of benevolence"[68] fails to overcome his skepticism. The pessimistic view of human nature so conducive to proslavery apologists allows for only one answer to the question the man in gray asks: "And are mankind so stupid, so wicked, that, upon the demonstration of these things they will not, amending their ways, devote their superfluities to blessing the world instead of cursing it?" Complacently "adjusting his gold sleeve-buttons," the insignia of his luxurious life, the gentleman oracularly announces: "Your sort of reasoning . . . seems all reasonable enough, but with mankind it won't do" (CM, 57).

Aptly summing up the gentleman with gold sleeve-buttons' attitude toward the man in gray's "world-wide scheme" are the reservations that a prominent southern apologist once expressed, in a letter to a British abolitionist, about human efforts to bring about

68. Charles Grandison Finney, *Sermons on Important Subjects* (3rd ed.; New York, 1836), 54.

the millennium: "I might say that ... I love perfection, and think I should enjoy a millennium such as God has promised. But what would it amount to? A pledge that I would join you to set about eradicating those apparently inevitable evils of our nature, in equalizing the condition of all mankind, consummating the perfection of our race, and introducing the millennium? By no means. To effect these things, belongs exclusively to a higher power. And it would be well for us to leave the Almighty to perfect his own works and fulfil his own covenants. Especially, as the history of the past shows how entirely futile all human efforts have proved."[69] The keynote of this southern litany, sounded in the gentleman with gold sleeve-buttons' every utterance, is its stony negativism. It is a cult of naysaying, formulated against an American creed southerners could no longer uphold if they were to preserve their menaced slave system. Through the laconic cavils of the gentleman with gold sleeve-buttons, Melville dramatizes the South's failure to transcend mere rejection of the dominant national ideals and to evolve a credo capable of existing independently of the one it denied. Not only does the gentleman with gold sleeve-buttons propound no values in the place of those he ridicules; he does not even cite any examples or arguments to support his pessimistic contentions. (To appreciate the shallowness of his dissent, one has only to contrast it with the substantive indictment of "free Ameriky" delivered by the ex-prisoner Thomas Fry.)

The one value that the gentleman with gold sleeve-buttons might seem to embody is charity. Yet while succumbing to the man in gray's fund-raising pleas, his heart, as the narrator pointedly tells us, has remained harder than the "granite" ones that the man in gray's eloquence "might crumble into gravel" (CM, 60). It thus becomes evident that his financial generosity is one of the very substitutes for charity that St. Paul dismisses as worthless: "And though I bestow all my goods to feed the poor ... and have not charity, it profiteth me nothing" (I Cor. 13:3). In the last analysis, the gentleman with gold sleeve-buttons shows himself "charitable ... only to the dreams of enthusiasm." He can well afford to patronize dreams so carefully censored of all elements threatening to a southern gentleman's security.

69. *The Pro-Slavery Argument*, 104.

236 SHADOW OVER THE PROMISED LAND

At the opposite pole of this dialectic, the moral bankruptcy of a millennialist faith animated by the "Wall street spirit" is too obvious to need further comment. More subtle is the role played by the gentleman with gold sleeve-buttons' Negro body servant in exposing the spuriousness of the benevolent movement as a means of bringing about the millennium. As the euphemism "servant" indicates, the Negro's enslavement is unacknowledged, his very presence overlooked by the man in gray, who instead weeps over the pagans in China and the paupers in London.[70] The reason for his conspicuous disregard of slavery is plain: the man in gray, like the benevolent organizations he represents, depends on a slaveholder to fund his World's Charity. This irony points up what is really wrong with the man in gray's panaceas for the "mob of misery" in London and the "pauper pagans" who die in the streets of China "like so many nipped peas in a bin of peas" (CM, 58). It betokens the essential fraudulence of a benevolent system financed, both directly and indirectly, by exploiting those it is supposed to benefit—directly by soliciting donations from the objects of its charity on their own behalf through a yearly "benevolence tax upon all mankind"of "one little dollar a head" (CM, 56);[71] indirectly by drawing on magnates who derive their "superfluities" from keeping their domestic labor forces at subsistence wages in factories, coal mines, and merchant ships, and from cheating, bullying, enslaving, and massacring the peoples they colonize abroad. In every respect, such a system taxes "the pauper not less than the nabob . . . to contribute to the relief of pauperism, and the heathen not less than the Christian to the conversion of heathenism" (CM, 57).

The dialectic this episode establishes between northern and southern variants of the national creed thus resolves itself into a consensus of betrayal. Embodying that betrayal, the unheeded Negro body servant, who gives the lie to the ideals of Yankee busybody and southern cavalier alike, epitomizes the significance of

70. This, I think, clearly distinguishes the man in gray from Wilberforce and from the evangelicals who became abolitionists. Hence I do not agree with Foster (ed.), *The Confidence-Man*, lv, 305–306, note 40.31, who sees the man in gray as a caricature of Wilberforce, denigrating his abolitionist efforts.
71. See *White-Jacket*, 158, where the Chaplain solicits money from the sailors for "building a seaman's chapel in China," paying the "salary of a tract-distributor in Greece," and raising "a fund for the benefit of an African Colonization Society."

slavery in the April Fools' Day apocalypse with which Melville dispels the expectation of inaugurating the millennium in America.

Symbolizing the central position that slavery occupies in Melville's indictment of America, and the pivotal role he ascribes to it in determining the nation's future, his most comprehensive historical review of the slavery question fittingly occurs at midpoint both in the *Fidèle*'s voyage from St. Louis to New Orleans and in his apocalyptic narrative of that voyage. Shortly before the *Fidèle* touches at her last "free" port on the voyage south, an argumentative frontiersman who calls himself "Pitch" disrupts the sectional entente that Yankee and cavalier have achieved at the expense of their respective scapegoats, and forces a thoroughgoing polemical showdown on slavery.

Pitch, who is introduced as "a Missouri bachelor" (CM, 146) and regularly called "the Missourian," drops several hints of a long residence in slave territory that has left its mark on him, notwithstanding his protestations to the contrary. The first is his casual reference to the doctors he has encountered in a Mobile, Alabama, hospital (CM, 147), which calls to mind the most famous doctor in Mobile, the ethnologist Josiah C. Nott. The second is Pitch's disclosure that he once owned a "plantation" on the Mississippi, until "Nature . . . absconded with ten thousand dollars' worth of my property . . . by one of those sudden shiftings of the banks in a freshet" (CM, 149). The third is his repeated use of the word "nigger," which Melville himself conscientiously avoided.[72]

The Missourian brings up the subject of labor problems—a constant preoccupation among southern planters[73] —almost as soon as he makes his entrance. After comparing his interlocutor, the herb-doctor (an avatar of Black Guinea), to "the last boy I had on my place," Pitch announces he is so fed up with the service of boys that "I am now started to get me made some kind of machine to do the sort of work which boys are supposed to be fitted for" (CM, 149). The idea of inventing a machine that could replace human labor

72. The only other instance I have found of Melville's using the word is in *White-Jacket*, 275, where May-Day calls Rose-Water a "*'nigger,*' which, among some blacks, is held a great term of reproach."
73. Stampp, *The Peculiar Institution*, 91, and Chap. 3, *passim*.

had long been lurking in the background of the slavery question. In 1833, an associationist pamphleteer named J. A. Etzler had petitioned Andrew Jackson and the American Congress for subsidies to design a mechanism capable of "superseding all human labor" by systematically harnessing the powers of nature. Promising Americans a "Paradise within the reach of all men" if they applied his principles, Etzler had envisioned a new order of society with "no fear of being robbed or cheated, no cares of managing the household, none even for the education of children . . . no anxiety for preserving or increasing property; no disgusting objects and occupations . . . no low vices and crimes, resulting from want, or fear of want, and poverty . . . no object, and no cause, any more for low cunning and deceit, for gaining advantage over his fellow-creature in fortune and rank . . . no more . . . selling as dear as possible, and buying as cheap as possible . . . [no more being] waited upon and surrounded by low, miserable, degraded beings, which he has to watch, to pity, or despise." [74]

Etzler had not oriented his mechanistic utopia specifically toward eliminating slavery, but by 1838, when the abolitionist movement was focusing national attention on this especially onerous form of human labor, the fantasy of supplanting the Negro with an automaton was apparently prevalent enough to find its way into an antiabolitionist satire. In Robert Montgomery Bird's *Peter Pilgrim*, an insane asylum inmate, formerly an inventor, relates how he had set out to liberate the slaves and make his own fortune by designing such an automaton, convinced that "substitutes once found . . . every body would come round to abolition in a moment, the Southerners in particular, who, the Lord knows, are sick of the bother of their labourers." Through "the invention (and a grand one it was,) of patent niggers" driven by horsepower, he proudly tells the narrator,

74. J. A. Etzler, *The Paradise within the Reach of All Men, without Labor, by Powers of Nature and Machinery* (Pittsburgh, 1833), 82–83. See also Henry David Thoreau's review of this book, "Paradise (to be) Regained," *United States Magazine and Democratic Review*, XIII (1843), 449–62; and Frederic I. Carpenter, " 'The American Myth': Paradise (To Be) Regained," *PMLA*, LXXIV (1959), 599–606. Associationists were utopian socialists who believed that the problems of class conflict and poverty could be solved by organizing society into small egalitarian communities. Robert Owen and François Marie Charles Fourier were the most famous exponents of Associationism, and Brook Farm the most famous Associationist community.

he actually succeeded in solving the problem technologically: "[My patent niggers were] men, sir, not of perishing and suffering flesh and blood, but of wood, iron, leather and canvas, so constructed as . . . to be a great deal better than the real niggers; because, sir, they were to do all kinds of work . . . and never get tired, or sick, or sulky—never die, or run away, or rise in insurrection—never require feeding, nor clothing, nor physicking—in short, sir, the best and cheapest niggers that human wit ever imagined!" Instead of winning him the fame and gratitude he thinks he deserves, however, this invention has landed its author in a madhouse, thanks to the machinations of the abolitionists, who "could not bear that they should lose the honour, and glory, and profit of completing the great work of emancipation."[75]

Despite its obvious failure to address the issue of the ex-slaves' future, the chimera of a technological escape from the slavery dilemma persisted. Barely a year before the outbreak of the Civil War, Thomas Ewbank, a former commissioner of patents, solemnly prophesied that "Inorganic Forces [were] Ordained to Supersede Human Slavery" and exhorted the "friends of the negro" to apply themselves to "mechanical science" as the surest means of hastening abolition.[76]

In contrast, Melville, as we have seen in "The Tartarus of Maids" and "The Bell-Tower," equated the hope of inventing mechanical substitutes for slave labor with the ongoing robotization of human beings through plantation and factory work. Thus Pitch's wish to "get some machine made to do [his] work" suggests from the start that he may actually be in quest of a slave like Bannadonna's automaton. The herb-doctor seems to suspect as much; for he asks Pitch point-blank: "Philanthropic scruples, doubtless, forbid your going as far as New Orleans for slaves?" (CM, 154).

Pitch's indignant response sounds unambiguous: " 'Slaves?' morose again in a twinkling, 'won't have 'em!' " His reasons, however, are not those of an abolitionist. Rather, they resemble the views of conservative northerners who, like James Fenimore Cooper, judged

75. Robert Montgomery Bird, *Peter Pilgrim: or A Rambler's Recollections* (2 vols.; Philadelphia, 1838), I, 106–107.
76. Thomas Ewbank, *Inorganic Forces Ordained to Supersede Human Slavery* (New York, 1860), 30–31.

the "American slave . . . better off, so far as mere animal wants are concerned, than the lower order of the European peasants."[77] Pitch declares that it is "bad enough to see whites ducking and grinning round for a favor, without having those poor devils of niggers congeeing round for their corn. *Though, to me, the niggers are the freer of the two*" (italics added). His very next words are: " 'You are an abolitionist, ain't you?' . . . squaring himself with both hands on his rifle, used for a staff, and gazing in the herb-doctor's face with no more reverence than if it were a target" (CM, 154–55). Since the herb-doctor has not given the slightest pretext for being thought an abolitionist (unless Pitch has misconstrued his allusion to "philanthropic scruples"), Pitch's abrupt and aggressive way of raising this question may betray the exacerbated sensitivity on the slavery issue and the hostility to abolitionists characteristic of conservatives. In their ensuing exchange of views on abolitionism, Pitch remains hard to place, sometimes sounding like an abolitionist, sometimes like a southerner.

The herb-doctor, for his part, adopts a position reminiscent of that held by the moderate churchmen whose guidance abolitionists had repudiated in the 1830s. Just as these churchmen had claimed to be against slavery, yet deplored "denunciatory" and "censorious" attacks on it as "calculated to injure religion" by provoking dissensions among Christians, the herb-doctor tries to define his stand on slavery in such a way as to conciliate all parties simultaneously:[78] "If by abolitionist you mean a zealot, I am none; but if you mean a man, who, being a man, feels for all men, slaves included, and by any lawful act, opposed to nobody's interest, and therefore, rousing nobody's enmity, would willingly abolish suffering (supposing it, in its degree, to exist) from among mankind, irrespective of color, then am I what you say" (CM, 155). In this masterfully noncommittal statement, the herb-doctor not only sets such stringent limitations on the kind of antislavery action he would support that it amounts to saying he would not support any, but he refrains from pronouncing himself in favor of abolishing slavery even under the conditions

77. Spiller, "Cooper's Defense of Slave-Owning America," 580; also cited in Franklin (ed.), *The Confidence-Man*, 154–55, note 12.
78. Finney, *Lectures*, 298–99; McLoughlin, *Modern Revivalism*, 108–12. The closest analogue to the herb-doctor, however, is Barbara M. Cross (ed.), *The Autobiography of Lyman Beecher* (2 vols., 1865; rpt. Cambridge, Mass., 1961), II, 240–60.

he has stipulated. All that he "would willingly abolish" is suffering in general, which he is loath to concede exists, and careful not to equate with slavery. The humanitarianism the herb-doctor caricatures is "irrespective of color" only in the sense that it embraces no one while ostensibly embracing everyone.

Pitch sums up our feelings about such shilly-shallying when he retorts: "You are the moderate man, the invaluable understrapper of the wicked man. You, the moderate man, may be used for wrong, but are useless for right." Yet when the herb-doctor "forgivingly" compliments him on being "without slave sentiments," though a Missourian and "living in a slave-state," Pitch strikes another suspicious note, echoing the drover's challenge to Black Guinea ("And who is your master, Guinea?"): "Aye, but are you? Is not that air of yours, so spiritlessly enduring and yielding, the very air of a slave? Who is your master, pray; or are you owned by a company?" (CM, 15, 155). Here Pitch seems to be speaking with the voice of the fiery southerners who boasted that they knew "too much of slavery to be slaves themselves," and who argued that the workers in the North were as much slaves as southern blacks, except worse off, being bound to a harsh, impersonal factory system, rather than to a humane, paternalistic master.[79]

The spirit of Pitch's concluding words, however, seems more akin to that of Ishmael's soliloquy in the first chapter of *Moby-Dick* ("Who aint a slave? . . . either in a physical or metaphysical point of view, that is; and so the universal thump is passed round, and all hands should rub each other's shoulder-blades, and be content"): "come from Maine or Georgia, you come from a slave-state, and a slave-pen, where the best breeds are to be bought up at any price from a livelihood to the Presidency. Abolitionism, ye gods, but expresses the fellow-feeling of slave for slave" (CM, 155–56).

Although Pitch emerges from this discussion looking much more attractive than his interlocutor, we must remember that the herb-doctor is Black Guinea in another guise, and that his probable motive here is to test the sincerity of Pitch's "philanthropic scruples," as he had earlier tested the merchant's and the clergymen's. Pitch has certainly shown enough ambiguity in his attitude toward slavery

---

79. Martineau, *Society in America*, II, 343; *The Pro-Slavery Argument*, 52–56, 61–62, 135–40, 162–64. See also Franklin (ed.), *The Confidence-Man*, 155, note 13.

242 SHADOW OVER THE PROMISED LAND

and the Negro to merit further probing. That is why, upon taking leave of Pitch with the double entendre *"but to return*; since, for your purpose, you will have neither man nor boy, bond nor free, truly, then some sort of machine for you is all there is left" (italics added), the herb-doctor returns to reopen the question, this time disguised as an expert on "the scientific procuring of good servants of all sorts, boys included, for the kind gentlemen, our patrons" (CM, 174).

Twenty minutes after the herb-doctor's supposed debarkation at Cape Girardeau, Pitch is accosted by "a round-backed, baker-kneed man, in a mean five-dollar suit, wearing, collar-wise by a chain, a small brass plate, inscribed P.I.O." (CM, 157–58). Somehow Pitch knows, without being told, that P.I.O. stands for "PHILOSOPHICAL INTELLIGENCE OFFICE" (employment agency). The way he latches onto the "novel idea" advertised in the firm's title reveals at once how preoccupied he is with finding disciplined servants, his pseudodemocratic bombast notwithstanding: "But how did you come to dream that I wanted anything in your absurd line, eh?" he inquires of his new acquaintance. The long debate on "boys" provoked by this leading question elaborates on the various issues Pitch and the herb-doctor have just been discussing, and sums up Melville's indictment of slavery.

Entitled "In the polite spirit of the Tusculan disputations," the chapter pitting the Missourian against the Philosophical Intelligence Office agent is cast in a form that proslavery apologists would have found particularly appropriate for a treatise on their time-honored institution: the form of a classical dialogue based on Plato's *Meno.*[80] In their pedantic encomiums of slavery, the apologists habitually appealed to the precedent of Greece and Rome, "where the spirit of liberty glowed with most intensity, [and] the slaves were more numerous than the freemen."[81] Their favorite authority on the natural law ordaining the enslavement of inferiors to superiors was Aristotle,[82] but the apologists also ransacked all of classical, biblical, and modern literature for pronouncements sanctioning the southern order. Thus Pitch cites "what Horace and others of the ancients say of servants," tracing his own views to "an immense hereditary ex-

80. Franklin (ed.), *The Confidence-Man*, 157–58, note 2.
81. *The Pro-Slavery Argument*, 461.
82. Jenkins, *Pro-Slavery Thought*, 137.

perience" (CM, 161). Similarly, the P.I.O. man, as H. Bruce Franklin has shown, advances his sordid theories on the potential for turning unpromising boys into model servants under the garb of a Socratic inquiry into the nature of virtue and the possibility of inculcating it.[83] Like the apologists, both Pitch and the P.I.O. man also rely heavily on the weight of religious testimony. Pitch, perhaps thinking, among other ramifications, of Augustine's view that slavery was a consequence of the Fall, instituted by God to cope with postlapsarian man's depravity,[84] asserts that "St. Augustine on Original Sin is my text book" (CM, 174). The P.I.O. man preens his firm on having conducted its studies of mankind "equally among all books of all libraries, as among all men of all nations" (as did the southern apologists and the racial theorists, archeologists, and ethnologists who collaborated with them); unlike his historical prototypes, however, he admits unabashedly "that these studies [have been] directed always to the scientific procuring of good servants." The examples he adduces as evidence that "rakish young waiters" may in time become "wonders of the world for anchoritish self-command" include St. Augustine, Ignatius Loyola, and the founder of the Trappists. Nor does he omit calling Christ himself to witness, in the apologists' tradition of quoting the New Testament in favor of slavery (CM, 173–74).

The classical format of this chapter does not serve merely to parody the proslavery argument, however. Its more integral function is to recall an inglorious aspect of classical slavery highly relevant to the South—the sexual exploitation of slaves. The licentiousness bred by the southern slave system was one of the abolitionists' prime targets. In countless tracts, books, and sermons, they told of light-skinned genteel girls being auctioned off as concubines, and defenseless slave women falling prey to their masters' lusts. Southerners sometimes denied these allegations, but more often they tried to turn the tables on abolitionists. Pointing to the "seventy thousand prostitutes of London, or of Paris, or the ten thousand of New York, or our other Northern cities," they contended that free society engendered far more immorality than existed under slavery. Indeed, piously intoned one apologist, "the intercourse which takes place

83. Franklin (ed.), *The Confidence-Man*, 157–58, note 2.
84. Jenkins, *Pro-Slavery Thought*, 136.

with enslaved females, is less depraving in its effects, than when it is carried on with females of their own caste"; for delinquent youths felt more "degradation in the act" and were less liable to the "allurements" offered by the sirens of their own race in the "haunts of vice."[85]

Classical literature, of course, shows slave boys, rather than slave women, to have been the chief victims of sexual exploitation, and it is on the classical abuse that Melville focuses in this chapter, as the clandestine means of dramatizing how completely slavery violated the manhood of the slave and perverted the moral being of the master. Foreshadowed in the herb-doctor's valedictory (which is delivered "with manly intrepidity forbearing each unmanly thrust" [CM, 156]), the homosexual innuendoes pervading this episode begin with the first sentence the P.I.O. man addresses to Pitch, in answer to the question "How did you come to dream that I wanted anything in your line?": "Oh, respected sir . . . from long experience, one glance tells me the gentleman who is in need of our humble services" (CM, 158). In explaining how his office helps clients like Pitch to find what, in the bachelor's words, "they jocosely call a good boy," the P.I.O. man emphasizes that the firm he represents is founded on physiological, as well as on philosophical principles.

Although Pitch now tries to disclaim any predilection for boys, his very words of denial betray the sexual fears and fantasies boys arouse in him: "Yes, a *thrice dear* purchase one of your boys would be to me. A *rot* on your boys!" (CM, 160; italics added). One hardly needs confirmation that this triple pun describes boys as sexually desirable, sexually disease-ridden ("rot" is another Elizabethan word for "pox,"[86] while the physical disease also symbolizes moral corruption), and financially, morally, and hygienically costly. Nevertheless, the ensuing exchange verifies and amplifies the pun with Shakespearean lavishness:

> "But, respected sir, if you will not have boys, might we not, in our small way, accommodate you with a man?"
> "Accommodate? Pray, no doubt you could accommodate me with

85. *The Pro-Slavery Argument*, 41–45.
86. Eric Partridge, *Shakespeare's Bawdy: A Literary & Psychological Essay and a Comprehensive Glossary* (rev. ed.; New York, 1969), 176.

a bosom-friend too, couldn't you? Accommodate! Obliging word accommodate: there's accommodation notes now, where one accommodates another with a loan, and if he don't pay it pretty quickly, accommodates him with a chain to his foot. Accommodate! God forbid that I should ever be accommodated."[87] (CM, 160)

When Pitch finally allows his interlocutor to expound the Philosophical Intelligence Office's method of reasoning "by analogy from the physical to the moral" (CM, 167), the P.I.O. man begins by comparing the "incipient" male baby, whom he insists on calling a "man-child," to a "little preliminary rag-paper study"—an image that recalls the elaborate sexual allegory Melville constructed around the papermaking process in "The Tartarus of Maids."[88] On advancing from the embryonic to the postnatal stage of the man-child's life cycle, the P.I.O. man drops the ragpaper figure for two suggestive metaphors "from the horticultural kingdom" (CM, 168). The first plant he associates with the "new-born man-child" is a "lily-bud," and he proceeds forthwith to evaluate the "points" of the infant male for their adult potential by likening them to the reproductive apparatus that the lily bud encloses within its petals: " 'Now, such points as the new-born man-child has—as yet not all that could be desired, I am free to confess—still, such as they are, there they are, and palpable as those of an adult. But we stop not here,' taking another step. 'The man-child not only possesses these present points, small though they are, but, likewise—now our horticultural image comes into play—like the bud of the lily, he contains concealed rudiments of others; that is, points at present invisible, with beauties at present dormant' " (CM, 168). Next taking the "downy-chinned little innocent" to the age where he will "eventually rival the goat in a beard" (CM, 169), the P.I.O. man replaces the lily bud with a similarly shaped, but larger and sturdier plant—Indian corn. Pitch's underlying motive for dissatisfaction with all the boys he has so far hired and fired, intimates the P.I.O. man, has been his impatience with the growth process. In the case of the thirtieth boy Pitch has been complaining about, for example, the bachelor may

---

87. See also pp. 284, 287–88, in the dialogue between Egbert and the cosmopolitan, where the homosexual overtones of these puns become still more obvious.

88. First pointed out by E. H. Eby, "Herman Melville's 'Tartarus of Maids,' " *Modern Language Quarterly*, I (1940), 95–100.

have dismissed him too early in his development. Instead of up-rooting his young plant, Pitch ought to have "cultivated" and "hoed round" his "sickly virtues,"[89] the P.I.O. man chides: "Who knows now, but that flexile gracefulness, however questionable at the time of that thirtieth boy of yours, might have been the silky husk of the most solid qualities of maturity. It might have been with him as with the ear of the Indian corn" (CM, 175). The bachelor himself indirectly corroborates the P.I.O. man's analysis. Whereas the lily bud image had visibly taxed his patience—eliciting from him the protest "cut it short, cut it short!"—the analogy with ripened Indian corn immediately appeals to Pitch: " 'Yes, yes, yes,' excitedly cried the bachelor, as the light of this new illustration broke in, 'yes, yes; and now that I think of it, how often I've sadly watched my Indian corn in May, wondering whether such sickly, half-eaten sprouts, could ever thrive up into the stiff, stately spear of August' " (CM, 168, 175).

Pitch's weakness for Indian corn proves his undoing in his bout with the P.I.O. man. Later, in attempting to understand how his philosophical adversary had "wormed into him, and made such a fool of him" as to induce him to invest in yet another boy, the bachelor all but admits to himself that his downfall came about not through default of "philosophy, knowledge, experience," but through a sexual impulse "unbeknown" to his rational self. "The entering wedge," he decides, must have been slipped into him "on the castle's south side, its *genial* one, where Suspicion, the warder, parleyed" (CM, 182; italics added).[90] Recognizing as the agent of his betrayal "his too indulgent, too artless and companionable nature," he resolves to "be a little splenetic in his intercourse henceforth."

The bawdy sexual imagery that enlivens this episode also serves a serious purpose: to establish an analogy between sexual and economic exploitation. Literally a prominent part of economic exploitation under every type of slave system, ancient and modern, sexual exploitation seems to have struck Melville as an apt and powerful symbol for the total expropriation the master made of the slave's

89. A play on the derivation of "virtue" from the Latin "virtus," meaning "manliness" (*OED*).

90. See Franklin (ed.), *The Confidence-Man*, 251, note 20, on the sexual and other meanings of "genial." "South side" also refers to the American South.

body, mind, and soul. At the same time, because the ugly realities of pederasty, *droit du seigneur*, rape, and prostitution so blatantly gave the lie to the philosophical and religious pretensions that the master class had used to justify slavery from time immemorial, Melville naturally found himself dramatizing the hypocrisy of the master class in sexual terms, as he had in "The Paradise of Bachelors and The Tartarus of Maids," which sheds light on many aspects of Pitch's confrontation with the P.I.O. man. Melville's commentary on the original Templars' fate, for example, provides a useful gloss on the Missouri bachelor's seduction, described in strikingly similar imagery: "a moral blight tainted at last this sacred Brotherhood. Though no sworded foe might outskill them in the fence, yet *the worm of luxury crawled beneath their guard*, gnawing the core of knightly troth, nibbling the monastic vow, till at last the monk's austerity relaxed to wassailing, and the sworn knights-bachelors grew to be but hypocrites and rakes" (PBTM, 203; italics added). Melville's observation on the indignity of "indiscriminately" calling "female operatives, of whatever age . . . girls, never women" (PBTM, 222), suggesting a parallel with the slaveowner's habit of calling all male blacks "boys" until well into old age, also redefines Pitch's term "boys." Most relevant to understanding the Missouri bachelor's attitude toward slavery, however, is the role machinery plays in enslaving the "girls" of this hellish paper mill to the old bachelor who owns it.

Despite the interest Pitch shows in the Philosophical Intelligence Office's recipes for making "good boys to order," he belligerently announces his preference for machines at the outset. "As I told that cousin-german of yours, the herb-doctor," he repeats to the P.I.O. man, "I'm now on the road to get me made some sort of machine to do my work. Machines for me" (CM, 156, 160).

Like the inventor Bannadonna, Pitch fancies machines because he finds human labor erratic and unreliable. "Boy or man," he tells the P.I.O. man, "the human animal is, for most work-purposes, a losing animal"—a conclusion "all thinking minds . . . now-a-days" are reaching. He adds, echoing Melville's catalogue of the qualities Bannadonna's "new serf" was to exhibit ("more useful than the ox . . . for industry an ant . . . in patience, another ass"): "Can't be trusted; less trustworthy than oxen; for conscientiousness a turnspit dog excels him" (CM, 161–62; BT, 233–34). The advantage of the machine, on the contrary, is its utter subordination to his will, its utter lack of independent desires or values, its utter limitation to the purpose it fulfills: "My cider-mill—does that ever steal my cider? My mowing-machine—does that ever lay a-bed mornings? My corn-husker—does that ever give me insolence? No: cider-mill, mowing-machine, corn-husker—all faithfully attend to their business. Disinterested, too; no board, no wages" (CM, 160). Machines, Pitch proclaims, are "the only practical Christians" he knows of: "doing good all their lives long; shining examples that virtue is its own reward." From a "moral point of view," a cornhusker is so far superior to a boy, asserts Pitch, that "a corn-husker, for its patient continuance in well-doing, might not unfitly go to heaven," whereas a boy could never meet the requisite standards of good conduct (CM, 160–61). Even the expletive with which the bachelor prefaces that statement articulates his belief that man ought to be a machine: "Start my soul-bolts!" In short, Pitch reduces the soul to a motor, virtue and goodness to mere mechanical performances, and the ideal Christian to a programmed automaton—just as apologists envisioned the perfect slave as the one whose happiness consisted first and foremost in "excel[ling] all . . . other slaves in the performance of his servile duties."[91]

Reacting with shock to the suggestion that "mere machine-work and puppet-work" deserve to go to heaven, and "things incapable of free agency, to receive the eternal reward of well-doing," the P.I.O. man puts his finger on a probable source of such "heresy": "Respected sir," he admonishes Pitch, "this way of talking as if heaven were a kind of Washington patent-office museum—oh, oh, oh!" (CM, 161).

Patent Commissioner Thomas Ewbank, during his three-year tenure from 1849 to 1852, had become a controversial exponent of the rising faith in technology—criticized in Congress for using the annual *Report of the Commisioner of Patents* as an organ for his theories; praised and publicized by the antislavery editor of the New York *Tribune*, Horace Greeley; anathemized by the evangelical abolitionist press for his "bad theology"; and bitterly attacked by proslavery southerners for prophesying that machinery was ordained

91. *The Pro-Slavery Argument*, 460.

to supersede slavery.[92] Ewbank proselytized for technology with the fervor of a religious convert. In his eyes, God was not the Great Spirit, but the Great Mechanic. The universe, "a collection of his inventions," unmistakably exhibited the Deity's "preference for the material and useful" as the truest embodiment of the "sublime." Science, consequently, was divine, and its application held the key to the millennium: "Not till mechanical as well as ethical science is fully explored and universally applied can man attain his destiny, and evil be swept from the earth."[93]

Although this apotheosis of mechanical science marked the age as a whole, Ewbank stood for its most extreme manifestation. In contrast to his precursor J. A. Etzler, who had stressed that labor-saving machinery must be collectively owned in order to benefit the working class, since otherwise "the price of their labors would sink almost to nothing, [and] dangers and violences would ensue,"[94] Ewbank airily dismissed the ravages that mechanization threatened to inflict on the working class. Instead, he took the lofty view that science ultimately tended to "eradicate evil," whatever momentary havoc it wreaked on its course toward earthly perfection. " 'Onward!' is the standing order of God," he hymned. "The inflexible fiat of Heaven" decreed that "those who refuse to obey must be pushed aside." And far be it from human sentimentalists to contest the laws God had set over the material universe. This philosophy lent itself to the same uses as ethnology in sanctioning the exploitation or extermination of races that proved "unprogressive." Hence Ewbank explained the "melting away of the red race" as the inevitable result of the Indians' failure to obey the law of progress. "No man's virtue makes his body bullet-proof," he moralized, "nor can the better qualities of an ignorant, idle, roving race, induce God to throw the world off its hinges to indulge them for ever in such habits." As he summed it up: "Races and nations are saved by works, not by faith." He meant, of course, mechanical works.[95]

92. Merle Curti, *The Growth of American Thought* (New York, 1943), 335; Arthur A. Ekirch, Jr., *The Idea of Progress in America, 1815–1860* (New York, 1951), 127–30; Filler, *The Crusade Against Slavery*, 196.
93. *Report of the Commissioner of Patents, for the Year 1849*, 31st Cong., 1st Sess., Ex. Doc. No. 20, Pt. 1, p. 488.
94. Etzler, *Paradise*, 5. See also Curti, *American Thought*, 336–37.
95. *Report of the Commissioner of Patents, for the Year 1849*, 31st Cong., 1st Sess., Ex. Doc. No. 20, Pt. 1, pp. 500–501. Ewbank was a founder of the American Ethnological

Ewbank's worship of the machine is thus the obverse of Pitch's contempt for the working or serving man's human intractability (CM, 162). Or rather, the two attitudes go hand in hand; for Pitch has also revealed himself to be an enthusiastic votary of the technological cult over which Ewbank presided as high priest. Through Pitch, Melville satirizes the views Ewbank had promulgated in the annual Patent Office Reports. Pitch's homage to machines as "practical Christians," for example, caricatures Ewbank's salute to the intrinsic "morality" of the mechanic arts, which the Patent Commissioner set above the highest achievements in literature and pronounced worthy of comparison with the Bible itself: "A steamer is a mightier epic than the Iliad; and Whittemore, Jacquard, and Blanchard, might laugh even Virgil, and Milton, and Tasso, to scorn. . . . A lever, hammer, pulley, wedge, and screw, are actual representations of great natural truths, and the men who revealed them may be said to have been inspired."[96] Similarly, Pitch travesties Ewbank's call for a millennium built on technological progress. Just as Ewbank had hailed the calculating machines, spinning machines, power looms, knitting machines, sewing machines, lacemaking machines, and embroidery machines whose "automatic fingers" performed "with a precision, regularity, despatch, delicacy of touch and finish, that no human organs can rival,"[97] so Pitch acclaims "these thousand new inventions—carding machines, horse-shoe machines, tunnel-boring machines, reaping machines, apple-paring machines, boot-blacking machines, sewing machines, shaving machines, run-of-errand machines, dumb-waiter machines, and the Lord-only-knows-what machines; all of which announce the era when that refractory animal, the working or serving man, shall be a buried by-gone, a superseded fossil" (CM, 162). But where Ewbank had simply shrugged off the massacre of the Indians and disregarded the destitution that lay in store for black chattels and white wage slaves once machines took over their respective functions, Pitch actively looks forward to the "glorious time" when obsolete human laborers will have become ripe for destruction at the hands of their

---

Society and delivered his *Inorganic Forces Ordained to Supersede Human Slavery* at one of their meetings.
96. *Ibid.*, 488.
97. *Ibid.*, 491.

former employers. "I doubt not," he tells the P.I.O. man, that "shortly prior" to the complete triumph of machinery, "a price will be put upon their peltries as upon the knavish 'possums,' especially the boys. Yes, sir," he adds, "(ringing his rifle down on the deck), I rejoice to think that the day is at hand, when, prompted to it by law, I shall shoulder this gun and go out a boy-shooting" (CM, 162). Thus Melville translates Ewbank's machine-worship into Pitch's man-hatred, Ewbank's mechanistic millennium into Pitch's genocidal apocalypse.

At this point, it may look as though Pitch wants contradictory things: on the one hand, well-disciplined servants who can also cater to his sexual needs; on the other hand, machines that can obviate forever his dependence on servants. Actually, these aspirations are complementary. Pitch's affinities with that other "cynic solitaire," the inventor Bannadonna, for example, suggest both a sexually and an economically exploitative relationship between wanting "good boys [made] to order" and wanting machines "made . . . to do the sort of work which boys are supposed to be fitted for" (BT, 228; CM, 149, 158). Sexually, as H. Bruce Franklin has shown in his analysis of "The Bell-Tower," "the creation of an automaton [is] a narcissistic act unconsciously intended to bypass the normal means of procreation."[98] Although the Missouri bachelor wishes to own, rather than to father, an automaton, he reveals an impulse to countervail nature and a hostility toward woman akin to Bannadonna's. He fiercely attacks the herb-doctor's assumption that nature is good by definition, claiming to owe his eyesight to an oculist who "counterplotted" nature. As evidence of nature's treachery, he instances the poisonous plant "deadly-nightshade," whose scientific name, "belladonna," means "beautiful woman" (CM, 147, 150). Even the machine he cites as superior to a boy, because it performs its assigned task without giving him "insolence," is sexually suggestive: the cornhusker (CM, 160).

In the socioeconomic sphere, Pitch's desire to supplant refractory boys with obedient machines symbolizes the desire to reduce boys to robots. Once again, as in "The Bell-Tower" and "The Paradise of Bachelors and The Tartarus of Maids," Melville has fused the

98. Franklin, *Future Perfect*, 143, 146.

master's domination of his slave in the South with the machine's domination of the worker in the North, presenting both as unnatural in every sense.

Although Melville defines Pitch's attitude toward slavery in terms of many other slave systems, ranging from the classical to the modern industrial models, ultimately he places the Missourian squarely in the context of southern slavery, as his repeated references to Missouri's slave status indicate. The most important of such cues sets the stage for the long debate on boys in which Pitch and the P.I.O. man recapitulate the current debate over slavery.

In answer to the question about where the Philosophical Intelligence Office is located, the P.I.O. man says, "'The branch one which I represent is at Alton, sir, in the free state we now pass,' (pointing somewhat proudly ashore)" (CM, 159). Two decades earlier, the abolitionist editor Elijah Lovejoy had likewise contrasted the "free" state of Illinois with the slave state of Missouri, while defending his right to publish antislavery views in Alton: "Is not this a free state? When assailed by a mob at St. Louis, I came hither, as to the home of freedom and of the laws."[99] Within three days, the citizens of Alton had replied with bullets, and Elijah Lovejoy had become the first martyr of the abolitionist crusade, and a potent symbol of slavery's threat to American democracy. Commenting on Lovejoy's slaying in his stirring *Narrative of Riots at Alton* (1838), the abolitionist Edward Beecher had prophesied: "From henceforth no boat will pass the spot where he fell, heedless of his name, or of his sentiments, or of the cause for which he died."[100] Lovejoy's and Beecher's words reverberate ironically through the P.I.O. man's heedless boast of coming from a free state, and through the Missourian's equally heedless reply, both belying the hope that Lovejoy's death would win the nation to the "cause for which he died," and testifying instead to the hold slavery continued to exert over "free" North and slave South alike.

If this political baiting has served to test the abolitionist sympathies Pitch appeared to voice in his parting jibes at the herb-

99. Edward Beecher, *Narrative of Riots at Alton*, 54.
100. *Ibid.*, 62.

doctor, Pitch's response tells the P.I.O. man all he needs to know. Far from reminding the P.I.O. man of Alton's sorry history, as an abolitionist would have, Pitch objects with the sectional pride of a southerner to the imputation that an Illinoisan is freer than a Missourian. For the second time, he resorts to the hackneyed southern strategy of turning the tables on the North: "Free, eh? You a freeman, you flatter yourself? With those coat-tails and that spinal complaint of servility? Free? Just cast up in your private mind who is your master, will you?" (CM, 159).

This time, while echoing the drover's words to Black Guinea ("And who is your master, Guinea?" "A free dog, eh? Well, on your account, I'm sorry for that, Guinea. Dogs without masters fare hard"), the Missourian seems literally to step into the drover's role and to reenact, in his own twilight encounter with the P.I.O. man, the drover's daybreak attempt to degrade and reenslave Black Guinea.

Of all Guinea's successors, the P.I.O. man most resembles the crippled Negro "cut down to the stature of a Newfoundland dog." Like Guinea, he is ill clad, his "mean five-dollar suit" corresponding to the Negro's "tow-cloth attire." As with Guinea, both his looks and his mannerisms "put him on a canine footing" (CM, 17). "Round-backed" and "baker-kneed," he wears "collar-wise by a chain, a small brass plate, inscribed P.I.O."—the equivalent of a dog tag marked with the owner's name. He behaves accordingly "with a sort of canine deprecation," crouching, slinking obliquely, ducking, groveling, and whining, "in his obsequiousness, seeming to wag his very coat-tails behind him, shabby though they were" (CM, 157–59). Just as Guinea gets himself treated like a dog by acting like one, the P.I.O. man's fawning posture incites Pitch to spurn him like a cur and to address him by "calling as if to his pointer" (CM, 157–58). Crowning the parallels between the two scenes are allusions to bakers and dough (CM, 158, 170) that recall Guinea's metaphor of the "good baker's oven" and the drover's view that black bread and "nice white rolls" ought to be baked separately (CM, 16).

These parallels teach the same lessons that abolitionists had drawn from the events at Alton: the cringing P.I.O. man personifies the consequences that enslaving one portion of a nation's citizenry leads to in undermining the freedom and dignity of all; the overbearing, arrogant Missourian illustrates how easily men who contract the habit of abusing one class of their fellows fall into the practice of indiscriminately abusing everyone.

Similar lessons emerge from Pitch's experiences with the thirty-five child laborers he seems to have held under a tenure amounting to slavery. Although he has employed American, Irish, English, German, Chinese, and Lascar, as well as African and mulatto boys, he speaks of them all in the terms that southern planters applied to their black slaves (CM, 162–63). The description he gives of his thirtieth boy, for example, whom he has ordered from the "Commissioners of Emigration, all the way from New York," in a process highly reminiscent of the African slave trade, conforms in almost every respect to the stereotype proslavery literature gave of the Negro in his ideal role: "But, such suavity! . . . always bowing and saying, 'Please sir!' In the strangest way, too, *combining a filial affection with a menial respect.* Took such warm, singular interest in my affairs. Wanted to be considered one of the family—sort of adopted son of mine, I suppose. Of a morning, when I would go out to my stable, with what *childlike good nature* he would trot out my nag" (CM, 163; italics added). The deceitfulness and "strong destructive propensities" Pitch discovers under this boy's "Chesterfieldian exterior" likewise tally with the experiences of slave duplicity that made many masters privately admit they could "never in a single instance decipher [the Negro's] character."[101] As for the conduct Pitch ascribes to himself in the face of the boy's misdeeds, it is, of course, the exemplary tolerance that the "kind master" prided himself on showing toward miscreants: "'But, he don't look very clean, does he?' unwilling to be downright harsh with so affectionate a lad; 'and he seems a little hollow inside the haunch there, don't he? or no, perhaps I don't see plain this morning'" (CM, 163).

Whereas Pitch claims to have discharged each of his thirty-five boys "for some wholly unforeseen species of viciousness peculiar to that one peculiar boy" (CM, 163), the delinquencies he reports of his thirtieth boy, at least, are precisely the ones planters most commonly complained of in their slaves: neglecting the livestock, "ac-

101. *The Pro-Slavery Argument*, 161; Stampp, *The Peculiar Institution*, 87–88, 131.

THE DEVIL IS NEVER SO BLACK 255

cidentally" breaking tools, damaging property, lying, stealing. Moreover, the word under which Pitch catalogues all these transgressions—"rascality"—was so closely associated with slaves that the ethnologist Samuel Cartwright actually diagnosed rascality as the chief symptom of a disease peculiar to the Negro.[102] Pitch's only departure from the viewpoint of the typical slaveholder is to characterize all boys—"polite boys or saucy boys, white boys or black boys, smart boys or lazy boys, Caucasian boys or Mongol boys"— as equally "rascals" (CM, 164). Yet contrary to what he maintains, the moral to which he unconsciously attests is not that rascality is an innate trait in "human nature of the juvenile sort," any more than it is a uniquely African disease; the moral is that all boys are equally liable to become rascals under a slave regime.

Ultimately, then, this long chapter (the longest in the book), which Melville has placed at the heart of his apocalyptic abnegation of America's millennial hope, is about the impact slavery has on the nation that sanctions it, on the master who profits from it, and on the slave who endures it. As the local seat of the office that supplies Pitch with his thirty-sixth boy—an office dedicated to furnishing "kind gentlemen" with well-drilled servants—Alton, Illinois, fitly embodies the fatal embrace in which slavery held South and North together. No other American city so dramatically testified to the North's complicity in slavery, and to the identity of interests which impelled northern merchants, bankers, academicians, politicians, and clergymen to placate southern opinion by violently suppressing public discussion of slavery.

As a professed nonslaveholder and an adopted Missourian, originally from the East (CM, 242), Pitch manifests the contaminating influence that a slave environment exerts over the entire population. He is Melville's sophisticated variant on the popular theme of the Yankee-turned-slaveholder. Though forswearing slave labor, he exploits children who, as minors and, for the most part, immigrants, are legally almost as much at his mercy as bona fide chattels would be. Critical of the northern factory system's wage slavery, he nevertheless longs to replace human labor with machinery. Meanwhile, he settles for "boys" advertised in the same terms as slaves ("likely," "tall," "stout," "industrious")[103] and offered on "scientific" principles as viable alternatives to robots.

The word *boys* itself, of course, expresses the slaves' eternal status as children in the minds of their white owners. More poignantly than any other metaphor Melville could have used, it conjures up the tragic mutilation that slavery inflicted on its victim's personality—infantilizing the slave emotionally, stunting him intellectually, emasculating him sexually, and debasing him morally.[104]

To this devastating indictment of the toll slavery took on all involved in it, Melville adds a final ironic twist. He makes Pitch's racial identity as enigmatic as the Confidence-Man's. The Missourian's name, on which he puns repeatedly ("My name is Pitch: I stick to what I say" [CM, 162, 175]) suggests blackness and links Pitch with both Black Guinea, a victim of slavery, and the Black Rapids man, a proslavery apologist and industrial slave master. Reinforcing these links and extending them to include the P.I.O. man are many plays on the etymology of the word that labels Pitch's philosophical stance—"cynic," originally meaning "dog." Pitch's associations with blackness and dogs seem to carry the same symbolic meaning as Black Guinea's, for a later character refers to the Missourian as a "queer 'coon" and nicknames him "Coonskins" (CM, 196, 220), recalling an epithet commonly applied to blacks— "Coon."[105] Perhaps the strongest evidence that this domineering Missourian may be a black passing for a white, however, is his deep tan, to which the herb-doctor draws attention: "by your complexion, I judge you live an out-of-door life" (CM, 150). If Pitch's racial identity is indeed ambiguous, he exemplifies still another lesson of Black Guinea's masquerade, and one borne out by the long historical

103. Franklin (ed.), *The Confidence-Man*, 154–55, note 12.
104. I am aware that recent scholarship has considerably modified this pessimistic view of the psychic injury slaves sustained. See, for example, John W. Blassingame, *The Slave Community: Plantation Life in the Antebellum South* (New York, 1972); Herbert G. Gutman, *The Black Family in Slavery and Freedom, 1750–1925* (New York, 1977); and to some extent Genovese, *Roll, Jordan, Roll*. Melville's view, however, was that of Frederick Douglass and the abolitionists, who emphasized psychic injury. Like Douglass, Melville saw the slave as escaping such injury only by actively resisting slavery.
105. Wentworth and Flexner (eds.), *Dictionary of American Slang*, gives 1887 as the earliest usage of this epithet, but it is probably much older (*e.g.*, a twentieth-century reference is given for "confidence-man").

THE DEVIL IS NEVER SO BLACK

view this chapter takes of slavery—that skin color does not distinguish the oppressors from the oppressed.

Pitch's encounter with the P.I.O. man climaxes the extended review of the slavery question that dominates the first half of *The Confidence-Man*. Like his predecessors, the good merchant and the clergyman, the Missouri bachelor has faced an apocalyptic test of his fellow feeling for the slave and has been found wanting. Viewed in these concrete historical terms, rather than in the abstract moral terms that have shaped the prevailing critical interpretation of *The Confidence-Man*, all of these seemingly sympathetic and well-meaning characters—so much like the middle-class readers to whom they appeal—have fallen victim not to the goodheartedness and trust in humankind that they at first appear to show, but to the greed, hypocrisy, racism, and insensitivity to human oppression that impel them to invest in slavery and to deny their brotherhood with the Negro on the day of reckoning.

Recognizing the centrality of slavery to the Confidence-Man's apocalyptic April Fools' Day masquerade thus entails relinquishing the accepted reading of the book as a nihilistic moral allegory dramatizing a malevolent trickster-god's entrapment of innocent human beings. Instead, *The Confidence-Man* emerges as Melville's most powerful indictment of nineteenth-century America—a nation that was bringing God's judgment on itself by enslaving and massacring its nonwhite citizens while posing as a religious and political haven.

EIGHT   *W*ounds of Fratricidal Strife
in Melville's Postwar Writings

The Confidence-Man was Melville's last statement
about slavery before the Civil War, but it was not quite his last
protest against racism. Oddly enough for someone who had learned,
as he lamented to his friend Evert Duyckinck, "that an author can
never—under no conceivable circumstances—be at all frank with
his readers,"[1] he delivered this final protest not covertly, in fiction,
but openly, on a lyceum platform.

Melville took up lecturing in lieu of writing soon after his return
from the long tour of Europe and the Holy Land on which he had
embarked after finishing *The Confidence-Man*. His eleven-year career as an author, during which he had published ten books and
enough tales, sketches, and reviews to fill up an eleventh, all the
while struggling to reconcile the demands of his conscience with
the financial and social pressures his family and milieu exerted on
him, had left him in a state of psychic exhaustion. Yet as a lecturer,
he faced even more acutely the problem of "try[ing] to get a living
by the Truth."[2] And once again, he opted for an uneasy compromise
that satisfied neither him nor his audience.

Of the three lectures Melville gave during his three years on the
lyceum circuit, the first, "Roman Statuary" (1857), flouted the
tastes of a lyceum audience, not to mention its expectations of the

1. Davis and Gilman (eds.), *Letters of Melville*, 96.
2. *Ibid.*, 127.

"man who lived among the cannibals."[3] The remaining two catered
to the appeal for "more modern and personal" subjects, but deliberately baited a public anxious to "arouse no jealous solicitude in
regard to . . . questions of current politics."[4]

In "The South Seas" (1858), an otherwise dismal rehash of the
books that had made him famous, minus the intimate adventures
the public thirsted to hear, Melville launched into a diatribe against
the white man's rape of Polynesia that made his notorious attacks
on the missionaries in *Typee* and *Omoo* seem tame by comparison.
The natives of Polynesia, he asserted, "are naturally of a kindly and
hospitable temper, but there has been planted among them an almost
instinctive hate of the white man. They esteem us, with rare exceptions, such as *some* of the missionaries, the most barbarous, treacherous, irreligious, and devilish creatures on the earth." Moreover,
Melville pointed out, they had ample cause. Had they not seen white
men's ships open their "batteries in indiscriminate massacre" on
seaside villages, "splattering the torn bamboo huts with blood and
brains of women and children, defenseless and innocent?" Were
they not being currently forced to "give up all that binds them
together as a nation or race—their language?" And what about
"those brutal and cruel vices" exhibited by American and European
adventurers, "which disgust even savages with our manners, while
they turn an earthly paradise into a pandemonium"? Judging by
the spectacle of the Sandwich Islands, Melville proclaimed, "the
result of civilization" was "productive to the civilizers, destructive
to the civilizees"—"very much on the principle of the old game,
'You lose, I win.'"[5] As if that weren't enough, Melville concluded
this lecture with a resounding plea against the contemplated an-
nexation of the Hawaiian Islands "until *we* have found for ourselves
a civilization morally, mentally, and physically higher than one
which has culminated in almshouses, prisons, and hospitals."[6]

The following year, in "Traveling: Its Pleasures, Pains, and Profits," his last effort to capture the lecture market, Melville formulated

3. *Ibid.*, 130 (Melville's rueful description of how he would go down to posterity).
My information about Melville's lectures is drawn from Merton M. Sealts's invaluable
Melville as Lecturer (Folcroft, Pa., 1970).
4. Sealts, *Melville as Lecturer*, 23, 27.
5. *Ibid.*, 168–69, 179–80.
6. *Ibid.*, 180.

the most explicit critique of racial prejudice that he had ever made, or would ever make again—one that summed up everything he had been saying in his fiction about the relativity of cultural values, the fallacy of ethnocentrism, the variability of alleged racial traits, and the brotherhood of mankind, but in language everyone could understand and no one mistake. The "legitimate tendency" of travel, he told his audience, "is to teach profound personal humility, while it enlarges the sphere of comprehensive benevolence till it includes the whole human race." The necessity of submitting to "the persecutions and extortions of guides" abroad, for example, may open the eyes of the American traveler to "the thousand times worse extortions practised on the immigrants here." At the same time, remarked Melville bluntly, travel served to "get rid of a *few* prejudices" by counteracting racial stereotypes:

> The Spanish matador, who devoutly believes in the proverb, "Cruel as a Turk," goes to Turkey, sees that people are kind to all animals . . . and comes home to his bull-fights with a very different impression of his own humanity. The stock-broker goes to Thessalonica and finds infidels more honest than Christians . . . the prejudiced against color finds several hundred millions of people of all shades of color, and all degrees of intellect, rank, and social worth, generals, judges, priests and kings, and learns to give up his foolish prejudice.[7]

This lecture was written in late October or early November, 1859. During those very weeks, the newspapers were full of an event that Melville later called the "meteor" of the impending Civil War— John Brown's raid on the federal arsenal at Harper's Ferry, Virginia.

The Civil War, which so many Americans experienced as the great divide in their lives, profoundly altered Melville's artistic vision and creativity. It is symptomatic of the impact the war had on him that he emerged from a ten-year silence in 1866 no longer a writer of prose fiction, but a poet—as if he had to find a new literary medium to express the trauma he and his compatriots had undergone.

The verse form he adopted in *Battle-Pieces and Aspects of the War* is harsh, grating, constricted, oppressive, like the perceptions it articulates about this unprecedented national bloodletting. Melville consciously strove to suit style to theme:

7. *Ibid.*, 183–84.

> Plain be the phrase, yet apt the verse,
> More ponderous than nimble;
> For since grimed War here laid aside
> His Orient pomp, 'twould ill befit
> Overmuch to ply
> The rhyme's barbaric cymbal.[8]

The effect is an extreme distancing of emotions, which the volume's most acute contemporary reviewer, William Dean Howells, singled out for criticism: "Is it possible—you ask yourself, after running over all these celebrative, inscriptive, and memorial verses—that there has really been a great war, with battles fought by men and bewailed by women? Or is it only that Mr. Melville's inner consciousness has been perturbed, and filled with the phantasms of enlistments, marches, fights in the air, parenthetic bulletin-boards, and tortured humanity shedding, not words and blood, but words alone?"[9] Howells construed the verse's strange "quality of remoteness" as an indication that Melville had "not often felt the things of which he writes."[10] However, the poem Howells quoted to illustrate this alleged failing, "The Portent" (a poem many modern critics consider the most outstanding piece of the collection), bespeaks rather a pain so intense as to numb all sensibility. Interestingly, that is precisely the emotional state pictured in its subject, John Brown:

> *Hanging from the beam,*
> *Slowly swaying (such the law),*
> *Gaunt the shadow on your green,*
> *Shenandoah!*
> *The cut is on the crown*
> *(Lo, John Brown),*
> *And the stabs shall heal no more.*

---

8. Herman Melville, *Battle-Pieces and Aspects of the War*, ed. Sidney Kaplan, 61. All citations from *Battle-Pieces* will be to this edition, and page references will be given parenthetically in the text. The poem cited is "A Utilitarian View of the Monitor's Fight." On the style of *Battle-Pieces*, see Robert Penn Warren, "Melville's Poems," *Southern Review*, n.s. III (1967), 804–12; Richard Harter Fogle, "Melville and the Civil War," *Tulane Studies in English*, IX (1959), 63–70; and Hennig Cohen (ed.), *The Battle-Pieces of Herman Melville* (New York, 1963), introduction and notes. I shall be drawing on all of these critics.
9. Cited in Kaplan (ed.), *Battle-Pieces*, xli.
10. *Ibid.*, xlii–xliii.

> *Hidden in the cap*
> *Is the anguish none can draw;*
> *So your future veils its face,*
> *Shenandoah!*
> *But the streaming beard is shown*
> *(Weird John Brown),*
> *The meteor of the war.*
>
> (BP, 11. Poem italicized in the original)

If Melville was seeking a stylistic mode of distancing pain, it was perhaps because the war had brutally confronted him with his own unresolved psychological and moral conflicts.[11] In the words of John Bernstein, who has focused on Melville's conflict between pacifism and rebellion, "the issue of the Civil War skewered Melville as firmly as it did more doctrinaire pacifists such as John Greenleaf Whittier, for though Melville may have been inexorably opposed to war, he was also inexorably opposed to slavery," and to oppose the one was implicitly to condone the other. Melville's fervent commitment to the side that "warred for Right" perpetually contends with his revulsion against the tragic waste of human life and potential on both sides. The tension between these two moral positions, as many critics have observed, is central to *Battle-Pieces*, which Bernstein has aptly characterized as "almost schizophrenic."[12]

Equally central is a related issue Melville raises—whether the civil strife that has cruelly divided brother from brother really has been a war between Right and Wrong, or only another senseless medieval feud, like that of York and Lancaster, Guelph and Ghibelline (BP, 73–74, 272). In *Battle-Pieces*, as in his antebellum fiction, with its recurrent motif of apocalyptic doom overtaking America, Melville frames the question primarily in terms of America's millennial myth. Thus poem after poem asks: how must we interpret this "tempest bursting from the waste of Time/ On the world's fairest hope linked with man's foulest crime" ("Misgivings")? Is

---

11. Warren, "Melville's Poems," 804–805, suggests rather that "the deep divisions of Melville's inner life . . . now found . . . in the fact of a *civil* war an appropriate image which might, in some degree, absorb and purge their pains."

12. John Bernstein, *Pacifism and Rebellion in the Writings of Herman Melville* (The Hague, 1964), 184, 187. See also Warren, "Melville's Poems," 805, 812–17; and Joyce Sparer Adler, "Melville and the Civil War," *New Letters*, XL (1973), 99–117. The quotation "warred for Right" is from the poem "Dupont's Round Fight," BP, 30.

it nothing but the Confidence-Man's ultimate "derision" of America's presumptuous millennial aspirations ("The Conflict of Convictions")? Or, on the contrary, "*is this the Age/ Of the world's great Prime*" and the war the long-heralded Armageddon needed to purify the nation before "the Giant of the Pool/ Heaves his forehead white as wool" to inaugurate America's millennial kingdom ("The Armies of the Wilderness," "A Canticle")? Melville, of course, offers no final answer to these questions, and the doubts and fears expressed in the poems with which *Battle-Pieces* opens persist up to the last paragraph of the prose Supplement with which it closes. Yet the final sentence of the book voices the prayer that "the terrible historic tragedy of our time may not have been enacted" without reeducating the whole nation, and that "fulfillment [may] verify in the end those expectations which kindle the bards of Progress and Humanity."

The task Melville set himself in *Battle-Pieces* was to initiate the process of reeducation that he hoped the war would bring about—first by restaging the tragedy from beginning to end, in all its sectional and political multifariousness, and second by explicitly inculcating the lessons he himself drew from the war and exhorting his countrymen to heed them in evolving their future policy of reconstruction. The striking range of viewpoints represented in *Battle-Pieces* suggests that Melville wanted to include all Americans—northern and southern, pro- and anti-Negro, black and white, young and old, idealistic and cynical, hopeful and pessimistic—in a comprehensive statement about what the war had meant to them.[13] Thus some poems, like "The Conflict of Convictions," take the form of a debate between dissenting factions (in this case youthful millennialists versus graybearded skeptics).[14] Others, like "Stonewall Jackson" and "Stonewall Jackson (Ascribed to a Virginian)," "The March to the Sea" and "The Frenzy in the Wake," are paired as northern and southern views of the war's leading heroes and campaigns. Still others, like the group "In the Turret," "The *Temeraire*," and "A Utilitarian View of the Monitor's Fight," explore one aspect of the war (the new technology of warfare) from several angles. Most important for our purposes, however, are five poems that, in

13. Cohen (ed.), *Battle-Pieces*, 19; Fogle, "Melville and the Civil War," 63, 71.
14. See the helpful explications of this difficult poem by Cohen (ed.), *Battle-Pieces*, 207–11 n.; and Fogle, "Melville and the Civil War," 65–69.

different ways, directly confront the incarnate issue of the war—the Negro.

The greatest of these poems, "The Swamp Angel," brings Melville's vision of the Negro as America's "black Angel of Doom" to its culmination. Personified as a fugitive slave turned apocalyptic destroying angel, the "Swamp Angel," as Melville's note informs us, is the Union soldiers' name for the "great Parrott gun . . . employed in the prolonged . . . bombardment of Charleston" (BP, 250 n.). Once "mocked" by the proud citizens of Charleston, the anthropomorphic iron black avenger (recalling Haman, the semihuman robot of "The Bell-Tower") now seals this ruling class's fate. "It comes like the thief in the gloaming" (night) of apocalyptic prophecy, and casts on its victims "a sleepless spell." "Deluding" them with its slow, unpredictable advance, the Swamp Angel "withers" and ironically "whitens" them with "a breath that is blastment." It reduces Charleston, like Babylon and Jerusalem, to weeds and ashes, while Charlestonians vainly appeal for aid to their patron saint, the "white man's seraph" Michael, who has abandoned them to join forces with the black "Angel over the sea."[15]

Serving as a pendant to "The Swamp Angel" is " 'Formerly a Slave,' " an "idealized Portrait," as the caption tells us, of a slave woman painted by the artist Elihu Vedder. This feminine image of the Negro (the only woman, except for the symbolic "America," mentioned in the book) stresses not the power of black rage, but the strength of black "sufferance"—a quality of endurance like that of the Chola widow Hunilla in "The Encantadas," to whom Melville had addressed one of his most moving tributes: "Humanity, thou strong thing, I worship thee, not in the laureled victor, but in this vanquished one."[16] Unlike the Swamp Angel, the former slave woman, "Sybilline, yet benign," prophesies healing rather than retribution. Although for her, "deliverance" has dawned "too late" to usher in a better life, she takes "prophetic cheer" in the prospect that "her children's children . . . shall know/ The good withheld from her." Her patience in allotting two generations for this consummation foreshadows the gradualist approach toward readjusting

15. See Adler, "Melville and the Civil War," 107–108, for a fine explication of this poem.
16. Berthoff (ed.), *Great Short Works of Herman Melville*, 132.

relations between blacks and whites in the South that Melville himself advocates in his prose Supplement.

Besides these two poems, which view the overthrow of slavery through black eyes—the eyes of the slave rebel and of the long-suffering black mother—three poems speaking for different classes of whites take stock of the price that whites have paid to undo the evil of slavery. "The March to the Sea," commemorating Sherman's march through Georgia, captures the initial mood of exultation with which "those of us who always abhorred slavery as an atheistical iniquity" (in the words of Melville's Supplement) greeted its downfall. Rejoicing slaves flock around the victorious northern armies, and nature itself seems to welcome the liberators:

> All nature felt their coming,
>   The birds like couriers flew,
> And the banners brightly blooming
>   The slaves by thousands drew,
> And they marched beside the drumming,
>   And they joined the armies blue.
>
>   . . . .
>   It was glorious glad marching
>   For every man was free.   (BP, 130)

Throughout the poem, however, sobering reminders of the depredations committed by the liberators temper the exultation, which yields to misgivings in the last stanza:

> For behind they left a wailing,
>   A terror and a ban,
> And blazing cinders sailing,
>   And houseless households wan,
> Wide zones of counties paling,
>   And towns where maniacs ran.
>   Was it Treason's retribution—
>   Necessity the plea?
>   They will long remember Sherman
>   And his streaming columns free—
>   They will long remember Sherman
>   Marching to the sea.   (BP, 132)

These misgivings are expressed even more strongly in the revisions Melville has written into his personal copy of *Battle-Pieces*, where he drops the word treason and asks instead, "Was the havoc, retri-

bution?", leaving the answer in doubt ("But howsoe'er it be
... "), so that the final accent of the poem falls heavily on the residue
of bitterness left by Sherman's march.[17]

Complementing "The March to the Sea," as "'Formerly a
Slave'" complements "The Swamp Angel," is "The Frenzy in the
Wake." This poem articulates the murderous hatred felt by the
southerners whose homes Sherman has devastated. Its southern
speaker rages against the oppression to which his peers have suddenly found themselves subjected in place of their slaves, and turns
in fury against the slaves whose tales of the slaveholders' brutality,
graphically illustrated by the instruments of torture Union soldiers
discovered on the plantations they liberated, were currently flooding
the North:[18]

> So strong to suffer, shall we be
> Weak to contend, and break
> The sinews of the Oppressor's knee
> That grinds upon the neck?
> O, the garments rolled in blood
> Scorch in cities wrapped in flame,
> And the African—the imp!
> He gibbers, imputing shame.　　　(BP, 133)

Striking a balance, finally, between northern and southern attitudes toward the war, and toward the Negro who symbolized it,
is "A Meditation," which the caption attributes to "a Northerner
after attending the last of two funerals from the same homestead—
those of a national and a confederate officer (brothers), his kinsmen,
who had died from the effects of wounds received in the closing
battles" (BP, 239). The concluding poem of Battle-Pieces, "A Meditation" voices the "strange remorse" that eventually overcame the
whole nation for "the sanctioned sin of blood," and above all for the
sanctioned sin of fratricidal warfare (BP, 241). To repent of the war
as a sin, of course, was also to question whether the brotherhood
of mankind transcended the brotherhood of race, and rightly dictated
that white Americans shed each other's blood on behalf of the Negro

---

17. Melville's revisions are listed in Kaplan (ed.), Battle-Pieces, xxv–xxviii.
18. See the diaries of Charlotte Forten and Thomas Wentworth Higginson, cited in
Edmund Wilson, Patriotic Gore: Studies in the Literature of the American Civil War (New
York, 1966), 250–51.

they have wronged. Thus the poem's imaginary speaker curses "the cause of war," and demands "Can Africa pay back this blood/ Spilt on Potomac's shore?" (BP, 242). Clearly, Melville intended to dissociate himself from this sentiment by putting it into the mouth of a fictional northerner directly involved in the war's fratricidal tragedy (as Melville was not).[19]

Nevertheless, the prose Supplement to *Battle-Pieces* reveals that Melville himself was not entirely free of such feelings, contrary though they were to the ideals that had animated his fiction. This Supplement, in which Melville comes forward in person to plead for "reasonable consideration for our late enemies" (BP, 264), has been praised by some critics as "one of the noblest public essays ever written by an American" and excoriated by others as a pathetic lapse of the uncompromising moral vision Melville had shown in his fiction and in the body of *Battle-Pieces*.[20] The chronological gap between these two varying evaluations, the former dating from 1962 (but echoing critics of the 1940s), the latter from 1973, tells us a lot about the influence that the civil rights, black power, and anti-Vietnam War movements have had on our perceptions of the Civil War and Reconstruction.

In 1962, the version of history that grew out of the impulses we find encapsulated in "A Meditation"—remorse for the fratricidal strife and a desire to atone for it by glossing over the slavery controversy and seeking reconciliation of North and South at the expense of the Negro—was still very prevalent. This version, in the words of a recent historiographer, represented the Civil War as a tragedy brought on by extremists on both sides, but redeemed by "the idealism and the nobility of the two contending forces": "Yankees and Confederates alike fought bravely for what they believed to be just causes." At the same time, it characterized Reconstruction as "the nadir of national disgrace" and the seedbed of the racial violence

---

19. This distinction seems to have been overlooked by Aaron, *The Unwritten War*, 77, in his otherwise excellent chapter on Melville's attitude toward the Civil War.

20. The first view is expressed by R. W. B. Lewis (ed.), *Herman Melville* (New York, 1962), 314, in a prefatory note to the Supplement; see also the eulogistic note by Howard P. Vincent (ed.), *Collected Poems of Herman Melville* (Chicago, 1947), 460. The second view is Adler's, "Melville and the Civil War," 100, 111–17. See also Kaplan, "Melville and the American National Sin," 36 (Kaplan is an exception among critics of the 1950s in objecting to the political message of the Supplement).

that henceforth stigmatized the South: an era when corrupt, self-serving northern politicians wreaked their spite on the South, in defiance of Lincoln's wish to "bind up the nation's wounds," while the Negro played the role of their unwitting tool.[21]

Over the past ten years, however, a diametrically opposite interpretation, originally advanced by Marxist historians during the 1930s, has won acceptance. The "revisionist" interpretation upholds nineteenth-century abolitionists' claims that southern intransigence had made free discussion of slavery impossible, peaceful coexistence of the slave system with the "free" North less and less feasible, and war inevitable as the sole means of ending slavery. It also judges that the positive accomplishments of Reconstruction—the legislation guaranteeing black men citizenship and voting rights, and the experience blacks gained in self-government and education—far outweighed its failures, many of which have been exaggerated. Indeed, the real failure of Reconstruction, according to some revisionists, was not that the Radicals went too far, but that they stopped short of dispossessing the big planters and allocating their land to the ex-slaves.[22]

Obviously, the new assessment of Reconstruction necessitates a new assessment of the "Christian" policy Melville calls for toward the defeated southerners and their ex-slaves. But before we can make

21. Kenneth M. Stampp, *The Era of Reconstruction, 1865–1877* (New York, 1965), 4. An instance of the influence the "tragic legend of reconstruction" has had on Melville scholarship is this historical judgment by Walter E. Bezanson (ed.), in his introduction to Melville's *Clarel: A Poem and Pilgrimage in the Holy Land*, cii–ciii: "During the twenty-five years that elapsed between the publications of *Moby-Dick* and *Clarel* . . . the nation plunged into civil war, forsook its humanitarian traditions in a brutal Reconstruction, and entered an orgy of economic self-exploitation. . . . Though recent scholarship has somewhat modified criticism of the quarter century before 1900 . . . no case has been made for the decade after the Civil War, nor does one seem possible." All citations from *Clarel* will be from this edition.
22. Richard O. Curry, "The Civil War and Reconstruction, 1861–1877: A Critical Overview of Recent Trends and Interpretations," *Civil War History*, XX (1974), 229, announces that the old stereotype of Reconstruction "has been consigned to the scrapheap of historical blindness . . . it so richly deserves." Representative of the view that the Radicals did not go far enough, are W. E. B. Du Bois, "Black Reconstruction," reprinted in Kenneth M. Stampp and Leon L. Litwack (eds.), *Reconstruction: An Anthology of Revisionist Writings* (Baton Rouge, 1969), 428–70; and C. Vann Woodward, "Seeds of Failure in the Radical Race Policy," and W. R. Brock, "The Waning of Radicalism," both reprinted in Edwin C. Rozwenc (ed.), *Reconstruction in the South* (2nd ed.; Lexington, Mass., 1972), 245–63, 263–84.

such a reassessment, we must familiarize ourselves with the political conditions and debates to which Melville was responding. The predominant reality of the day was the determination of the slaveholding oligarchy—abetted by President Andrew Johnson—to remain in power and to reinstitute some form of slavery. Faced with the defiant reelection of ex-Confederate leaders, the refusal of several southern states to ratify the Thirteenth Amendment outlawing slavery, general opposition to repudiating the Confederate war debt, and most ominous of all, the passage of Black Codes and the emergence of white terrorist organizations like the Ku Klux Klan, growing numbers of Republicans had come to feel that only by disfranchising ex-Confederates and enfranchising blacks could pro-Union, Republican governments be set up in the South and the fruits of victory over the slave power be secured.

Many who favored Negro suffrage in the South opposed it in their own states, however—as did their constitutents, who regularly voted against Negro suffrage amendments to northern state constitutions. Even among the radical vanguard, support for universal Negro suffrage only evolved gradually. Wendell Phillips was exceptional in having advocated it publicly by 1863. In contrast, William Lloyd Garrison, a year later, pronounced the "elective franchise . . . a conventional, not a natural right," and maintained that it was "not practicable" to translate "chattels personal" straight "from the auction block . . . to the ballot-box." If Negro suffrage were enforced on the South, he argued, it might be "submitted to as a necessity," but would certainly be overturned once southern states were left to manage their own affairs. Throughout 1865, Garrison continued to insist that "so long as most Northern states denied the ballot to Negroes the North had no *moral* right to impose equal suffrage on the South." Although some of Garrison's erstwhile followers expressed dismay at these conservative statements, many others, including Charles Sumner, confessed to doubts about the wisdom of enfranchising illiterate blacks and toyed with the idea of making Negro suffrage contingent on literacy. As late as December, 1865, Thaddeus Stevens, soon to become the foremost congressional champion of Negro suffrage, held that the ex-slaves were not ready for the vote, since the constraints of slavery had "prevented them from acquiring an education, understanding the commonest laws of contract, or of managing the ordinary business of life."[23]

Clearly, Republicans found it easier to disfranchise southern whites than to enfranchise southern, let alone northern, blacks. The Fourteenth Amendment, passed shortly before *Battle-Pieces* came off the press, reflected this; instead of conferring suffrage on blacks, it merely penalized southern states for not doing so, by reducing their representation in Congress. Three sections of the amendment, in fact, dealt with disabilities for ex-Confederates, and only one section with citizenship rights for blacks. Not until the Reconstruction Act of 1867 did Congress explicitly award southern blacks the vote, and not until 1870 did the nation ratify the Fifteenth Amendment, making Negro suffrage the law throughout the land. Meanwhile, Congress multiplied legislative sanctions against southern whites, and radicals like Phillips and Stevens pressed for the measures they considered essential to effecting a true "social revolution" in the South—prolonged military occupation and confiscation and redistribution of the large estates among the ex-slaves and poor whites.[24] This, then, is the political context in which we should read Melville's Supplement.

As a political analysis of the Civil War, the Supplement concurs fully with the revisionist view. Melville minces no words in asserting that the cause for which southerners had fought was "the erecting in our advanced century of an Anglo-American empire based upon the systematic degradation of man" (BP, 261). "It was in subserviency to the slave-interest that Secession was plotted," he emphasizes; states' rights had been nothing but a pretext by which "conspirators" had "entrapped" the "people of the South" into supporting their attempt to "perpetuate the curse of slavery, and even

23. James C. Mohr, *The Radical Republicans and Reform in New York during Reconstruction* (Ithaca, N.Y., 1973), Chaps. 7–8, tells of how the battle for Negro suffrage in Melville's home state of New York was given up for lost by the Radicals. Particularly interesting is the impact racist ethnology had on the debate (p. 231). See also James M. McPherson, *The Struggle for Equality: Abolitionists and the Negro in the Civil War and Reconstruction* (Princeton, 1964), 239–40, 294–95, 297, 328, 333–34. Garrison is cited in McPherson, 294–95, 297, and Stevens is in C. Vann Woodward, *The Burden of Southern History* (Rev. ed.; New York, 1969), 73.

24. J. G. Randall and David Donald, *The Civil War and Reconstruction* (2nd ed.; Lexington, Mass., 1961), Chaps. 33–34, 37; Stampp, *The Era of Reconstruction*, Chap. 5; McPherson, *The Struggle for Equality*, 370–72.

extend it" (BP, 261, 266). Melville also affirms categorically that slavery could not have been abolished without violence: "we should remember that emancipation was accomplished not by deliberate legislation; only through agonized violence could so mighty a result be effected" (BP, 268).

Where Reconstruction policy is concerned, however, Melville takes a stand somewhere between that of contemporary radicals and moderates. He raises three main issues in the Supplement: what conditions of reunion to impose on the ex-Confederate states, what civil rights to legislate for blacks, and what role the federal government ought to play during the "present transition period for both races in the South" (BP, 269).

On the first issue, Melville's position is more conciliatory toward the South than the Republican party's was in 1866—far too conciliatory from a revisionist standpoint. "No consideration," Melville warns, "should tempt us to pervert the national victory into oppression for the vanquished. Should plausible promise of eventual good, or a deceptive or spurious sense of duty, lead us to essay this, count we must on serious consequences" (BP, 269). Specifically, Melville urges the repeal of the test-oath disqualifying former secessionists from holding office, and the admission, as soon as feasible, of congressmen duly "elected by the people of the South" to "represent the populations lately in revolt" (BP, 270–71). While acknowledging the likelihood that northern and southern congressmen would then clash over the same sectional interests that had led them to wage war, Melville finds it unrealistic to imagine that "the political existence of the millions of late Secessionists can permanently be ignored by this Republic" (BP, 271).

On the issue of civil rights and Negro suffrage, I believe that Melville's position is closest to Garrison's. Like Garrison, who argued that northerners should not impose Negro suffrage on the South if they were unwilling to enfranchise blacks in their home states, Melville stanchly opposes unequal application of the laws on the grounds that it is both unjust and impolitic. Instead, he calls upon his compatriots to aspire toward "that kind of pacification, based upon principles operating equally all over the land, which lovers of their country yearn for, and which our arms, though signally triumphant, did not bring about, and which law-making, however anxious, or energetic, or repressive, never by itself can achieve" (BP, 266). Melville does not deny that "some revisionary legislation and adaptive is indispensable"—presumably, as he later spells out, "to confirm the benefit of liberty to the blacks" (BP, 266, 268). Yet he implies that no amount of legislation can achieve this without a fundamental change in American racial attitudes, such as he had endeavored to promote through his fiction. It is in this spirit that he exhorts Americans to "take . . . to heart" the role that "generosity of sentiment public and private" can play in bringing about true national unity.

Melville's chief concern is that "our natural solicitude" to guarantee basic civil liberties to blacks should not find expression in "measures of dubious constitutional rightfulness toward our white countrymen—measures of a nature to provoke, among other of the last evils, exterminating hatred of race toward race" (Melville may have been thinking of the antiblack riots that had erupted in Memphis in May, 1866). He pleads: "In imagination let us place ourselves in the unprecedented position of the Southerners—their position as regards the millions of ignorant manumitted slaves in their midst, for whom some of us now claim the suffrage. Let us be Christians toward our fellow-whites, as well as philanthropists toward the blacks, our fellow-men. In all things, and toward all, we are enjoined to do as we would be done by" (BP, 268).

Some critics have construed this to mean that Melville opposed Negro suffrage.[25] I find it more plausible, however, that the words "measures of dubious constitutional rightfulness toward our white countrymen" refer specifically to the disfranchisement of southern whites. After all, when Melville writes "some of *us* now claim the suffrage" (as three sentences earlier he had written "Those of *us* who always abhorred slavery"), he seems to number himself among the supporters of Negro suffrage.[26] The whole passage makes better

25. Adler, "Melville and the Civil War," 113–15.
26. Another passage in which Melville appears to link himself with the proponents of equal rights legislation is BP, 269–70, where he warns of "divisions among the Northern adherents of the Union" should the Radicals go too far in penalizing the South: "Assuredly, if any honest Catos there be who thus far have gone with *us*, no longer will they do so, but oppose *us*, and as resolutely as hitherto they have supported" (italics added). The abolitionist John Greenleaf Whittier takes a stand almost identical with Melville's in his poem "To the Thirty-ninth Congress" (*Poetical Works*, ed. Waggoner, 347–48). Exhorting Congress to forego vengeance against the South and to claim only "the guaranty/ Of union,

sense if we interpret it as arguing simply that the extension of civil rights to blacks ought not to be accompanied by their withdrawal from southern whites, even on the pretext of lessening the disadvantage at which blacks would otherwise find themselves vis-à-vis their former masters.

Unlike the radicals, Melville seems to have felt that repression would have no more success in reconciling southerners to treating their ex-slaves as equals than it had had in quenching the desire for liberty that had driven thousands of black slaves to run away, strike out against their masters and overseers, and even revolt in the face of certain defeat. Far from hastening the transformation of the South into an egalitarian society, Melville apparently believed, the radical effort to break the power of the old slaveowning class would only unite southerners in undying enmity toward both their conquerors and their former slaves. At least that is how I understand the caveat with which the above-quoted passage concludes: "Nor should we forget that benevolent desires, after passing a certain point, can not undertake their own fulfillment without incurring the risk of evils beyond those sought to be remedied. Something may well be left to the graduated care of future legislation, and to heaven" (BP, 269).

On the third issue—how far the federal government's "guardianship" over the freedmen should extend, particularly in view of the antiblack riots and terrorist attacks then sweeping the South[27] —Melville is hardest to situate historically. To modern ears, a comment like this sounds intolerably paternalistic: "The blacks, in their infant pupilage to freedom, appeal to the sympathies of every humane mind. The paternal guardianship which for the interval government

freedom, peace," he proposes that Congress address the South as follows:
We urge no conqueror's terms of shame.

Make all men peers before the law,
Take hands from off the negro's throat,
Give black and white an equal vote.
Keep all your forfeit lives and lands.

27. The most serious outbreaks were the antiblack riots in Memphis and New Orleans, in May and July, 1866. Terrorist attacks on individual blacks were also occurring frequently, at the behest of organizations like the Ku Klux Klan, founded in Tennessee in 1866. See Stampp, *The Era of Reconstruction*, 199–203; Randall and Donald, *The Civil War and Reconstruction*, 587–88; and John Hope Franklin, *From Slavery to Freedom: A History of Negro Americans* (3rd ed.; New York, 1967), Chap. 18.

exercises over them was prompted equally by duty and benevolence" (BP, 267). Joyce Adler rightly objects that Melville might more appropriately have termed the "former supporters of slavery" in "infant pupilage to freedom."[28] Although Melville does say that southerners have been "for years politically misled by designing men" (BP, 266), one must concede that he tends to present white southerners as adults and blacks as minors. The image of blacks that emerges from the Supplement is a far cry from the "erect, lofty-minded African" depicted in Melville's antebellum fiction.

Melville's paternalism needs to be put in historical context, however. Even proponents of equal justice, rather than "benevolence," toward blacks acknowledged that some type of temporary guardianship, such as that which the Freedmen's Bureau was furnishing, was necessary, "not because these people are negroes, only because they are men who have been, for generations, despoiled of their rights."[29] Wendell Phillips, for example, the greatest abolitionist spokesman for racial equality, used words quite similar to Melville's in defining the duty of abolitionists after emancipation: "to watch for the welfare of this victim race, guard it during its pupilage, shelter it by patronage, by protection, by privilege, by recognizing its claim to an equal manhood."[30] The alternative to paternalism in the post-Civil War era was what came to be known as the "root hog or die" approach: to give blacks formal equal rights without compensating for the socioeconomic handicaps of slavery and pariah status, and then exhort them to compete successfully with whites or go under.[31]

From the standpoint of contemporary radicals, Melville would have appeared not too paternalistic toward blacks, but too laissez faire in his attitude toward the South's interracial "trouble" when he philosophizes:

> In one point of view the coexistence of the two races in the South—whether the negro be bond or free—seems (even as it did to Abraham Lincoln) a grave evil. Emancipation has ridded the country of the reproach, but not wholly of the calamity. Especially in the present

28. Adler, "Melville and the Civil War," 114.

29. American Freedmen's Inquiry Commission Report, cited in McPherson, *The Struggle for Equality*, 186–88.

30. Cited in *ibid.*, 154.

31. Fredrickson, *Black Image in the White Mind*, Chap. 6.

transition period for both races in the South, more or less of trouble may not unreasonably be anticipated; but let us not hereafter be too swift to charge the blame exclusively in any one quarter. With certain evils men must be more or less patient. Our institutions have a potent digestion, and may in time convert and assimilate to good all elements thrown in, however originally alien. (BP, 269)

Melville's laissez faire attitude is based on his repeatedly expressed fear of prolonged civil and interracial strife: "Why is not the cessation of war . . . attended with the settled calm of peace? . . . In the recent convulsion has the crater but shifted?" (BP, 267–68). However warranted by the mounting violence of what one historian has called the "guerilla warfare . . . against both Negroes and whites who represented the Washington government in the South,"[32] fear, in Joyce Adler's words, acted "not only as a limitation on [Melville's] vision of the future but as a rein on his creative imagination" in the Supplement to Battle-Pieces[33] —and indeed in all his later writing about the Civil War. Nowhere is this more apparent than in the passage cited above, with its disturbing implication that blacks, incarnating as they do the "calamity" of slavery, are such an alien element in the American body politic as to require special powers of digestion.

Equally disturbing is another passage that attempts to justify subordinating the welfare of blacks to that of the nation as a whole (a policy we have learned to equate with the indefinite postponement of social justice): "Yet such kindliness [toward blacks] should not be allowed to exclude kindliness to communities who stand nearer to us in nature. For the future of the freed slaves we may well be concerned; but the future of the whole country, involving the future of the blacks, urges a paramount claim upon our anxiety. Effective benignity, like the Nile, is not narrow in its bounty, and true policy is always broad" (BP, 267). It is indeed dismaying to find the Melville who had pleaded so eloquently for human brotherhood in Moby-Dick, and attacked the concept of racial distinctions so brilliantly in "The 'Gees" and The Confidence-Man, lapsing here into the fallacy

32. Franklin, From Slavery to Freedom, 326–27. Randall and Donald also maintain that in the summer of 1866, "many sober men feared a renewal of civil strife," or even a military coup d'état (The Civil War and Reconstruction, 588).
33. Adler, "Melville and the Civil War," 112.

that "communities" who appear to share the same "racial" features we do are "nearer to us in nature" than "communities" who superficially differ from us. But we should not let the racist overtones we hear in these two passages obscure the genuine commitment Melville makes to the ideal of a multiracial America "involving the future of the blacks"—an ideal beautifully symbolized by the Nile, the African river that fertilized the cradle of an empire claimed as the progenitor of both European and African civilization.

To appreciate the significance of Melville's reaffirmation that blacks are part of America's destiny, we must remember how many of his contemporaries had cherished the fantasy of expatriating blacks en masse after emancipation. Lincoln, for example, had told a deputation of blacks as late as 1862 that white Americans would never willingly allow "free colored people to remain with us," and had persisted in promoting colonization schemes until thwarted at last by the fiasco of an attempt to plant a black colony on an insalubrious Caribbean island where the majority died of disease.[34] Thus, even while Melville advocates putting the "future of the whole country" above that of blacks, he is exorcising once and for all the chimera of America as a white man's country. In contrast to Lincoln's America—and to most of his white compatriots'—Melville's America remains what he had envisioned before the war as "a piebald [black-and-white] parliament, an Anacharsis Cloots congress of all kinds of that multiform pilgrim species, man" (CM, 14).

Having taken stock of what Melville was trying to accomplish in *Battle-Pieces* by recreating a comprehensive experience of the war, and having done our best to assess in contemporary terms the lessons he sought to draw from it, we still cannot help feeling that Melville's response to the Civil War as a creative artist and thinker falls short of the extraordinary prescience, insight, and versatility he had shown in dealing with slavery and race in his antebellum fiction. The crux of the weakness we sense in *Battle-Pieces* is that Melville's anguish is focused almost entirely on the fraternal bond linking the white men fighting for Right with those fighting for Wrong.[35] The equally

---

34. Stampp, *The Era of Reconstruction*, 46–48; McPherson, *The Struggle for Equality*, 155–56; Litwack, *North of Slavery*, 276–79; Basler (ed.), *Works of Lincoln*, II, 405–409, III, 145–46, V, 370–75.
35. This is also Aaron's criticism of *Battle-Pieces* in *The Unwritten War*, 90.

intense drama of the blacks whose fate the war was deciding, and who were laying down their lives for the Union cause by the thousands, no longer seems to touch Melville's imagination.

Although slavery continues to dominate his perception of the war in *Battle-Pieces* (contrary to his late poetry and prose sketches, where he loses sight of everything but the tragedy of fratricidal strife), we are aware of it only as an abstract issue. It is symptomatic, for example, that the sole black "characters" in *Battle-Pieces* are not real people, but personified abstractions: a cannon in "The Swamp Angel," a painting in "Formerly a Slave." Even more revealing, in a volume of poems commemorating almost every major event that occurred between John Brown's hanging in 1859 and Lee's testimony before the Reconstruction Committee in 1866, including a number of secondary battles, is the conspicuous absence of tributes to the two most significant political milestones of the war: the Emancipation Proclamation and the arming of America's first Negro regiment.[36] The prose Supplement, with its implication that the brotherhood of race overrides the brotherhood of humanity, merely verbalizes a sentiment unconsciously expressed in the very conception of *Battle-Pieces*. We are forced to conclude that the powerful egalitarian convictions that Melville had dramatized with greater acumen than any other writer of his time were not rooted deeply enough in his psyche to withstand the shock of a war that brought his deepest personal conflicts into play.

As we approach the portion of Melville's literary career that *Battle-Pieces* inaugurates, the question we find ourselves asking is: what has eclipsed the uncompromising egalitarianism, the activist social conscience, and the passionate commitment to human solidarity and brotherhood that animated all his antebellum fiction? One answer, I believe, lies in the guilt Melville seems to have shared with most of his contemporaries at having endorsed a war to which the entire nation imputed a fratricidal character. In a culture where bitter sibling rivalry is so prevalent, it is suggestive that the national imag-

36. The importance of these two events is stressed by Fredrickson, *The Inner Civil War*, Chaps. 8 and 10; McPherson, *The Struggle for Equality*, Chaps. 3–5, 9; Franklin, *From Slavery to Freedom*, Chap. 16; and Benjamin Quarles, *The Negro in the Civil War* (2nd ed.; Boston, 1969), Chaps. 1, 2, 7, 8.

ination should so quickly have translated the Civil War from a moral and political conflict over slavery into a tragic and perhaps senseless quarrel between brothers. It is all the more suggestive to find this impulse in a writer as intellectually sophisticated as Melville, and as cognizant as he had previously shown himself to be of the ideological issues at stake in the war. One has the impression that for many Americans, the fantasy of brother murdering brother may have represented something deeper than mere metaphor; that it may have involved a hidden guilt at having acted out the murderous hatred of childhood. Documenting the connection in Melville's case provides an opportunity to test this hypothesis, which I am offering as an explanation not merely of Melville's individual psychology, but of a cultural phenomenon he may exemplify.[37]

We know from surviving parental letters that throughout his youth and early manhood, Melville had played second fiddle to his elder brother Gansevoort. During their childhood, Gansevoort had always been considered the genius of the family, whereas Herman, whatever his achievements at school or his popularity with uncles, aunts, and grandparents, could never overcome his parents' image of him as "backward in speech & somewhat slow in comprehension," though "of a docile & amiable disposition."[38] Later, after their father's bankruptcy and death, their mother's hopes of recovering the family's lost wealth and prestige had been pinned on Gansevoort. Even when Gansevoort's fur business, which had seemed to promise renewed prosperity for the family, failed in the Panic of 1837, these hopes were not transferred to Herman, who now seemed bent on fulfilling the family expectations of him as a drifter and ne'er-do-well. While Herman was knocking around the world as a common sailor, Gansevoort was making a name for himself as a campaigner for the Democratic presidential candidate, James K. Polk.[39] Herman

37. Aaron, *The Unwritten War*, xiii–xix, 327–40, generalizes about American writers' attitudes toward the war and suggests other reasons why the war was "unfaced," if not "unfelt"—chief among them being an "emotional resistance" on the race issue that blurred "literary insight."

38. Leyda, *Melville Log*, I, 25, 32, 43. For an extensive analysis of Melville's relationship with Gansevoort, see Miller, *Herman Melville*, 90–103, 355–56.

39. Gansevoort's political career and oratorical style are analyzed in detail by Hershel Parker, "Gansevoort Melville's Role in the Campaign of 1844," *New York Historical Society Quarterly*, XLIX (1965), 143–73. See also Leyda, *Melville Log*, I, 168, 174, 181–88, 194–97, and II, 911–13.

arrived home on board the *United States* just in time to witness the triumphant climax of the election of 1844, for which Gansevoort took no little credit. In July of the following year, Gansevoort received his reward: the post of secretary at the American legation in London. Meanwhile, Herman's manuscript of *Typee* had been rejected by Harper and Brothers. In the end, it was Gansevoort who succeeded in launching *Typee* from London, where he showed the manuscript to Washington Irving and contracted for its English and American publication. Although with *Typee*'s instantaneous popularity Herman at last came into his own, his gratification must have been somewhat marred by the knowledge that he owed even his literary début partly to Gansevoort's good offices. He did not realize, of course, that his seemingly brilliant brother had in fact become persona non grata with his ambassador in London, who was desperately trying to get Polk's irresponsible young protégé reassigned to a country where his jingoistic oratory would pose less of a danger to American diplomatic relations. Nor was Herman aware, on receiving the pathetic letter in which Gansevoort complained "I sometimes fear I am gradually breaking up," that his brother was in the grip of a severe depression, or "nervous derangement," as the doctor termed it, that would soon culminate in his death. By the time Herman wrote to cheer his brother up, Gansevoort was already dead.[40]

If Melville had ever secretly wished his brother out of the way, he must have felt tremendous guilt at Gansevoort's sudden death. At the same time, he may also have resented his brother for once again stealing the show, since the family mourning would naturally have cast a damper on rejoicings over *Typee*'s success—a success none of Melville's subsequent books would match.

These feelings, apparently, remained buried for decades. Not until the last years of Melville's life did they resurface. Yet when they did, it was with a clarity that sheds much retrospective light on why the Civil War was so traumatizing for Melville, and why remorse over the fratricidal strife came to haunt him as obsessively after the war as the sin of slavery had before, ultimately clouding his understanding of what the war had been about.

40. Leyda, *Melville Log*, I, 196–204, 208, 213.

Our first clue to the guilt-ridden relationship with Gansevoort that Melville seems to have projected onto his southern brothers is a Balzac novel called *The Two Brothers*, in which Melville marked several evocative passages about a mother's preference for her elder son, a dashing "blackguard" whom she saw as a hero and "a man of genius," over her younger son, an ugly duckling whom she "simply was unable to understand," and whose dreams of "an artist's glory," she thought, "would only bring her ... worries and anxieties."[41] Some time between 1887, when the English translation Melville read of this novel came out, and 1891, the year of his death, Melville composed the poem "Timoleon," in which he linked the private theme of rivalry for a mother's love with the political issue that the Civil War had raised—whether loyalty to the public good could oblige a man to kill his erring brother.

It is impossible to read Melville's description of the two Corinthian brothers Timophanes and Timoleon, presented through the eyes of their ambitious mother, without recalling both the old parental letters praising Gansevoort at Herman's expense and the fictional portrait Melville had long ago drawn of his mother in *Pierre* as the haughty Mary Glendinning:

> Timophanes was his mother's pride—
> Her pride, her pet, even all to her
> Who slackly on Timoleon looked:
> Scarce he (she mused) may proud affection stir.
>
> . . . .
> When boys they were ...
> I made the junior feel his place,
> Subserve the senior, love him, too;
> And sooth he does, and that's his saving grace.
> But me the meek one never can serve,
> Not he, he lacks the quality keen
> To make the mother through the son
> An envied dame of power, a social queen.[42]

The ensuing story of fratricide and "a mother's ban" also reminds us irresistibly of the Civil War and of Melville's poem "America,"

41. *Ibid.*, II, 829; also Wilson Walker Cowen, "Melville's Marginalia" (11 vols.; Ph.D. dissertation, Harvard, 1965), II, 216, 219.

42. "Timoleon" gives its title to the volume of poems Melville published privately in 1891, reprinted in Vincent (ed.), *Collected Poems*, 209–15.

in which he conceived his country as a "lorn Mother . . . / Pale at the fury of her brood" (BP, 161). "Because of just heart and humane," the younger brother Timoleon, like the North with whom Melville also identifies, hates "crimes of pride and men-of-prey/ And impious deeds that perjurous upstarts do." As he contemplates his brother's reign of terror, "revulsion racks the filial heart" of Timoleon, "the loyal son, the patriot true." In response to a "voice whose mandate calls,/ Or seems to call, peremptory from the skies," Timoleon resolves to "adjure the tyrant" (as abolitionists had adjured the slaveholder) and to deliver him to the vengeance of the citizens if he will not repent. After vainly exhorting his brother, Timoleon at last "sobs the predetermined word,/ And Right in Corinth reassumes its place." (Revealingly, Melville slurs over the murder.) Now, however, Timoleon finds himself ostracized by Corinth, rejected by his mother, and dogged by "his playfellow's reproachful face." The gods from whom he demands "some little sign" that he has acted according to their bidding answer him with silence. Only after long years as an outcast is Timoleon at length "absolved."

It seems likely that in writing this infelicitous poem about sibling rivalry and political fratricide, Melville was belatedly confronting the guilt over his resented elder brother's death which apparently underlay his remorse at having sanctioned the North's fratricidal crusade (and which may also account for the poem's stilted diction). In any case, "Timoleon" expresses the compunctions that drove many northerners besides Melville to seek reconciliation with the South.

In various ways, the ideological distance between *Battle-Pieces* and Melville's next work, the long narrative poem *Clarel*, published ten years later, seems greater than the gap between *The Confidence-Man* and *Battle-Pieces*. For one thing, *Clarel* is virtually silent on slavery. Only twice do the multifarious pilgrims who debate the nature of man, the fate of religion, and the course of contemporary politics against the backdrop of a blighted Holy Land mention slavery: once when Mortmain, the disillusioned Swedish revolutionary who has become obsessed with human evil as a result of his experiences with "Judases" in revolutionary ranks, conjectures that slave trading must have been among the "sins refined, crimes of the spirit" for which Sodom and Gomorrah were overthrown (II.xxxvi.44, 74–85); and a second time (indirectly), when the narrator tells us that the embittered ex-Confederate soldier Ungar had "in years bygone" defied "the prejudice of kin/ And custom" to voice "his heart's belief" about slavery (which turns out to be the watered-down, morally impotent creed of the southern cavalier):

> That holding slaves was aye a grief—
> The system an iniquity
> In those who plant it and begin;
> While for inheritors—alas,
> Who knows? and let the problem pass.

(IV.vi.145–53)

Another omission in *Clarel* marking the distance Melville has traveled since *Battle-Pieces* is that there are no blacks among the thirty-odd pilgrims who constitute his latest fictional microcosm of religions and races, ranging from an East Indian Jew to a European Turk, from an Englishman of the pure Saxon strain to an American with Red Indian blood in his veins. The sole black referred to in the narrative is a mysterious passenger, a Moor, whom the old Greek timoneer Agath recalls as the Jonah of an ill-starred voyage ending in shipwreck. Like Ishmael, Agath is the lone survivor of this wreck, but his story suggests a moral diametrically contrary to Ishmael's. In contrast to Queequeg and Pip, those dark-skinned bridegrooms whose embrace might have saved their shipmates from disaster, the Moor smuggled on board the timoneer's ship (ironically christened *The Peace of God*) proves to be "a black lieutenant of Lucifer," an armorer whose secret freight of poisoned blades attracts the lightning that deflects the ship's compass during a storm and thus swerves her off course and onto the breakers (III.xii.57–130). The tale is a transparent allegory about how the Negro, smuggled into the New World aboard slavers, had brought about the foundering of America's ship of state[43] and the ironic fulfillment of Christ's apocalyptic warning: "Think not that I am come to send . . . peace, but a sword. For I am come to set a man at variance

43. James Russell Lowell's *The Biglow Papers [First Series]*, ed. Thomas Wortham (DeKalb, Ill., 1977), 98 (V. "The Debate in the Sennit"), provides a striking parallel: "I think that no ship of state was ever freighted with a more veritable Jonah than this same domestic institution of ours. Mephistopheles himself could not feign so . . . satirically sad a sight. . . . Perhaps our suspicious passenger is no Jonah after all, being black."

against his father, and the daughter against her mother, and the daughter in law against her mother in law. And a man's foes shall be they of his own household" (Matt. 10:34–36). In telling it through Agath, a sailor sharing the same memories of a voyage to the Encantadas, Melville comes much closer to owning the resentment of the Negro as "the cause of war," that he had attributed in "A Meditation" to a fictional northerner.

The most striking difference between *Clarel* and Melville's preceding works, however, is that it presents the vanquished southerner, rather than the Negro, as the victim of American history to whom reparation is due, and the Civil War, rather than slavery, as the sin for which the nation must seek absolution. Thus the ex-Confederate soldier Ungar, a refugee from the reconstructed South, elicits guilt feelings in the narrator and the other American pilgrims as soon as he appears on the scene:

> Ay me, poor Freedom, can it be
> A countryman's a refugee?
> What maketh him abroad to roam,
> Sharing with infidels a home?
> Is it the immense charred solitudes
> Once farms? and chimney-stacks that reign
> War-burnt upon the houseless plain
> Of hearthstones without neighborhoods?
> . . . .
> Is't misrule after strife? and dust
> From victor heels? Is it disgust
> For times when honor's out of date
> And serveth but to alienate? (IV.v.38–53)

Throughout their discussions with Ungar, guilt pervades the pilgrims' attitude toward him and muzzles them in the face of his splenetic outbursts. Not even the character most critics see as Melville's self-portrait dares take exception, for example, when Ungar erupts into an impassioned tirade against the North's refusal to let the South secede peaceably, of which he is reminded by the sight of two Palestinian shepherds who appear to be halving the land, like Abraham and Lot (IV.ix.66–82).

As this suggests, in embracing the southerner and seeking to make amends for the wrong done to him in the war and its aftermath,

Melville inevitably ends up embracing the view of the war that he had once pitied southerners for having been "cajoled" into accepting: "the plea, plausibly urged, that certain inestimable rights guaranteed by the Constitution were directly menaced." Instead of condemning the "slave-interest"—the true cause of the war, as he had stated in the Supplement to *Battle-Pieces* (BP, 261)—Melville now condemns the war itself as a tragic dispute "touching construction of a pact,/ A paper pact, with points abstruse/ As theologic ones—profuse/ In matter for an honest doubt" (IV.v.87–90).

By the same token, he also endorses the neo-Calvinistic creed that had served to rationalize the southern Hamlet's pathetic resignation to slavery, as well as the proslavery apologists' belligerent opposition to the efforts of reformers to abolish it: that mankind is innately and incorrigibly depraved, that all human endeavors aimed at "eradicating those apparently inevitable evils of our nature" are hence doomed to failure, and that "it would be well for us to leave the Almighty to perfect his own works and fulfil his own covenants."[44] Thus Ungar, though lacerated by the social evils against which Melville had once urged his countrymen to act, continually takes refuge in a morbid obsession with evil in general that only succeeds in consuming his inner vitality. Coming across a group of escaped Arab convicts who have been mutilated by their captors to mark them for easy identification, Ungar does not see in them (nor does anything indicate that Melville does) a parallel to the branded fugitive slaves whose descriptions had once filled the advertisement columns of southern newspapers. Instead, the sight merely feeds his "angry sense/ Of evil, and malevolence/ In man toward man" (IV.xiii.228–30). Similarly, his indignation at the misery of "Pauperism's unhappy sons/ In cloud so blackly ominous,/ Grimy in Mammon's English pen—/ Collaterals of his overplus" only makes him bemoan the decline of private charity that has accompanied the decline of Christian faith, and lament that "Poverty, erst free from shame,/ Even sacred through the Savior's claim," has now become degrading (IV.xx.85–97). Again, no other character points out, as Melville had in sketches like "Poor Man's Pudding and Rich Man's Crumbs," how arrogant it is for the rich to sentimentalize poverty and how degrading charity itself is toward the poor. Whereas Redburn and Pierre had interpreted the Sermon on the Mount as a social gospel and had tried (granted ineptly) to live by it, Ungar maintains that Christ's message contains only a promise of heaven, and "no thought to mend a world amiss" (IV.xx.44).

There is, nevertheless, one important aspect of the southerner's moral philosophy that Melville does not endorse, however much his sense of guilt may have driven him to identify with the victim of his fratricidal impulses. That aspect is the southerner's racism. Nothing, apparently, could fully suppress the side of Melville that had created Queequeg and Babo and envisioned White-Jacket and Steelkilt as analogues to the "erect, lofty-minded African" who refuses to submit to slavery. Indeed, it still pervades the unique conception of the southerner that Melville substituted in *Clarel* for the stereotyped cavalier. The "self-exiled" Ungar, descended from an English Catholic and a "wigwam maid" whose "lineaments" and "latent nature" he inherits, is doubly an alien in the land of his birth (IV.v.108–109, 135–55). Though his Indian ancestry may owe something to the legend of John Randolph (a scion of the Indian princess Pocahontas, as Melville had recalled in *Pierre* [P, 10]), Ungar, unlike Randolph, is more Indian than southern, as the "forest name" for which, "in freak," he has abandoned his English cognomens indicates. The bitterness of "an Indian's hopeless feud/ Under the white's aggressive reign" thus infuses the bitterness of his defeat as a southerner with a special meaning, which accounts for his exile. In contrast to his compatriots in the South, who were taking out their rage on the Negro—like the southerner Melville pictured in "The Frenzy in the Wake"—and forming paramilitary groups in defense of white supremacy,[45] Ungar, with his "Indian heart," has reserved his hatred for the Anglo-Saxon oppressor of all nonwhite peoples, with whom he has joined forces by leaving his country to fight for the Egyptians and the Turks (IV.v.27–34), currently the prey of European imperialist powers. The tirade Ungar hurls against the Anglo-Saxon oddly echoes Melville's own language in his lectures on "The South Seas" and "Traveling":[46]

45. See note 27, above.
46. Sealts, *Melville as Lecturer*, 168–69, 179–80, 183–84 (cited at the beginning of this chapter).

286 SHADOW OVER THE PROMISED LAND

"*As cruel as a Turk*: Whence came
That proverb old as the crusades?
From Anglo-Saxons. What are they?

. . . .

The Anglo-Saxons—lacking grace
To win the love of any race;
Hated by myriads dispossessed
Of rights—the Indians East and West.
These pirates of the sphere! grave looters—
Grave, canting, Mammonite freebooters,
Who in the name of Christ and Trade
(Oh, bucklered forehead of the brass!)
Deflower the world's last sylvan glade! " (IV.ix.113–26)

It is obvious, in short, that Melville's hatred of racism remains as
fierce as ever. All that has happened is that he has transferred it to
spheres that would not conflict with his overwhelming need to atone
for the fratricidal passions the Civil War had reawakened in him.
Here, I believe, lies the reason for the strange absence of the Negro
in *Clarel*, which strikes us with particular forcefulness in a passage
that omits Africa from the catalogue of the white man's depredations.

So far we have been exploring the element of guilt in Melville's
identification with the southerner. Yet there is also another element,
which Daniel Aaron has explained as the projection of Melville's
personal sense of defeat onto his country's beaten rebels. In Aaron's
words: "Defeated and misunderstood himself, Melville must have
found in the mixture of rage, hurt, and despair that marked the
unforgiving and unyielding ex-Confederates . . . an analogue to his
private wounds and disappointments. . . . The still recalcitrant South
became an outlet for his own rebellious notions."[47]

By 1876, however, there was no longer anything "rebellious" in
attacking American democracy, since all the best minds of the day
were sharing Melville's revulsion from the unprecedented graft and
cynicism of the Gilded Age. Far from representing the kind of
deviation from the spirit of the age that *The Confidence-Man* had
been when it had appeared in 1857, *Clarel* stood squarely in the
intellectual company of Whitman's *Democratic Vistas*, Mark Twain's
The Gilded Age, and Henry Adams' *Democracy*, all written within

47. Aaron, *The Unwritten War*, 89.

the same decade.[48] There is a poignant irony, moreover, in Melville's translating the men he had once called "zealots of the Wrong" (BP, 93) into symbols of his own thwarted rebelliousness; for the rebellion of southerners, of course, had consisted in defying the egalitarian principles Melville held dearest in the American heritage, whereas Melville's rebellion had consisted largely in taking these principles more seriously than most of his peers and in defending them against men like his father-in-law, Judge Shaw. This strange inversion bespeaks better than anything else the nature of the defeat Melville had experienced in bowing to the family consensus that he had failed as a literary man, and in abandoning the creative effort to "preach the Truth to the face of Falsehood" (MD, 50) for the dull routine of making a living as a customs inspector: he had come to internalize the oppressive worldly authorities he had been contending with all his life.

Clarel, in effect, writes the epitaph of Melville's democratic faith. In the place of the Redburns, White-Jackets, Steelkilts, Ishmaels, and Pierres who had articulated and tried to live out Melville's passionate homage to "that democratic dignity which, on all hands, radiates without end from God" and apotheosizes the meanest of men (MD, 104), Clarel confronts us with a collection of disillusioned revolutionaries who curse democracy as the "arch strumpet of an impious age" (IV.xix.145) and who explicitly abjure their quondam faith in man, even going so far as to rant: "Man's vicious; snaffle him with kings;/ Or, if kings cease to curb, devise/ Severer bit" (II. iii.189–91).

There is the Swedish Mortmain, for example, who had once thought to heal the wounds of an unloved childhood by resorting to "the vague bond of human kind" and throwing himself into the revolutionary movement of 1848 in Paris: "That uncreated Good/ He sought, whose absence is the cause/ Of creeds and Atheists, mobs and laws" (II.iv.25, 49–51). Having discovered that "the vain, foolhardy, worthless, blind" and treacherous outnumbered the "strong hearts" and "superior mind[s]" in the movement, Mortmain had been further shaken by the bloody repression that had overtaken

48. See Woodward, The Burden of Southern History, 83–103, for a provocative discussion of Clarel, Democracy, and Henry James's The Bostonians.

the revolutions of 1848. Like Melville, he recoiled from the prospect
of fighting the enemies of his ideals with their own weapons:

> Be many questionable wrongs:
> By yet more questionable war,
> Prophet of peace, these wouldst thou bar?
>
> (II.iv.54–59, 74–76)

Mortmain had also taken to heart the same lessons that Melville
drew from the Civil War and Reconstruction:

> Though even shouldst thou triumph, see,
> Prose overtakes the victor's songs:
> Victorious right may need redress:
> No failure like a harsh success.　　　(II.iv.78–81)

Concluding that the "new prospects" his crusade had opened "to
Adam's kind" had but given "ampler sway" to the corruption inherent in human nature, Mortmain now believes that the only course
open to men like him is ascetic withdrawal from an evil world, and
he spends his last days in the Holy Land "under ban/ Of strange
repentance and last dearth," brooding over the meaning of Christ's
betrayal, which he sees as the ultimate proof of man's irredeemable
depravity. His is "the dire *Vox Clamans* of our day," whose message
is:

> "Repent! repent in every land
> Or hell's hot kingdom is at hand!
> 　　　　　　Yea, yea,
> In pause of the artillery's boom,
> While now the armed world holds its own,
> The comet peers, the star dips down;
> Flicker the lamps in Syria's tomb,
> While Anti-Christ and Atheist set
> On Anarch the red coronet!"　　　(II.xxxiv.30–38)

　　Parallel to Mortmain's experience, but even more tragic in that
it emerges from the New World, are those of Ungar and his comic
counterpart Don Hannibal, both of whom have returned to the Old
World in search of "some blest asylum from the New!" Don Hannibal, crippled in Mexico's war of independence from Spain and
disabused of his hopes for a better society in its aftermath, has
become, he announces, a "*reformado* reformed" (IV.xix.46, 77):

> "Hidalgos, I am, as ye see,
> Just a poor cripple—that is all;
> A cripple, yet contrive to hop
> Far off from Mexic liberty,
> Thank God! I lost these limbs for that;
> And would that they were mine again,
> And all were back to former state—
> I, Mexico, and poor Old Spain."   (IV.xix.65–72)[49]

Like Mortmain, Don Hannibal has come to execrate man. "Disparage him with all my heart!" he exclaims. "What villain takes the rascal's part?" But in preference to Mortmain's ascetic withdrawal, Don Hannibal opts for retreating into epicureanism. The only reforms in which he now believes, he says, are "wine and the weed!" As for democracy, it is nothing but an eternal destroyer: "Woe is me,/ She lopped these limbs, Democracy" (IV.xix.98–99, 122, 125–26).

The most articulate of the disillusioned democrats and defeated rebels Melville portrays in *Clarel*, however, is Ungar, who is given the last word in a debate with the other pilgrims about the nature of man, the fate of the New World, and the end result of democracy. In answer to their hopes of seeing "belief revised/ Men liberated—equalized/ In happiness," Ungar contends that the world is hastening toward an apocalyptic outbreak of class war whose upshot will "yield to one and all/ New confirmation of the fall/ Of Adam" (IV.xx.29–31, xxi.96, 131–33). The stage on which that cataclysm will be enacted, he believes, is the New World, provided by the gods "in satire" of the presumptuous notion that "the excellence of man" would prevail if he were given a fresh start and were "left to himself, his natural bent,/ His own devices and intent" (IV.xxi.50–63, 110–23). Meanwhile, America was fast breeding the "combustibles" of her "Thirty Years (of) War," what with her "rival sharp communities/ Unchristianized" and the "hundred thousand" demagogues who represented them, backed with the power of universal male suffrage:

> Sequel may ensue,
> Indeed, whose germs one now may view:

---

49. Note the resemblance between Don Hannibal and the cripple in *The Confidence-Man* who masquerades as an American veteran of the Mexican War (Chap. 19).

Myriads playing pygmy parts—
Debased into equality:
In glut of all material arts
A civic barbarism may be:
Man disennobled—brutalized
By popular science—Atheized
Into a smatterer . . .
Yet knowing all self need to know
In self's base little fallacy;
Dead level of rank common-place:
An Anglo-Saxon China, see,
May on your vast plains shame the race
In the Dark Ages of Democracy." (IV.xxi.133–48)

Although Ungar speaks only for one side of Melville, as Daniel Aaron points out,[50] it is clearly the side that is uppermost in *Clarel*. None of the other pilgrims, including Rolfe, Melville's idealized younger self, have the heart to answer Ungar, knowing as they do that his acrimony is the product of the violence his homeland has suffered in the Civil War and Reconstruction. Nor can they help admitting to themselves that they, too, have misgivings:

They felt how far beyond the scope
Of elder Europe's saddest thought
Might be the New World's sudden brought
In youth to share old age's pains—
To feel the arrest of hope's advance,
And squandered last inheritance;
And cry—"To Terminus build fanes!
Columbus ended earth's romance:
No New World to mankind remains!" (IV.xxi.160–69)

For northerners as well as southerners, the beautiful dream of a new Eden has ended, and the millennial hope that had lighted the America of their youth has gone out like the waning solar lamp at the end of the Confidence-Man's apocalyptic April Fools' Day visitation.

Except for the apocalyptic denunciation of America, all the tendencies we see in *Clarel*—the de-ideologizing of the Civil War in the interests of reconciliation with the South; the disappearance of

50. Aaron, *The Unwritten War*, 89.

the Negro; the appearance, in his place, of the southerner as the new victim of American history; and the internalization of the authority figure in the defeated rebel—reach their logical culmination in that nostalgic poem of Melville's old age, "Bridegroom Dick," published in 1888.[51] A dramatic monologue in vivid nautical dialect, affectionately addressed by an old salt to his wife, "Bridegroom Dick" furnishes a striking contrast to *Moby-Dick*. In it, Melville makes his peace with all his youthful antagonists, beginning with his wife. As the speaker reminisces with his "old woman" about his days aboard a man-of-war and about the shipmates he has left behind, we recognize in the shipmates dubbed Jack Genteel, the Anak Finn, Captain Turret, Rhyming Ned, Guert Gan, and Tom Tight, many of the characters from *White-Jacket*—Jack Chase, Mad Jack, Captain Claret, Lemsford the poet—as well as Melville's cousin Guert Gansevoort, a navy lieutenant. Yet how thinned and whitewashed are their ranks, and how changed the incidents they reenact! Gone is Tawney, the universally admired black veteran whose tales of the War of 1812 had aroused White-Jacket's indignation against the barbarism of warfare, and gone the cast of minor black and Cape Verdean crewmen. The Melville who in 1850 had jotted down the names of at least three blacks and several "Portuguese" among his former shipmates of the *Acushnet*, and noted what became of them,[52] has apparently forgotten that he ever had any but white shipmates. The hated Captain Claret, who imposed so many floggings aboard the *Neversink* and lashed out against sailors like White-Jacket for showing manly dignity, has become a lovable old tippler in "Bridegroom Dick" who decides of his own accord to let off a sailor he has condemned to a flogging:

> "Flog? Never meant it—hadn't any heart.
> Degrade that tall fellow?"—Such, wife, was he,
> Old Captain Turret, who the brave wine could stow.
> Magnanimous, you think?—but what does Dick see?
> Apron to your eye! Why, never fell a blow,
> Cheer up, old wifie, 't was a long time ago. (BD, 178)

Guert Gansevoort, that other rival for the family esteem Melville

---

51. Leyda, *Melville Log*, II, 804, dates the completion of the poem December 4, 1887. It was published privately in *John Marr and Other Sailors* (1888), reprinted in Vincent (ed.), *Collected Poems*, 167–82.

52. Leyda, *Melville Log*, I, 399–400.

could never seem to earn, against whose acquiescence in the hanging of three alleged mutineers at sea, in the notorious *Somers* case, White-Jacket had taken a firm stand,[53] has become both the gallant Mexican War veteran Guert Gan and the stanch naval officer "Tom Tight, no fine fellow finer," "true to himself and loyal to his clan" (BD, 174–75). The horror of war and the distrust of American imperialism that had pervaded Melville's antebellum fiction have given way to a glorification of America's military and naval heroes and of the famous battles they have fought:

> But where's Guert Gan? Still heads he the van?
> As before Vera-Cruz, when he dashed splashing through
> The blue rollers sunned, in his brave gold-and-blue,
> And, ere his cutter in keel took the strand,
> Aloft waved his sword on the hostile land!
> Went up the cheering, the quick chanticleering;
> All hands vying—all colors flying:
> "Cock-a-doodle-doo!" and "Row, boys, row!"
> "Hey, Starry Banner!" "Hi, Santa Anna!"—
> Old Scott's young dash at Mexico.   (BD, 169–70)

Most revealing is the treatment of the Civil War, whose sentimental obfuscation is now complete:

> But ah, how to speak of the hurricane unchained—
> The Union's strands parted in the hawser over-strained;
> Our flag blown to shreds, anchors gone altogether—
> The dashed fleet o' States in Secession's foul weather.

The causes of the war no longer interest Melville in "Bridegroom Dick." Even the garbled explanations of it offered in *Clarel* have vanished. All that remains is the tragedy of fratricidal strife, the heroism of the contestants, and the pathos of the southerner torn by conflicting loyalties:

> We sailors o' the North, wife, how could we lag?—
> Strike with your kin, and you stick to the flag!
> But to sailors o' the South that easy way was barred.
> To some, dame, believe (and I speak o' what I know),
> Wormwood the trial and the Uzzites black shard;
> And the faithfuller the heart, the crueller the throe.

---

53. *White-Jacket*, 294, 303. For documentary résumés of the *Somers* case, see Leyda, *Melville Log*, I, 157–61; and Harrison Hayford (ed.), *The Somers Mutiny Affair* (Englewood Cliffs, N.J., 1959).

Duty? It pulled with more than one string,
This way, and that, and anyhow a sting.
The flag and your kin, how be true unto both?

(BD, 170–71)

In the end, the poem simply dismisses this "intestine war"—though with a touch of Melville's old wry humor—as nothing but a "troublous colic" that "sets the bowels o' affection ajar" (BD, 173). Rather than dwell on those "racking days/ Since set up anew are the ship's started stays," Bridegroom Dick prefers to "booze on the days/ Ere the Old Order foundered in these very frays,/ And tradition was lost and we learned strange ways" (BD, 173–74). Fortunately for his peace of mind, Melville does not remember that his younger self had envisioned that "Old Order" as a soot-streaked steamer floating toward the slave capital of New Orleans, which her passengers have mistaken for the New Jerusalem.

Although "Bridegroom Dick" is Melville's last word on the Civil War, it is not his last look at the life on board a man-of-war that he had once represented as analogous to slavery. Whether or not Melville was troubled by the sentimentality of Bridegroom Dick's view of the past, he apparently felt compelled to reexamine it more closely. Before publishing the collection of sea poetry in which "Bridegroom Dick" appears, he had already started work on a prose narrative about a man-of-war's-man named Billy Budd and his relationship with his captain that reopened the chief questions Melville had raised in the novels of his prime.[54]

Billy Budd has probably stirred more controversy than any other work of Melville's with the possible exception of "Benito Cereno." Critics on one side of the fence have interpreted this short novel as Melville's "testament of acceptance," his final reconciliation with all the tyrannies against which he had chafed since his youth: God, Christ, father, captain, naval discipline, and the harsh ways of a flawed world. On the opposite side, critics have cited *Billy Budd* as Melville's "testament of resistance," his deathbed reiteration of the "Everlasting Nay" he had sounded in all the works of his young

54. Herman Melville, *Billy Budd, Sailor (An Inside Narrative)*, ed. Harrison Hayford and Merton M. Sealts, Jr. (Chicago, 1962). I will be relying throughout on the editors' chronological analysis of the stages the manuscript went through.

manhood, from *Typee* to *The Confidence-Man*. It is no accident, of course, that the battle lines between the two camps have often been political, since one can see why conservatives or moderates would agree more readily with the austere, intellectual Captain Vere in setting law and order above the subversive promptings of private conscience, while radicals would tend to find this stand abhorrent and to sympathize rather with the young sailor victimized by the hatred of his superior officer and the tyranny of martial law.[55] Yet the controversy could never have arisen had not Melville himself been as deeply divided at heart as his critics among themselves; for the moral dilemma central to *Billy Budd*—the dilemma of the Sermon on the Mount versus the Articles of War, justice versus expediency, freedom and human dignity versus authority, rebellion versus conformity, social ferment versus despotism, son versus father, Jobian or Promethean man versus God—is none other than the conflict Melville had struggled unsuccessfully to resolve throughout his life.

In his early works through *Moby-Dick*, as we have seen, Melville sided unequivocally with the victims of injustice. Identifying with common sailors in their rebellion against autocratic commanders, he consistently drew analogies between the shipboard tyranny he had experienced at first hand and the tyranny of chattel slavery that millions of American blacks were then enduring, and a vocal mi-

---

55. This critical controversy is summed up by Hayford and Sealts (eds.), *Billy Budd*, 25–27. Representative of the "testament of acceptance" school are: Matthiessen, *American Renaissance*, 508–14; Stern, *Fine Hammered Steel of Melville*, 26–27, 206–39 (with reservations); and R. W. B. Lewis, *The American Adam: Innocence, Tragedy, and Tradition in the Nineteenth Century* (Chicago, 1955), 146–52. Representative of the opposite school are Phil Withim, "*Billy Budd*: Testament of Resistance," and Leonard Casper, "The Case against Captain Vere," both reprinted in William T. Stafford (ed.), *Melville's "Billy Budd" and the Critics* (Rev. ed.; Belmont, Calif., 1968), 140–52, 212–15; Merlin Bowen, *The Long Encounter: Self and Experience in the Writings of Herman Melville* (Chicago, 1960), 216–33; Dryden, *Melville's Thematics of Form*, 209–16; Widmer, *The Ways of Nihilism*, 16–58; and Franklin, *The Victim as Criminal and Artist*, 67–70. The battle lines are not always political, of course. Two recent radical critics, for example, reiterate the pro-Vere interpretation: Gilmore, *The Middle Way*, 182–94; and Ann Douglas, *The Feminization of American Culture* (New York, 1977), 323–26. And the most clear-cut example of an endorsement of Vere growing out of political conservatism comes not from a Melville critic but from a political philosopher: Hannah Arendt, *On Revolution* (New York, 1963), 77–83. The best interpretation I have seen of *Billy Budd*, and one that transcends this dichotomy, is Joyce Sparer Adler's "*Billy Budd* and Melville's Philosophy of War," *PMLA*, XCI (1976), 266–78.

nority of his contemporaries defying. Again and again in these novels, however, Melville confronted the issue of whether an oppressed subaltern might justifiably resort to violence against his oppressor, only to draw back at the brink from endorsing such an act. So strong a hold, apparently, did some inner authority exert over his imagination that he was never able to let his sailor heroes consummate a successful rebellion. White-Jacket faced the equally unbearable alternatives of submitting to the degradation of an unmerited flogging or leaping overboard with his hated captain in his arms, thus making the supreme reparation for the "privilege" of killing his oppressor. Steelkilt thwarted the mutiny he had set in motion by electing imprisonment in lieu of violence and only consenting to violence when it meant certain death. Daggoo's vengeance against his white detractor was forestalled by a storm at sea.

As the slavery crisis had come to a head, making the threat of civil war ever more real, Melville's writings revealed correspondingly less sympathy with rebels and greater foreboding about the consequences of the "agonized violence" needed to overthrow so deep-rooted an iniquity. While he allowed the slave rebels of his short fiction to act out the murderous impulses that White-Jacket and Steelkilt had merely fantasied, Melville denied them, too, the fruits of their rebellion. The insurrection of the Dog-King's subjects in "The Encantadas" eventuated in a "riotocracy" from which many of them sought refuge in the shipboard discipline they had originally fled. Both the slave revolt led by Babo and the revenge that Bannadonna's robot took against his master ended in their deaths. Of these rebels, whose triumph portended the total destruction of the nation, the only one Melville was able to portray at all sympathetically as a human being—and even then solely at the moment of his defeat—was Babo. Yet Melville continued throughout this period to recognize the inevitability, and indeed the necessity, of the revolution his stories heralded, and when the long dreaded Civil War at last broke out, he repressed his misgivings about its outcome, throwing himself heart and soul behind the Union side he perceived as battling for the "Right."

The aftermath of the war, however, seemed to Melville to confirm his darkest fears about the perils of seeking to abolish one wrong by means of another. Overcome by a sense of guilt at the fratricidal passions the war had aroused in him and his countrymen, Melville repudiated radical Reconstruction, with its punitive measures against the South, as a misguided attempt to "pervert the national victory into oppression for the vanquished" (BP, 269) and began to identify, as we have noticed, with the southerners he had previously seen as oppressors. At the same time, the blatant corruption of the Grant administration discredited the positive accomplishments of the reconstructionists in his eyes, and like so many of his contemporaries, Melville became disaffected with reformist crusades in his revulsion from their by-products. Hence the characters who became his spokesmen in his postwar poetry were no longer stymied rebels, but disillusioned revolutionaries who upheld the necessity for autocratic governments to control the evil they had come to fear in the human heart.

What this poetry suggests, in short, is that in growing old with the nation, Melville had also grown imperceptibly into the role of the oppressive father against whose authority he had been rebelling in his antebellum fiction. As his letters and other family documents of the 1860s and 1870s tell us, Melville had become a father who, writing home from the middle of the Pacific Ocean, could graphically describe to his eleven-year-old son how a sailor had fallen from the yardarm in a gale off Cape Horn and been buried at sea in a piece of sailcloth weighted with cannon balls, reinforcing the threat implied in such a letter with this cruel admonition: "Now is the time to show . . . whether you are a good, honorable boy, or a good-for-nothing one. Any boy, of your age, who disobeys his mother, or worries her, or is disrespectful to her—such a boy is a poor shabby fellow; and if you know any such boys, you ought to cut their acquaintance."[56] Thus by the time Melville again undertook to formulate in prose the conflict between rebellious youthful idealism and repressive worldly authority that had dominated his literary career, he was writing out of the experience not just of a son thwarted in his efforts to fulfill his ideals, but of a father whose harshness and insensitivity to his children's needs may have driven one son

---

56. Davis and Gilman (eds.), *Letters of Melville*, 203.

to suicide and the other to a series of flights from home, and from one job to another (uncannily reenacting Melville's own youthful wanderings), that culminated in a lonely death in San Francisco at age thirty-five.

The version of *Billy Budd* that Melville left heavily revised and possibly unfinished on his death poignantly reflects these unreconciled aspects of his personality. The tale had its origin, according to the editors who have made the most thorough study of the manuscript, as a headnote to a ballad recited by a sailor "condemned for fomenting mutiny and apparently guilty as charged" (BB, 2), a sailor who, like Babo, had been vanquished after carrying out the rebellion contemplated by White-Jacket and abortively attempted by Steelkilt, and whom one might think of as representing the defeated rebel in Melville. In subsequent stages of the story's composition,[57] this hero gave way to the Billy Budd we now know: the Handsome Sailor, idol of his shipmates, and innocent victim of a false accuser against whom he has retaliated impulsively with a mortal blow, for which he must hang. Meanwhile, two new characters came to the forefront: the evil master-of-arms Claggart, who seeks to destroy Billy because he envies the youth, beauty, and manliness that have won Billy the status of Handsome Sailor; and the ambiguous Captain Vere, who affirms his belief in Billy's moral innocence, but decrees his execution on the grounds that he has committed a capital crime which, regardless of provocation or intent, cannot go unpunished without setting the whole crew a dangerous example, especially during a period of mutinous outbreaks in the navy. As superior officers, the one about fourteen years older than Billy and the other "old enough to have been Billy's father" (BB, 115), Claggart and Vere both play the role of the oppressive authority figure Melville had once pitted against his White-Jackets and Steelkilts. Yet here that authority figure is clearly split into two halves, onto one of whom Melville could project all his hatred while seeking reconciliation with the other, a purified and softened image of the father.

Hence the central problem of interpretation that *Billy Budd* poses is this: to what extent has Melville actually succeeded in separating

---

57. Hayford and Sealts (eds.), *Billy Budd*, 1–12.

the bad father from the good and in dramatizing what one critic has called a "reconciliation between an erring son and a stern but loving father-figure"?[58]

To answer that question, one must first look with an open mind at the evidence on both sides. There is no denying that *Billy Budd*, as it now stands in its perhaps still tentative state, includes contradictory assessments of Captain Vere. Many narrative statements about the captain are unmistakably positive and can only be construed otherwise by reading irony into them, as some critics have attempted to do.[59] A smaller, but crucial number of statements are extremely negative, and it is hard to explain their inclusion except as a means of casting doubt on the rightness of the captain's decision. A few passages, finally, can be interpreted either way, depending on a critic's personal bias.

On the positive side we find: the assertion that Vere had "always acquit[ted] himself as an officer mindful of the welfare of his men," though "never tolerating an infraction of discipline" (BB, 60); Vere's "unobtrusiveness of demeanor," which "may have proceeded from a certain unaffected modesty of manhood sometimes accompanying a resolute nature" (BB, 60); his "honesty" and "directness" (traits Melville also attributed to himself and for which he had a rueful admiration [BB, 63][60]); his repute in the navy as a commander especially suited to handling "unforeseen difficulties," where "a prompt initiative might have to be taken in some matter demanding

---

58. Simon O. Lesser, *Fiction and the Unconscious* (Boston, 1957), 92, cited in *ibid.*, 183–84, n.

59. See, for example, Withim, *"Billy Budd*: Testament of Resistance," 140–52.

60. See Melville's self-portrait as Rolfe in *Clarel* (both the similarities and the differences between Rolfe and Vere are revealing):

> One read his superscription clear—
> A genial heart, a brain austere—
> And further, deemed that such a man
> Though given to study, as might seem,
> Was no scholastic partisan
> Or euphonist of Academe,
> But supplemented Plato's theme
> With daedal life in boats and tents,
> A messmate of the elements;
> And yet, more bronzed in face than mind,
> Sensitive still and frankly kind—
> Too frank, too unreserved, may be,
> And indiscreet in honesty. (I.xxxi.13–25)

knowledge and ability, in addition to those qualities implied in good seamanship" (BB, 90); and to be sure, the affirmation that "something exceptional in the moral quality of Captain Vere made him, in earnest encounter with a fellow man, a veritable touchstone of that man's essential nature" (BB, 96)—an affirmation dramatically borne out by Vere's intuitive distrust of Claggart and his acuteness in divining Billy's "liability to vocal impediment" (BB, 93–94, 99). In addition to the virtues the narrator imputes to Vere, various incidents serve to put Vere in a positive light: the admiration Vere expresses for Billy's spirit on hearing how his new recruit, in an apparent "satiric sally," had bade farewell to his former ship with the words "and good-bye to you too, old *Rights-of-Man*" (BB, 49, 95—an admiration one must contrast with the instinctive dislike of the manly sailor that White-Jacket had ascribed to the average sea-officer); the episode in the cabin when Vere, noticing Billy's speech impediment, lays "a soothing hand" on the young sailor's shoulder and says to him in a "fatherly . . . tone," " 'There is no hurry, my boy. Take your time, take your time'" (BB, 99); the trial scene in which Vere, betraying his "suppressed emotion" in his voice, makes the unorthodox gesture of publicly assuring Billy that he believes in his innocence of mutinous intent (BB, 106); the picture the narrator conjures up of Vere's possible behavior during his closeted interview with the condemned Billy, when "the austere devotee of military duty, letting himself melt back into what remains primeval in our formalized humanity, may in end have caught Billy to his heart, even as Abraham may have caught young Isaac on the brink of resolutely offering him up in obedience to the exacting behest" (BB, 115); and correspondingly, the peaceful look the narrator describes on Billy's face as a result of "something healing" in the meeting with Vere (BB, 119). Finally, there is a passage in which Melville, under the guise of "a writer whom few know," all but directly exonerates Vere:[61]

> Forty years after a battle it is easy for a noncombatant to reason about how it ought to have been fought. It is another thing personally and under fire to have to direct the fighting while involved in the

61. Hayford and Sealts (eds.), *Billy Budd*, 34–35, and 183, note 282. Recently, however, Stanton Garner, "Fraud as Fact in Herman Melville's *Billy Budd*," *San Jose Studies*, IV (1978), 95–96, has argued convincingly in favor of interpreting this passage ironically.

obscuring smoke of it. Much so with respect to other emergencies involving considerations both practical and moral, and when it is imperative promptly to act. The greater the fog the more it imperils the steamer, and speed is put on though at the hazard of running somebody down. Little ween the snug card players in the cabin of the responsibilities of the sleepless man on the bridge. (BB, 114)

The weight of all this evidence that Melville endorses Vere is considerable, and it is not surprising that many critics have found it conclusive. Yet the evidence on the negative side is equally convincing, if at times subtler. There is, first of all, the simple fact that Vere is a Man of War, professionally committed to the violence Melville had always abhorred,[62] as he emphasized in changing the name of Vere's ship from *Indomitable* (with its approbative overtones) to *Bellipotent* (with its stark connotation of brute force). There are also the less attractive traits the narrator cites in Vere: a demeanor evincing "little appreciation of mere humor" (BB, 60; surely a failing in Melville's eyes, judging by the prominent place humor enjoys in his writings); a reputation among his colleagues for "lacking in the companionable quality" (another quality Melville ranked high), and for exhibiting "a queer streak of the pedantic" in his intercourse with men to whom the "remote" literary and historical allusions he liked to make were "altogether alien" (BB, 63);[63] "settled convictions" that "were as a dike against those invading waters of novel opinion, social, political, and otherwise, which carried away as in a torrent no few minds in those days, minds by nature not inferior to his own" (BB, 62); and not least significant, given its bearing on Vere's alacrity in settling Billy's case in a way that would earn him a name for keeping a close rein on his men in this mutinous era, the possibility that the captain "may yet have indulged in the most secret of all passions, ambition" (BB, 129).

62. I am indebted for this suggestion to H. Bruce Franklin's comments on my manuscript.
63. See, for example, Melville's description of John Marr: "to a man wonted . . . to the free-and-easy tavern-clubs . . . in certain old and comfortable sea-port towns of that time, and yet more familiar with the companionship afloat of the sailors . . . something was lacking [in the company of his neighbors]. That something was geniality, the flower of life springing from some sense of joy in it, more or less" (Vincent [ed.], *Collected Poems*, 161); also Melville's disparagement of Emerson's lack of convivial geniality (Davis and Gilman [eds.], *Letters of Melville*, 80). Contrast this with the description of Rolfe cited in note 60, above.

As with the positive evidence, however, the most telling counts against Vere emerge indirectly, through little vignettes: the tableau of him covering his face on ascertaining that Claggart is dead, and then slowly uncovering it, to reveal that "the father in him, manifested towards Billy thus far in the scene, was replaced by the military disciplinarian" (BB, 100)—a dramatic example of the phenomenon White-Jacket had labeled "*shipping . . . the quarter-deck face*," when an officer "assumes his wonted severity of demeanor after a casual relaxation of it" (WJ, 276); the untoward excitement Vere betrays to the ship's surgeon, and the haste with which he pronounces his verdict while in this agitated state of mind—"Struck dead by an angel of God! Yet the angel must hang!"—a verdict he will subsequently present as coldly reasoned, urging the members of his drumhead court not to let "warm hearts betray heads that should be cool" (BB, 101, 111); and most damning of all, the suggestion the narrator advances through the surgeon and invites the reader to "determine for himself by such light as this narrative may afford": "Whether Captain Vere, as the surgeon professionally and privately surmised, was really the sudden victim of any degree of aberration" (BB, 101–102)—whether, in short, his decision to hang Billy, however rationally argued, may not have been the product of temporary insanity.

As several critics have pointed out, this suggestion becomes all the more plausible when juxtaposed with the narrator's analysis of the "mania" he attributes to Claggart, who shares several of Vere's most salient characteristics: an "exceptional nature," austerity, intellectuality, respectability, secretiveness (BB, 64, 67, 74–76).[64] Of this mania the narrator writes:

Though the man's even temper and discreet bearing would seem to intimate a mind peculiarly subject to the law of reason, not the less in heart he would seem to riot in complete exemption from that law, having apparently little to do with reason further than to employ it as an ambidexter implement for effecting the irrational. That is to say: Toward the accomplishment of an aim which in wantonness of atrocity would seem to partake of the insane, he will direct a cool judgment sagacious and sound. These men are madmen, and of the

64. Withim, "*Billy Budd*: Testament of Resistance," 147; Bowen, *The Long Encounter*, 218–21; Franklin, *The Victim as Criminal and Artist*, 68–69.

most dangerous sort; for their lunacy is not continuous, but occasional, evoked by some special object; it is protectively secretive, which is as much as to say it is self-contained, so that when, moreover, most active it is to the average mind not distinguishable from sanity, and for the reason above suggested: that whatever its aims may be—and the aim is never declared—the method and the outward proceeding are always perfectly rational. (BB, 76)

Of course this passage applies specifically to Claggart, rather than to Vere, and occurs amidst the narrator's attempt to define "Natural Depravity," which it would be going too far to ascribe to Vere. But the narrator does ask, with regard to the captain: "Who in the rainbow can draw the line where the violet tint ends and the orange tint begins? . . . So with sanity and insanity" (BB, 102). And Melville could not but have been aware that in raising the same question about both men, he was at least drawing a partial analogy between them, if not actually vilifying Captain Vere by association.

Thus the upshot of this exercise in sifting the evidence for and against Captain Vere seems to be an irreconcilably ambiguous view of him. Unsatisfying though such a conclusion may appear at first glance, this very ambiguity guides us to the heart of the conflict the story embodies; for the key fact, according to the most reliable editors of the *Billy Budd* manuscript, is that the negative view of Vere arises almost entirely from late revisions Melville made in his "final" version of the tale, where Vere assumes a prominent role.[65] That is, Melville apparently introduced Vere in order to dramatize the reconciliation between rebellious sailor and autocratic captain, "erring son" and "stern but loving father-figure," that so many critics have seen in *Billy Budd*. He conceived Vere as a captain who "suffered" more in inflicting the death penalty than the young sailor he condemned to die (BB, 115), a father who pleaded "it hurts me more than it hurts you" while delivering his son the mortal blow. And he fantasied this lethal authority-figure, now internalized in himself, receiving forgiveness from a defeated rebel "generous" enough to "feel even for us on whom in this military necessity so heavy a compulsion is laid" (BB, 113).[66] Yet at the moment of dramatizing

65. Hayford and Sealts (eds.), *Billy Budd*, 9–12, 34–39.
66. For a similar interpretation, see Widmer, *The Ways of Nihilism*, 35–36.

their embrace, Melville recoiled—just as he had always before recoiled on the verge of dramatizing a successful rebellion.

As some critics have observed, the climactic scene of Vere's closeted interview with Billy is fatally marred by "a failure of artistry
in its rendering"[67] —a failure to *show* Vere "frankly disclos[ing]
to [Billy] the part he himself had played in bringing about the
decision, at the same time revealing his actuating motives"; to *show*
Billy greeting these tidings "not without a sort of joy . . . [at] the
brave opinion of him implied in his captain's making such a confidant
of him"; to *show* Vere at last taking Billy into his arms. Patently
evading the inherent drama of the scene on the flimsy pretext that
"what took place at this interview was never known" and that the
sacramental embrace of nature's noblemen ought to remain "in-
violable" (BB,114–15), Melville substituted what one critic has
called "a paragraph of thin summarized conjecture" about how Vere
and Billy might have acted.[68] He then proceeded, after writing this
part of the story, to insert into the recopied manuscript the crucial
passage that casts doubts on Vere's sanity and implicitly identifies
the self-righteous captain with his malignly jealous master-of-arms,
thus fusing the two authority figures into whom Melville had split
the ambivalent father image that haunted him. It is as if the rebellious
son in Melville resisted to the last the triumph of the father in him
who had imagined young Billy going to his death with the cry "God
bless Captain Vere!" on his lips (BB, 123).

Indeed, true to the younger self who, forty-odd years earlier, in
that other man-of-war narrative echoed throughout *Billy Budd*, had
pictured himself on the brink of "locking souls" with his tyrannical
captain in death (WJ, 280), Melville could not end his story without
meting out to Captain Vere the death sentence the latter had pronounced against Billy Budd. Shortly after Billy's execution, the
Bellipotent falls in with the French warship *Athée* ("the aptest name
. . . ever given to a warship"), and Captain Vere is mortally wounded
in the ensuing battle. His last words, spoken under the influence
of an anaesthetizing drug, though "not [in] the accents of remorse,"

67. Royal A. Gettmann and Bruce Harkness, *"Billy Budd, Foretopman,"* in *Teacher's Manual for "A Book of Stories"* (New York, 1955), 71–74, cited in Hayford and Sealts (eds.), *Billy Budd*, 184, note 287; also Widmer, *The Ways of Nihilism*, 34.
68. Gettmann and Harkness, *"Billy Budd,"* 74.

are "Billy Budd, Billy Budd" (BB, 129). For Melville, apparently, the deathbed was the only place where a reconciliation between the father and the son in himself, so inextricably intertwined, could be brought to consummation.

If *Billy Budd* ultimately emerges neither as "testament of acceptance" nor as "testament of resistance," at least where the central moral issue it raises is concerned, it does reaffirm the democratic faith of Melville's youth. Unlike Melville's late poetry, with its obsessive focus on human evil, the view of man *Billy Budd* presents is profoundly humanistic, even heroic.

The novel opens with a two-page description of the nautical archetype its title character will personify: the "Handsome Sailor," a sea-faring Hercules and a figure of "natural regality," to be recognized by the "bodyguard" of admiring shipmates surrounding him (BB, 43). The Handsome Sailor, explains Melville, typifies the qualities sailors value most highly:

> Invariably a proficient in his perilous calling, he was also more or less of a mighty boxer or wrestler. It was strength and beauty. Tales of his prowess were recited. Ashore he was the champion; afloat the spokesman; on every suitable occasion always foremost. Close-reefing topsails in a gale, there he was, astride the weather yardarmend, foot in the Flemish horse as stirrup, both hands tugging at the earing as at a bridle, in very much the attitude of young Alexander curbing the fiery Bucephalus. A superb figure, tossed up as by the horns of Taurus against the thunderous sky, cheerily hallooing to the strenuous file along the spar. (BB, 44)

He is the apotheosis of the working man, whose "democratic dignity . . . radiat[ing] without end from God" Melville had celebrated in *Moby-Dick* (MD, 104).

No mere paragon of virility, the Handsome Sailor also manifests a "moral nature . . . seldom out of keeping with the physical make." Without the crowning attribute of virtue, indeed, he could "hardly . . . have drawn the sort of honest homage" his fellow sailors pay him (BB, 44). Billy's comrades, for example, "instinctively" feel that he must have been "as incapable of mutiny as of wilful murder," even if the death penalty "was somehow unavoidably inflicted from the naval point of view," and the image they forever cherish of him is that of a "face never deformed by a sneer or subtler vile freak of the heart within" (BB, 131).

Fittingly, this latter-day epic figure who reincarnates Melville's long-dead faith in the essential nobility of man also embodies once again the ardent racial egalitarianism and the commitment to human brotherhood that had always been part and parcel of that faith. The very first instance Melville cites of the Handsome Sailor—three paragraphs before focusing on the Anglo-Saxon Billy Budd—is a majestic African seaman who seems literally to step out of Melville's past. Melville introduces him in his own narrative voice (which he uses in only one other passage of the novel, also reminiscing about a black seaman),[69] and the date and place of the encounter correspond exactly with those of Melville's first voyage to Liverpool, in July, 1839:

> A somewhat remarkable instance recurs to me. In Liverpool, now half a century ago, I saw under the shadow of the great dingy street-wall of Prince's Dock . . . a common sailor so intensely black that he must needs have been a native African of the unadulterate blood of Ham—a symmetric figure much above the average height. The two ends of a gay silk handkerchief thrown loose about the neck danced upon the displayed ebony of his chest, in his ears were big hoops of gold, and a Highland bonnet with a tartan band set off his shapely head. It was a hot noon in July; and his face, lustrous with perspiration, beamed with barbaric good humor. In jovial sallies right and left, his white teeth flashing into view, he rollicked along, the center of a company of his shipmates. (BB, 43)

The biographical references recall the experience that long ago liberated Redburn (and perhaps Melville himself) from racism: the encounter with the ship's "black steward, dressed very handsomely and walking arm in arm with a good-looking English woman," which crystallized Redburn's observation that "in Liverpool . . . the negro steps with a prouder pace, and lifts his head like a man; for here, no such exaggerated feeling exists in respect to him, as in America" (R, 202).

The scene Melville depicts in *Billy Budd*, however, where sailors and wayfarers alike pay "spontaneous tribute" to the beauty and

---

69. Hayford and Sealts (eds.), *Billy Budd*, 66. Hayford and Sealts, 135, note 3 (*In Liverpool*), and 156, note 97, also point out these "directly autobiographical reminiscences."

manliness of a fellow being, regardless of race, contrasts vividly with his lament in *Redburn* that "for the mass, there seems no possible escape" from racism (R, 202). Fulfilling the dream of brotherhood once fleetingly glimpsed by White-Jacket while communing with Tawney in the maintop, and acted out by Ishmael and Queequeg as the alternative to apocalyptic doom, the black Handsome Sailor unites around him "such an assortment of tribes and complexions as would have well fitted them to be marched up by Anacharsis Cloots before the bar of the first French Assembly as Representatives of the Human Race" (BB, 43). Moreover, his is the sole Anacharsis Cloots procession in Melville's fiction to accomplish the purpose of its original, unlike both the "Anacharsis Clootz deputation" Ahab leads to death and destruction, and the "Anacharsis Cloots congress" of April Fools the *Fidèle* transports to the wrong New Jerusalem. By creating harmony among his shipmates through their allegiance to him, as the fleshly image of "certain virtues pristine and unadulterate" that once characterized mankind "prior to Cain's city and citified man," this black sailor plays the same role Billy Budd does aboard the *Rights-of-Man*, whose captain describes Billy as "my peacemaker" (BB, 47, 53).

The black Handsome Sailor's most obvious fictional antecedents are the "gigantic, coal-black negro savage" Daggoo, who likewise sports "two golden hoops" in his ears and displays the "barbaric virtues" and pride of the native African, and the "grand and glorious" Queequeg, who twice bears witness to human solidarity in this "mutual, joint-stock world" by risking his life to save another's (MD, 61, 107, 289). Although the black Handsome Sailor occupies only the first two pages of *Billy Budd*, he surpasses his more fully delineated predecessors in triumphing over race prejudice—indeed over the very consciousness of race. He testifies that the conjunction of extraordinary prowess, beauty, and virtue that make up the Handsome Sailor can be found—and universally recognized—in men of any race. Even when he fades into his white counterpart Billy Budd, as the lamb-like man fades into Black Guinea, he demonstrates more affirmatively than the Confidence-Man's masquerade that black and white are identical.

Thus in this brief epiphanic opening scene of *Billy Budd*, which fuses the humanistic spirit of *Moby-Dick* with the critical insight of

The Confidence-Man, Melville has achieved his finest—and final—statement about race. Having transcended both the rage that embittered his devastating attacks on racism in the late 1850s and the paralyzing guilt that marred his vision after the war, he has at last become free to dismiss the phantasm of race with complete serenity, and to embrace once again the dark brothers of his youth.

*B*ibliography

Primary

MANUSCRIPT COLLECTIONS OF MELVILLE FAMILY MATERIALS

Gansevoort-Lansing Collection. New York Public Library. New York City.
Melville Collection. Houghton Library, Harvard University, Cambridge, Mass.
Shaw Collection. Massachusetts Historical Society. Boston, Mass.

WORKS OF MELVILLE

Melville, Herman. *Battle-Pieces and Aspects of the War*, ed. Sidney Kaplan. Amherst: University of Massachusetts Press, 1972.
———. *The Battle-Pieces of Herman Melville*, ed. Hennig Cohen. New York: Thomas Yoseloff, 1963.
———. *Melville's "Benito Cereno": A Text for Guided Research*, ed. John P. Runden. Lexington, Mass.: D. C. Heath, 1965.
———. *Billy Budd, Sailor (An Inside Narrative)*, ed. Harrison Hayford and Merton M. Sealts, Jr. Chicago: University of Chicago Press, 1962.
———. *Clarel: A Poem and Pilgrimage in the Holy Land*, ed. Walter E. Bezanson. New York: Hendricks House, 1960.
———. *Collected Poems of Herman Melville*, ed. Howard P. Vincent. Chicago: Packard, 1947.
———. *The Confidence-Man: His Masquerade*, ed. Hennig Cohen. New York: Holt, Rinehart and Winston, 1964.
———. *The Confidence-Man: His Masquerade*, ed. Elizabeth S. Foster. New York: Hendricks House, 1954.
———. *The Confidence Man: His Masquerade*, ed. H. Bruce Franklin. Indianapolis: Bobbs-Merrill, 1967.
———. *The Confidence-Man: His Masquerade*, ed. Hershel Parker. New York: W. W. Norton, 1971.
———. *Great Short Works of Herman Melville*, ed. Warner Berthoff. New York: Harper & Row, 1970.

———. "Hawthorne and His Mosses." Harrison Hayford and Hershel Parker, eds. *Moby-Dick; or, The Whale.* New York: W. W. Norton, 1967, pp. 535–51.
———. *Herman Melville,* ed. R. W. B. Lewis. New York: Dell, 1962.
———. *Israel Potter: His Fifty Years of Exile,* ed. Lewis Leary. New York: Sagamore Press, 1957.
———. *The Letters of Herman Melville,* ed. Merrell R. Davis and William H. Gilman. New Haven: Yale University Press, 1960.
———. *Mardi: and A Voyage Thither,* ed. Harrison Hayford, Hershel Parker, and G. Thomas Tanselle. Evanston and Chicago: Northwestern University Press and Newberry Library, 1970.
———. *Moby-Dick; or, The Whale,* ed. Charles Feidelson, Jr. Indianapolis: Bobbs-Merrill, 1964.
———. *Moby-Dick; or, The Whale,* ed. Harrison Hayford and Hershel Parker. New York: W. W. Norton, 1967.
———. *Omoo: A Narrative of Adventures in the South Seas,* ed. Harrison Hayford, Hershel Parker, and G. Thomas Tanselle. Evanston and Chicago: Northwestern University Press and Newberry Library, 1968.
———. *The Piazza Tales.* New York: Dix & Edwards, 1856.
———. *Pierre; or, The Ambiguities,* ed. Harrison Hayford, Hershel Parker, and G. Thomas Tanselle. Evanston and Chicago: Northwestern University Press and Newberry Library, 1971.
———. *Pierre; or, The Ambiguities,* ed. Henry A. Murray. New York: Hendricks House, 1949.
———. *Redburn: His First Voyage, Being the Sailor-boy Confessions and Reminiscences of the Son-of-a-Gentleman, in the Merchant Service,* ed. Harrison Hayford, Hershel Parker, and G. Thomas Tanselle. Evanston and Chicago: Northwestern University Press and Newberry Library, 1969.
———. *Typee: A Peep at Polynesian Life,* ed. Harrison Hayford, Hershel Parker, and G. Thomas Tanselle. Evanston and Chicago: Northwestern University Press and Newberry Library, 1968.
———. *White-Jacket: or The World in a Man-of-War,* ed. Harrison Hayford, Hershel Parker, and G. Thomas Tanselle. Evanston and Chicago: Northwestern University Press and Newberry Library, 1970.

EIGHTEENTH- AND NINETEENTH-CENTURY IMPRINTS ON SLAVERY, RACE, AND RELIGION

"About Niggers." *Putnam's Monthly Magazine,* VI (December, 1855), 608–12.
Adams, Francis Colburn. *Manuel Pereira; or, The Sovereign Rule of South Carolina; with Views of Southern Laws, Life, and Hospitality.* Washington, D.C.: Buell & Blanchard, 1853.
Beecher, Edward. *Narrative of Riots at Alton.* Introd. Robert Merideth. 1838. Reprint. New York: E. P. Dutton, 1965.
Beecher, Lyman. *The Autobiography of Lyman Beecher,* ed. Barbara M. Cross. 2 vols. 1865. Reprint. Cambridge, Mass.: Harvard University Press, Belknap Press, 1961.
———. *A Plea for the West.* 1835. Reprint. New York: Arno Press, 1977.
Bird, Robert Montgomery. *Peter Pilgrim: or A Rambler's Recollections.* 2 vols. Philadelphia: Lea & Blanchard, 1838.

Cartwright, Samuel A. "Diseases and Peculiarities of the Negro Race." *De Bow's Review*, XI (July, 1851–January, 1852), 64–69, 209–13, 331–36, 504–508.
———. *Essays, Being Inductions Drawn from the Baconian Philosophy Proving the Truth of the Bible and the Justice and Benevolence of the Decree Dooming Canaan To Be Servant of Servants*. . . . Vidalia, La., n. p., 1843.
———. "How to Save the Republic, and the Position of the South in the Union." *De Bow's Review*, XI (August, 1851), 184–97.
———. "Slavery in the Light of Ethnology." E. N. Elliott, ed. *Cotton Is King, and Pro-Slavery Arguments: Comprising the Writings of Hammond, Harper, Christy, Stringfellow, Hodge, Bledsoe, and Cartwright, on This Important Subject*. . . . Augusta, Ga.: Pritchard, Abbott & Loomis, 1860.
Channing, William Ellery. "Slavery." *The Works of William Ellery Channing*. 6 vols. Boston: James Munroe, 1841, II, 5–153.
Child, Lydia Maria. *An Appeal in Favor of [That Class of] Americans Called Africans*. 1833. Reprint. New York: Arno Press and New York *Times*, 1968.
Cogswell, William. *The Harbinger of the Millennium*. Boston: Peirce & Parker, 1833.
Colton, Calvin. *History and Character of American Revivals of Religion*. London: Frederick Westley and A. H. Davis, 1832.
———. *A Voice from America to England*. London: Henry Colburn, 1839.
Cooper, James Fenimore. *The American Democrat*. 1838. Reprint. Baltimore: Penguin Books, 1969.
Dana, Richard Henry, Jr. *The Journal of Richard Henry Dana, Jr.*, ed. Robert F. Lucid. 3 vols. Cambridge, Mass.: Harvard University Press, Belknap Press, 1968.
Defoe, Daniel. *The Four Years Voyages of Capt. George Roberts . . . With a . . . Description and Draught of the Cape de Verd Islands*. . . . London: A. Bettesworth, 1726.
Douglass, Frederick. *My Bondage and My Freedom*. 1855. Reprint. New York: Dover, 1969.
———. *Narrative of the Life of Frederick Douglass, an American Slave. Written by Himself*. 1845. Reprint. Garden City, N.Y.: Doubleday, 1963.
Edwards, Jonathan. *The Works of Jonathan Edwards*. Edited by Perry Miller. New Haven: Yale University Press, 1957–77. Vol. 4, *The Great Awakening*, edited by C. C. Goen, 1972.
Estes, Matthew. *A Defence of Negro Slavery As It Exists in the United States*. Montgomery, Ala.: Press of the *Alabama Journal*, 1846.
Etting, Frank M. "The Old Liberty Bell." *American Historical Record*, II (January, 1873), 9–14.
Etzler, J. A. *The Paradise within the Reach of All Men, without Labor, by Powers of Nature and Machinery*. Pittsburgh: Etzler and Reinhold, 1833.
Ewbank, Thomas. *Inorganic Forces Ordained to Supersede Human Slavery*. New York: William Everdell, 1860.
———. "Origin and Progress of Invention" and "The Motors: Chief Levers of Civilization." *Report of the Commissioner of Patents, for the Year 1849*. 31st Cong., 1st Sess., Ex. Doc. No. 20, Pt. 1, pp. 483–511.
Finney, Charles Grandison. *Lectures on Revivals of Religion*, ed. William G. McLoughlin. 1835. Reprint. Cambridge, Mass.: Harvard University Press, Belknap Press, 1960.

———. *Sermons on Important Subjects.* 3rd ed. New York: John S. Taylor, 1836.

Fitzhugh, George. *Cannibals All! or, Slaves Without Masters,* ed. C. Vann Woodward. 1857. Reprint. Cambridge, Mass.: Harvard University Press, Belknap Press, 1960.

———. *Sociology for the South, or The Failure of Free Society.* 1854. Reprint. New York: Burt Franklin, n. d.

Garrison, William Lloyd. *Selections from the Writing and Speeches of William Lloyd Garrison.* 1852. Reprint. New York: Negro Universities Press, 1968.

Goodell, William. *The American Slave Code in Theory and Practice: Its Distinctive Features Shown by Its Statutes, Judicial Decisions, and Illustrative Facts.* 1853. Reprint. New York: Negro Universities Press, 1968.

Imprisonment of Coloured Seamen under the Law of South Carolina: A Tract Containing the Cases of Manuel Pereira and Reuben Roberts; and of John Glasgow, A Free British Subject Who Was Sold into Slavery in Georgia. London: British and Foreign Anti-Slavery Society, 1854.

"Is Man One Or Many?" *Putnam's Monthly Magazine,* IV (July, 1854), 1–14.

Jefferson, Thomas. *Notes on the State of Virginia.* Introd. Thomas Perkins Abernethy. 1785. Reprint. New York: Harper Torchbooks, 1964.

Lincoln, Abraham. *The Collected Works of Abraham Lincoln,* ed. Roy P. Basler. 8 vols. New Brunswick, N. J.: Rutgers University Press, 1953.

Lowell, James Russell. *The Biglow Papers.* [*First Series*], ed. Thomas Wortham. DeKalb, Ill.: Northern Illinois University Press, 1977.

Martineau, Harriet. *Society in America.* 3 vols. 1837. Reprint. New York: AMS Press, 1966.

Mayhew, Henry. *The Religious, Social, and Political History of the Mormons, or Latter-day Saints,* ed. Samuel M. Smucker. New York: Miller, Orton & Mulligan, 1856.

Mercier, Henry James. *Life in a Man-of-War: or Scenes in 'Old Ironsides' during Her Cruise in the Pacific, By a Fore-Top-Man.* Philadelphia: Lydia R. Bailey, 1841.

"The Negro." *De Bow's Review,* III (May, 1847), 419–22.

Nelson, Truman, ed. *Documents of Upheaval: Selections from William Lloyd Garrison's "The Liberator," 1831–1865.* New York: Hill and Wang, 1966.

Nott, Josiah Clark. "Nature and Destiny of the Negro." *De Bow's Review,* X (March, 1851), 329–32.

———. "Statistics of Southern Slave Population. With Especial Reference to Life Insurance." *De Bow's Review,* IV (November, 1847), 273–91.

Nott, Josiah Clark, and George R. Gliddon. *Types of Mankind: or, Ethnological Researches, Based upon the Ancient Monuments, Paintings, Sculptures, and Crania of Races, and upon Their Natural, Geographical, Philological, and Biblical History. . . .* 1854. Reprint. Miami: Mnemosyne Publishing Co., 1969.

Olmsted, Frederick Law. *A Journey in the Back Country.* Introd. Clement Eaton. 1860. Reprint. New York: Schocken Books, 1970.

———. *A Journey in the Seaboard Slave States, with Remarks on Their Economy.* 1856. Reprint. New York: Negro Universities Press, 1968.

"On a Chinaman in Broadway." *United States Magazine and Democratic Review,* n.s. IV (May, 1855), 411–12.

The Pro-Slavery Argument; as Maintained by the Most Distinguished Writers of the Southern States, Containing the Several Essays, on the Subject, of Chancellor

Harper, Governor Hammond, Dr. Simms, and Professor Dew. 1852. Reprint. New York: Negro Universities Press, 1968.

Sewall, Samuel. *The Selling of Joseph: A Memorial*, ed. Sidney Kaplan. 1700. Reprint. Amherst: University of Massachusetts Press, 1969.

Simms, William Gilmore. *"Mardi: and a Voyage Thither."* Southern Quarterly Review, XVI (October, 1849), 260–61.

————. "The Morals of Slavery." *The Pro-Slavery Argument.* . . . 1852. Reprint. New York: Negro Universities Press, 1968.

————. *"White-Jacket; or the World in a Man-of-War."* Southern Quarterly Review, XVII (July, 1850), 514–20.

————. *The Wigwam and the Cabin.* New York: Wiley and Putnam, 1845.

————. *Woodcraft; or, Hawks about the Dovecote. A Story of the South at the Close of the Revolution.* 1854. Reprint. New York: W. W. Norton, 1961.

Sprague, William B. *Lectures on Revivals of Religion.* New York: Daniel Appleton, 1833.

Stowe, Harriet Beecher. *Uncle Tom's Cabin; or, Life Among the Lowly*, ed. Kenneth S. Lynn. 1852. Reprint. Cambridge, Mass.: Harvard University Press, Belknap Press, 1962.

Thoreau, Henry David. "Paradise (to be) Regained." *United States Magazine and Democratic Review*, XIII (November, 1843), 449–62.

Tucker, St. George. *A Dissertation on Slavery: with A Proposal for the Gradual Abolition of it, in the State of Virginia.* 1796. Reprint. Westport, Conn.: Negro Universities Press, 1970.

Weld, Theodore Dwight. *American Slavery As It Is: Testimony of a Thousand Witnesses.* 1839. Reprint. New York: Arno Press and New York *Times*, 1969.

————. *The Bible Against Slavery.* . . . New York: American Anti-Slavery Society, 1837.

————. *The Letters of Theodore Dwight Weld, Angelina Grimké Weld, and Sarah Grimké, 1822–1844*, ed. Gilbert H. Barnes and Dwight L. Dumond. 2 vols. Gloucester, Mass.: Peter Smith, 1965.

Whittier, John Greenleaf. *The Poetical Works of John Greenleaf Whittier*, ed. Hyatt H. Waggoner. Boston: Houghton Mifflin, 1975.

Secondary

BOOKS

Aaron, Daniel. *The Unwritten War: American Writers and the Civil War.* New York: Alfred A. Knopf, 1973.

Addison, James Thayer. *The Episcopal Church in the United States, 1789–1931.* New York: Charles Scribner's Sons, 1951.

Anderson, Charles R. *Melville in the South Seas.* New York: Dover, 1966.

Aptheker, Herbert. *American Negro Slave Revolts.* New York: International Publishers, 1969.

Araujo, Norman. *A Study of Cape Verdean Literature.* Wetteren, Belgium: Cultura Press, 1966.

Arendt, Hannah. *On Revolution.* London: Faber and Faber, 1963.

Arvin, Newton. *Herman Melville.* New York: Viking Compass Books, 1957.

Baird, James. *Ishmael: A Study of the Symbolic Mode in Primitivism.* New York: Harper Torchbooks, 1960.

Barnes, Gilbert H. *The Antislavery Impulse, 1830–1844.* New York: Harcourt, Brace, 1964.

Bercovitch, Sacvan. *The Puritan Origins of the American Self.* New Haven: Yale University Press, 1975.

Berlin, Ira. *Slaves without Masters: The Free Negro in the Antebellum South.* New York: Vintage Books, 1976.

Bernstein, John. *Pacifism and Rebellion in the Writings of Herman Melville.* The Hague: Mouton, 1964.

Bickley, R. Bruce, Jr. *The Method of Melville's Short Fiction.* Durham: Duke University Press, 1975.

Blassingame, John W. *The Slave Community: Plantation Life in the Antebellum South.* New York: Oxford University Press, 1972.

Bowen, Merlin. *The Long Encounter: Self and Experience in the Writings of Herman Melville.* Chicago: University of Chicago Press, 1960.

Braswell, William. *Melville's Religious Thought: An Essay in Interpretation.* New York: Octagon Books, 1973.

Curti, Merle. *The Growth of American Thought.* New York: Harper and Brothers, 1943.

Dillingham, William B. *Melville's Short Fiction, 1853–1856.* Athens, Ga.: University of Georgia Press, 1977.

Douglas, Ann. *The Feminization of American Culture.* New York: Alfred A. Knopf, 1977.

Drake, Thomas E. *Quakers and Slavery in America.* Gloucester, Mass.: Peter Smith, 1965.

Dryden, Edgar A. *Melville's Thematics of Form: The Great Art of Telling the Truth.* Baltimore: Johns Hopkins University Press, 1968.

Du Bois, W. E. B. *The Suppression of the African Slave-Trade to the United States of America, 1638–1870.* 1896. Reprint. New York: Dover, 1970.

Ekirch, Arthur A., Jr. *The Idea of Progress in America, 1815–1860.* New York: Peter Smith, 1951.

Ellison, Ralph. *Invisible Man.* New York: New American Library, 1952.

Fiedler, Leslie A. *Love and Death in the American Novel.* Rev. ed. New York: Stein & Day, 1966.

Filler, Louis. *The Crusade Against Slavery, 1830–1860.* New York: Harper Torchbooks, 1963.

Fisher, Marvin. *Going Under: Melville's Short Fiction and the American 1850s.* Baton Rouge: Louisiana State University Press, 1977.

Fletcher, Robert S. *A History of Oberlin College.* 2 vols. Oberlin: Oberlin College Press, 1943.

Flibbert, Joseph. *Melville and the Art of Burlesque.* Amsterdam: Rodopi N. V., 1974.

Floan, Howard R. *The South in Northern Eyes, 1831 to 1861.* New York: Haskell House, 1973.

Franklin, H. Bruce. *Future Perfect: American Science Fiction of the Nineteenth Century.* New York: Oxford University Press, 1966.

———. *The Victim as Criminal and Artist: Literature from the American Prison.* New York: Oxford University Press, 1978.

————. *The Wake of the Gods: Melville's Mythology.* Stanford: Stanford University Press, 1963.

Franklin, John Hope. *From Slavery to Freedom: A History of Negro Americans.* 3rd ed. New York: Alfred A. Knopf, 1967.

Fredrickson, George M. *The Black Image in the White Mind: The Debate on Afro-American Character and Destiny, 1817–1914.* New York: Harper & Row, 1971.

————. *The Inner Civil War: Northern Intellectuals and the Crisis of the Union.* New York: Harper Torchbooks, 1965.

Freehling, William W. *Prelude to Civil War: The Nullification Controversy in South Carolina, 1816–1836.* New York: Harper Torchbooks, 1968.

Genovese, Eugene D. *Roll, Jordan, Roll: The World the Slaves Made.* New York: Vintage Books, 1976.

Gettmann, Royal A., and Bruce Harkness. "Billy Budd, Foretopman," in *Teacher's Manual for "A Book of Stories."* New York: Rinehart, 1955.

Gilmore, Michael T. *The Middle Way: Puritanism and Ideology in American Romantic Fiction.* New Brunswick, N.J.: Rutgers University Press, 1977.

Grejda, Edward S. *The Common Continent of Men: Racial Equality in the Writings of Herman Melville.* Port Washington, N.Y.: Kennikat Press, 1974.

Gutman, Herbert G. *The Black Family in Slavery and Freedom, 1750–1925.* New York: Vintage Books, 1977.

Hayford, Harrison, ed. *The Somers Mutiny Affair.* Englewood Cliffs, N.J.: Prentice-Hall, 1959.

Heimert, Alan. *Religion and the American Mind, from the Great Awakening to the Revolution.* Cambridge, Mass.: Harvard University Press, 1966.

Henderson, Harry B., III. *Versions of the Past: The Historical Imagination in American Fiction.* New York: Oxford University Press, 1974.

Hoffman, Daniel G. *Form and Fable in American Fiction.* New York: Oxford University Press, 1961.

Howard, Leon. *Herman Melville: A Biography.* Berkeley: University of California Press, 1967.

Jenkins, William Sumner. *Pro-Slavery Thought in the Old South.* Gloucester, Mass.: Peter Smith, 1960.

Jordan, Winthrop D. *White Over Black: American Attitudes Toward the Negro, 1550–1812.* Baltimore: Penguin Books, 1969.

Kenney, Alice P. *The Gansevoorts of Albany: Dutch Patricians in the Upper Hudson Valley.* Syracuse: Syracuse University Press, 1969.

Keyssar, Alexander. *Melville's ISRAEL POTTER: Reflections on the American Dream.* Cambridge, Mass.: Harvard University Press, 1969.

Kraditor, Aileen S. *Means and Ends in American Abolitionism: Garrison and His Critics on Strategy and Tactics, 1834–1850.* New York: Vintage Books, 1969.

Lesser, Simon O. *Fiction and the Unconscious.* Boston: Beacon Press, 1957.

Levine, Lawrence W. *Black Culture and Black Consciousness: Afro-American Folk Thought from Slavery to Freedom.* New York: Oxford University Press, 1977.

Levy, Leonard W. *The Law of the Commonwealth and Chief Justice Shaw.* Cambridge, Mass.: Harvard University Press, 1957.

Lewis, R. W. B. *The American Adam: Innocence, Tragedy, and Tradition in the Nineteenth Century.* Chicago: University of Chicago Press, 1955.

————. *Trials of the Word: Essays in American Literature and the Humanistic Tradition.* New Haven: Yale University Press, 1965.

Leyda, Jay. *The Melville Log: A Documentary Life of Herman Melville, 1819–1891.* 2 vols. New York: Gordian Press, 1969.

Litwack, Leon L. *North of Slavery: The Negro in the Free States, 1790–1860.* Chicago: University of Chicago Press, 1961.

Lyall, Archibald. *Black and White Make Brown: An Account of a Journey to the Cape Verde Islands and Portuguese Guinea.* London: William Heinemann, 1938.

Marx, Leo. *The Machine in the Garden: Technology and the Pastoral Ideal in America.* New York: Oxford University Press, 1964.

Matthiessen, F. O. *American Renaissance: Art and Expression in the Age of Emerson and Whitman.* New York: Oxford University Press, 1968.

McLoughlin, William G. *Modern Revivalism: Charles Grandison Finney to Billy Graham.* New York: Ronald Press, 1959.

McPherson, James P. *The Struggle for Equality: Abolitionists and the Negro in the Civil War and Reconstruction.* Princeton: Princeton University Press, 1964.

Metcalf, Eleanor Melville. *Herman Melville: Cycle and Epicycle.* Westport, Conn.: Greenwood Press, 1970.

Miller, Edwin Haviland. *Melville: A Biography.* New York: George Braziller, 1975.

Miller, Perry. *The Raven and the Whale: The War of Words and Wits in the Era of Poe and Melville.* New York: Harcourt, Brace, 1956.

Miller, Wayne Charles. *An Armed America: Its Face in Fiction: A History of the American Military Novel.* New York: New York University Press, 1970.

Milne, Gordon. *George William Curtis and the Genteel Tradition.* Bloomington: Indiana University Press, 1956.

Mohr, James C. *The Radical Republicans and Reform in New York during Reconstruction.* Ithaca, N.Y.: Cornell University Press, 1973.

Nnolim, Charles E. *Melville's "Benito Cereno": A Study in Meaning of Name Symbolism.* New York: New Voices, 1974.

Nye, Russel B. *Fettered Freedom: Civil Liberties and the Slavery Controversy, 1830–1860.* Rev. ed. Urbana: University of Illinois Press, 1972.

Olson, Charles. *Call Me Ishmael: A Study of Melville.* San Francisco: City Lights Books, 1947.

Partridge, Eric. *Shakespeare's Bawdy: A Literary & Psychological Essay and a Comprehensive Glossary.* Rev. ed. New York: E. P. Dutton, 1969.

Quarles, Benjamin. *The Negro in the Civil War.* 2nd ed. Boston: Little, Brown, 1969.

Rampersad, Arnold. *Melville's ISRAEL POTTER: A Pilgrimage and Progress.* Bowling Green: Bowling Green University Popular Press, 1969.

Randall, J. G., and David Donald. *The Civil War and Reconstruction.* 2nd ed. Lexington, Mass.: D. C. Heath, 1961.

Ratner, Lorman. *Powder Keg: Northern Opposition to the Antislavery Movement, 1831–1840.* New York: Basic Books, 1968.

Sabin, Joseph. *Bibliotheca Americana: A Dictionary of Books Relating to America, from Its Discovery to the Present Time.* 29 vols. New York: J. Sabin's Son, 1868–1936.

Schweitzer, Albert. *The Mystery of the Kingdom of God: The Secret of Jesus' Messiahship and Passion.* Introd. Walter Lowrie. New York: Schocken Books, 1964.

———. *The Quest of the Historical Jesus: A Critical Study of Its Progress from Reimarus to Wrede.* Introd. James M. Robinson. New York: Macmillan, 1968.

Sealts, Merton M. *Melville as Lecturer.* Folcroft, Pa.: Folcroft Press, 1970.

Sedgwick, William Ellery. *Herman Melville: The Tragedy of Mind*. Cambridge, Mass.: Harvard University Press, 1944.

Stampp, Kenneth M. *The Era of Reconstruction, 1865–1877*. New York: Vintage Books, 1965.

———. *The Peculiar Institution: Slavery in the Ante-Bellum South*. New York: Vintage Books, 1956.

Stanton, William. *The Leopard's Spots: Scientific Attitudes toward Race in America, 1815–59*. Chicago: University of Chicago Press, 1960.

Starobin, Robert S., ed. *Demark Vesey: The Slave Conspiracy of 1822*. Englewood Cliffs, N.J.: Prentice-Hall, 1970.

———. *Industrial Slavery in the Old South*. New York: Oxford University Press, 1970.

Stern, Milton R. *The Fine Hammered Steel of Herman Melville*. Urbana: University of Illinois Press, 1957.

Stewart, Randall. *Nathaniel Hawthorne: A Biography*. New Haven: Yale University Press, 1948.

Swaney, Charles Baumer. *Episcopal Methodism and Slavery, with Sidelights on Ecclesiastical Politics*. New York: Negro Universities Press, 1969.

Takaki, Ronald T. *A Pro-Slavery Crusade: The Agitation to Reopen the African Slave Trade*. New York: Free Press, 1971.

Taylor, William R. *Cavalier and Yankee: The Old South and American National Character*. New York: Harper Torchbooks, 1969.

Thompson, Lawrance. *Melville's Quarrel with God*. Princeton: Princeton University Press, 1952.

Tuveson, Ernest Lee. *Redeemer Nation: The Idea of America's Millennial Role*. Chicago: University of Chicago Press, 1968.

Wentworth, Harold, and Stuart Berg Flexner, eds. *Dictionary of American Slang*. New York: Thomas Y. Crowell, 1967.

Weseen, Maurice H., ed. *Dictionary of American Slang*. New York: Thomas Y. Crowell, 1934.

Widmer, Kingsley. *The Ways of Nihilism: A Study of Herman Melville's Short Novels*. Los Angeles: Anderson, Ritchie & Simon (Publication of the California State Colleges), 1970.

Wilson, Edmund. *Patriotic Gore: Studies in the Literature of the American Civil War*. New York: Oxford University Press, 1966.

Winters, Yvor. *In Defense of Reason*. Denver: Alan Swallow, 1947.

Woodward, C. Vann. *The Burden of Southern History*. Rev. ed. New York: New American Library, 1969.

Wright, Nathalia. *Melville's Use of the Bible*. New York: Octagon Books, 1969.

Wright, Richard. *Black Boy: A Record of Childhood and Youth*. New York: New American Library, 1964.

Yellin, Jean Fagan. *The Intricate Knot: Black Figures in American Literature, 1776–1863*. New York: New York University Press, 1972.

Zoellner, Robert. *The Salt-Sea Mastodon: A Reading of "Moby-Dick."* Berkeley: University of California Press, 1973.

ARTICLES

Adler, Joyce Sparer. "*Billy Budd* and Melville's Philosophy of War." *PMLA*, XCI (March, 1976), 266–78.

———. "Melville and the Civil War." *New Letters*, XL (Winter, 1973), 99–117.

———. "Melville on the White Man's War Against the American Indian." *Science & Society*, XXXVI (Winter, 1972), 417–42.

———. "Melville's *Benito Cereno*: Slavery and Violence in the Americas." *Science & Society*, XXXVIII (Spring, 1974), 19–48.

Arnaud-Marçais, Dominique. "*The Confidence-Man: His Masquerade* et le problème noir." Viola Sachs, ed. *Le Blanc et le Noir chez Melville et Faulkner*. Paris: Mouton, 1974.

Bond, William H. "Melville and *Two Years before the Mast*." *Harvard Library Bulletin*, VII (Autumn, 1953), 362–65.

Bowen, Merlin. "Tactics of Indirection in Melville's *The Confidence-Man*." *Studies in the Novel*, I (Winter, 1969), 401–20.

Braswell, William. "The Early Love Scenes in Melville's *Pierre*." *American Literature*, XXII (November, 1950), 283–89.

———. "Melville as a Critic of Emerson." *American Literature*, IX (November, 1937), 317–34.

———. "The Satirical Temper of Melville's *Pierre*." *American Literature*, VII (January, 1936), 424–38.

Brock, W. R. "The Waning of Radicalism." Edwin C. Rozwenc, ed. *Reconstruction in the South*. 2nd ed. Lexington, Mass.: D. C. Heath, 1972, pp. 263–84.

Cardwell, Guy. "Melville's Gray Story: Symbols and Meaning in 'Benito Cereno.'" John P. Runden, ed. *Melville's "Benito Cereno": A Text for Guided Research*. Lexington, Mass.: D. C. Heath, 1965, pp. 133–42.

Carpenter, Frederic I. "'The American Myth': Paradise (To Be) Regained." *PMLA*, LXXIV (December, 1959), 599–606.

Carsel, Wilfred. "The Slaveholders' Indictment of Northern Wage Slavery." *Journal of Southern History*, VI (November, 1940), 504–20.

Casper, Leonard. "The Case against Captain Vere." William T. Stafford, ed. *Melville's "Billy Budd" and the Critics*. Rev. ed. Belmont, Calif.: Wadsworth, 1968, pp. 212–15.

Cohen, Hennig. "Melville's Tomahawk Pipe: Artifact and Symbol." *Studies in the Novel*, I (Winter, 1969), 397–400.

Costello, Jacqueline A., and Robert J. Kloss. "The Psychological Depths of Melville's 'The Bell-Tower,'" *ESQ: A Journal of the American Renaissance*, XIX (4th Qt., 1973), 254–61.

Curry, Richard O. "The Civil War and Reconstruction, 1861–1877: A Critical Overview of Recent Trends and Interpretations." *Civil War History*, XX (September, 1974), 215–38.

Demos, John. "The Antislavery Movement and the Problem of Violent 'Means,'" *New England Quarterly*, XXXVII (1964), 501–26.

Donaldson, Scott. "The Dark Truth of *The Piazza Tales*." *PMLA*, LXXXV (October, 1970), 1082–86.

Du Bois, W. E. B. "Black Reconstruction." Kenneth M. Stampp and Leon L. Litwack (eds.). *Reconstruction: An Anthology of Revisionist Writings*. Baton Rouge: Louisiana State University Press, 1969, pp. 428–70.

Eby, E. H. "Herman Melville's 'Tartarus of Maids.'" *Modern Language Quarterly*, I (March, 1940), 95–100.

Feltenstein, Rosalie. "Melville's 'Benito Cereno.'" John P. Runden, ed. *Melville's "Benito Cereno": A Text for Guided Research*. Lexington, Mass.: D. C. Heath, 1965, pp. 124–33.

Flint, Allen. "Hawthorne and the Slavery Crisis." *New England Quarterly*, XLI (September, 1968), 393–408.

Fogle, Richard Harter. "Melville and the Civil War." *Tulane Studies in English*, IX (1959), 61–89.

Foster, Charles H. "Something in Emblems: A Reinterpretation of *Moby-Dick*." *New England Quarterly*, XXXIV (March, 1961), 3–35.

Garner, Stanton. "Fraud as Fact in Herman Melville's *Billy Budd*." *San Jose Studies*, IV (May, 1978), 82–105.

Gilmore, Michael T. "Melville's Apocalypse: American Millennialism and *Moby-Dick*." *ESQ: A Journal of the American Renaissance*, XXI (3rd Qt., 1975), 154–61.

Guttmann, Allen. "The Enduring Innocence of Captain Amasa Delano." John P. Runden, ed. *Melville's "Benito Cereno": A Text for Guided Research*. Lexington, Mass.: D. C. Heath, 1965, pp. 179–88.

Hart, James D. "Melville and Dana." *American Literature*, IX (March, 1937), 49–55.

Heimert, Alan. "*Moby-Dick* and American Political Symbolism." *American Quarterly*, XV (Winter, 1963), 498–534.

————. "Puritanism, the Wilderness, and the Frontier." *New England Quarterly*, XXVI (September, 1953), 361–82.

Higgins, Brian. "Mark Winsome and Egbert: 'In the Friendly Spirit.'" Hershel Parker, ed. *The Confidence-Man: His Masquerade*. New York: W. W. Norton, 1971, pp. 339–43.

Hillway, Tyrus. "In Defense of Melville's 'Fleece.'" *Extracts*, XIX (September, 1974), 10–11.

Kaplan, Sidney. "Herman Melville and the American National Sin: The Meaning of 'Benito Cereno.'" *Journal of Negro History*, XLI (October, 1956), 311–38, and XLII (January, 1957), 11–37.

Karcher, Carolyn L. "Melville's 'The 'Gees': A Forgotten Satire on Scientific Racism." *American Quarterly*, XXVII (October, 1975), 421–42.

————. "Spiritualism and Philanthropy in Brownson's *The Spirit-Rapper* and Melville's *The Confidence-Man*." *ESQ: A Journal of the American Renaissance*, XXV (1st Qt., 1979), 26–36.

Le Duc, Thomas H. "Grahamites and Garrisonites." *New York History*, XX (April, 1939), 189–91.

Lucid, Robert F. "The Influence of *Two Years before the Mast* on Herman Melville." *American Literature*, XXXI (November, 1959), 243–56.

Margolies, Edward L. "Melville and Blacks." *CLA Journal*, XVIII (March, 1975), 364–73.

Nicol, Charles. "The Iconography of Evil and Ideal in 'Benito Cereno.'" Raymona E. Hull, ed. *Studies in the Minor and Later Work of Melville*. Hartford: Transcendental Books, 1970, pp. 25–31.

Oliver, Egbert S. "Melville's Picture of Emerson and Thoreau in *The Confidence-Man*." *College English*, VIII (November, 1946), 61–72.

Parker, Hershel. "Gansevoort Melville's Role in the Campaign of 1844." *New York Historical Society Quarterly*, XLIX (April, 1965), 143–73.

————. "Melville's Satire of Emerson and Thoreau: An Evaluation of the Evidence." *American Transcendental Quarterly*, VII (Summer, 1970), 61–67.

Putzel, Max. "The Source and the Symbols of Melville's 'Benito Cereno.'" John

P. Runden, ed. *Melville's "Benito Cereno": A Text for Guided Research*. Lexington, Mass.: D. C. Heath, 1965, pp. 153–66.

Roper, Laura Wood. "Frederick Law Olmsted in the 'Literary Republic.'" *Mississippi Valley Historical Review*, XXXIX (December, 1952), 459–82.

Rosenfeld, William. "Uncertain Faith: Queequeg's Coffin and Melville's Use of the Bible." *Texas Studies in Literature and Language*, VII (Winter, 1966), 317–27.

Rowland, Beryl. "Melville's Bachelors and Maids: Interpretation through Symbol and Metaphor." *American Literature*, XLI (November, 1969), 389–405.

Saxton, Alexander. "Blackface Minstrelsy and Jacksonian Ideology." *American Quarterly*, XXVII (March, 1975), 3–28.

Sealts, Merton M., Jr. "Herman Melville's 'I and My Chimney.'" *American Literature*, XIII (May, 1941), 142–54.

——. "Melville's Short Fiction." *ESQ: A Journal of the American Renaissance*, XXV (1 Qt., 1979), 43–56.

Shroeder, John W. "Indian-hating: An Ultimate Note on *The Confidence-Man*." *Books at Brown*, XXIV (1971), 1–5.

——. "Sources and Symbols for Melville's *Confidence-Man*." Hershel Parker, ed. *The Confidence-Man: His Masquerade*. New York: W. W. Norton, 1971, pp. 298–316.

Simpson, Eleanor E. "Melville and the Negro: From *Typee* to 'Benito Cereno.'" *American Literature*, XLI (March, 1969), 19–38.

Sowder, William J. "Melville's 'I And My Chimney': A Southern Exposure." *Mississippi Quarterly*, XVI (Summer, 1963), 128–45.

Spiller, Robert E. "Fenimore Cooper's Defense of Slave-Owning America." *American Historical Review*, XXXV (April, 1930), 575–82.

Staiger, C. Bruce. "Abolitionism and the Presbyterian Schism of 1837–1838." *Mississippi Valley Historical Review*, XXXVI (December, 1949), 391–414.

Stern, Milton R. "*Moby-Dick*, Millennial Attitudes, and Politics." *Emerson Society Quarterly*, LIV (1st Qt., 1969), 51–60.

Stone, Edward. "The Whiteness of the Whale." *CLA Journal*, XVIII (March, 1975), 348–63.

Strauch, Carl F. "Ishmael: Time and Personality in *Moby-Dick*." *Studies in the Novel*, I (Winter, 1969), 469–83.

Vanderhaar, Margaret M. "A Re-Examination of 'Benito Cereno.'" *American Literature*, XL (May, 1968), 179–91.

Vauthier, Simone. "'Marie ou l'esclavage aux Etats-Unis.' par Gustave de Beaumont: Ambiguités américaines, ambiguité française." *Recherches anglaises et américaines*, III (décembre, 1970), 99–126.

Warren, Robert Penn. "Melville's Poems." *Southern Review*, n.s. III (Autumn, 1967), 799–855.

Withim, Phil. "*Billy Budd*: Testament of Resistance." William T. Stafford, ed. *Melville's "Billy Budd" and the Critics*. Rev. ed. Belmont, Calif.: Wadsworth, 1968, pp. 140–52.

Woodruff, Stuart C. "Stubb's Supper." *Emerson Society Quarterly*, XLIII (2nd Qt., 1966), 46–48.

Woodward, C. Vann. "Seeds of Failure in the Radical Race Policy." Edwin C. Rozwenc, ed. *Reconstruction in the South*. 2nd ed. Lexington, Mass.: D. C. Heath, 1972, pp. 245–63.

Yellin, Jean Fagan. "Black Masks: Melville's 'Benito Cereno.' " *American Quarterly*, XXII (Fall, 1970), 678–89.

Zirker, Priscilla Allen. "Evidence of the Slavery Dilemma in *White-Jacket*." *American Quarterly*, XVIII (Fall, 1966), 477–92.

UNPUBLISHED PAPERS AND DISSERTATIONS

Carothers, Robert L. "Herman Melville and the Search for the Father: An Interpretation of the Novels." Ph.D. dissertation, Kent State University, 1969.

Cowen, Wilson Walker. "Melville's Marginalia." 11 vols. Ph.D. dissertation, Harvard University, 1965.

Lorant, Laurie Jean. "Herman Melville and Race: Themes and Imagery." Ph.D. dissertation, New York University, 1972.

Lucid, Robert F. 1969. Melville and Dana. Paper read at Special Meeting of the Melville Society, 5–8 September 1969, at Nantucket, Massachusetts.

*I*ndex